MARKETING IN
A CHANGING
ENVIRONMENT

The Wiley Marketing Series

WILLIAM LAZER, Advisory Editor
Michigan State University

MARTIN ZOBER, *Marketing Management*

ROBERT J. HOLLOWAY AND ROBERT S. HANCOCK
  The Environment of Marketing Behavior—
  Selections from the Literature

GEORGE SCHWARTZ, Editor
  Science in Marketing

EDGAR CRANE
  Marketing Communications—A Behavioral
  Approach to Men, Messages, and Media

JOSEPH W. NEWMAN, Editor
  On Knowing the Consumer

STEUART HENDERSON BRITT, Editor
  Consumer Behavior and the Behavioral
  Sciences—Theories and Applications

DONALD F. MULVIHILL AND STEPHEN PARANKA
  Price Policies and Practices

DAVID CARSON
  International Marketing: A Comparative
  Systems Approach

BRUCE E. MALLEN
  The Marketing Channel: A Conceptual
  Viewpoint

RONALD R. GIST
  Management Perspectives in Retailing

JOHN K. RYANS AND JAMES C. BAKER
  World Marketing: A Multinational
  Approach

JOHN M. BRION
  Corporate Marketing Planning

NORTON E. MARKS AND ROBERT M. TAYLOR
  Marketing Logistics: Perspectives and
  Viewpoints

JAMES BEARDEN
  Personal Selling: Behavioral Science
  Readings and Cases

FRANK M. BASS, CHARLES W. KING, AND
  EDGAR A. PESSEMIER, Editors
  Applications of the Sciences in Marketing
  Management

ROBERT J. HOLLOWAY AND ROBERT S. HANCOCK
  Marketing in a Changing Environment

MARKETING IN A CHANGING ENVIRONMENT

Robert J. Holloway

School of Business Administration
University of Minnesota

Robert S. Hancock

School of Business
Southern Illinois University

John Wiley & Sons, Inc.   New York · London · Sydney

Copyright © 1968 by John Wiley & Sons, Inc.

All Rights Reserved
This book or any part thereof must not
be reproduced in any form without the
written permission of the publisher.

Library of Congress Catalog Card Number: 68–11408
Printed in the United States of America

This book is dedicated to:

Roland S. Vaile
Emeritus Professor of Economics and Marketing
University of Minnesota

Harvey W. Huegy
Emeritus Professor of Marketing
University of Illinois

Who shaped the thinking and intellectual curiosity of a multitude of marketing students and who shared their time, abundant knowledge, and wisdom so generously with the authors.

Preface

Several years ago the authors were impelled to examine the content of the introductory course in marketing and the approach they had been taking in teaching it. At the University of Minnesota, as at most universities, the approach was either in the traditional pattern or attempts were made to make the subject matter managerially operational. Although this approach has the respect of the authors, it does little to develop basic concepts and generalities about marketing. It often leaves the student with a mass of facts and descriptive ideas that are presented neither in coherent nor organized form.

After much thought and discussion with colleagues and students, and between ourselves, we thought it possible to lend more order to the body of knowledge known as marketing. One of our goals was to tell *why* marketing exists in this and other economies and *why* it does adjust and change to meet social and economic needs.

In this book marketing is conceived as a social/economic phenomenon. It adjusts and adapts to needs through the set of forces generated by its environment. We therefore refer to our structure and content as the "environmental approach" to marketing. The ultimate method which this book represents grows out of refinement and adaptation of our original thoughts after their trial with numerous American and foreign graduate students and undergraduates. Whether there is soundness and order to the material in this book may thus be to their credit. They represented many disciplines and were an invaluable source of help.

The reader may find several useful devices in the chapters that follow. First, a schematic showing of the marketing environment as being social, economic, technological, legal, and ethical is presented early in the text. This device is somewhat refined as the material progresses leading to a final incorporation of marketing activities. These activities which are so importantly influenced by their environment are product development, pricing, market persuasion, and the logistical aspect of the firm. Perhaps a second feature of this book is its illustrations and bordered pages referred to as "boxes." The illustrations which have direct relevance to the text material are in abundance and are intended to reduce the amount of written material. The serious student will get more mileage from the course through study and understanding of the illustrative material. The boxes illuminate the text, show what someone else believes or has learned and, in some cases, raise controversy. These too may be used by the more serious student to seek out other points of view and to explore literature not always widely read.

The user of this book will find little text material on marketing institutions. Rather than discuss the several marketing institutions, the authors devised Appendix A to Chapter 2 to provide supplementary statistical information for the interested instructor and student. Other appendices are similarly included to further the thinking of the reader. The Appendix to Chapter 6 deals with consumer decision making; several other appendices supplement marketing research, product development, persuasion, and international marketing. A glossary of marketing definitions not incorporated into the text material appears after Chapter 22. This was thought a useful addition to the text in order to provide the reader with precise terminology.

The authors wish to acknowledge their gratitude to their many former graduate students who contributed to the clarity, refinements, and details of the manuscript through instructional and academic interest in our work. In particular we wish to acknowledge the help of Assistant Professors David M. Gardner, University of Illinois; James Taylor, University of Michigan; Meenakshisunder Venkateson, University of Massachusetts; Laurence Feldman, University of Illinois at Chicago Circle; Donald J. Hempel, University of Connecticut; and John Faricy, University of Florida. We wish also to acknowledge our appreciation to Jeanne Bartels who was particularly helpful in typing the manuscript and in handling the load of correspondence attendant to a book of this nature.

Robert J. Holloway
Robert S. Hancock

Contents

PART I. THE BASIS AND CONCEPTUAL FRAMEWORK OF   1
    MARKETING

    CHAPTER 1. Marketing and Society   3
    CHAPTER 2. The System of Marketing   15
    CHAPTER 3. Marketing in Capitalistic and Planned Economies   41

PART II. MARKETING ENVIRONMENT AND MARKET FORCES   51

    CHAPTER 4. The Environment of Consumer Behavior—I   53
    CHAPTER 5. The Environment of Consumer Behavior—II   73
    CHAPTER 6. The Environment of Consumer Behavior—III   89
    CHAPTER 7. The Visible and Dynamic Force of Technology   119
    CHAPTER 8. The Economic Environment—Competition   143
    CHAPTER 9. Demand Analysis   161
    CHAPTER 10. Marketing and the Law   177
    CHAPTER 11. The Ethical Dimension in Marketing   201

PART III. MARKET DEVELOPMENT   219

    CHAPTER 12. Marketing Intelligence—I   221
    CHAPTER 13. Marketing Intelligence—II   239
    CHAPTER 14. Planning for Marketing Development   269
    CHAPTER 15. Market Development: The Product   287
    CHAPTER 16. Market Development: The Price   313
    CHAPTER 17. Marketing Logistics   341
    CHAPTER 18. Persuasion in the Market Place—I   357
    CHAPTER 19. Persuasion in the Market Place—II   379

PART IV. MARKETING IN PERSPECTIVE   401

    CHAPTER 20. Universality of Marketing and Economic Development   403
    CHAPTER 21. International Marketing   421
    CHAPTER 22. An Evaluation of Marketing   451

Glossary of Marketing Definitions   465

Name Index   487

Subject Index   491

MARKETING IN
A CHANGING
ENVIRONMENT

The Basis and Conceptual Framework of Marketing

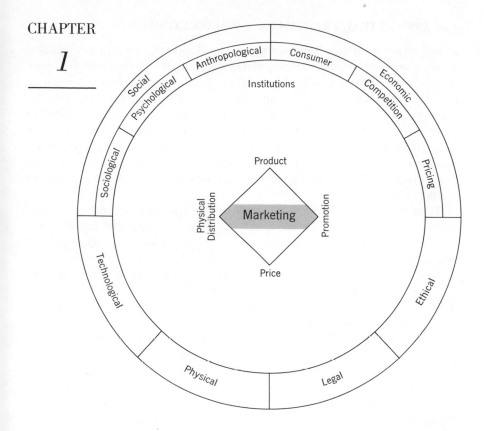

Marketing and Society

WHAT IS MARKETING? • SPECIALIZATION GIVES RISE TO MARKETING • MARKET-
ING ADVANCES SOCIAL AND ECONOMIC WELFARE • MARKETING IS MULTIDISCI-
PLINARY • THE CHARACTER OF MARKETING IS SOCIAL • THE CHARACTER OF
MARKETING IS ECONOMIC • THE CHARACTER OF MARKETING IS POLITICAL AND
ETHICAL • THE CHARACTER OF MARKETING IS TECHNOLOGICAL • THE PLAN
OF STUDY • MARKETING—A RESPONSE TO THE SOCIAL SYSTEM

In any economy at an advanced stage of development, marketing constitutes a major segment. As the economy develops, complex forces come into play to which man responds with the creation of many forms of social organization. The political system, the monetary system, the corporation, and the marketing system are a few of the social organizations man has devised to serve his fellowmen. A marketing system provides economic values which rank in quantity and quality with those of manufacturing, banking, agriculture, medicine, and others. Though not as tangible as many other values affecting our daily lives, the economic values of a marketing system are nonetheless highly significant.

Their significance derives from marketing's capacity to provide goods and services to consumers, industrial plants, political organizations, and all other institutions functioning in an economy. Even the exporting and importing activities of a nation depend on the existence of a marketing system.

How advanced a nation's marketing structure may be and how the activities are carried on within it depend on the level (or stage) of economic and social development, and the immediate and long-range goals of the society. To most Americans economic growth and development means continuing gains in their standards of living, increasing personal and real incomes, and new jobs for an expanding population. It means TV sets, washing machines, jet-set vacations, and college educations. To the Libyan, Ecuadorian, or Malayan, however, economic growth and development means something else. It probably means the production and distribution of enough food to keep him from being hungry. Similarly other economies may have more and better medical care, better housing, or education as their most immediate and basic economic needs. In accomplishing these ends marketing must play a significant if not dominant role. Quite obviously, the aggregate of a society's specific demands will determine the character of its marketing system and marketing structure.

WHAT IS MARKETING?

We define marketing as *those activities necessary and incidental to bringing about exchange relationships.* The activities may be those of business firms or of consumers which directly influence and exchange process. As its focal point, marketing has exchange—or put another way, exchange is the center of marketing. Buying and selling are the activities commonly associated with exchange; yet many other functions and events facilitate the exchange process and these are included in the concept of marketing.

SPECIALIZATION GIVES RISE TO MARKETING

For marketing, a society must have *specialization.* Specialization helps to explain the phenomenon of marketing. The important proposition that specialization is prerequisite to marketing stems from the fact that exchange cannot exist without specialization. Exchange makes sense only because everyone does not have, or make, the same things. It is easy to imagine a society in which everyone has the same or produces essentially the same things. Even today exchange plays little or no role in the economies of many societies. Societies of this kind are usually the economically depressed and underdeveloped ones where everyone raises his own food, makes his own clothing, and provides only his own needs. No exchange is possible, since everyone has the same things and it is foolish to exchange identical goods. In such a society every family is self-sufficient, and no exchange occurs in the usual sense of the term. Clearly, the need for exchange rests on the proposition that individuals, regions, and nations possess different things and similarly possess different skills.

To say that specialization is essential to exchange, however, does not necessarily explain the phenomenon of marketing. Although specialization is fundamental to exchange as well as to marketing, there remains another question: *Why* do we exchange? The reason is that we recognize exchange as a means of accumulating wealth. The following schematic diagram illustrates this proposition:

Skills $\longrightarrow$ Specialization $\longrightarrow$ Exchange $\longrightarrow$ Wealth

Possessing different skills, each of us devotes the bulk of his time to using his skill once he recognizes the advantage of not being "a jack of all trades and a master of none." People use their skills to specialize when a benefit of some kind is recognized. Even in primitive societies some individuals are recognized as skilled in fishing, skilled in weaving, skilled in hunting. Their specialization in one of these activities creates more for the whole society than if each person divided his time among the several tasks needed to keep him and his society alive. In a complex and economically advanced society the occupations (skills) are very numerous. In the United States, for example, about 15 million people are engaged in manufacturing, about 7 million in agriculture, over 10 million in trade activities, and more than 11 million in the various service industries. These millions of people are *specializing* because they can best serve themselves and society by working for salaries or wages, in turn exchanging their money for the goods and services they need and desire. Most of these millions of Americans are neither capable nor desirous of being sufficient unto themselves. If, for example, we lived only unto ourselves and produced only our own immediate needs, we would be very poor indeed. It is because of our complex system of specialization and exchange that we and others enjoy the abundances and luxuries of a modern-day economic system.

Marketing activities and a marketing system make it possible for people to enjoy the full fruits of specialization and exchange. It is marketing that provides the institutions, the market communication, the prices, the order, the standards, and the direction for the tasks essential to a workable exchange mechanism. Marketing converts the outputs of producers into the standard of living of consumers. Therefore marketing is defined as "those activities necessary and incidental to bringing about exchange relationships."

MARKETING ADVANCES SOCIAL AND ECONOMIC WELFARE

Perhaps the most glaring error in economic reasoning is the common view that the economic process is one of *production* and *consumption*. Production does *not* involve the satisfaction of human wants except when some mechanism of distribution (or marketing) channels the inputs to the firm and the outputs to the consumers. The notion that the economic process is one of production and consumption has undoubtedly contributed to such shopworn clichés as "middlemen are parasites," "the only real value is the product," and "any activity not producing a physical commodity is unproductive."

In examining these fallacies it is essential to broaden our narrow concepts of utility. Utility in the economic sense refers to any object that can satisfy a human need. Marketing and distribution authorities have for many years emphasized production as the creation of *form utility*. It was noted that production does not satisfy human wants. A necessary corollary to the satisfaction of human wants is a marketing system and an exchange mechanism. Hence, marketing and exchange create the utilities essential to satisfying human wants. Marketers refer to the utilities created by marketing as *time* utility, *place* utility, and *possession* utility. These three kinds of utilities are intangible values created by the marketing system, but they are no less important than form utility. Thus, milk on the farm, automobiles at the factory, and lumber at the mill are not the same commodities as milk in the supermarket, automobiles at the dealer's showroom, and lumber at the construction site. Time utility and place utility have been added to the commodities, and all that remains is for the consumer to gain possession. Only then can a human want be satisfied. Although the physical aspects of a commodity are certainly important, who can judge the relative values of the several utilities?

Is form utility of greater value than those utilities created by marketing? It is commonly believed that the value or worth of anything is dependent on its physical properties. Kenneth E. Boulding, an economist at the University of Michigan, states:

Popular economic discussion often assumes that things have an "intrinsic" worth. As soon as we perceive the truth of the above proposition, however, it becomes clear that what a thing is worth to us depends on how much of it we have, and that therefore the "worth" is not anything "in" a commodity. It is not a physical property of an object like weight or volume, but is simply "how we feel about it." Things are "valuable" because somebody thinks they are, and for no other reason whatever. This is true, . . . , even of gold—a commodity which people are inclined to think has an "intrinsic" value. Gold, like everything else, is valuable only because people think it is.[1]

In following Professor Boulding's reasoning it is the contention of the authors of this book that a physical product has no value *per se*. Things have value only when a marketing system exists to create the other necessary utilities and when a market mechanism functions to convert the physical thing into satisfaction of human wants. If our economic process was only one of *production* and *consumption*, there would be a vast gap between the physical output of firms and the eventual satisfaction of human wants. Production, which creates the physical properties or form utility of an object, must be complemented by a marketing system; otherwise an economy will fall short of satisfying needs and wants. Furthermore, the objects of production cannot have value unless a demand for the objects is made *effective*. By creating time, place, and possession utilities, marketing turns the objects of production into a valued satisfaction.

The consequence of trade is that the parties in the transaction become better off. Without exchange of goods while we specialize, our storehouses would only bulge with our outputs. Because we can produce a large number of things, we are eager to exchange what we have for the things we lack. In other words, an actual purchase means that we value the object or service purchased greater than the money equivalent we pay. Correspondingly, the merchant who sells the object values the money more than the object exchanged. In this way we satisfy ourselves by acquiring the things we cannot provide alone.[2] We not only *feel* better off—we are! When this simple explanation is extended to an entire economy, one better understands our complex system of specialization and exchange and the means whereby we enjoy the many conveniences and luxuries of modern life. Not all marketing

---

[1] Kenneth E. Boulding, *Economic Analysis*, 3rd Ed. (New York: Harper & Row, 1955), p. 22.

[2] The reader should be aware that many people could provide some things more efficiently than the person from whom he makes the purchase. We are quite willing to forego the work of doing many things which could just as well satisfy us because we are even better off to practice our professions and occupations and not spend the time (less wisely) on some other endeavor. The basic economic *principle of best advantage* and the *principle of comparative advantage* contribute to this discussion. See Kenneth E. Boulding, *Economic Analysis*, 3rd Ed. (New York: Harper & Row, 1955), pp. 24–27.

It should also be pointed out that few people will exchange all they have. Some of their receipts (either money or goods) gained from specialization may be withheld. For example, a grower of apples may sell most of his yield, but retain some for his own use. The well-known economic principle of diminishing utility functions to influence the acquisitions and holdings of most people. It functions similarly in most economies on the globe.

necessarily enhances social and economic welfare, but more often than not it does.

MARKETING IS MULTIDISCIPLINARY

Seen as part of a total social organization, marketing takes on broad dimensions. This text regards the marketing system and marketing activities as evolving in response to a social and economic system. That the precise character of marketing differs from one society to another may be discerned from the varied levels of socioeconomic development which are readily observable from country to country. Yet common influences are at work in all societies, and in particular those societies organized on the basis of private ownership. Such economies are sometimes loosely referred to as "free-enterprise" economies, but with governments playing an increasingly important role in social and economic life, "mixed-enterprise system" may be a more appropriate designation.

Despite this lack of precise identification, when private ownership is the basis of organization, production decisions are heavily influenced by market opportunities. Market opportunities set the basis for production, which then flow to a market by means of a marketing system. In such a manner a society enjoys the products and services of an economy. Given the resources, abundance often typifies these societies as freedom of choice forces recognition of individual desires. Contrary to popular belief, individuality (in contrast to conformity) can be more fully expressed in societies where the market is a directing force and abundance is the response.

To understand marketing it becomes necessary to have knowledge of its nature and many interrelationships, for marketing is multidisciplinary. Of itself marketing does not provide a basis for understanding or studying the human and institutional activities involved. For this reason it is said that its character is *social, economic, technological,* and *political.* Closely allied to the political nature of marketing is the ethical framework in which marketing occurs. These disciplines, all contributing to a basic understanding of marketing, have a good deal of universality—that is, they function, but not with the same forcefulness, in all societies that can be catagorized as private-enterprise systems.

The schematic diagram in Figure 1-1 summarizes the multidisciplinary dimensions of marketing. This diagram will be further developed and modified in Chapter 2. This becomes necessary as some of the specifics of the disciplines become known and the principal components of marketing are discussed.

It is often assumed that one who practices marketing has an understanding of the subject. More likely, the practitioner comprehends the impact which his direction of marketing activities might have on the market place. To understand the *why of marketing* and the *why of a marketing system* requires

.Figure 1-1.

a study of the influences and forces that create marketing and give it observable dimensions. By studying the contributions of the disciplines summarized in Figure 1-1, one gains insight into why people, markets, and marketing institutions behave as they do. Once an individual knows the influences that explain marketing phenomena, he can better appreciate the adjustment and change so often needed to meet marketing's objectives.

THE CHARACTER OF MARKETING IS SOCIAL

The social aspects of marketing acquire importance because markets directly involve either people or institutions in which decisions are made by people. The social structure of a market is influenced by interpersonal and intergroup relationships. The response of people to market stimuli is most properly analyzed in terms of demographic factors, psychological influences, and the influences generated by a society's culture and traditions. Thus, when a market is said to have social influences, it means that the disciplines of sociology, psychology, and cultural anthropology can be utilized to understand some of its phenomena. This does not mean that all knowledge of these disciplines gives us insight. On the contrary, one must be eclectic in determining the significant contributions to an understanding of marketing.

In economics the student learns to accept the wants and desires of a market as given. In marketing this cannot apply, for underlying all markets and marketing activities is the matter of individual choice. Choices made in the market have determinants that are not solely economic. Variations and distortions in demand are responses which, among other things, can be explained by individual and group behavior. The family life cycle, where and how people live, their tendency to accept new and technologically complex things, variations in education and occupation, and cultural patterns—these are a few examples of market influences not in the economic domain. An examination of the socio-psychological influences relevant to marketing affords insight into the consumer's behavior in the marketplace.

THE CHARACTER OF MARKETING IS ECONOMIC

Although the economic influences in marketing are many, the essential ones are (1) the economic status of consumers, (2) the kind of competition that permeates the market, and (3) price determination.

Even though many influences in the market are not economic, the economic status of a society's populace is the ingredient that turns desires into effective demand. Without money income and money to spend, the socio-psychological aspects of an economy would lie dormant. Money income remains the most fundamental basis for the functioning of the social variables, and as such it gives impetus to other market influences.

The United States and other advanced economies have experienced marked rises in consumer income. Further reinforcement of consumer incomes has come from the decline in their concentration. This permits a vast array of goods to occupy an important position in the family budget. Family outlays differ from one income level to another and become quite pronounced when the material necessities are easily acquired by virtue of high incomes. Thus when incomes are relatively high outlays for material things represent a diminishing share of the budget. The principal effect at this stage of consumer welfare seems to be the declining importance of income and a rising importance of the socio-psychological variables. Hence, consumption patterns cannot be attributed solely to economic influences, but the economic welfare of consumers plays a dominant role in giving birth and reality to the behavioral influences.

In turning to the nature of competition and pricing, we find rival companies trying to take sales from one another. Individual firms' decisions and market strategies are influenced by their reactions to rival market offerings and vice versa. At the core of exchange transactions reside the influences of competition and pricing. Marketing has always respected the effect of the economist's theoretical descriptions on production, consumption, and the distribution of goods and services. To this end economic theory contributes to what is produced, and how outputs can be distributed to a market. Marketing and economics share common interests in the analyses of competition and pricing. Through insight into these economic functions, explanations about who participates, how they behave, and what their impact is on the market are more clearly understood.

THE CHARACTER OF MARKETING IS POLITICAL AND ETHICAL

The political character of marketing lies in the legal nature of marketing activities which lead to exchange processes. No business, and particularly if it is engaged in marketing, can operate very long without contact with the legal framework. Marketing functions within the framework of law. The legal dimension is one of the most highly formalized and complex influences on marketing behavior. It regulates pricing, competitive activities, the degree of market control exercised by industries and individual firms, and the nature of promotional activities, all of which are designed to have an impact on the sale of goods and services.

The ethical aspect of marketing has subtler impact than the legal framework. However, it is closely related to the political character of marketing, for often the alternative to ethical behavior of business is legislative enactments. Law and ethics, though free of identical interpretation, set the boundaries of operation for marketing.

THE CHARACTER OF MARKETING IN TECHNOLOGICAL

Modern technology has wrought many changes in man and has profound effects on an economic system. It is the basis for today's production and distribution methods: the source of new inventions, improved products, and product and service innovations. When the state of modern technology is considered together with the advancement of the socioeconomic factors, its influence is recognized as related to our standard of living. With the broad implications of technology identified, it becomes apparent not only that must production change and adjust to technological genius and skill, but that enormous pressures are also built up in the marketing system. For the most part, marketing has responded well to these pressures. In doing so, the physical movement of goods, the kinds and sizes of institutions, and the communicative skills have kept pace and given balance to the production-marketing structure. Even though the state of technology and its impact on marketing have seldom been a concern of marketing, technology becomes an integral force, along with the others, in the scheme of this book.

THE PLAN OF STUDY

Now that some of the specific subjects of discussion have been added to the broad multidisciplinary character of marketing, it is appropriate to revise Figure 1-1. Figure 1-2 depicts the more detailed concepts which lend themselves to understanding the *why* of marketing phenomena.

It should be observed that Chapters 4 through 11 contain detailed discussions of the subjects outlined in Figure 1-2. Despite the necessity of treating each subject separately, the several disciplines combine to form marketing's environment and relevant forces.

This volume is a study of the basic principles, concepts, and forces that help to explain the phenomenon of marketing. Although we emphasize marketing in a setting which is socially and economically advanced, our approach is also intended to be useful in understanding and analyzing marketing in less advanced economies. Both purposes are served, because a major portion of this volume provides an analytical framework which explains why marketing is necessarily complex and why it adjusts to changing social and economic stimuli.

MARKETING—A RESPONSE TO THE SOCIAL SYSTEM

The authors believe that marketing comes about and evolves in response to the social structure. Whenever man or a society rises above the level of

Figure 1-2. The environment and forces of marketing.

self-sufficiency, marketing is likely to emerge and attain increasing importance as the society continues to advance. As a nation (or society) develops, the need for an abundance of social organizations is soon felt. The populace comes to need medical and dental care, a legal framework within which to live and act, productive skills and capacities to create the items demanded, a monetary structure and, of course, a system to distribute goods and services which in turn satisfy the demands of the people. Such a system, whether extremely simple or large and complex, is referred to as a *marketing system*.

Questions

1. Compare your marketing environment with that which your parents experienced at your age.
2. How would you quantify the marketing task?
3. Examine the marketing of several consumer and industrial products and determine which factors are common to the marketing processes.
4. What is meant when one argues that goods and services do not have intrinsic value?
5. Explain why one of the first important forces in the marketing environment was the recognition of the advantages of specialization.

Statements to Consider

Marketing is any activity which actualizes the potential market relationship among the market users of economic goods and services.

The final objective of marketing is to make goods and services available for use.

In marketing terms, it is somewhat more precise to say that exchange takes place in order to increase the utility of the assortments held by each party to the transaction.

It follows, then, that the two principal or most basic tasks of marketing are (1) to direct the use of resources and allocate scarce supplies in conformity with existing demand, and (2) to aid in making consumption dynamic in conformity with changes in our ability to cater to human wants.

SELECTED REFERENCES

Martin L. Bell, *Marketing: Concepts and Strategy* (Boston: Houghton Mifflin Company, 1966).
Cyril S. Belshaw, *Traditional Exchange and Modern Markets* (Englewood Cliffs, N.J.: Prentice-Hall, 1965).

Alfred Kuhn, *The Study of Society* (Homewood, Ill.: Irwin-Dorsey Series, 1963).

Karl Polanyi, Conrad M. Arensberg, and Harry W. Pearson, *Trade and Markets in the Early Empires* (Glencoe, Ill.: The Free Press, 1957).

Roland S. Vaile, E. T. Grether, and Reavis Cox, *Marketing in the American Economy* (New York: The Ronald Press Company, 1952).

° George W. Robbins, "Notions About the Origins of Trading," *Journal of Marketing,* Vol. 11, No. 3, January 1947, pp. 228–236.

° Arch W. Shaw, "Some Problems in Market Distribution," pp. 35–53 in Hugh G. Wales (ed.), *Changing Perspectives in Marketing* (Urbana: University of Illinois Press, 1951).

Generalizations Were Taken From:

William C. McInnes, "A Conceptual Approach to Marketing," in Reavis Cox, Wroe Alderson, and Stanley Shapiro (eds.), *Theory in Marketing,* Second Series (Homewood, Ill.: Richard D. Irwin, 1964).

Roland S. Vaile, E. T. Grether, and Reavis Cox, *Marketing in the American Economy* (New York: The Ronald Press Company, 1952).

Wroe Alderson, *Marketing Behavior and Executive Action* (Homewood, Ill.: Richard D. Irwin, 1957).

° Readings marked by an asterisk appear in the authors' selected readings, R. J. Holloway and R. S. Hancock, *The Environment of Marketing Behavior* (New York: John Wiley and Sons, 1964).

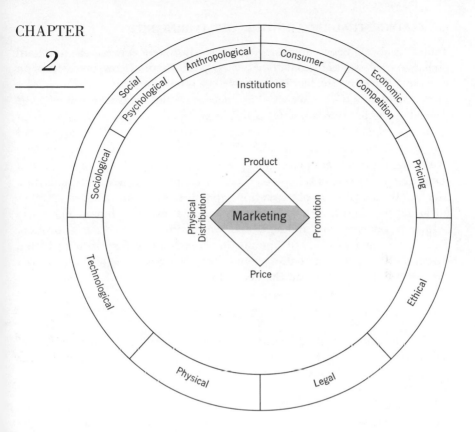

The System of Marketing

THE FLOW OF GOODS IN THE ECONOMY • MARKETING NETWORK IN THE ECO-
NOMY • THE FIRM—A SUBSYSTEM • THE COMPONENTS OF MARKETING   *The*
Offer   The Market   The System   The Forces
ADDENDUM: SUPPLEMENTARY INFORMATION ON MARKETING INSTITUTIONS

There has always been a tendency, particularly among economists, to regard exchange processes as the only device needed to distribute the products of an economy. However, the fact is that exchange is only one element of a broader marketing system. Other activities are necessary, and for this reason we have defined marketing as *those activities necessary and incidental to bringing about exchange relationships.* The definition suggests that marketing is a set of activities. Some activities become readily apparent when we reflect that marketing creates time, place, and possession utilities. Space gaps between the actual production of things and their consumption suggest other activities. Much of the actual work of marketing is physical, since our definition implies a transfer of things from one hand to another. It also will have much to do with how resources are allocated and who is involved in their allocation. Thus, prices and profits will operate in the system. Before turning to the specifics of marketing activities, it may help the reader to have an overall view of the flow of goods in the economy.

THE FLOW OF GOODS IN THE ECONOMY

The colossal task of distributing goods and services in a multibillion-dollar economy is depicted in Figure 2-1. At first glance the figure may appear bewildering and complex, but on examination it is quite simple, condensed, and yet comprehensive.

Goods and services pour into the economy from one of the four sources shown at the left of Figure 2-1—agriculture, imports, extractive, and the public utility, transportation, and service industries. The outputs are taken out at the right by households, government, capital formation, and exports. Manufacturing, intermediate trade (mostly wholesalers), and retail trade function within the system, but they neither bring things into it nor take things out of it.[1]

The size of the bands or lines are approximate values of the purchases by a sector or the sales to a sector, whichever is the case. Contrary to popular belief, a large amount of trade occurs with groups in a seller's own sector. Such trade and their magnitudes are shown by the "backflows" emanating from the top of the blocks. The buying and selling among members of the same sector is of major proportions in manufacturing, construction, and intermediate trade.

Another interesting aspect shown in the figure is the differences in band widths between inflows into a sector and outflows. The outflows are of greater magnitude than the inflows. This difference is referred to as "roughly equiva-

[1] Reavis Cox *et al., Distribution in a High Level Economy* (Englewood Cliffs, N.J.: Prentice-Hall, 1965), p. 37.

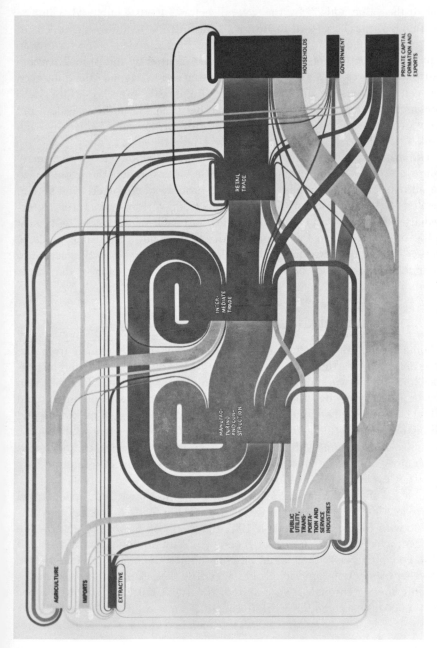

Figure 2-1. The flow of ownership. (Reprinted by permission of Prentice-Hall, Inc.)

lent to the value added" by the several sectors.[2] Each sector adds value to the things it purchases and in turn sells. From time to time the student of marketing will be confronted with the term "value added." The term is an approximate measure of the additional value created by the productive and distributive processes. It avoids double counting since it signifies the difference between shipments (or sales) and the cost of materials, supplies, utilities, and containers purchased. Thus the difference between the outflows (sales) and inflows (purchases) represents a rough measure of the value added by each block.

The main point to be gained from Figure 2-1 is the knowledge that many groups are involved in getting goods and services through the economy to the ultimate markets. Numerous exchange processes take place even among members of the same sector. Manufacturers trade with manufacturers, intermediaries trade with other intermediaries, and each sector trades with most of the others shown in the diagram. All of these flows from one place to another involve the performance of marketing activities. Marketing activities are highly important to the efficiency and smooth functioning of the whole system.

MARKETING NETWORK IN THE ECONOMY

Some idea of the dimensions of the marketing task is gained from the large number of participants in the system.[3] Marketing agencies and institutions form the network and they function in each of the ten sectors shown in Figure 2-1. Any agency that enters into exchange processes of buying and selling can be identified as a marketing institution. In carrying on buying and selling, other marketing activities become essential. Some agencies, however, specialize in marketing. Their principal activity is the marketing of goods which other units of the network produce. Agencies engaged in intermediate and retail trade are of this kind.

Table 2-1 shows the approximate number of firms for each of the identified sectors in Figure 2-1. Although the data in Table 2-1 are not strictly comparable with Figure 2-1 (based on 1947 transactions), they do dramatize the total task necessary in our kind of economy. With a population of over 190 million people in more than 53 million households, the number of cumulative activities, transactions, and goods is staggering. One estimate of the number of items flowing through such a system records 3,750,000. Of this number about 1,000,000 are goods available to civilians and military. About 500,000

---

[2] *Ibid.*, p. 38.
[3] For the interested reader, the Addendum to this chapter includes selected and detailed information on marketing institutions. See pp. 29–39.

Table 2-1. Number of Agencies in Marketing Network

		Economic Sector		
	Manufacturing and	Trade		Consumption
Origin	Construction	Intermediate	Retail	and Use
Agriculture (4,783,021)		Wholesalers, agents and other (285,996)	Retail (1,707,931)	Households (53,021,000)
	Manufacturers (331,000)			Governments (91,237)
Imports (n.a.)				
	Construction (476,000)			
Extractors (75,026)		·		Private capital formation and exports (n.a.)
Public utility and service (n.a.)				

SOURCES: 1963 Census of Business, *Retail Trade: United States Summary*, United States Department of Commerce, and *Statistical Abstract of the United States*, 1965.

items are used by civilian agencies alone whereas the remainder are exclusively military goods.[4]

The magnitude of the marketing task and the nature of the activities in the marketing system vary, of course, from one economy to another. This was implied earlier. In underdeveloped economies the objectives of the system differ from those of advanced economies, but marketing activities may be similar. People in an underdeveloped society look to the system for better housing, improved health, more and better clothing, and the relief of misery. In an economy of abundance, on the other hand, people look to the system for a continued stream of goods and services for the improvement and maintenance of an already high living standard. Although a high living standard is not universally enjoyed in the United States, this goal will be supplied by marketing when the means become available for the nonsharing

[4] See Dickson Reck, *Government Purchasing and Competition* (Berkeley: University of California Press, 1954), p. 9.

residents to share in the abundance. In the broadest sense, the goal of marketing is to bridge the available resources of production with their use and consumption. Satisfaction is the end of the system. A marketing network is one of the elements needed to attain both goal and end.

THE FIRM—A SUBSYSTEM

Much of the preceding discussion has emphasized the aggregate aspect of marketing. Within an economy's network of marketing the firm constitutes a subsystem. In the individual firm, production and marketing decisions are made, and in particular, firms carry out marketing activities. Through marketing materials, supplies, and other resources flow to the firm. In turn, goods and services are produced and then moved to the various markets. Flowing from the markets is the money from use and consumption expenditures. Marketing thus produces the revenue for the firm and hence its profits.

Given the resources, what set of marketing activities must the firm perform to convert goods into money? If the firm is responsive to market conditions, its products will be approximately compatible with market demand. Hence, *product*[5] is one marketing activity. The firm feels the pulse of the market through its marketing system, and as a result numerous product characteristics reflect market demand. Certainly many aspects of a product are not marketing, but more properly fall into the realm of engineering and other technological skills. There are, however, many marketing aspects to most products, such as quality, features, design, use, brand name, package, and the like. Marketing is thus concerned with the development of products, changes in existing products and product lines, and the uncovering of new uses for them.

Another marketing activity is *price*. The products of all firms must be priced. Price has traditionally been considered a key marketing variable and has both internal and external implications for the firm. Internally it contributes to determination of the magnitude of the firm's revenue, assuming that it is a price which does not hamper sales goals. External influences are general business conditions and the actions and reactions of competitors in the market place. Another and equally important influence is the customer's responses to the price of the offering. Price, therefore, must also be compatible with the socio-psychological variables that influence customer behavior. For example, the belief that the lowering of price will expand the quantity sold in the market is often untrue. The lowering of price may be viewed by customers as a reduction in quality. Pricing also has legal and

---

[5] The term *product* most often has the connotation of physical goods. As used here it means goods or services, whichever is applicable. In some of the discussion which follows, it is not possible to equate the two. This is particularly true in the physical distribution of actual products, but this is perhaps obvious to the reader.

ethical implications. For now it is adequate merely to note that price is another marketing variable with which the firm must contend.

Distribution is yet another marketing activity. In order for the firm to engage eventually in an exchange process, its goods have to be physically moved from one place to another. This suggests as a minimum both transportation and storage. But goods are not sold directly to users and consumers. Figure 2-1 shows that goods flow through a complicated network of intermediate traders and agencies. So it is with the firm as a subsystem. Its products flow through certain intermediate agencies within the network. The particular agency selected for the handling of the firm's goods is referred to as the *channel of distribution* or *marketing channel*. A wide range of combinations faces the firm, and its choices influence its success in the market place. The marketing activity encompassing all the aspects of the movement and flow of goods and attendant services is called *physical distribution*.

Finally, there is *promotion*. The market must be informed of the firm's offer in the market place. This the firm does through promotion activity.

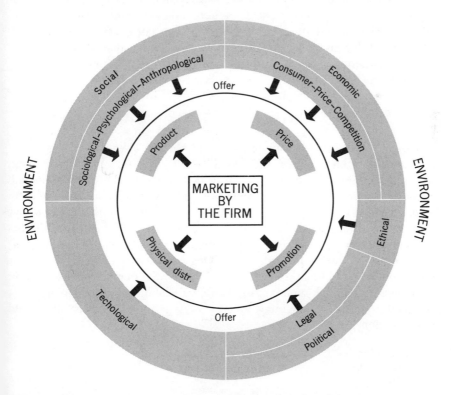

Figure 2-2. The environment, forces, and activities of marketing.

Promotion can take the form of advertising or personal selling or a combination of the two.

Among these activities there is a high degree of interaction. The determination of price, the promotion, and the physical distribution activities are governed by the actual product, however. There has to be a starting point for marketing activities, and this logically rests with first having a product to sell.

Now that the marketing activities common to all marketing firms have been introduced, it is again appropriate to revise our earlier schematic diagram, Figure 1-2 (see Chapter 1). Figure 2-2 is a complete schematic representation of our approach to marketing. The marketing activities of the firm have been cast within an environmental framework.

The firm and its marketing activities are the central focus in Figure 2-2. Hence, they become the central focus of this book and our view of marketing derives from that standpoint. We treat marketing as an integral group of activities, all of which are conditioned, given impetus, and influenced by the environmental framework and forces. This approach corresponds closely with our early definition of the subject. A band labeled "Offer" surrounds the various marketing activities. In this way they are portrayed as integral and interacting. Whereas Part II of this volume is concerned with the environment of marketing, Part III discusses the offer, with individual chapters devoted to each of its parts.

THE COMPONENTS OF MARKETING

In any approach to the study of marketing there is always the danger that the student will be confused and bewildered by the subject's far-reaching and multidisciplinary character. Some of this is due to the often-presented quantitative data showing the dimensions and results of marketing and to the discussion of minor facets too numerous for orderly comprehension. Minimization of such an occurrence may come about if one knows precisely the components of marketing. If the components are known and understood, a greater possibility exists for orderly thinking on the subject at hand.

The components of marketing have been suggested in much of the preceding discussion. Through summarizing them and elaborating on them, a somewhat better understanding may emerge of what marketing is all about. These components are:

1. The offer.
2. The market.
3. The system.
4. The environment and forces.

The Offer

An offer is a result of economic and marketing activities of the firm. The term encompasses every conceivable variable that might influence the offer's acceptance or rejection by a buyer. It is an *offer* that people and institutional buyers purchase. It is not too shocking to learn that a product such as a pair of shoes, an automobile, or a pound of rice is not *all* that a purchaser accepts. What he really accepts is an offer which includes every facet that might encourage or discourage his purchase. Included in the term, of course, is product, but so are its package, market information, method of distribution, price, the image of the selling firm, and the like. Briefly, it includes the what, when, who, how, and by and through whom of the purchase.

The Market

The term "market" has been used widely in the preceding discussion. Because of its frequent use it is undoubtedly of importance to marketing thought and understanding. The American Marketing Association defines a market in two ways. First, a market is *"the aggregate of forces or conditions within which buyers and sellers make decisions that result in the transfer of goods and services."* Second, it is *"the aggregate demand of the potential buyers of a commodity or service."*[6] Other definitions of a market are also stated in aggregate terms. Two other commonly held definitions are (1) that a market is people with money and an inclination to buy, and (2) that a market is the place (or geographical area) where the exchange process occurs.

One of the difficulties encountered in each of the foregoing definitions is that they are stated in aggregate terms and thus do little more than point out *where* a market might be or of *what* it might consist. It is a basic necessity to be able to identify the aggregate market, but that market is not the ultimate concern of the firm. More important, the market for any particular firm is a *segment* of the aggregate market. In automobile manufacturing, for example, the market for automobiles may have a potential of nine million new vehicles. As no single automobile manufacturer can hope to capture the entire market, a more meaningful and specific terminology is used. Reference is therefore made to the market for General Motors vehicles, the market for cars of the Ford Motor Company, and so on, until a market for a specific model and a specific name can be identified. A definition of the market which seems to overcome the deficiencies of earlier ones is the following:

A market is a group of buyers and sellers within a geographical area: (a) for a product or reasonable substitutes; (b) at a particular stage in the trade channel, such

---

[6] Ralph S. Alexander, Chairman of Committee of Definitions, *Marketing Definitions* (Chicago: American Marketing Association, 1960).

as manufacturers selling to retailers, or consumers buying from retailers; and (c) at a particular time.[7]

This definition is more detailed than others and implies that a market has both sellers and buyers, that the demand is for specific goods, that the market can exist in many particular places, and that time is a necessary element. As a meaningful component of marketing, a market should be defined by the greater detail and implied specifics of this definition. Some idea of the complexity in defining an actual market is illustrated by Box 2-1.

In addition to having a somewhat precise concept of a market, it has been implied that it is useful to understand the segmentation of markets. Box 2-1 also helps the reader to grasp this concept. Market segmentation is of little concern in economies that can be characterized as having a homogeneous demand. When a homogeneous demand exists, vast numbers of the population demand almost identical things. However, when a market is one of abundance and luxury, such as in the United States and other highly developed economies, many opportunities exist for a firm to segment the market. The markets of the United States are highly segmented. This is another way of saying that our heterogeneous demands are met by the market's heterogeneous offers.

The concept of market segmentation can be viewed as the opportunity for a manufacturer to obtain a strong hold on a portion of the market by means of product differentiation. Hence, the producer makes a strong appeal to a market segment rather than to the aggregate market. This is one of the practical applications of the concept, but it does not explain *why* markets can be segmented. One reason markets are susceptible to segmentation resides in diverse demographic characteristics. Differences in age, sex, geography, and money available to spend are examples of demographic segmentation. Occupational differences, education, and ethnic group also help to explain market segments. Many of us have actually observed these elements functioning in a market. Another and somewhat subtler reason for this phenomenon may be found in buyer attitudes. The attitudes of buyers are influenced by their motivations, cultural patterns, aesthetic preferences, and sense of values. Differences in attitudes may be equally or more important in explaining that behavior which permits a market to be segmented.

The System

The task of distributing goods and services to an entire economy has been depicted in Figure 2-1, and the accompanying discussion has pointed out the complicated network of agencies and intermediaries. This was referred to as

---

[7]Paul D. Converse, Harvey W. Huegy, and Robert V. Mitchell, *Elements of Marketing* (Englewood Cliffs, N.J.: Prentice-Hall, 1965), p. 7 (Reprinted by the permission of Prentice-Hall, Inc.).

BOX 2-1

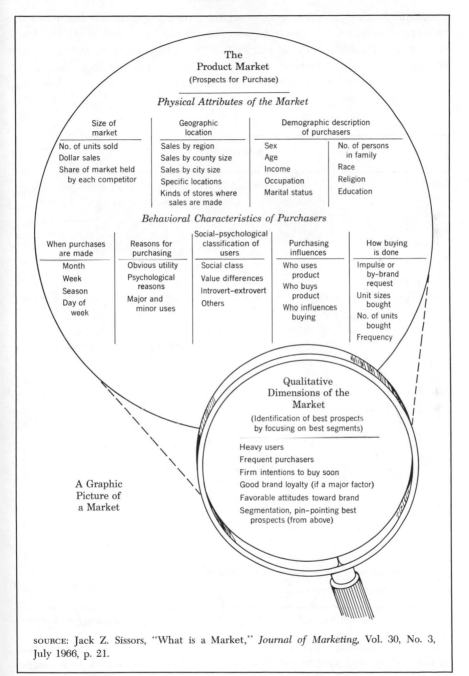

The Product Market
(Prospects for Purchase)

Physical Attributes of the Market

Size of market	Geographic location	Demographic description of purchasers	
No. of units sold	Sales by region	Sex	No. of persons in family
Dollar sales	Sales by county size	Age	Race
Share of market held by each competitor	Sales by city size	Income	Religion
	Specific locations	Occupation	Education
	Kinds of stores where sales are made	Marital status	

Behavioral Characteristics of Purchasers

When purchases are made	Reasons for purchasing	Social-psychological classification of users	Purchasing influences	How buying is done
Month	Obvious utility	Social class	Who uses product	Impulse or by-brand request
Week	Psychological reasons	Value differences	Who buys product	Unit sizes bought
Season	Major and minor uses	Introvert–extrovert	Who influences buying	No. of units bought
Day of week		Others		Frequency

Qualitative Dimensions of the Market
(Identification of best prospects by focusing on best segments)

Heavy users
Frequent purchasers
Firm intentions to buy soon
Good brand loyalty (if a major factor)
Favorable attitudes toward brand
Segmentation, pin-pointing best prospects (from above)

A Graphic Picture of a Market

SOURCE: Jack Z. Sissors, "What is a Market," *Journal of Marketing,* Vol. 30, No. 3, July 1966, p. 21.

25

a *system*. Similarly, but in more specific terms, a system for the physical movement of the firm's products must be selected or developed. The *how* of getting goods from a manufacturer to any market can be answered in one of two ways. A manufacturer can develop his own marketing channel by owning and operating the intermediate and retail (if the product is one sold to consumers) facilities. Few manufacturers are inclined to expend their

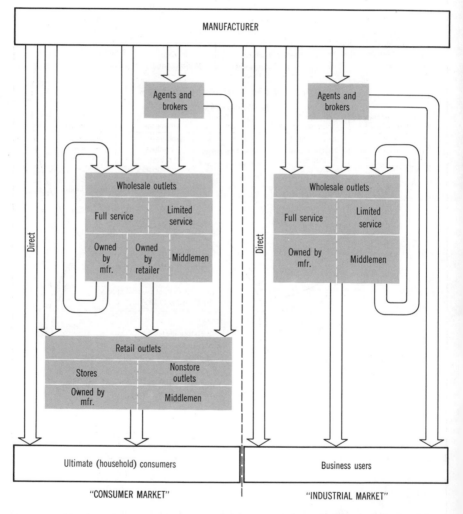

Figure 2-3. Schematic diagram of possible marketing channels for manufactured products. (Copyright 1962 by the President and Fellows of Harvard College. Reproduced from Note on Marketing Channels ICH 10M 65(EA M 480) by permission.)

resources for this purpose and instead adopt a substitute method. The substitute method means that the manufacturer selects firms already operating in the distributive structure.

Figure 2-3 illustrates the array of distribution channels open to the manufacturer of either consumer goods or industrial goods. The options available to him are often combined so that more than a single channel may be used. The selection of a channel or a combination of channels is dependent upon the nature of the product, the kind of market segment to be approached, and the kind and amount of effort needed for effective marketing.

The important point at this time is that each firm producing goods will have to adopt some system of distribution compatible with its marketing goals. Such a system is essential to the creation of time, place, and possession utilities, or to those values born of marketing. The *system* adopted will carry the *offer* to the *market*.

The Forces

This final component of marketing refers to the environment in which marketing takes place. It is conceived as the final component because environmental forces influence the nature and character of the offer, the market, and the system. In preceding sections much has been implied or specifically noted as an influence on marketing behavior. As one pursues the study of marketing, one should bear in mind that the environmental forces contribute to every facet of change and adjustment in a marketing network. Little if any substantive understanding of marketing in an economy or marketing by a firm can be had without a perception of the principal influences that shape the behavior of marketing itself.

Questions

1. Describe the flow of a product from its beginning to the time it is consumed. What role does marketing play?
2. What really is a *market?* Describe its many meanings.
3. How can the concept of a "system" be applied to marketing?
4. Why is the change in ownership emphasized in the study of marketing?
5. Do you agree that marketing activities begin where production activities end?

Statements to Consider

On balance, cost is the most important consideration in determining any middleman's place in the channel of distribution.

Technical products of high unit value tend to have a short channel of distribution.

The tendency of manufacturers to locate near markets is further strengthened by their marketing requirements. Marketing tends to increase in relative cost as goods move through the successive stages of production toward ultimate consumers.

Since retailing comprises the activities and organizations of marketing that sell goods and services directly to consumers, it must be in some sense as widespread as the people it serves.

Organizations are inherently vulnerable to change because fixed patterns of behavior cannot be expected to persist indefinitely.

Possibly the most essential function of a marketing firm is that of handling information and acting as a kind of switchboard connecting the consumer who has a specialized need with the specialized product which can satisfy his need.

SELECTED REFERENCES

Ralph S. Alexander, James S. Cross, and Ross M. Cunningham, *Industrial Marketing*, Revised Edition (Homewood, Ill.: Richard D. Irwin, 1961).

Richard M. Clewett (ed.), *Marketing Channels* (Homewood, Ill.: Richard D. Irwin, 1954).

Robert D. Entenberg, *Effective Retail and Market Distribution: A Managerial Economic Approach* (New York: The World Publishing Company, 1966).

Richard M. Hill, *Wholesaling Management: Text and Cases* (Homewood, Ill.: Richard D. Irwin, 1963).

Stanley C. Hollander, *Explorations in Retailing* (East Lansing,: Bureau of Business and Economic Research, Graduate School of Business Administration, Michigan State University, 1959).

Schuyler F. Otteson, William G. Panschar, and James M. Patterson, *Marketing: The Firm's Viewpoint* (New York: The Macmillan Company, 1964).

Jac L. Goldstucker, "A Study of Wholesale Trading Areas," *Journal of Marketing*, Vol. 26, No. 2, April 1962, pp. 22–25.

° Industrial Marketing Committee Review Board, "Fundamental Differences Between Industrial and Consumer Marketing," *Journal of Marketing*, Vol. 19, No. 2, October 1954, pp. 152–158.

Bernard Lester, "Changing Methods in the Marketing of Industrial Equipment," *Journal of Marketing*, Vol. 1, No. 1, July 1936, pp. 46–52.

° Pierre Martineau, "The Personality of the Retail Store," *Harvard Business Review*, Vol. 36, No. 1, January–February 1958, pp. 47–55.

Gerald B. Tallman and Bruce Blomstrom, "Retail Innovations Challenge Manufacturers," *Harvard Business Review*, Vol. 40, No. 5, September-October 1962, pp. 130–143.

Generalizations Were Taken From:

Rayburn D. Tousley, Eugene Clark, and Fred E. Clark, *Principles of Marketing* (New York: The Macmillan Company, 1962).

Theodore N. Beckman, Nathaniel H. Engle, and Robert D. Buzzell, *Wholesaling* (New York: The Ronald Press Company, 1959).

Roland S. Vaile, E. T. Grether, and Reavis Cox, *Marketing in the American Economy* (*New York: The Ronald Press Company, 1952*).

Wroe Alderson, Marketing Behavior and Executive Action (Homewood, Ill.: Richard D. Irwin, 1957).

ADDENDUM. *Supplementary Information on Marketing Institutions*

Additional information on United States marketing institutions and consumer expenditures is provided in this addendum. Useful insights can be gained from a study of the data, but the reader should recognize that marketing institutions are constantly changing as they adjust to the dynamic environmental conditions.

List of Addendum Tables

2–1. Personal Consumption Expenditures, 1946–1964

2–2. Retail Trade, United States, 1958 and 1963

2–3. Number of Retail Establishments, Sales and Population, 1963

2–4. Retail Sales by Geographic Division, 1963

2–5. Retail Sales, Standard Metropolitan Statistical Areas, 1963

2–6. Retail Sales, SMSA's, Cities, and Central Business Districts, 1958 to 1963

2–7. Selected Services, United States, 1958 and 1963

2–8. Selected Services, Geographic Division, 1963

2–9. Selected Services, SMSA's, 1963

2–10. Wholesale Trade, Establishments and Sales, 1958 and 1963

2–11. Wholesale Trade, United States, 1963

2–12. Wholesale Trade, Geographic Division, 1963

Addendum Table 2-1. Personal Consumption Expenditures, 1946–1964

		Billions—Constant Dollars		
Year	Total	Durable Goods	Nondurable Goods	Service
1946	$203.5	20.5	110.8	72.1
1947	206.3	24.7	108.3	73.4
1948	210.8	26.3	108.7	75.8
1949	216.5	28.4	110.5	77.6
1950	230.5	34.7	114.0	81.8
1951	232.8	31.5	116.5	84.8
1952	239.4	30.8	120.8	87.8
1953	250.8	35.3	124.4	91.1
1954	255.7	35.4	125.5	94.8
1955	274.2	43.2	131.7	99.3
1956	281.4	41.0	136.2	104.1
1957	288.2	41.5	138.7	108.0
1958	290.1	37.9	140.2	112.0
1959	307.3	43.7	146.9	116.8
1960	316.2	44.9	149.7	121.6
1961	322.6	43.9	153.1	125.6
1962	338.6	49.2	158.4	131.1
1963	352.4	53.2	161.8	137.3
1964	372.1	58.5	169.4	144.2

SOURCE: United States Bureau of Census, Biennial Supplement to *The Survey of Current Business, Business Statistics, 1965* (Washington, D.C.: United States Government Printing Office, 1965).

Addendum Table 2-2. Retail Trade, United States, 1958 and 1963

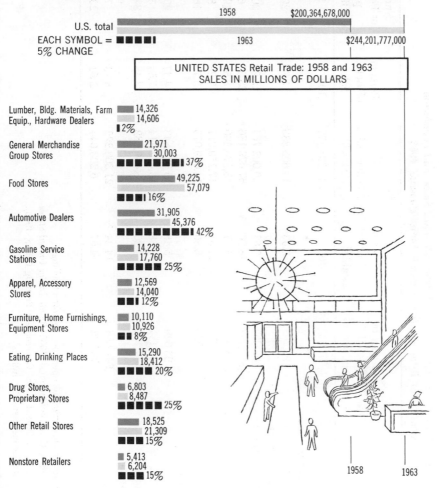

1958 $200,364,678,000

U.S. total

EACH SYMBOL = ■ ■ ■ ■ I   1963 $244,201,777,000
5% CHANGE

UNITED STATES Retail Trade: 1958 and 1963
SALES IN MILLIONS OF DOLLARS

Lumber, Bldg. Materials, Farm   14,326
Equip., Hardware Dealers   14,606
I 2%

General Merchandise   21,971
Group Stores   30,003
■■■■■■■I 37%

Food Stores   49,225
57,079
■■■I 16%

Automotive Dealers   31,905
45,376
■■■■■■■I 42%

Gasoline Service   14,228
Stations   17,760
■■■■■ 25%

Apparel, Accessory   12,569
Stores   14,040
■■I 12%

Furniture, Home Furnishings,   10,110
Equipment Stores   10,926
■■ 8%

Eating, Drinking Places   15,290
18,412
■■■■I 20%

Drug Stores,   6,803
Proprietary Stores   8,487
■■■■■ 25%

Other Retail Stores   18,525
21,309
■■■ 15%

Nonstore Retailers   5,413
6,204
■■■ 15%

1958   1963

1963 CENSUS OF BUSINESS, U.S. Department of Commerce, Bureau of the Census

Addendum Table 2-3. Number of Retail Establishments, Sales, and Population in Relation to Total Number of Retail Establishments, 1963

Type of Establishment	Number of Retail Establishments	Percent of Retail Establishments	Dollar Sales ($1,000)	Percent of Retail Sales	Number of Persons per Establishment
Total	1,707,931	100	244,201,777	100	110
Lumber, building materials, hardware, and farm equipment dealers	92,703	5.43	14,605,836	5.98	2038
General merchandise stores (department stores, limited price variety stores, etc.)[a]	62,063	3.63	30,002,764	12.29	3039
Food stores	319,433	18.70	57,079,186	23.37	691
Automobile dealers	98,514	5.77	45,376,290	18.58	1915
Gasoline stations	211,473	12.38	17,759,917	7.27	892
Apparel and accessory stores	116,223	6.80	14,039,979	5.75	1623
Furniture, home furnishings, and equipment	93,649	5.48	10,925,843	4.47	2015
Eating and drinking establishments	334,481	19.58	18,412,414	7.54	562
Drug stores and propriety stores	54,732	3.20	8,486,682	3.48	3447
Other retail stores (liquor, antique, bookstores, etc.)	244,868	14.34	21,309,222	8.73	770
Nonstore retailers[b]	79,792	4.67	6,203,644	2.54	2367

[a] Included in nonstore category.

[b] Nonstore includes mail-order houses, vending machine operators, and direct selling.

SOURCE: United States Bureau of Census, Census of Business, 1963. *Retail Trade: United States Summary*, BC63–RA1, (Washington, D.C.: United States Government Printing Office, 1965). Ratios and estimated persons per establishment are the authors'.

Addendum Table 2-4. Retail Sales by Geographic Division, 1963

Geographic Division	Number of Retail Units	Sales ($1,000)	Percent Change in Sales, 1958 to 1963
Total United States	1,707,931	244,201,777	21.9
New England	102,713	15,087,951	21.2
Middle Atlantic	336,700	46,947,929	16.2
East North Central	333,723	50,611,215	20.0
West North Central	158,275	21,054,215	15.6
South Atlantic	239,167	32,364,547	27.0
East South Central	111,565	12,351,046	25.7
West South Central	162,262	20,991,111	18.8
Mountain	69,263	10,147,423	28.1
Pacific	194,263	34,646,339	32.1

SOURCE: United States Bureau of Census, Census of Business, 1963. *Retail Trade: United States Summary*, BC63-RA1, (Washington, D.C.: United States Government Printing Office, 1965).

Addendum Table 2-5. Top Twenty Standard Metropolitan Statistical Areas Ranked by Retail Sales with Accompanying Population Rank and Per Capita Sales, 1963

SMSA and Rank	Sales ($1,000)	Population Rank	Per Capita Sales ($)
New York City	15,646,307	1	1,663
Los Angeles–Long Beach	10,687,367	3	1,770
Chicago	9,889,061	2	1,590
Philadelphia	5,737,442	4	1,321
Detroit	5,393,024	5	1,433
San Francisco–Oakland	4,511,342	6	1,703
Boston	3,972,873	7	1,531
Washington, D.C. (Maryland–Virginia)	3,366,922	10	1,682
Pittsburgh	2,878,235	8	1,197
St. Louis, Missouri–Illinois	2,847,475	9	1,353
Cleveland	2,715,566	11	1,422
Newark, New Jersey	2,582,485	13	1,529
Baltimore, Maryland	2,265,647	12	1,312
Minneapolis–St. Paul	2,194,393	14	1,481
Houston	1,961,557	17	1,578
Paterson–Clifton–Passaic, New Jersey	1,871,219	19	1,577
Dallas	1,809,047	22	1,669
Seattle–Everett	1,747,818	20	1,579
Milwaukee	1,706,994	18	1,385
Kansas City, Missouri	1,682,887	21	1,540

SOURCE: United States Bureau of Census, Census of Business, 1963. *Retail Trade: United States Summary*, BC63-RA1, (Washington, D.C.: United States Government Printing Office, 1965).

Addendum Table 2-6. Retail Sales: 1958 to 1963 Number of SMSA's, Cities, and CBD's, by Percentage Change Groups

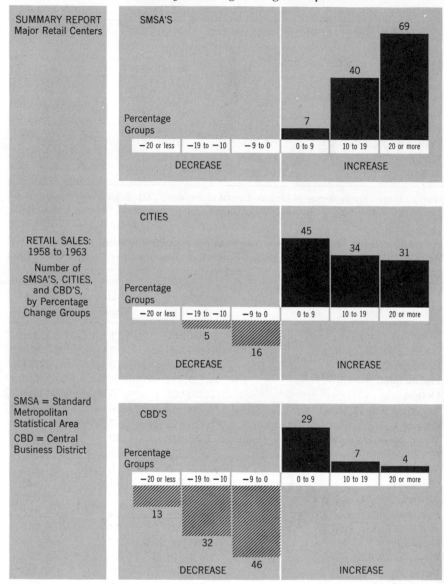

SUMMARY REPORT
Major Retail Centers

RETAIL SALES:
1958 to 1963

Number of
SMSA'S, CITIES,
and CBD'S,
by Percentage
Change Groups

SMSA = Standard
Metropolitan
Statistical Area
CBD = Central
Business District

SMSA'S

69

40

7

Percentage
Groups

| −20 or less | −19 to −10 | −9 to 0 | 0 to 9 | 10 to 19 | 20 or more |

DECREASE   INCREASE

CITIES

45

34

31

Percentage
Groups

| −20 or less | −19 to −10 | −9 to 0 | 0 to 9 | 10 to 19 | 20 or more |

5

16

DECREASE   INCREASE

CBD'S

29

7

4

Percentage
Groups

| −20 or less | −19 to −10 | −9 to 0 | 0 to 9 | 10 to 19 | 20 or more |

13

32

46

DECREASE   INCREASE

SOURCE: United States Bureau of Census, Census of Business, 1963, *Major Retail Centers Summary Report*, BC63–MRC-1, (United States Government Printing Office, Washington, D.C., 1965).

Addendum Table 2-7. Selected Services, United States, 1958 and 1963

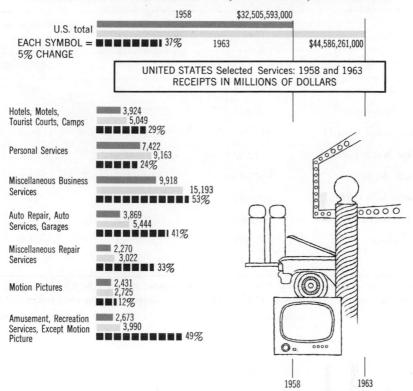

	1958	$32,505,593,000
U.S. total		
EACH SYMBOL = ■■■■■■■■ 37%	1963	$44,586,261,000
5% CHANGE		

UNITED STATES Selected Services: 1958 and 1963
RECEIPTS IN MILLIONS OF DOLLARS

Hotels, Motels,
Tourist Courts, Camps
3,924
5,049
■■■■■■ 29%

Personal Services
7,422
9,163
■■■■■ 24%

Miscellaneous Business
Services
9,918
15,193
■■■■■■■■■■ 53%

Auto Repair, Auto
Services, Garages
3,869
5,444
■■■■■■■■ 41%

Miscellaneous Repair
Services
2,270
3,022
■■■■■■ 33%

Motion Pictures
2,431
2,725
■■■ 12%

Amusement, Recreation
Services, Except Motion
Picture
2,673
3,990
■■■■■■■■■ 49%

1958   1963

1963 CENSUS OF BUSINESS, U.S. Department of Commerce, Bureau of the Census

Addendum Table 2-8. Selected Services, Geographic Division, 1963

Geographic Divisions	Total Establishments	Total Receipts, All Establishments ($1,000)	Percent Change in Total Receipts, 1958 to 1963
New England	62,768	2,196,722	36.2
Middle Atlantic	206,384	12,722,915	35.1
East North Central	210,897	8,426,857	28.5
West North Central	92,230	2,802,908	31.8
South Atlantic	140,049	5,044,310	44.2
East South Central	56,849	1,534,616	40.3
West South Central	96,661	2,945,589	32.2
Mountain	48,051	1,916,823	44.9
Pacific	147,784	6,995,521	50.3

SOURCE: United States Bureau of Census, Census of Business, 1963, Vol. 6, *Selected Services— Summary Statistics* (Washington, D.C.: United States Government Printing Office, 1966).

Addendum Table 2-9. Selected Services, All SMSA's Combined and Remainder of United States, by Kind of Business Group: 1963

Kind of Business Group	United States			All SMSA's			Remainder of United States		
	Number of Establishments	Receipts ($1,000)	Payroll, Entire Year ($1,000)	Number of Establishments	Receipts ($1,000)	Payroll, Entire Year ($1,000)	Number of Establishments	Receipts ($1,000)	Payroll, Entire Year ($1,000)
Total	1 061 673	44 586 261	12 192 105	692 012	36 850 004	10 395 229	369 661	7 736 257	1 796 876
Hotels, motels, tourist courts, camps	84 706	5 049 255	1 439 496	34 255	3 449 134	1 072 126	50 451	1 600 121	367 370
Personal services	447 080	9 163 208	2 932 752	297 075	7 050 260	2 381 051	150 005	2 112 948	551 701
Miscellaneous business services	147 668	15 192 622	4 103 006	120 478	14 162 227	3 771 804	27 190	1 030 395	331 202
Auto repair, auto services, garages	139 611	5 443 937	1 135 091	86 151	4 216 179	940 096	53 460	1 227 758	194 995
Miscellaneous repair services	146 776	3 021 988	744 459	92 323	2 337 099	636 789	53 953	684 889	107 670
Motion pictures	16 381	2 724 965	731 963	9 602	2 453 454	670 676	6 779	271 511	61 287
Amusement, recreation services, except motion pictures	79 451	3 990 286	1 105 338	51 628	3 181 651	922 687	27 823	808 635	182 651

SOURCE: United States Bureau of Census, Census of Business, 1963, Vol. 6, *Selected Services—Summary Statistics* (Washington, D.C.: United States Government Printing Office, 1966).

37

Addendum Table 2-10. Wholesale Trade, Establishments and Sales, 1958 and 1963

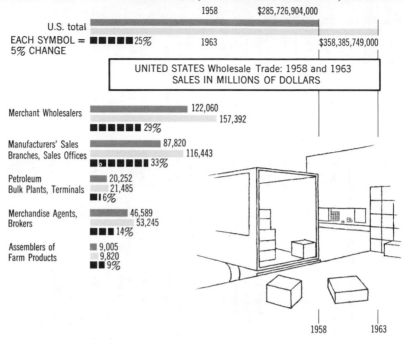

1958 $285,726,904,000

U.S. total

EACH SYMBOL = ■■■■■25%   1963 $358,385,749,000
5% CHANGE

UNITED STATES Wholesale Trade: 1958 and 1963
SALES IN MILLIONS OF DOLLARS

Merchant Wholesalers   122,060
157,392
■■■■■■ 29%

Manufacturers' Sales   87,820
Branches, Sales Offices   116,443
■■■■■■ 33%

Petroleum   20,252
Bulk Plants, Terminals   21,485
■16%

Merchandise Agents,   46,589
Brokers   53,245
■■■14%

Assemblers of   9,005
Farm Products   9,820
■■9%

1958   1963

1963 CENSUS OF BUSINESS, U.S. Department of Commerce, Bureau of the Census

Addendum Table 2-11. Wholesale Trade, by Type of Operation, Establishments and Sales, 1963, United States

Type of Operation	Number of Establishments	Percent of Establishments	Sales	Percent of Sales
Total—All Types of Operation	308,177	100	358,385,749	100
Merchant Wholesalers	208,997	67.7	157,391,769	44.2
Mfg.'s Sales Branches, Sales Offices	28,884	9.3	116,443,312	32.4
Petroleum Bulk Stations, Terminals	30,873	10.0	21,485,414	5.9
Merchandise Agents, Brokers	25,313	8.2	53,245,009	14.8
Assemblers of Farm Products	14,110	4.8	9,820,245	2.7

SOURCE: United States Bureau of Census of Business, 1963, *Wholesale Trade: United States Summary:* BC63–WA1 (Washington, D.C.: United States Government Printing Office, 1965).

Addendum Table 2-12. Wholesale Trade, by Regions and Geographic Divisions, 1929–1963

Geographic Region or Division	Sales, All Types of Operation (Including Merchant Wholesalers)					
	1963	1958	1954	1948	1939	1929
United States Total	100.0%	100.0%	100.0%	100.0%	100.0%	100.0%
New England	4.7	4.8	5.0	5.0	5.7	6.0
Middle Atlantic	27.1	28.0	29.3	30.5	34.3	33.9
East North Central	20.5	20.8	21.7	21.5	20.3	20.1
West North Central	9.6	9.9	10.1	11.6	10.5	12.6
South Atlantic	10.6	10.0	9.3	8.7	8.3	6.7
East South Central	4.2	4.2	4.4	4.2	3.6	3.7
West South Central	7.8	7.8	7.3	6.9	6.2	7.1
Mountain	2.7	2.8	2.5	2.3	2.0	1.7
Pacific	12.8	11.7	10.4	9.3	9.1	8.2

SOURCES: United States Bureau of Census, *United States Census of Business: 1958. Vol. 1, Retail Trade—Summary Statistics* (Washington, D.C.: United States Government Printing Office, 1961), and United States Bureau of Census of Business, 1963, *Wholesale Trade: United States Summary:* BC63–WA1 (Washington, D.C.: United States Government Printing Office, 1963).

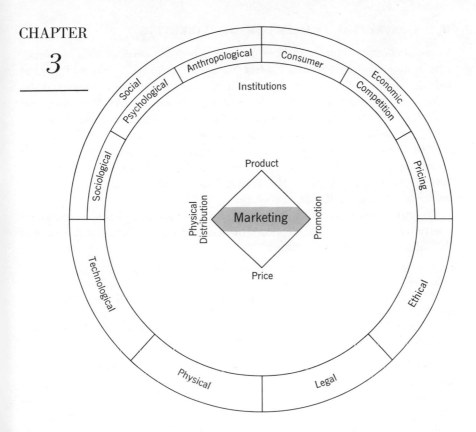

Marketing in Capitalistic and Planned Economies

THE ROLE OF MARKETING IN COMPARATIVE SYSTEMS • RESPONSE OF MARKETING
TO A CAPITALISTIC SYSTEM • SATISFACTIONS WITH MARKETING IN THE TWO
SYSTEMS • A LOOK TO THE FUTURE •

Every economic system somehow gets the job done, whether it is a capitalistic system, like that of the United States, or a centrally planned system, like that in the USSR. Even economies of much less sophistication and development have a means of accomplishing economic tasks. The principal differences in the economic systems of the United States and the USSR are found in the *means of accomplishing the task, the allocation of resources, and the bases for measurement of their respective accomplishments*. Other economies, such as Japan, Britain, and India, lie more or less between the private-ownership system of the United States and the public (collective)-ownership system of the Soviet Union.

Despite rather marked differences in economic systems, the basic economic questions to be answered remain the same. Every economic system has the following common questions:[1]

1. What is to be produced? In other words, how are natural resources to be allocated?

2. How are products to be produced and to what or whom are they to be distributed?

3. How much of a society's resources should be allocated to current consumption, and how much should go to future growth (investment)?

In the United States most productive resources are privately owned and directed in part by the price system and in part by the nonprice variables functioning in the market. All production decisions are made in response to the market. Conversely, in the Soviet Union most productive resources are collectively owned, and the economic processes of resource use, production, and distribution are centrally planned and controlled by the state.

When economists measure and evaluate an economic system, they almost always include similar criteria. One well-known economist, in setting the criteria for a good economic system, seeks a *yes* response to the following questions:[2]

1. Does the system provide a progressively higher standard of living for all—economic stability and growth?

2. Does it provide economic freedom for the individual?

3. Does it provide economic security for all?

4. Does it produce goods and services consumers want?

5. Does it provide an equitable distribution of income?

The Soviet Union does not measure up to these criteria, but its planners have set somewhat different objectives. Paying lip service to a higher standard of living, they have given this criterion a lower priority than the rapid develop-

[1] George Leland Bach, *Economics—An Introduction to Analysis and Policy*, 3rd Ed. (Englewood Cliffs, N.J.: Prentice-Hall, 1960), pp. 812–813.
[2] *Ibid.*, p. 813.

ment of heavy industry and military strength. None of the objectives of a Soviet plan says anything about individual economic freedom. But by emphasizing higher literacy and cultural standards, improved health, and reduction in insecurity, the Soviets have approached the other elements of the aforementioned criteria.

THE ROLE OF MARKETING IN COMPARATIVE SYSTEMS

In any economic system the objectives of a marketing system are the same as those of the economy. Some qualification of this contention is necessary because the cited set of criteria is quite broad, and it would be incorrect as well as biased to credit marketing with contributing to each of them. Marketing's major contribution to our economy lies in its ability to provide a higher standard of living and to function as the impetus in getting consumers the goods and services they want. Similarly in the Russian and other planned systems, marketing is directly involved with delivering the standard of living even though decisions as to what to produce lie with the state.

The fact that public ownership and central planning are deep contrasts to private ownership and decentralized decisions does not preclude other similarities in the two systems. Upon examination one finds the need for similar marketing activities in all economic systems. Among the marketing activities cited in Chapter 2, product, price, and physical distribution are universally performed. Products, as remarked, are dictated by the planners in the Soviet world and hence their kind, character, and quality reflect the goals of the state. With the centralized decision of what is to be produced and which sector(s) of the economy is to be supplied, price is also set by the state. Price is used, not as a device to allocate goods, but to fulfill planned goals. If, for example, television sets are deemed desirable to the cultural development of the people and television production is forthcoming, the price is set to encourage their purchase. Conversely, state-set prices discourage consumption and use when set relatively high.

The one marketing activity not regarded as essential to the goals of a planned state is promotion. Promotion activities, which are an intregal part of market development by American firms, have had little place in the Soviet system. In some ways the Soviet Union has relaxed its hold on the consumer market. Each consumer has always been able to choose how he will spend his income. And this choice is indirectly influenced, of course, by the kinds of goods permitted to flow into the market. Recently, some attention has been given to individual differences, tastes, and desires. Promotion has been introduced to inform the people of improved styles but not to develop market goals; it is promotion which implies a better life as permitted by the state. Some advertising calls attention to products in adequate supply, but again its aim concerns information more than market development. Market development activities in a capitalistic system comprise not only promotion but also price, product, and distribution strategies which are all designed to be compatible with market demand. If market development functioned in the Soviet system, it would upset the workings of the planned economy. Thus, this is a major distinction between the two systems.

RESPONSE OF MARKETING TO A CAPITALISTIC SYSTEM

The achievements of communist Russia have been nothing short of spectacular. Since the 1920s it has made remarkable strides in converting the economy from a rural backward system to a highly industrialized state. All this has been done by a political and economic philosophy which is alien to western society. The test of an economic system, from our eyes, rests not in industrialized accomplishments but in the choices it offers. One author summarized this view by saying:

When the choices are limited by coercion of one sort or another, the system must fall short of meeting the test in greater or less degree. The virtue of a free system— i.e., competitive capitalism—is that it allows energy to flow uncoerced into a thousand-and-one different forms, expanding goods, services, and jobs in myriad, unpredictable ways. Every day, under such a system, a consumer's plebiscite (the phrase is von Mise's) is held, the vote being counted in whatever money unit is the handiest. With his votes the consumer directs production, forcing or luring energy, brains, and capital to obey his will.[3]

The direct implication is that the alternatives open to the people living in the economy have much to do with its economic accomplishments. A strong case can be made for those societies built on a foundation of free choice, the concept that the goal of production is consumption and that goods are made to satisfy human wants.

When private ownership prevails, an individual has the right to manufacture and sell any product, provided he does not violate the laws enacted for the good of society. As a businessman, he is driven to reap the profits and other incentives available through the system. He must also assume the burden of risks and losses. Consumers, too, have much freedom. They are free to choose the seller and the products, all of which are in competition with one another. With consumers having freedom of choice, the production and marketing systems must be highly efficient; otherwise the seller faces the danger of displacement in the market. Freedom of choice is the basis for the

[3]John Chamberlain, *The Roots of Capitalism*, (Princeton, N.J.: D. Van Nostrand Company, 1959), p. 165.

development of our industries and our marketing complex. Over time, both our production and our marketing institutions have adjusted to the dynamics of the marketplace. All of this has taken place with little or no centralized authority.[4] Box 3-1 is a clever characterization of the principal workings of a capitalistic system.

SATISFACTIONS WITH MARKETING IN THE TWO SYSTEMS

The principal merit to the planned economy derives from its ability to set priorities and direct the growth of certain economic sectors. The remarkable growth of industrialization in the Soviet Union can be seen in this light. On the other hand, the living-standard test and the availability of goods demanded by consumers fall totally short and leave much to be desired. This is depicted in the following observation of the consumer goods market in the USSR:

In the United States, we most frequently have a situation which can perhaps be best described as a buyers' market, where sellers are ever searching for potential buyers; in the Soviet Union, the reverse situation prevails chronically. There is a sellers' market with potential buyers chasing frequently unavailable commodities. As a result, despite some long-run improvement in the quality of Soviet consumer goods, our products and retail services are undoubtedly generally superior quality-wise. The range of commodities, grades, and models from which Soviet consumers are able to select is also much narrower than is the case in the United States. To some extent, this is counterbalanced by the fact that many more consumer durables are purchased on time in the United States, so that a rather substantial interest charge should be added to some of our prices. Finally, a considerable amount of food must be purchased on the collective farm markets in the USSR, where prices are ordinarily considerably higher, especially in winter when food supplies are short.[5]

The marketing environment in the USSR has recently changed. One observer wrote in 1966:

. . . summer dresses are brighter, gayer and of better material; spiked heels have replaced the heavy shoes of earlier days. . . . The women look prettier, trimmer, and better groomed. . . . Food has become better and more varied. There is more meat, and fruit is imported in greater quantities to supplement the staple diet. . . . Hairdos, too, have become more elaborate. . . . The first Beatle haircuts for boys have made their appearance in Moscow. . . . The twist now is taught in dancing

---

[4] An economy may be founded on freedom of choice and yet centrally planned. The United States economy during the Second World War is an example. More recently, social and economic legislation has given some new direction to incentives and industry. The system, however, still rests on freedom of choice.

[5] United States Congress Joint Economic Committee, Comparisons of the United States and Soviet Economies, (Washington, D.C., United States Government Printing Office, 1959), p. 337.

BOX 3-1

SOURCE: E. I. Dupont DeNemours & Company, *Better Living*, Vol. 19, No. 6, November–December 1965.

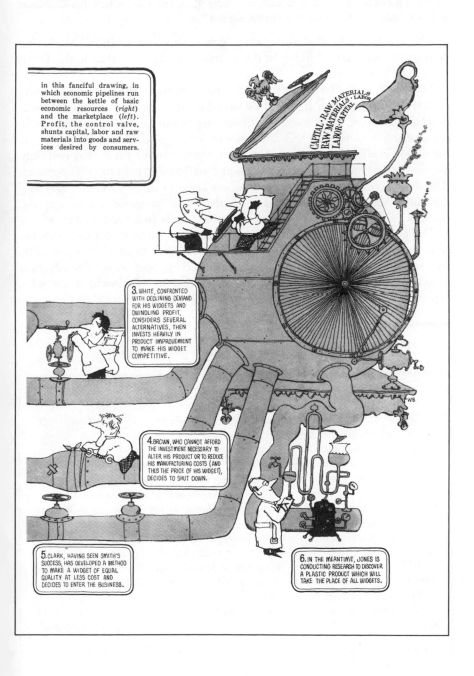

in this fanciful drawing, in which economic pipelines run between the kettle of basic economic resources (*right*) and the marketplace (*left*). Profit, the control valve, shunts capital, labor and raw materials into goods and services desired by consumers.

CAPITAL · RAW MATERIALS
RAW MATERIALS · LABOR
LABOR · CAPITAL

3. WHITE, CONFRONTED WITH DECLINING DEMAND FOR HIS WIDGETS AND DWINDLING PROFIT, CONSIDERS SEVERAL ALTERNATIVES, THEN INVESTS HEAVILY IN PRODUCT IMPROVEMENT TO MAKE HIS WIDGET COMPETITIVE.

4. BROWN, WHO CANNOT AFFORD THE INVESTMENT NECESSARY TO ALTER HIS PRODUCT OR TO REDUCE HIS MANUFACTURING COSTS (AND THUS THE PRICE OF HIS WIDGET), DECIDES TO SHUT DOWN.

5. CLARK, HAVING SEEN SMITH'S SUCCESS, HAS DEVELOPED A METHOD TO MAKE A WIDGET OF EQUAL QUALITY AT LESS COST AND DECIDES TO ENTER THE BUSINESS.

6. IN THE MEANTIME, JONES IS CONDUCTING RESEARCH TO DISCOVER A PLASTIC PRODUCT WHICH WILL TAKE THE PLACE OF ALL WIDGETS.

schools for children. . . . But it will take more than trimmer girls, taller buildings and new paint to transform the Soviet capital.[6]

The consumer is obviously being given some recognition. Marketing delivers the standard of living to the people, and this is as true in the USSR as in the United States.

Though it would be comforting to think that the USSR is fast becoming capitalistic, and though it would be amusing to think that the consumer is as whimsical there as in western nations, one has to be realistic and remember that the Soviets have had a number of swings of the pendulum and that the nation is still clearly state-controlled. On the other hand, it is certainly interesting that marketing research is being used now to help forecast demand. It is also interesting that Soviet consumers are now more sovereign and that they have some choice. But many of the basic questions concerning the changes in marketing have not been resolved, as is indicated in Box 3-2.

The principal satisfaction deriving from our operation of private enterprise marketing rests in our standard of living. The innumerable products, conveniences, and services give a continued and growing sense of satisfaction to most Americans. Marketing, as well as production, has provided new jobs, higher incomes, and opportunities for self-expression.

[6]Henry Tanner, *New York Times*, July 5, 1966.

BOX 3-2

Questions about Marketing in the USSR

Will nonprofitable state enterprises be permitted—or even forced—to go out of business?

Will free labor markets be permitted?

Will several manufacturers of similar goods actually be allowed to compete in selling to the *same* distributive channels and the *same* stores? (This would upset the inherited system of planned links between production and distribution and, in effect, introduce a market economy at the wholesale as well as the retail stage.)

Will the Russians tolerate such seemingly indispensable ingredients of free markets as mass advertising, brands, and trademarks?

Will stores be allowed to integrate backward, and will manufacturers be allowed to integrate forward and create their own outlets? What about mergers?

Will antitrust laws be enacted?

Will pressure from the market be permitted to generate an expansion of the consumer goods industries at the cost of heavy industry and producer goods?

SOURCE: Hans B. Thorelli, "Libermanism is Not Liberalism," *Business Horizons*, Vol. 8, No. 2, Summer 1965, p. 46.

As with most freedoms, though, they are sometimes abused. There are sellers in the market who take liberties which violate accepted business practices, traditions, culture, and beliefs in fair play. The unethical and unlawful prey on the lack of wisdom and human frailities of consumers. Another observable dissatisfaction stems from the market-development efforts of manufacturers. Without being unethical or illegal, these efforts sometimes register negative attitudes among the consuming public. The widespread use of superlatives, claims, and clichés has often given grounds for the remark "there ought to be a law." These, together with practices that invade human privacy, give fuel to the attackers of American marketing.

A LOOK TO THE FUTURE

The imperfections in American marketing are traced to the economic and political system under which we operate. Abuses of freedom and attendant wastes will probably continue to bring attacks on the marketing sector of the economy. Few of us, however, would willingly accept the greater imperfections of planned economies.

With the maturing of marketing thought and basic understanding of market behavior, it is hoped that abuses will diminish. Once a seller recognizes the futility of insidious efforts among an increasingly knowledgeable group of consumers, he should adjust his methods to the better informed public. Competition, free choice, and better information will all combine toward long-run improvements and even greater satisfaction with the system. To this end marketing people should direct their energies.

Questions

1. Could you devise an economic system without including marketing?
2. Do you see any conflicts between the goals of society and the goals of a corporation insofar as marketing is concerned?
3. What basically are the differences in marketing in the USSR as opposed to the United States?
4. Is the United States marketing in wartime similar to the USSR marketing in peacetime?
5. Do you think that the USSR economic system is becoming more capitalistic?

Statements to Consider

Sales results are the function of organized marketing effort applied to market opportunity. Management of marketing operations should begin with this fundamental equation.

Allocating marketing effort is the same thing as selecting a marketing program. The core of the market offers the firm a place to get started and continues to be the foundation of its security in the market, no matter how great its sales expansion.

Every transaction in the marketplace is an attempt to match a segment of demand with an appropriate segment of supply.

SELECTED REFERENCES

Marshall I. Goldman, *Soviet Marketing: Distribution in a Controlled Economy* (New York: Free Press of Glencoe, 1963).

° Francis M. Boddy, "Soviet Economic Growth," in Robert T. Holt and John E. Turner (eds.), *Soviet Union: Paradox and Change* (New York: Holt, Rinehart and Winston, 1962), pp. 62–89.

Philip Hanson, "The Assortment Problem in Soviet Retail Trade," *Soviet Studies*, Vol. 14, April 1963, pp. 347–364.

Hans B. Thorelli, "Libermanism Is Not Liberalism," *Business Horizons*, Vol. 8, No. 2, Summer 1965.

GENERALIZATIONS WERE TAKEN FROM:

Wroe Alderson, *Marketing Behavior and Executive Action* (Homewood, Ill.: Richard D. Irwin, 1957).

Marketing Environment and Market Forces

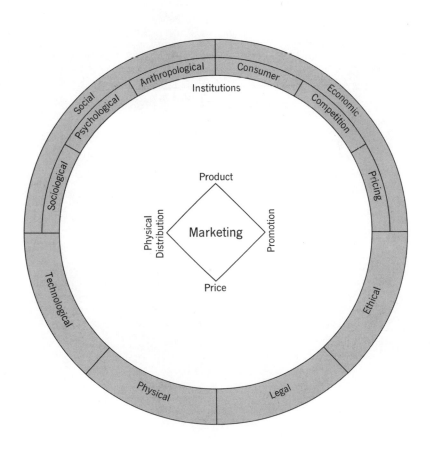

CHAPTER

4

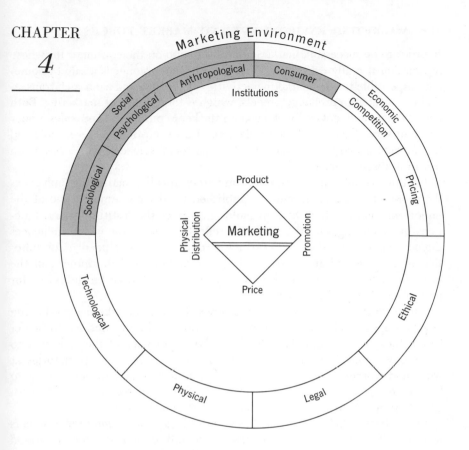

The Environment of Consumer Behavior—I

BUYING AND CONSUMING · ENVIRONMENTAL FORCES OF CONSUMPTION *Selected Consumption Forces* · *Marketing Impact*

In order to be successful, marketing must depend on the consumer for whose satisfaction it really exists. Every purchase by a consumer is a sale by someone responsible for the marketing activities of the firm and each such transaction constitutes an exchange process, which is the essence of marketing. Both businessmen and government economists keep purchases and sales under constant surveillance, and the whole area of consumption has been subjected to continuing study by scholars in all of the social sciences, which has given it a multidisciplinary cast.

Consumers influence marketing and, reciprocally, marketing influences the consumer. The environment established by the consumer is one of the important factors which help to mold and direct the institutions and functions of marketing, and the marketing effort is one factor which influences the consumer. More than 150 years ago, Adam Smith concluded: "Consumption is the sole end and purpose of all production; and the interest of the producer ought to be attended to only so far as it may be necessary for promoting that of the consumer."[1]

Although the questions of consumer sovereignty and marketing-production relationships have been with us for a long time and may continue to be debated, there is nothing debatable about the importance of the consumer to society. We may hear that we must consume simply to keep factories at work and workers on the payroll, that Madison Avenue can persuade us to buy anything, or that consumers are soft, willing to buy in order to earn group approval. Any student of the consumer knows better.

On a strictly dollar-and-cents basis, state, local, and federal governments in the United States spend more than $120 billion annually for goods and services. Business firms spend over $30 billion on durable equipment, and personal expenditures for consumption exceed $360 billion. As the consumer does not exist for national income but national income goes to the consumer, the significance of marketing to the economy, through consumption, is self-evident.

BUYING AND CONSUMING

In any field of study, terminology is often confusing. Therefore some care should be taken to differentiate a buyer from a consumer because they are not necessarily the same. The housewife frequently buys all the food for her family, but consumes only a share. The remainder of her family are consumers but not buyers. The student who purchases a textbook, his instructor hopes, is both buyer *and* consumer. The buyer for an industrial firm purchases many items that will be consumed in the manufacturing process;

[1] Adam Smith, *The Wealth of Nations* (London: Methuen and Company, 1904), p. 159.

he also purchases items that will become components of the final product. The wholesaler buys goods for resale to nonconsuming retailers who then sell to buyers and buyer-consumers. The Boeing Aircraft Corporation is both buyer and consumer, as are the government of the Philippines, the city of Cairo, the Tennessee Valley Authority, the National Aeronautics and Space Agency, the United States Marines, and all ordinary citizens of all nations.

As marketing students, we strive for principles to guide us in the understanding of all kinds of buying and consumption, whether industrial, military, governmental, or household in origin. As his knowledge of marketing expands, the individual comes to appreciate the marketing differences among the various kinds of goods and services. Pricing, distribution, advertising, packaging, and financing—all aspects of the marketing process—may be quite different. Furthermore, there can be important marketing differences between selling camera film to the ordinary consumer and to a Hollywood studio. Some of these differences may be of great significance, others may not (see Box 4-1).

ENVIRONMENTAL FORCES OF CONSUMPTION

The consumer is probably as baffling to the marketer as he is essential. As a result, predictions of plant and equipment expenditures or personal consumption expenditures often miss their mark. The unexpected happens: consumers go on a buying spree when their personal income is at an all-time low; a war in some part of the world flares up and consumers react to this danger by buying; a new product replaces an existing one; a strike closes down the steel industry; a killing frost ruins the fruit crop. Both the factors over which we have some control and those over which we have none hamper the forecasting of buying behavior. Some superficial answers are provided in Box 4-2. Marketers continue to search for the clues that will enable them to forecast more accurately than before. They look into the reasons why the Boeing 707s were so successful, why some powered toothbrushes have failed and others succeeded, or why the color trends in clothing are what they seem to be at the end of the summer. The clues aid management in making marketing decisions. Should, for example, the ABC Company introduce a new dietary beverage product in France? What clues point to a positive or negative answer?

Both aggregate and individual consumption patterns are difficult to predict. Even brand preference is not a simple concept or statement of fact. In a world of expanding population, growing complexity, new horizons of technical achievements, and swirling currents of forces on the human being and his culture, it is not surprising that consumer behavior is challenging. All consumers live in a world of buying encouragement; that is, they are

BOX 4-1

Selected Principal Characteristics of Industrial Marketing

1. Characteristics of the market or buyers:

   a. Derived demand
   b. Rational buying motives
   c. Small number of buyers
   d. Geographic concentration
   e. Volume purchasing
   f. Multiple-buying responsibility

2. Product characteristics:

   a. Technical
   b. Small fluctuations in price
   c. Specifications for details
   d. Bidding system
   e. Standardization

3. Characteristics of the operational setup:

   a. Short channels
   b. Trade publications for advertising
   c. Reciprocity
   d. Seller makes contact
   e. Production for inventory

4. Other characteristics:

   a. Speed and dependability of delivery
   b. Extensive sales training
   c. Low sales promotion expense
   d. Small number of women buyers
   e. Predominance of raw and semifinished products

SOURCE: Adapted from Industrial Marketing Committee Review Board, "Fundamental Differences Between Industrial and Consumer Marketing," *Journal of Marketing*, Vol. 19, No. 2, October 1954, pp. 142–158.

under constant pressure to buy. Whether a person contemplating the purchase of a new lawn mower, an Air Force committee considering a new type of missile, or a company purchasing agent deciding on material for engine bearings, the consumer makes the marketing world an exciting one.

Before exploring the forces that make us want to buy, let us review our own attitudes toward buying and consumption. Probably one thing all of us have in common is that we do not want to have to regret our purchase. (Few of us will concede that we made a bad buying decision.) Most of us desire our limited funds to go as far as possible and to give us as much satisfaction as possible. Probably most of us approach the subject of marketing with ambivalence. On the one hand, we have a buyer-beware attitude; every seller and advertiser is attempting to persuade the consumer, sometimes even through contrivance, cheating, soft sell, hard sell, persistence, and domination. Perhaps he may sell us items we neither want nor can afford. On the other hand, we study at college in order to acquire a good job which will provide us with an income sufficient to buy a large number of commodities. Every student who enters industry must become interested in his firm's sales. Indeed *all companies sell.*

We may agree that buyers make buying decisions to gain satisfaction and to fulfill their wants and needs. Even if marketers refrained from all kinds of persuasive acts, consumers would still seek out sources of supply for many items of their own choosing because of consumption forces. Each buy-sell transaction is consummated because *both* the buyer and seller find the exchange desirable.

Blatant advertising, tasteless commercials, and persistent salesmen represent only some of the pressures or forces in our environment. More important are the forces that emanate from our heritage, our culture, and our immediate situation. These forces are of many types: they may be anthropological, psychological, economic, sociological, or multidisciplinary in nature. The study of these disciplines brings knowledge to bear on the problems of the consumer. Through it the student can attempt to understand how these forces interrelate and how they act on the consumer.

Critics of marketing may imply that all consumption can be manipulated by marketing executives who know exactly how to make willing subjects of millions of intelligent people. Experience indicates that consumption cannot be so easily explained. Marketers have failed repeatedly to sell people items which they have not wanted. They have failed when they tried to go

BOX 4-2

Why Women Buy

Women buy: (1) because her husband says she cannot have it; (2) it makes her look thin; (3) it comes from Paris; (4) her neighbors cannot afford it; (5) nobody has one; (6) everybody has one; (7) it's different; (8) because . . . .

SOURCE: Cedric Adams' Column, *Minneapolis Star,* date unknown.

against the current of a consumption trend; they have failed when they have tried to change a habit. In this connection, a firm several years ago test-marketed a new aspirin tablet which could be chewed and swallowed without the usual drink of water. It was not accepted because people liked to take water with their pills. As any marketing student or practitioner knows, an understanding of the consumer requires one to be aware of the existing forces which influence consumer buying habits.

Selected Consumption Forces

One of the most basic environmental forces affecting consumption is the *culture*. An examination of the influence exerted on consumption by the cultural environment would yield a long list of items that might be considered culturally motivated. But more important than the items themselves is the need to recognize the power of the culture toward consumers. Indeed it is possible to differentiate Americans from other nationalities in part by their consumption patterns. Even segments of a nation's population can thus be identified in some cases. For this reason, to be acceptable, products must conform to the culture and so must their package design and color.

Within families the power structure is cultural in nature. The cultural forces can act in a positive manner and thrust an individual into the position of desiring some particular article. For example, a young man and lady become engaged and an engagement ring typically becomes an important aspect of the event. In one Pacific culture, a human head was formerly used to serve as a symbol of good intentions. Broadly speaking, modern man has been called a victim of his culture. He may find it necessary, or desirable, to buy a new home in the suburbs, a second automobile, a boat and trailer, a power mower, barbecue, and carpetlike lawn. Cultural influences can become evident in numerous ways and in many purchases.

The most important consumer forces also, as a rule, include *physical* or biological needs. Food, clothing, and shelter are the items most commonly mentioned. The pressure for them varies markedly from culture to culture, climate to climate, and person to person. A large man requires several thousand calories to sustain himself, whereas a small woman may get by on 1,500. The Igorot in the Philippines finds a G-String satisfactory; Alaskans require something more substantial. However, biological needs are common to all; they vary only in degree. Although not as glamorous as socio-psychological factors, biological needs are most basic to consumption and, as such, should be carefully considered by anyone studying the consumer environment.

Personality has some impact on the desire to consume. An individual's need for security may cause him to take extra flight insurance. His aesthetic sense may be reflected in a house full of paintings; curiosity may have prompted his buying a new novel. Because he enjoys expressing his gratitude, he sends a gift to his host. His faith prompts him to support the church, his desire to be a little "showy" may be the reason he purchases a gas light for his front lawn. His intellectual leanings are fed by subscriptions to scholarly magazines. The list can be long: a person's personality can lead to consumption of a variety of products.

As we mature, we become a bundle of *attitudes*. We place *values* on almost all things with which we come into contact. These attitudes and values affect our consumption. If we are optimistic about the football team's chances, we may buy a season ticket. If we place great value on owning our home, we shall likely buy instead of renting. Some of the things we value most become our goals, and these become strong motivating forces.

Goals or *aspirations* play interesting roles. One is often willing to work overtime or take a "moonlighting" job in order to achieve some aspiration. We save for silver, a trip, and a dishwasher. Once they are purchased, our interest turns from aspiring to enjoying the satisfaction from the purchases, and the degree of satisfaction determines whether each item is repurchased. We shift our aspirations upward or downward according to our successes; just as a golfer shifts his expectations according to his present game, a consumer shifts his aspirations according to his achievement and satisfaction. His aspiration may shift from a second-hand automobile to a new compact, to a larger car, and on to the most expensive car on the market. Shifting aspirations contribute to the difficulty in applying the principle of diminishing utility to consumption. It is not as simple as saying that once we achieve our goal of owning a radio we stop buying radios. Instead, we may want larger and better ones, one for the car, one for the kitchen, and a transistor to carry with us. We change our aspirations as we change our consumption patterns. Typically, our aspirations remain reality-oriented. Some consumers do buy more than they can handle, but installment buying is built on the successful achievement of realistic aspirations. Realistic or unrealistic, aspirations provide a potent force for consumption.

For most of us, *prestige* is an important aspiration. Corporation executives construct buildings and lay expensive carpets in their offices in order to gain prestige. Governments subsidize airlines, consumers buy products for purposes of prestige. Even children do this. Sometimes the prestige item is something expensive and showy, sometimes it is not. Thorstein Veblen in 1899 wrote of "conspicuous consumption." Later, the automobile with its chromium typified this kind of consumption. In the early days of television, an aerial denoted the ownership of a prestige item, often in the low income household. Many times we purchase items which we hope will enhance our prestige, and this desire to impress and gain recognition is likely to continue. There are interesting twists to the conspicuous-consumption concept, as shown by the people who go to extremes to avoid any kind of a purchase which could be construed as conspicuous. They become conspicuous by their inconspicuousness.

The desire for prestige plays tricks on market researchers. Persons like to impress interviewers, even when not acquainted with them. Respondents will often indicate that they enjoy the repertoire theatre, the symphony, Scotch, and the *Saturday Review of Literature*. Further investigation may reveal that the respondent has not been to the theatre "this year," has a refrigerator full of beer, cannot recall the name of any composer, and really meant *TV Guide*.

Consumer requirements for prestige vary among the *social classes*. A particular brand and style of automobile is thought to fit a particular social class, although there is not complete agreement on this point. Some products do not fit a certain social class, but cut across several classes. Logically, one would expect the products to flow from higher to lower social classes, but this is not always the case. (Television had almost a reverse flow.)

Consumers may keep their identity with a social class by residence, style of home, and the items they purchase. The identification of a social class is not always a simple chore, for the identity depends on a complicated network of interrelated attitudes and characteristics. One's awareness of one's position within a given social class can be the springboard to a number of purchases (see Box 4-3). Greatly oversimplified, it can be said that each social class functions as a stimulant to purchasing.

Belonging to a social class is closely related to the concept of *affiliation* with *reference* and *membership* groups. We belong to some groups and refer to other groups. Each of these groups has consumption norms to which one is obliged to adapt if one wants to maintain status. It may be necessary to own a hi-fi set to "belong" to one group, a camping tent, to another, a suburban home or lake cabin, to another, and to attend a particular college to belong to another group.

Not all products are susceptible to reference group influence. The product must be one that is observable or noticed and is not universally possessed.[2] Some products are susceptible to reference-group influence both for the product itself and its brand (Box 4-4). An automobile is a good example of such a product; canned peaches are not. A product can change in susceptibility over a period of time. Sometimes saturation of a market encourages a group to drop a product from its acceptable list: black-and-white television may give way to color television. A reference group may, however, drop a

[2]Francis S. Bourne, "Group Influence in Marketing and Public Relations," in Rensis Likert and Samuel P. Hayes, Jr., (eds.), *Some Applications of Behavioral Science Research* (Paris: UNESCO, 1957), p. 217.

BOX 4-3

The Social Perspectives of the Social Classes

As the class sees itself	As another class sees it
U-U "Old aristocracy"	"Society or the folks with the money (U-U as seen by L-L)
L-U "Aristocracy but not old"	"Society but not old families" (U-M)
U-M "People who should be upper class"	"People who think they are somebody" (L-M)
L-M "We poor folks"	"Way high-ups but not society" (L-L)
U-L "Poor but honest folks"	"Po' whites" (U-U)
L-L "People just as good as anybody"	"Shiftless people" (U-L)

Key

U-U—upper-upper
L-U—lower-upper
U-M—upper-middle
L-M—lower-middle
U-L—upper-lower
L-L—lower-lower

SOURCE: Allison Davis, Burleigh B. Gardner, and Mary R. Gardner, *Deep South; A Social Anthropological Study of Caste and Class* (Chicago: University of Chicago Press, 1941).

product long before saturation takes place—for example, in the case of fashion items.

The force of reference groups is powerful indeed. It is probably not possible to ascertain the precise influence of the groups to which we belong or desire to belong, but it is possible to gain some notion of their importance by noticing how many items that we have are also possessed by groups members. Yet the importance of the reference group to marketers is not well understood. It is clear that people can have several reference groups, and that group norms do include the possession of certain items, but it is frequently difficult to identify the group. Current research may provide greater insight into the roles of groups and group leaders.

Group leaders exert *personal influence* over the members. The leaders themselves have to conform to the norms of the group, just like the followers, but it is assumed that leaders can influence the norms a good deal. By identifying and understanding the leaders, the marketers feel they can do a

BOX 4-4

Reference Group Influence on Products and Brands

	Weak −	Strong +	
Strong + Reference Group Influence Relatively: Weak −	Clothing Furniture Magazines Refrigerator (type) Toilet soap	Cars Cigarettes Beer (prem. vs. reg.) Drugs	+ Brand or Type
	Soap Canned peaches Laundry soap Refrigerator (brand) Radios	Air conditioners Instant coffee TV (black and white)	−
	−	+	
	Product		

SOURCE: Francis S. Bourne, *Group Influence in Marketing and Public Relations*, (Ann Arbor, Mich.: Foundation for Research on Human Behavior, 1956), p. 8.

more efficient job of forecasting the masses' wants. A few years ago, by surveying graduating college seniors and getting their ideas about style, one firm hoped that it could establish a lead over the competition.

Personal influence can be a strong consumption force. We are influenced by our peers, our reference groups, our family members, our neighbors. Relatives, too, can exert a good deal of personal influence on consumer decisions. Each social class tends to have its own leaders and their influence varies from product to product and person to person. For marketers, however, personal influence is a force with which to reckon. Probable success for a product is greater when the marketing decision can move downstream with personal influence, which can be far more effective than an advertising campaign.

Personal influence, reference-group affiliation, and aspirations all relate to consumption. Interrelated with these forces is *conformity*. As with Willy Loman in *Death of a Salesman*, we want to be well liked, to fit into the group, and to be accepted. We may be careful not to do or say anything that will rub others the wrong way. "Amid these uncertainties, word of mouth is tremendously important, for it above all is the best guide in the delicate job of keeping in tune with the life style. . . ."[3] There is social pressure for

[3] William H. Whyte, Jr., "The Web of Word-of-Mouth," *Fortune*, November 1954, p. 204.

conformity; the individual faces the group and the group exacts some degree of conformity from him. Even a beatnik conforms to his group. With reference to consumers, we have long been aware of the importance of current modes and manners. Do we consume as others want us to consume? Do we deviate in our consumption only in those areas where a group norm is not established? (See Fig. 4-1.)

Conformity in consumption represents a drive cutting across all kinds of goods and people, including industrial buyers. Advertising, personal selling, and new products reflect the force of conformity as people achieve satisfaction from purchasing a product which conforms to some norm; with this kind of product they are at ease. Nor is all conformity undesirable; much of it is simply the easy way to handle unimportant buying decisions. By making mass marketing possible, conformity increases the efficiency of the marketing process and lowers production costs through the long production runs that one style and color make possible.

Few of us, however, would care to be complete conformists in our consumption patterns. Yet few would deny that we do conform in some ways. Probably most of us like to think that we conform in those situations where it "makes sense," but that we deviate in many ways. One of these is to be the first to try a new product; others then conform to us. Another way is to purchase different brands, different colors, different variations of the product in question. Some years ago, for example, the girls in one neighborhood purchased expensive contact lenses. Though each girl purchased a different color and in this way maintained for herself some feeling of independence, the girls conformed to the group by purchasing the product. Marketing thus takes place in an atmosphere of conformity, and marketers should be prepared to deal with this significant force.

The psychological and biological stimuli are certainly manifested in *fashion*. Our desire to be "appropriate" leads us into stores to buy the currently adopted style. We may want to conform or to be distinctive through expressions of fashion. Corporations hire motivational researchers to do image studies because these are popular. It becomes fashionable to hire an outside man for the presidency of the firm or to add the position of vicepresident of marketing. It may be fashionable to possess a horse, a foreign car, a parakeet, a colored refrigerator, two-toned shoes, and one-color automobiles. Even food habits can be fashionable. Fashion is an all-persuasive manifestation of drives which results in consumers buying, doing, singing, wearing, or viewing the same general style.

That consumers act in such a way as to make fashion an almost universal phenomenon is extremely important to marketers and businessmen everywhere. One can confidently predict a reversal of almost any trend. The difficulty lies in predicting the precise turning point and in distinguishing long-run general trends from shorter-run specific fashion trends. Regardless, the desire on the part of consumers to be fashionable offers opportunities as well as problems to those who sell. The correct estimate of a fashion change can encourage company expansion; an incorrect estimate can put a firm out of business.

Figure 4-1. The X's in this picture mark the houses that have air conditioners. The X's also mark the great power of word of mouth. This neighborhood, in the Overbrook Park area in Philadelphia, is fairly homogeneous; most of the people are white-collar couples between twenty-five and forty who earn between $5,000 and $7,000 and live in nearly identical $12,000 houses. Despite this homogeneity, however, the conditioners are not equally distributed. They cluster. Note the street running diagonally across the middle of the picture; on one side only three of the forty-two families have bought conditioners, and the lone box sticking out near the middle is a conspicuous exception in an otherwise unbroken facade. Just on the other side of the street, however, there are eighteen conditioners—or six times as many.

SOURCE: William H. Whyte, Jr., "The Web of Word-of-Mouth," *Fortune*, November 1954, pp. 140–141.

One student of fashion, Laver, has described the existence of a fashion cycle and then, with tongue in cheek, he indicated the clothing cycle shown in Box 4-5.

It may be that every trend has already sown the seeds which will in time reverse it. When large automobiles are fashionable, a trend for small autos is developing, and vice versa. The same may be true with light and dark colors, dietary fashions, hair styles, and length of hemline on a dress. There is, moreover, opportunity for a few producers to buck the trend. At opposite extremes, we have seen two successful automobile manufacturers, Rolls Royce and Volkswagen, keep their basic design when most others were emphasizing style change.

Fashion is important to consumers, to producers, and to marketers. If not a basic drive in itself, it is at least a manifestation of other psychological and biological drives which can "wear out" one's present article faster than one can consume it.

Many other forces influence and encourage consumption. Several of these are closely related and may be considered together: *age, marital status, family size,* and *life cycle.* Our preferences and consumption patterns change with age and as we progress through the various stages of the life cycle. In the early years, there is an expansion of wants and needs in addition to the changes that take place. Perhaps in later years it is more a matter of change than expansion. It is relatively easy to look back on the things con-

BOX 4-5

The Clothing Cycle

The same costume will be:

Indecent	10 years before its time
Shameless	5 years before its time
Daring	1 year before its time
Smart	at present
Dowdy	1 year after its time
Hideous	10 years after its time
Ridiculous	20 years after its time
Amusing	30 years after its time
Quaint	50 years after its time
Charming	70 years after its time
Romantic	100 years after its time
Beautiful	150 years after its time

SOURCE: James Laver, *Taste and Fashion,* (London: George G. Harrap and Company, 1938), p. 202.

sumed; changes have taken place each year. Take the transportation needs for example: wagons, tricycles, bicycles of various sizes, motor scooters, second-hand cars, new small cars, new large cars, and perhaps finally another new small car. The medical field offers us first an obstetrician, then a pediatrician, generalist, and specialists of all kinds. The budget is constantly under strain caused by one's entering each new phase of the life cycle. Although there is no one classification for a life cycle, we should have some notion of its development. The following classification used by Lansing and Morgan will suffice.[4]

1. The bachelor stage
2. Marriage
   a. Newly married couples with no children
   b. Full nest—married couple with dependent children
      (1) Infancy
      (2) Childhood
      (3) Adolescence
      (4) Launching period
   c. Empty nest—married couple after the children have left home
3. The solitary survivor

The forces of age, marital status, family size, and life cycles are easy to grasp. The single person may buy many clothes; young married people buy many of the new cars; young girls consume a great deal of shampoo; married women spend a relatively large amount for food; older people travel and buy travel magazines; young married families purchase labor-saving devices for the home; and of course, babies consume most of the baby food, reaching their peak before they are a year old.

It is obvious why marketers have given much attention to these forces which relate to the life cycle. Knowledge of them helps the marketer in planning his entire marketing program, and it aids the firm in determining directions for its research and development. A comparison of the possessions of a bachelor with those of a family in "full nest" illustrates the magnitude of the consumption forces which are released during changes in the life cycle. The "two can live as cheaply as one" concept becomes a mockery as one person contemplates how he can find room in his budget for riding lessons, music lessons, a new furnace, a lakeside cabin, YMCA membership, the church, United Fund, symphony, summer vacation, magazine subscriptions, television, food, and clothing. Securing a college wardrobe may seem like a problem today, but consider the problem of providing for one's children's wardrobe in addition to one's own and that of one's spouse.

Our expectations are that we will have jobs which will provide adequate

[4] John B. Lansing and James N. Morgan, "Consumer Finances Over the Life Cycle," in Lincoln Clark (ed.), *The Life Cycle and Consumer Behavior* (New York: New York University Press, 1955), p. 37.

incomes for the many items we will want to purchase. In this light, it should be recognized that *occupation per se* is a powerful consuming force. It affects our aspirations, our reference groups and, of course, our ability to buy. For the working-class wife, most of what is bought finds its way into the home to be consumed, but the home—and what it represents—stands as a kind of umbrella under which the variegated acts of consuming take on meaning and significance.[5] Upper-income wives are motivated quite differently and it is not only a matter of income. It stands to reason that different forces will affect each group's consumption because occupation is a composite of educational attainment, income, reference groups, and other factors. Perhaps the consumer in each occupation plays the expected role, not in a precise but in a general way, and collectively, occupational distinctions can be significant. For example, a city which has a high percentage of its employed in retailing will be a better market for airline travel than a city with a high percentage of its employed in manufacturing. Occupation is a useful indicator for sociological and marketing analyses, and is certainly a force having an impact on marketing.

Location and *climate* are also forces influencing consumption. Consumers purchase antifreeze and overshoes in the northern climates; in the south they purchase air conditioners. Rural families have to buy a number of items which their city cousins do not need, and the converse is also true. Laws in one state may require a company to place antismog devices on its fleet cars, whereas another state requires seat belts. Rainfall; temperature; population density; nearness to the sea, mountains, lakes, or rivers; and many other factors serve as significant forces on consumption behavior. The city of Minneapolis owns and operates much expensive snow-removal equipment, whereas Manila, in the Philippines, equips and operates typhoon stations. London may buy products to combat the fog menace while Moscow is concerned with the snow. Environments are different from the physical standpoint, and we react to these differences by buying items most suitable to the situation.

The differences in physical environments become apparent whenever people move from one place to another. Sometimes complete new wardrobes are necessary and many other items must also be purchased. This suggests another force on consumption, *mobility*. There are many kinds of mobility, most of which exert force on our buying behavior. Mobility means more than a change in residence; it refers to mobility in job and income, and even a break with the older generation.[6] The attainment of a college degree contributes to mobility; a second degree contributes further to it. This better-

[5] Lee Rainwater, Richard P. Coleman, and Gerald Handel, *Workingman's Wife* (New York: MacFadden-Bartell Corporation, 1959), p. 161.

[6] Opinion Research Corporation, *America's Tastemakers*, Tastemaker Research Report No. 1, (Princeton, N.J.: Opinion Research Corporation, 1959), p. 6.

ment concept of mobility permeates much of our lives and its impact is substantial. Consider the effect of advancing from a salesman's job to that of sales manager, or the difference between having a college degree and not having one. Leaving one's parents' home to make a home of one's own also generates a host of changes which affect the individual's buying.

One study of mobility has resulted in the hypothesis that mobile people are the ones who first consume the new products on the market. It may be that the betterment aspects of mobility are reflected in the purchases of new items. Traditionally, marketers have attributed much buying behavior to emulation, but it is likely that the desire for bettering one's position is also a proper explanation of the urge to buy. Corporations are mobile in a multiple sense, changing their locations, moving into new product areas, merging, adding new models, and breaking with the past by changing the corporate name and symbol. Mobility, apparently, is a marketing force for most of us (see Box 4-6).

Technology is considered in Chapter 7 as a part of the marketing environment. However, because it fits the mobility and betterment concepts, we briefly insert the idea of technological impact at this point. Technology is an important factor in consumption. The head of a household may trade in black-and-white television for color; another may replace his AM car radio with a portable FM model. We read of the Air Force scrapping an obsolete plane to make room for a newer model. The Post Office Department pleased millions of people when it replaced the old scratchy pens with new ballpoints. The university responds to enrollment pressures by utilizing the technology of closed-circuit television. A steady stream of new products serves to stimulate consumption, touching every group and force previously mentioned.

The final force to be considered in this chapter is *buying power*. In the aggregate, the sum of retail sales fluctuates with changes in disposable personal income. For the individual, changes in his buying power can very well increase his consumption. Likewise with business; in a good year, a firm may decide to build a new plant, raise its quantity of advertising, and increase salaries and commissions. Given increased appropriations, the military signs new contracts with a number of business firms. Early in his term the late President Kennedy ordered GI insurance dividends paid as soon as possible to stimulate more spending. Additional income tends to provide a new incentive to spend more, for to the adult, it may serve as a buying stimulant just as the nickel "burns a hole in the pocket" of the child.

MARKETING IMPACT

This chapter has dealt with those forces that encourage consumption. Some marketing efforts are meant to be persuasive acts, as in the case of advertising. Although the effectiveness of advertising has never been accurately measured, it is surely believed that it does persuade people to buy. Personal selling is in the same category. Less obvious marketing efforts which induce people to buy include a variety of actions such as the opening of a new service station which encourages people to buy there. A manufacturer

BOX 4-6

High Mobiles and a Tastemaker Theory

The underlying concept of the tastemaker theory of change is *mobility*. Mobile people are those who are on the move with reference to:

| Occupation | Education | Travel | Politics |
| Residence | Ideas | Economics | New ventures |

High Mobiles lead in new product buying.

Example—*WILD RICE*

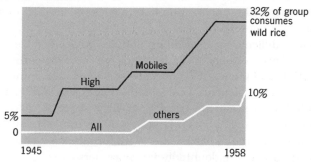

As adoption fans out, the High Mobiles account for a dwindling share of the total market.

Example—*Wall-to-Wall Carpeting*

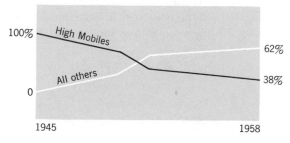

SOURCE: By permission of the copyright owners, Opinion Research Corporation, *America's Tastemakers* (Princeton, N.J.: Opinion Research Corporation, 1959), p. 6.

may set up his own selling force, thus eliminating the selling agent, and in this way may have a more persuasive man calling on customers. A new credit system represents encouragement, as does the installation of a vending machine in a heavily traveled corridor. One manufacturer hopes to add customers by selling through mail-order outlets for the first time while another speeds up delivery time by using air freight, and still another sets up a system of repair facilities to service small motors. A retailer may develop a complete line of private-brand clothing while a competitor signs a contract for an exclusive line of shoes.

All these are examples of the ways in which marketing, by its own efforts, can influence consumption. This suggests a kind of feedback system, which does exist. Combined with the forces discussed earlier, marketing forces represent powerful factors. There is a difference, however, between the marketing forces and the others, in that most of the other forces encourage consumption in a basic sense, whereas much of marketing persuasion is spent in competitive efforts. For example, the desire to conform forces one into a decision to purchase a small boat and motor: much of the marketing effort persuades one to purchase one brand instead of another, and vice versa.

It is extremely difficult for marketing activity to commence a buying trend, stop one, or even change it. Basic trends are more powerful than the forces of marketing, and some critics give advertising too much credit indeed for influencing consumer demand. Undoubtedly these individuals have never been responsible for arresting the trend from large to small cars or for increasing the purchase of men's hats. Marketing forces can certainly be effective in some situations, but the basic force of conformity, hunger, or achievement of some aspiration is undoubtedly far more persuasive.

The importance of the consumer to marketing, whether industrial, governmental, or household, is perhaps obvious. Less obvious is the need for appreciating the difficulty involved in understanding and predicting consumer behavior. We have seen some of the forces at work in the environment which urge the individual to consume. No magic formulas have been tried which enable the seller to hold the consumer in his palm, and none is known. The consumer may not be supreme in our society, but likewise he is not obscure.

Questions

1. State in as few words as possible your understanding of a theory of consumer behavior.
2. Why are there problems today in predicting fashion? Is it easier today than it was thirty or forty years ago?
3. Do industrial buyers take the same basic buying approach as consumer buyers?

4. Is conformity a desirable characteristic of the members of our society? Do the activities of marketing further the influence of conformity? In what areas is the force of conformity most noticeable or more prevalent?
5. What reference groups influence the purchases made by college students?

Statements to Consider

What our friends own we own also, or shall soon own.

As the size of the purchase increases, the planning period of buying lengthens.

Even with an affluent society, consumers still are obliged to make choices.

Reference groups are powerful influences. Members are well aware what the members think and what the members would say if one did not conform to the norms.

Custom and habit are perhaps the strongest forces in determining specific wants at any particular time and place.

A fashion cannot be forced upon consumers unless they find it attractive and desire to adopt it.

SELECTED REFERENCES

Steuart Henderson Britt, *Consumer Behavior and the Behavioral Sciences: Theories and Applications* (New York: John Wiley and Sons, 1966).
° Francis S. Bourne, "The Concept of Reference Group Influence," in Francis S. Bourne, *Group Influence in Marketing and Public Relations* (Ann Arbor, Mich.: Foundation for Research on Human Behavior, 1956), pp. 1, 2, 7–11.
James Coleman, Elihu Katz, and Herbert Menzel, "The Diffusion of an Innovation Among Physicians, " *Sociometry*, Vol. 20, No. 4, December 1957, pp. 253–270.
° Philip M. Hauser, "Business Implications of Population Growth," *Business Horizons*, Vol. 3, No. 2, Summer 1960, pp. 87–96.
° Robert J. Holloway, "Which Automobiles Will Be Here Tomorrow?" *Journal of Marketing*, Vol. 25, No. 3, January 1961, pp. 35–36.
° Pierre Martineau, "Social Classes and Spending Behavior," *Journal of Marketing*, Vol. 23, No. 2, October 1958, pp. 121–130.
° Opinion Research Corporation, *America's Tastemakers*, Tastemaker Research Report 1 (Princeton, N.J.: Opinion Research Corporation, April 1959).
° Charles Winick, "Anthropology's Contributions to Marketing," *Journal of Marketing*, Vol. 25, No. 5, July 1961, pp. 53–60.

Generalizations Were Taken From:

Adaptations by students from general statements in a number of published sources.

CHAPTER

5

_____

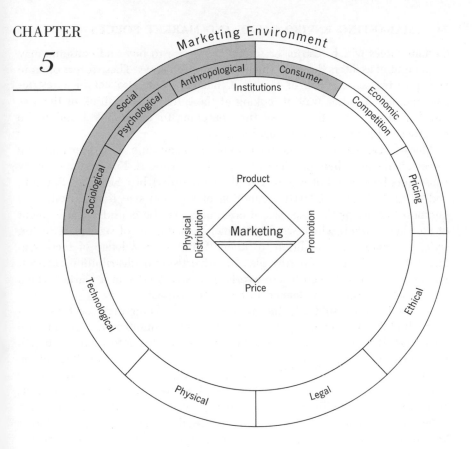

The Environment of Consumer Behavior—II

SELECTED DISCRIMINATING FORCES • RESTRAINING FORCES • DISCRIMINATING
FORCES AND THE MARKETING PROCESS

Certain forces which restrict or screen the desire to buy and consume may be thought of as filters through which consumption flows. These forces operate in a positive sense much of the time, but they can also act in a restrictive manner. Another way of looking at these forces is to think of them as discriminators, since they cause the consumer to discriminate and to be selective in his buying, as we shall see.

Many forces encourage consumers to buy and consume, with discriminating forces channeling their purchases in specific directions. For example, many consumers buy Size 6 of Brand A while many others buy Size 7 of Brand B, and so forth. This is in part a function of age and size if the product in question is shoes or the like. Size 6 customers may be considered a segment of the shoe market, which would also include segments of size, price, color, style, and material in addition to others. Without knowledge of these segments, the marketer can hardly plan his advertising or distribution channels intelligently. He is forced to use overly extensive tactics in a market which may in fact be precisely defined in terms of segments.

As products are sold into the markets, the marketer may see these segments building up. Through research, he counts a number of segments and then plans his operations to take advantage of this information, though frequently he overlooks the force behind the segment. As an illustration, consider the shoe firm which found that it was selling a certain style in large quantities in one city in the United States. The firm increased its advertising efforts with the hope of doing even better. It was some time before the firm learned that Negroes were the principal buyers. Had it known this sooner, it could have made special plans to develop the market faster and to a greater extent. There was present in this situation an acceptance of the style, probably some personal influence, conformity, and maybe reference-group influence. The result was a market segment which could be defined on the basis of race, sex, age, and geographic location.

A number of discriminating forces have the power to determine certain kinds of purchases which can ultimately be cast into a segment of the market. This permits us to view marketing forces in another manner.

SELECTED DISCRIMINATING FORCES

As we have seen, progression into the next stage of the *life cycle* can often signal the purchase of many new items. Now it is suggested that these stages can be seen as discriminating forces. The retired couple may seek an apartment suitable for two, whereas the family looks for a house. The mother of several youngsters may purchase enriched food items, but the teen-ager consumes soft drinks. A student in junior high may need a particular kind of notebook, while his older brother, in college, may require one of a quite different type. Needs for housing, food, and writing paper exist for most of our lives, but vary according to life cycle. Many products bought and consumed can be categorized according to life-cycle stage. Thus the life cycle can be considered a discriminating force. Not only does a new stage call for additional purchases, it also calls for certain types of purchases (Box 5-1).

Consumers also vary in buying abilities, susceptibilities to advertising, and reliance on advertised brands in accordance with their position in the life cycle. We would not expect the new bride to be the world's best shopper; she might, however, be quite susceptible to the advertising of branded items. The middle-aged woman, on the other hand, has many years of experience to draw upon and, as a result, is a different type of buyer in many ways. A younger person may shop around a good deal, whereas a less energetic consumer may buy largely because of convenience. As the consumer proceeds through life, he feels pressures to consume many items and also to discriminate in his buying of these items. The life-cycle force serves as both a screening force and motivation for consumption.

The screening forces are also evident in *racial* differences in consumption patterns. There exists the stereotype of the nonwhite who drives an expensive automobile and parks it outside a dilapidated rented house. Behind this stereotype may be a person who has a strong desire to be accepted, to have some element of prestige, and to own something worthwhile. Since many of the good homes are not available to him, he purchases a fine automobile. In a study of racial differences, Marcus Alexis points out that "the alleged differences in Negro and white spending behavior is attributed to the social and economic discrimination which has been part of the Negro's heritage since emancipation. Not being able to live, relax or dine where they please, American Negroes are said to have developed consumption patterns different from those of their white counterparts." He further states that these observed differences in market behavior will continue to be influenced by the socioeconomic environment. Several findings from Alexis' study should be noted.

1. Total consumption expenditures of Negroes are less than for comparable income whites.

2. Negro consumers spend more for clothing and nonautomobile transportation and less for food, housing, medical care, and automobile transportation than do comparable income whites.

3. There is no consistent racial difference in expenditures for either recreation and leisure or home furnishings and equipment at comparable income levels.[1]

Social class can also be considered a discriminating force. As we know, consumers tend to buy additional items as they climb the social-class ladder.

[1] Marcus Alexis, "Racial Differences in Consumption Patterns," *Business News Notes,* University of Minnesota, No. 50, 1960, p. 4.

BOX 5-1

Discriminations in Buying Behavior

(average annual household expenditures)

Life Cycle

	No Children and Head under 40	Younger Children	Older Children Only	No Children and Head over 40 Married Head	No Children and Head over 40 Single Head
Beverages (soft)	$ 21	$ 28	$ 31	$ 16	$ 10
Furniture	135	69	61	54	16
Women's and girls' clothing	236	196	298	195	158

Education of Household Head

	Some Grade School or Less	Finished Grade School	Attended High School	Finished High School	Some College or Beyond
Baby foods	$ 1	$ 3	$ 6	$ 6	$ 7
Baking ingredients	32	26	24	21	19
Tobacco products	113	115	125	136	116

Occupation of Household Head

	Professional– Semiprofessional	Clerical Sales	Service Worker	Retired or not Employed
Sports goods, equipment	$ 74	$12	$ 4	$ 4
Major appliances	127	83	68	45
Drugs, remedies	56	56	44	48

Geographic Location of Metropolitan Household

	Northern	Central	Southern	Western
Home heating	$173	$166	$124	$150
Men's and boys' clothing	157	131	119	129
Medical and personal care— total	248	235	206	301

SOURCE: *Life Study of Consumer Expenditures,* Volume One, LIFE, New York, 1957.

BOX 5-2

Food Consumption Differences by Urbanization

(Based on purchases for one
week during April–June 1955)

	Urban	Rural Nonfarm	Rural Farm
Total food	$29.99	$24.29	$17.15
Milk, cream, ice cream, cheese	3.56	3.10	1.69
Bakery products	1.70	1.59	1.33
Sugar, sweets	0.64	0.77	0.92
Commercially frozen fruits and vegetables	0.25	0.16	0.07
Meat, poultry, fish	8.09	6.25	3.50

SOURCE: United States Department of Agriculture, *Food Consumption of Households in the United States* (Washington, D.C.: United States Government Printing Office, 1956).

Seen from the standpoint of market segments, belonging to a class puts certain pressures on the consumer which make him a discriminating buyer. Income itself cannot be readily exhibited and thus we prove our social standing in part by our purchases (Box 5-2). We might not guess that a neighbor earns $50,000 annually until he purchases a new Rolls Royce!

The social-class force has far-reaching consumption effects. For example, the lower-class workingman's wife has aspirations quite distinct from the higher groups, and her goals and her buying decisions reflect these differences. Purchase patterns can symbolize the social class.

Upper-Upper or Social register class—The force here is to buy items which uphold the family reputation and which permit gracious living.

Lower-Upper or *nouveau riche* class—The image of this small class is well known. Consumption is similar to the upper-upper but it is combined with more of a drive to move upward in the social world.

Upper-Middle class—The persons making up this class are rather successful people. The group is growing and is representing a strong market for many goods. The group desires most of the same items as the two groups above but some things are clearly out of reach.

Lower-Middle class—One of the largest of the social groups, the lower-middle class are very much concerned with being accepted. They are striving for the better things which puts them in the market for many consumer items.

Upper-Lower class—The largest of the groups, the average man class, spend differently than the lower-middle. They are more interested in keeping up with the times than in gaining respect; they want to enjoy their lives. Some consumption decisions on their parts may be rather surprising.

Lower-Lower class—Many in this group have gradually lowered their levels of aspiration. They are apathetic toward events about them. They do not have the income to purchase many items others purchase in stride.[2]

Those in marketing may enjoy poking fun at the social-class concept but they cannot lightly dismiss it. Some products can be sold to one class but not to another. There are, of course, products which can be sold to persons in all classes. For many items, acceptance by groups below our class is the signal for us to change consumption patterns. Agnes Young has stated: "There is no doubt that the tendency on the part of the inferior to assimilate themselves to their superiors is always in conflict with a tendency on the part of the superiors to differentiate themselves from inferiors."[3] Regulations exist in some situations which prevent classes from having the same privileges as those in the upper groups. For example, transportation by land, sea, and air has several classes of travel. We have seen the companies with dining rooms restricted to the top executives, and the plush restaurant which requires diners to wear evening clothes.

Whether because of social class, race, or life-cycle stage, consumers see or *perceive* products and needs very differently from one another. Products, brands, and even corporations are imbued with personalities. Each product can be described in detail by someone who adds to it all the things he perceives. Recently the governor of one state used a Ford as his official car, perceiving this as adequate and comfortable. It was actually desirable because it was the car of the common man, in addition to having been built in his state. The succeeding governor ordered a Cadillac because he perceived the governor's car as an important way to convey the prestige of the office.

Perceptions vary from person to person and perhaps from group to group. Pass interference on the football field is seen quite differently by home and visiting team supporters. An umpire calls the balls and strikes as he sees them, although some umpires would argue, "As they are." Many women would perceive a new automatic washing machine as a wonderful birthday gift; those of the upper-upper group may perceive it as a necessary item for the maid. An interesting experiment has been reported on the relationship between the motorist's impression of acceleration and the softness of the gas-pedal spring. Motorists perceived greater acceleration with the softer

[2] Richard P. Coleman, "The Significance of Social Stratification in Selling," *Proceedings of the American Marketing Association,* ed. Martin L. Bell, December 1960, pp. 171–184.

[3] Agnes Young, *Recurring Cycles of Fashion,* (New York: Harper & Brothers, 1937), p. 196. (Quotation from A. H. Biggs.)

gas-pedal spring and low-power acceleration than with a hard spring.[4] Consumers also perceive brands differently. Rather strong arguments can be made by the supporters of a Ford automobile as well as supporters of other makes. Each may perceive his preferred brand quite differently from the other person (Box 5-3). One's perception helps to make distinctions between products and between brands.

Perception applies to many attributes of a product, brand, or even a corporation. A consumer may perceive prices in one way and his neighbor in another. Pricing based on psychological principles has many supporters who firmly believe in its effectiveness. They believe that $19.95 is preferred to $19.50 or $20.00. The recent successful experience with the Chrysler Windsor is testimony to how differently people reacted to the automobile before and after it was advertised as "Less than $3,000." Market experience also shows that sometimes consumers perceive a low price as an indicator of low quality. In some cases manufacturers have had to raise the price of their products in order to convince the population that the quality was indeed satisfactory.

Our perceptions of brand, product, company, and other images play an

[4] Alfred Politz, "Science and Truth in Marketing Research," *Harvard Business Review,* Vol. 35, Number 1, January–February 1957, p. 121.

BOX 5-3

Who is Loyal to Brands?

There are no socio-economic characteristics associated with different degrees of brand loyalty for low price, frequently purchased items (tentative). "In the absence of positive evidence to the contrary, manufacturers had better check carefully before they make the assumption that . . . they can distinguish between high-loyalty and low-loyalty families in their particular market by certain socio-economic characteristics."

There is *not* a significant proportion of loyalty-prone families, that is, housewives who tend to have the same degree of brand loyalty in various product classes.

No truly significant correlation exists between brand loyalty behavior and store loyalty behavior.

There is no relationship between size of purchase and brand loyalty.

SOURCE: Ross M. Cunningham, "Brand Loyalty—What, Where, How Much?" *Harvard Business Review,* Vol. 34, No. 1, January–February 1956, pp. 116–128.

important role in buying. We may believe that products made in Sweden are of long life, that Italian products are stylish, that Dutch products are non-technical and durable, that German items are unaesthetic but sound in construction, that those from France are elegant but not durable, that English products are utilitarian, and that products from the United States are practical but rapid-wearing.[5] It is futile to prove the consumer wrong in his perception. The consumer, after all, will buy the product in question if he perceives it to meet best his requirements. The consumer has to make his decisions the way he "sees" the situation, and this may or may not be entirely rational from another person's viewpoint, but the consumer is his own best judge of his satisfactions.

Another discriminating influence is *experience*, which enables the consumer to accumulate a reservoir of information about products and sources of supply. The industrial buyer may have elaborate files of vendors, complete with ratings on delivery time, prices, quality, and even credit; the household consumer may keep this information in her head. Successful experience with vendors and products becomes a most important force in the next decision-to-buy process. Attempts by other sellers to switch the consumer will, for the most part, be unsuccessful if the consumer is indeed quite satisfied with his experience. At least the selling (switching) task is much more difficult than with a consumer who has had unsuccessful experience with a product and who, in fact, is searching for alternatives.

Our own experiences represent one of our strongest discriminating forces. Experience does not necessarily encourage consumption but rather screens our buying so that it falls into already proven patterns. The issuance of free samples is an attempt to woo the consumer away from his existing pattern of consumption and is perhaps the best way for a marketer to coax him to try a new brand. Successful experience with the new brand may cause brand switching; at least it puts the consumer in a more receptive attitude for making a change.

One must recognize that the consumer is constantly changing. Basic and discriminating forces, advertising and personal selling efforts, and neighbor influences keep him in a fluid state. Lazarsfeld has pointed out that individuals are changed by every kind of influence. Consumer A becomes Consumer A_1 when he sees a billboard, for example. He becomes A_2 when he speaks with a friend, and so forth.[6] His attitudes toward buying any product undergo constant change so that the complex bundle of motives may become even more complex. The consumer, in effect, reflects the net result of these many influences, and he changes his consumption along the time line. This concept

[5] Market Facts, *The Made In* . . . . *Image* (Chicago: Roc International, 1960).
[6] See Box 6-9.

BOX 5-4

Is the Industrial Buyer an Emotional Buyer?

(Conclusions based upon a study among
metalworking executives)

1. Fear is one of the major influences in industrial buying. Fear of displeasing the boss. Fear of making the wrong decision. Fear of committing the company to large outlays. Fear of losing status.

2. The buyer needs personal reassurance. He needs confidence. He needs to have faith in people.

3. As products and services become more objectively alike, the buyer's final decisions are based more on subjective, emotional factors.

4. Industrial marketers are not doing a sufficiently creative job of changing needs into wants.

SOURCE: Hector Lazo, "Emotional Aspects of Industrial Buying," in Robert S. Hancock (ed.), *Dynamic Marketing For A Changing World* (Chicago: American Marketing Association, 1960), pp. 258–266.

is much more accurate than that of the impulsive consumer who dashes out of the house bent on purchasing every gadget and bargain in sight. The consumer, after all, has accumulated an abundance of experience, information, and attitudes in the process of maturing. He could not possibly react to every attempt to influence him, any more than he could resist them all. He may deviate from what he considers his proper role of buyer, but for most consumers these deviations represent minor instances, since the consumer is both sane and cautious as he adapts himself to constantly changing conditions.

RESTRAINING FORCES

Up to this point we have considered discriminating or screening forces. Forces can go beyond this to where they restrict consumption. *Economic* forces are among the most important of these. A family's assets, their quantity and liquidity, surely exert a powerful influence over the consumer's ability and even desire to buy. Lack of assets restrains and restricts; we postpone, cancel, and fail to consider purchases when our assets do not permit purchasing the item; we may not buy if we have previously acquired certain household assets, for example. Of course, the reader will recognize that this is the same concept as marginal utility and indifference-curve analysis. If a consumer already has purchased a complete set of glassware, it is unlikely that she is going to be interested in another set. In this sense her assets restrict her buying.

It is apparent that economic forces can act in the opposite direction. The affluent consumer with ample assets may be encouraged to buy. And, in the case of *credit*, the lack of adequate credit restricts consumption whereas its abundance can encourage it. It is not uncommon to find a consumer willing to spend several thousands of dollars more on a house or several hundred dollars more on an automobile because of the credit arrangements. Like a two-edged sword, credit availability can cut both ways.

Income is commonly used to explain consumer buying behavior. Usually the explanation is oversimplified, leaving the notion that expenditures always follow income in a linear relationship. Aggregate data show this tendency over time, but income *per se* is not the complete answer to understanding buying behavior (Box 5-5).

Engel's laws (1848) have been used to illustrate a stable relationship between income and expenditures. On the basis of these laws, we would expect expenditures for most categories to increase as income rose. The percentage spent (according to recent modifications) would decrease for food, remain constant for housing, and increase for clothing, transportation, recreation, health, and education. It has been suggested that Engel's laws probably held satisfactorily during the relative social stability of the period 1887 to 1914, but that in recent years the social and economic changes have often more than counterbalanced the effect of changed incomes on expenditures. Benjamin Loeb, who suggested this, "tested" the applicability of Engel's laws on a year-to-year basis from 1929 to 1953. The laws conformed only 45 percent of the time.[7] Thus, consumer expenditure predictions require some appreciation of noneconomic factors.

Many theories relate income and consumption. The *absolute-income hypothesis* was stimulated by Keynes: "Men are disposed, as a rule and on the average, to increase their consumption as their income increases, but not by as much as the increase in their income."[8] Aggregate consumption expenditures over time correlate highly with aggregate disposable income. This hypothesis has been questioned, however, because budget data have been difficult to reconcile in regard to savings. The *relative-income hypothesis* assumes that the savings rate depends not only on the level of income but also on the relative position of the individual on the income scale. This hypothesis recognizes the drive of people to attain a higher standard of living. Consumers want to close the gap between themselves and their

[7] Benjamin S. Loeb, "The Use of Engel's Laws as a Basis for Predicting Consumer Expenditures," *Journal of Marketing*, Vol. 20, No. 1, July 1955, pp. 20–27.

[8] J. M. Keynes, *The General Theory of Employment Interest and Money* (New York: Harcourt, Brace and Company, 1936), p. 96.

BOX 5-5

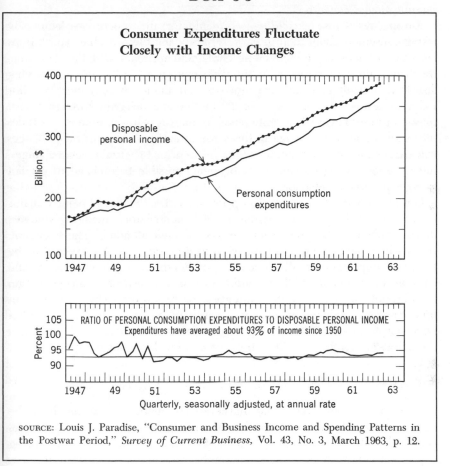

**Consumer Expenditures Fluctuate
Closely with Income Changes**

SOURCE: Louis J. Paradise, "Consumer and Business Income and Spending Patterns in the Postwar Period," *Survey of Current Business*, Vol. 43, No. 3, March 1963, p. 12.

neighbor. If comparison with their neighbor is unfavorable, they want to alleviate this disparity. Furthermore, once a given level of consumption is reached, there is a tendency to stay with it if at all possible even though one's income decreases.

A more recent income hypothesis is the *permanent-income theory.* Friedman divides income into two parts: permanent and transitory. A consumer determines his standard of living according to his expectations involving his returns from resources over a long period of time. These returns would be rather constant from year to year. The transitory-income factors account for deviations in consumption from year to year. They amount to nuisance factors as far as the basic relationship between permanent income and consumption is concerned.

Katona has stressed a *willingness to buy* or an expectations factor. By asking consumers about their intentions to buy and their income expectations for future periods, he combines a psychological approach with the economic. He stresses the importance of habitual purchasing for many items, believing that it is difficult to generalize motives that influence consumer behavior and that instead it is better to examine specific behavior through actual consumer interviewing. It is quite possible that for many consumers, attitudes and expectations may change in the same direction. These attitude changes (toward buying, for example) may take place prior to actual income changes, and by interviewing consumers, it becomes possible beforehand to predict changes in buying behavior.

Despite new insights into consumption activities, the human being remains a complex and inconsistent organism. Each contribution made by students on consumer behavior adds some degree of understanding. The economic forces which have received a great deal of attention can at a given time be the most important of all forces. At other times, the consumer hardly considers the economics of the situation. Income can restrict, it can encourage, and certainly it can force discrimination or selectivity. The consumer, in some manner, melds the noneconomic with the economic forces and makes a decision to buy, not to buy, or to buy a certain brand at a certain price. The economic forces, as well as the psychological, cannot be ignored.[9]

DISCRIMINATING FORCES AND THE MARKETING PROCESS

It has been demonstrated that marketers try deliberately to influence the consumer. Manufacturers would like to manipulate demand, or as critics would have it, "to warp, twist, and mold consumer demand." Advertising may direct consumers to "Eat more cranberries this Christmas Season." Or, it may suggest, "Next time, buy Eatmore cranberries." In other instances, the retailer assembles what he considers the most attractive selection of merchandise for the consumer, and his selection of merchandise may be adequate to encourage patronage. The manufacturer's salesmen may carry bulky catalogs full of alternatives for the customer. All such activities on the part of marketers are influencing forces and most of the time they are of the discriminating kinds.

A consumer may decide to concentrate his purchasing with one department store because he likes to carry one charge account or because he likes to

---

[9] For an excellent coverage of consumer economics, see: Robert Ferber, "Research Household Behavior," *The American Economic Review*, Vol. 52, No. 1, March 1962.

buy with maximum convenience. Locations, credit policies, arrays of goods, and price lines cause consumers to discriminate in their selection of retailers. The same is equally true with industrial goods and their suppliers. A price appeal may be sufficient to activate buying on the part of consumers, but this appeal will not be universally received; only some consumers will be moved by it.

Probably every marketing activity can serve as a discriminating force for some consumers. Every marketing institution can also serve as a selective or discriminating force. These forces are merged with all the others previously mentioned as the purchase is considered.

It is important at this time to raise an important generality. Consumption needs can be satisfied by any one of several *alternatives*. Technology frequently gives us a newer and better way of satisfying a need. Each consumer becomes aware of a need and then of the alternative ways to solve the problem. A family may choose a new automobile from perhaps fifty brands and a thousand models in total; it chooses a Dodge, let us assume. The telephone company has need for many trucks, and it may choose Chevrolets. The state patrol may order specially built Fords; the taxi company may buy Checker cabs; and a corporation may settle on a fleet of Ramblers for its city salesmen. Each of these consumers was aware of forces to buy automobiles; each satisfied the need differently from a variety of alternatives. Some marketers even feature their alternatives as reasons why a consumer should purchase their brand.

It has also been suggested that marketing forces are important in the consumer environment. Marketing makes possible the distribution of the alternatives desired by the consumers and calls attention to these alternatives through advertising and personal selling. Some persons who do not know marketing frequently exaggerate the importance of these persuasive functions. Others ignore them.

Perhaps the best way to conclude this discussion of the forces of the consumer environment is to quote from Vaile's 1940 article on consumption.

Demand manipulation by its very name suggests that something is being done to consumers; that consumption programs are being fashioned, molded, twisted, or warped by some force outside of consumers themselves. Offering is pitted against offering, taste against taste, thrill against thrill, until the reader of advertisements may well be dizzy. This function of marketing is directed at the determination rather than the implementation of consumption. Consumption is the end and aim of sales promotion, right enough, but to *manipulate* demand does not necessarily *further* consumption. This is, however, one of the strongest forces influencing consumption. It plays upon the emotions, the prejudices, the whims, and the fancies of consumers; it creates mirages and will-o'-the-wisps; it leads to jealousy and covetousness and the drive to "keep up with the Joneses." But it also fires ambition, leads people out of the humdrum, and puts color into merchandise and thus into homes and into life itself. It leads people to aspire for a return from their income beyond the provision of food and shelter. If any point in industry merits the term "Business, the Civilizer," this is it.[10]

Questions

1. Trace the buying of an individual over his or her life cycle.
2. Explain how aspiration may influence one's buying patterns.
3. Is satisfaction dependent only upon a rational analysis of product performance?
4. How would you describe the "best" kind of consumer?
5. Make a list of the basic information needed before one could intelligently purchase a camping trailer.
6. Why might a measure of brand loyalty be inadequate as a gauge of consumer satisfaction with a product?

Statements to Consider

Purchasing a known brand or a brand recommended by friends may be as intelligent a method of buying as carefully investigating the alternatives yourself.

Unfortunately, consumers desire and expect only slightly more than they presently have.

We have witnessed a change in marketing influence. The retailers have become more passive and our friends have become more influential.

A leveling process exists and in time consumers will be buying more and more like all others.

Market saturation may occur but it need not last very long. Consumers can simply change their desires for products and buy a second or a third or a fourth of the item which was once thought to have reached market saturation.

The husband makes the primary decision to buy the product and then the wife makes all the sequential decisions concerned with product details.

New products are almost always preferred to the old.

SELECTED REFERENCES

Perry Bliss, *Marketing and the Behavioral Sciences* (Boston: Allyn and Bacon, 1963).
° Warren J. Bilkey, "A Psychological Approach to Consumer Behavior Analysis," *Journal of Marketing*, Vol. 18, No. 1, July 1953, pp. 18–25.

[10]Roland S. Vaile, "Consumption, the End of Marketing," *The Annals*, Vol. 209, May 1940, pp. 17–18.

° Nelson N. Foote, "The Autonomy of the Consumer," in Lincoln H. Clark (ed.)., *Consumer Behavior: The Dynamics of Consumer Reaction* (New York: New York University Press, 1955), pp. 15–24.

Donald A. Laird, "How the Consumer Estimates Quality by Subconscious Sensory Impressions," *Journal of Applied Psychology,* Vol. 16, No. 3, June 1932, pp. 241–246.

° Walter A. Woods, "Psychological Dimensions of Consumer Decision," *Journal of Marketing,* Vol. 24, No. 3, January 1960, pp. 15–19.

GENERALIZATIONS WERE TAKEN FROM:

Adaptations by students from general statements in a number of published sources.

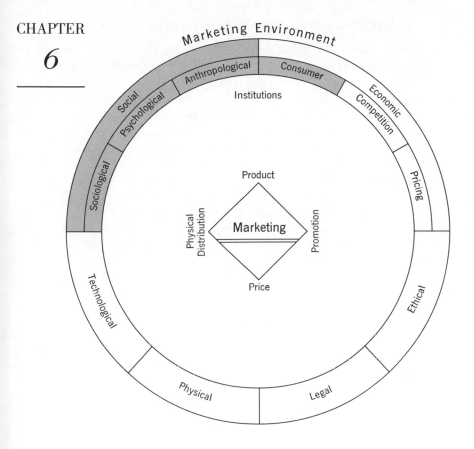

The Environment of
Consumer Behavior—III

CONSUMER DECISIONS TO BUY · INFORMATION FOR DECISIONS · INTERACTION
· A PICTURE OF THE DECISION-MAKING PROCESS · ADDENDA: 1. PERSONAL
CONSUMPTION EXPENDITURES BY TYPE OF PRODUCT, 1929 AND 1962 · 2. A
DIAGRAM OF CONSUMER DECISION MAKING · 3. CONSUMER BEHAVIOR PROPOSI-
TIONS

Whether the purchase is a ball of string for the household, a drill press for an auto plant, or an antitank missile for the government, someone has to make the decision to buy or not to buy, and invariably that someone is the consumer. Marketing therefore has to adapt itself to the kaleidoscopic world of the consumer, for the sum total of these decisions determines consumer satisfaction, influences the level of economic activity, and makes a business profitable or unprofitable. It is our intention to examine this decision-making process, since a clear understanding of it is one avenue toward more efficient marketing operations and increased consumer buying satisfaction.

Consumers are subjected to all kinds of pressures to buy, of which the most important are the physical and environmental forces. Somehow over his lifetime the consumer deals with these many forces and arrives at decisions for thousands of products. Many of these decisions involve an element of

BOX 6-1

The Consumer Needs an Education

The plight of today's consumer was recognized by President Kennedy in his Consumer Message of March 15, 1962, when he said, "Many of the new products used every day in the home are highly complex. The housewife is called upon to be an amateur electrician, mechanic, chemist, toxicologist, dietician, and mathematician—but she is rarely furnished the information she needs to perform these tasks proficiently" . . . .

It is my conclusion from a good many years of experience in the fields of economics and home economics, that the basic problem underlying all so-called "consumer problems" is the lack of education. It is not enough, in fact it is impossible, to represent consumers in a meaningful way if they are ill-informed and irresponsible. It is not enough to offer them isolated pieces of information about specific problems, if they do not have a broad framework of understanding about their role in our economy as responsible consumers and citizens . . . .

I am convinced that if our economic system is to survive, it will come not only by training specialists and leaders but primarily by acquainting the average citizen with simple basic economic truths. For the first time in human history, a world without poverty and without war is *technically* possible. But it would be the greatest of all tragedies if in our ignorance and fear we should turn this into an age of mass suicide.

SOURCE: Helen G. Canoyer, "The Consumer Advisory Council: Its Origin, Purpose and Problems," Speech before the American Home Economics Association, Kansas City, Missouri, June 27, 1963. Dean Canoyer, the first Chairman of the Consumers Advisory Council, was appointed by President Kennedy in 1962.

risk and uncertainty, for the consumer cannot always know if his decision is the best one. He wants it to reduce the risk involved as much as possible, and yet increase the satisfaction he derives from the product. But to make intelligent decisions, the consumer needs a good deal of information. He must become an educated consumer, and this is not always an easy accomplishment (Box 6-1). Certainly it is expected of the industrial buyer, but not of the household consumer, at least to the same degree.

Every purchase is the result of a decision to buy. Pan American Airways may decide to acquire six new jets for its fleet, statesmen in India may decide to erect a government steel mill, or the housewife may decide to purchase a quart of milk. Regardless of the item, in each situation a decision has been made to buy.

CONSUMER DECISIONS TO BUY

At the outset, decisions to buy differ from one another in various ways. The *product* under consideration can serve as one classification. Some products, for example, are purchased by habit: since Pepsi Cola satisfies us, we do not carefully weigh our decision in buying the next soft drink. This may signify brand or patronage loyalty or it may simply represent convenience. India's decision to buy the steel mill implies a buying situation in which careful decision making would occur, a procedure that takes place whenever the item involves a rather high cost. Many purchases reflect decisions to try something new or different; here the decision making may be deliberate.

The decision process may be influenced in other ways, depending on the type of product. The product in question is most important. For a price-appeal item the consumer may go through one decision-making process, and for an item purchased on impulse or on the basis of emotion he may go through another. Furthermore, a new product would be viewed differently from a well-known one. Those responsible for procuring weapons for the United States Marines certainly experience a different process from those procuring routine food items. The consumer may have a number of decision processes; one type may operate for the repetitive buying of food, another for recreation expenditures, another for education, and still another for expensive durables.

The degree of planning or *deliberation* is another aspect of decision-making. This may be simply a function of the cost of the product under consideration and may reflect the degree of satisfaction with products purchased in the past or personality distinctions and differences in educational attainment. The amount of deliberation can also suggest one's income, age, and occupation.

Some purchase decisions represent long planning processes, whereas others are made on impulse (Box 6-2). A family may spend many evenings planning

BOX 6-2

Do Consumers Buy on Impulse?

(Findings based on survey of 5300 Canadians in six cities.)

Impulse Purchases (as a per cent of all purchases)

Product Group	Food Stores	Drug Stores	Variety Stores	Dept. Stores	Avg. All Stores
Candy and nuts	69.6	34.1	82.8	77.1	65.8
Baked goods (sweet)	67.1	—	68.7	76.7	70.1
Cosmetics	—	24.3	61.5	49.7	41.8
Drugs and sundries	—	32.2	—	44.0	38.0
Stationery	—	19.8	48.8	57.3	41.9
Toilet articles	—	27.5	37.8	47.6	37.6
Notions	—	—	37.2	54.7	46.0
Dress accessories	—	—	28.5	22.8	25.5
Jewelry	—	—	50.0	49.1	49.5
Hardware and electrical supplies	—	—	28.5	34.6	41.5
Cutlery, kitchenware, glassware	—	—	47.8	31.2	39.5
Toys	—	—	57.9	53.0	55.5
Hosiery	—	—	25.2	50.2	37.6
Wearing apparel	—	—	27.5	20.7	24.1
°GENERAL AVERAGES—ALL ITEMS	43.5	26.6	41.5	33.6	36.7

°These averages are for all products surveyed in each of these outlets. They are not averages of only the product classifications shown above. Last figure shows that 36.7 per cent of all purchases in the four types of outlets in all *six cities* are made on impulse.

SOURCE: C. John West, "Results of Two Years of Study Into Impulse Buying," *Journal of Marketing*, Vol. 15, No. 3, January, 1951, p. 363.

its next summer's vacation, but one of the children may buy a package of chewing gum on impulse the next time he is sent to the store. Similarly some industrial purchases are made after long and detailed planning, bids are submitted, estimates are made, and planning costs run into thousands of dollars, whereas other industrial items are bought more routinely. For example, when the supply of S.A.E. 10 lubricating oil reaches the reorder point, a replenishment is automatically ordered.

Some items are bought repetitively, while others are purchased once or twice in a lifetime. The deliberation process reflects which of these patterns prevails in a given buying situation. The average person may personally inspect two or three houses before deciding to buy a home, although there are exceptions. A colleague of one of the authors told recently of examining forty-five homes before reaching a decision to buy. An individual can do this for a few purchases, but time would run out if he did it for many. He may visit several automobile dealers before making a buying decision (Box 6-3), but for other items he may buy at the most convenient place with or without carefully examining alternatives.

Decisions differ according to the *decision maker*. In addition to considerations of income, personality, education, and age, there is the multiple versus the single process. Business firms and governments have regulations for buying which enable one person to buy small items without multiple approval but which require group approval for many other items. The family probably has no set procedure although in effect it does this same kind of thing. For many items the housewife and the husband may, without realizing it, have a division of labor since each purchases certain items for the household. For other items, the husband and wife may seek approval of the other; for still other items, the entire family may become involved. Recently a family of five decided to purchase a dog. For this family there were five preferences, and the decision became an involved group matter. The process was definitely different from others in which the husband or the wife had made the decision for the family without consultation having taken place. Who makes the decision and how many persons are involved are two substantial aspects of the overall decision process.

BOX 6-3

Length of Planning Period for Durable Goods Purchases

The question was: "Could you tell me how long you people were thinking or talking about buying a _____ before you actually bought it?

Length of Planning Period	Percent of buyers
Several years	8
One or two years	13
Several months	30
One or two months	9
A few weeks	19
A few days	13
One day or less	4
Not ascertained	4
All cases	100

SOURCE: Lincoln H. Clark (ed.), Era Mueller and George Katona, "A Study of Purchase Decisions," in *Consumer Behavior* (New York: New York University Press, 1955), p. 44.

This raises another question. When is the decision made? Certainly the housewife makes a decision when she puts a box of Wheaties into her shopping cart. But the child who asked her to buy that brand may have made the decision for the housewife, who only acted as "buying agent." The Congress, in appropriating funds for a project to send a manned spacecraft to the moon, makes the basic decision, but another government agency implements the Congressional will. Many decisions to buy are really implementing decisions after the real decisions have been made by someone else.

For one product there are several decisions required. A family or firm may decide to buy Product X, then there are decisions to buy from Source A, and to buy Brand Z. The timing may also require a decision involving credit terms, delivery, installation, and other facets of the purchase. A purchase thus is not necessarily a single process, but a sequential affair. From the marketer's standpoint, each part of this sequence is important, for the decision to buy a candy bar does not become relevant to Hershey until that brand is chosen. The product decision is undoubtedly the most basic one, but to a marketer, the retailer and brand are also important.

The consumer decision to buy is thus not a simple concept. There are many types of decisions to be made which could, perhaps, be classified in a variety of ways—product, deliberation time, degree of planning, the decision maker, multiple versus singular decisions, and sequential decision making. A decision may be made in an instant or it may take years. The consumer may enter the decision process joyously—"We received the raise, now we can decide on our remodeling"—or the decision may be painful if the item is a forced purchase, as would occur following a fire or collision. We may be almost unaware that we are making a decision (for example, the housewife quickly buys a week's supply of groceries), or we may relish the entire process.

For marketers, the decision to buy is the culmination of the market development process. An understanding of the buying process can surely aid him in planning his advertising copy, distributive mechanism, appeals, and other features of the marketing process. Moreover, the marketer has to make decisions relevant to the consumer decision-making process. He must decide whether to appeal to consumers at a point of time when they may not even be considering the product or whether to direct his appeal when they are weighing alternative brands or sources of supply. To be effective, marketing operations must dovetail with the consumer's decision-making process.

INFORMATION FOR DECISIONS

Probably no consumer is entirely ignorant about a purchase, yet few consumers are completely informed about their actual needs, the alternatives, and the other factors of the decision process. Many purchases are made without the consumer's deliberately attempting to use information; the housewife may use rules of thumb or long-established procedures, or she may purchase from habit. Other purchases are made after considering as many factors as possible; it would be expected that an industrial buyer would assemble information on pricing, sources of supply, delivery time, financing, quality control, and other factors.

It should be kept in mind that one may accumulate buying information over a long period of time. The fact that a consumer does not spend hours gathering data does not mean that he is uninformed. He has experience with one or more brands. Advertising, store visits, and discussions with friends, neighbors, and relatives provide a great deal of information. It is probably true that if a consumer wants to exert the effort, he can accumulate as much information as he needs to make an intelligent purchase (Box 6-4). Unfortunately, information is not always easy to find, and it may require much effort to get both the quality and the quantity desired. Many times a good deal of useless information is readily available, whereas useful information must be gleaned from hard-to-find specifications.

Some consumers find helpful information in such sources as *Consumer Reports, Changing Times,* and *Consumer Bulletin.* These sources are used by thousands of people, some employing the information as a "buying bible" while others treat it as a less important buying guide (Box 6-5).

The desire for information changes over time. If no desire exists to buy an air conditioner, the consumer may be quite oblivious to information concerning air conditioners. When he becomes aware of a need and decides that an air conditioner is both a feasible and a desirable product to purchase, he may open his mind to information sources and indeed will probably seek them. He may gather information until he thinks he has a sufficient amount on each product, then he cuts off the supply. It may be that he keeps the supply of information shut off even after the purchase has been made. In this way, he permits only the flow of information that reinforces his decision. If he purchased a Carrier unit, he would welcome information favorable to Carrier but would dread information about the negative aspects of this brand and the positive aspects of another. Thus, the use of information may change considerably from the onset of the desire to buy to the postdecision period. As consumers, we do have some control over the flow of information to us.

Often times when seeking information, we find it difficult to locate, inadequate in its coverage, and lacking in objectivity, but at other times we are virtually overwhelmed with it. (Try counting the number of individual advertisements to which we are exposed in one day.) This information is usually a form of marketing persuasion and seldom provides all the intel-

BOX 6-4

What Else Does a Consumer Need to Know?

Mail-order catalogs provide most if not all of the vital information.

WAS $16.66 **$14⁴⁴**

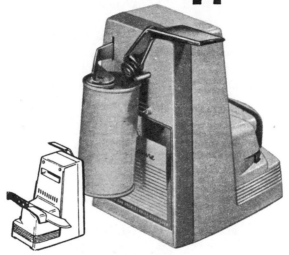

Electrically Opens Cans and Sharpens Knives

- Opens Any Size, Shape Can Automatically in Seconds
- Sharpener Puts Keen Edge on Knives and Scissors

Smart Shopping 3 Ways . . . Save $2.22 at Our Anniversary Sale Price and get a work-saving 2-in-1 appliance.

Easy, One-Control Operation. Just insert can, touch lever . . . starts motor, pierces lid, opens can, holds can in place until released. Rolls cut edge back smoothly. Powerful magnet lifts and holds lid so it can't fall into can. Stainless steel cutting wheel removes to clean.

Fine Grinding Wheel Swiftly Sharpens Knives and Scissors to razor-sharp edge (see sketch), keeps them like new.

White Styrene Plastic Case with MW Thrush Beige front panel; no-mar feet. Cord storage compartment. Slot for easy carrying. About 6½x4½x7½ in. AC only.

86 G 2298—Ship. wt. 6 lbs. Was $16.66.....Now **$14.44**

SOURCE: Montgomery Ward & Co. 91st Anniversary Sales Catalog, 1962, p. 162.

BOX 6-5

Are Consumer Research Bulletins and Consumer Union Reports Used?

(Selected results from a survey of 1,353 consumers)

Percent Buying Recommended Products

	CU Subscribers and Consulters	Non-consulters	CR Subscribers and Consulters	Non-consulters
Automatic clothes washer	18.6	8.4	22.0	19.8
Electric shaver (men's)	26.1	21.6	23.3	24.2
Television (table)	15.7	8.8	4.8	5.1
Vacuum (tank)	10.2	4.2	8.0	4.7
Total durables studied	17.6	12.9	15.0	13.0
Children's Shoes	41.5	40.0	27.0	28.3
Detergent	72.8	68.3	20.7	29.1
Floor wax	60.8	66.2	62.3	61.3
Razor blades	0.2	0.4	81.9	84.8
Total nondurables studied	61.9	60.9	45.8	47.6

(Not all respondents were buyers during this period. For example, 581 reported purchases of floor wax. Of these, 358 persons or 61.8% purchased recommended brands.)

Reading households have incomes higher than nonreading families.

	CR Subscribers	Nonconsulters
Over $15,000	15.9	8.9
$10–15,000	19.7	12.8
$7,500–10,000	23.5	20.3
$5,500–7500	18.8	24.6
$3,500–5500	18.9	25.6
Under $3500	0.8	4.2
No answer	2.4	3.6
	100	100

SOURCE: Hugh W. Sargent, "Consumer-Product Rating Publications and Buying Behavior," *University of Illinois Bulletin*, Vol. 57, No. 31, 1959, pp. 24–27, 46.

ligence needed. Its message is more of an inducement to buy than a careful appraisal of the buying factors. Frequently, however, marketers do provide informative advertising about their products. Automobile dealers have provided detailed comparisons and hi-fi companies have given every conceivable kind of specification (Box 6-6), but it is not clear whether this kind of advertising sells more merchandise than the inducement variety.

Sometimes information is very subtle. It may come to us from trusted friends, it may come accidentally, and it may come without our being conscious of it. Information provides cues of all kinds, which may be the knobs on a television set, the dashboard instruments of an automobile, the package of cigarettes, or something more basic in nature. Some cues are valued more than others. If valued lightly, a cue will probably be used as a basis for product evaluation. Since most consumers know little about the complicated inner workings of an automatic washer, it seems reasonable to expect them to make some value judgments on the basis of the control dials and the shell which surrounds the mechanics of the washer. Donald Cox relates that suds serve as a cue for washing effectiveness of soaps, and color for the richness of ice cream.[1] Copper pipes help to sell a new house; they become visible cues for the buyers.

The marketer should understand the various uses of information. He must recognize that some information makes the consumer aware of needs, some helps to narrow the alternatives, some helps the consumer to decide on price line, some helps him to select the source of purchase, and some information can reinforce the consumer after he has made the purchase. Properly disseminated by the marketer and properly used by the consumer, information can lead to buying decisions that are satisfactory from all points of view. It is possible, of course, that information can complicate the purchase process. If, for example, the consumer knew of only the Eastman Kodak brand of camera, no alternatives would have to be considered. Information concerning the Leica and Canon might complicate the decision process. In general, awareness of alternatives is considered to be desirable, since the consumer can select the best alternative for himself (at least as he perceives it).

INTERACTION

Individual consumer decision making takes place thousands of times each day. It is not limited to the bachelor, since many individuals decide on items without group consultation of any kind. The father may buy life insurance with absolutely no interaction, except with the insurance salesman; the

---

[1] Donald F. Cox, "The Measurement of Information Value," Speech before the American Marketing Association, Pittsburgh, December 1962.

purchasing agent in the business firm may place many orders without advice from others; the purchasing officer in a government agency can procure many items on his own.

Nevertheless, interaction among consumers is common. Families, industrial buyers, and government buyers typically discuss the items they propose to buy. Frequently it becomes necessary to obtain group agreement before a purchase can be approved. Interaction among consumers can primarily constitute the passage of information or the appraising of relevant alternatives and can occur at almost any time within the family or with friends, colleagues, or members of any group. The interaction changes over time since the roles of the group members change. College students report, for example, that they frequently have more buying influence after they have left home to attend college.

Elements in the interaction process are depicted in Box 6-7. This diagram suggests the interaction between the physical forces and personality on the left side and the cultural and environmental forces on the right side. All during this period of interaction the consumer plays various roles, buying as a father at one time, as a husband at another time, as the outdoor man, or as a grateful son. Just as his role changes in the ordinary sense of social interaction, so does it change in consumer interaction.

Hare explains that interaction is an essential ingredient of a group. Without it, families would merely be collections of people. Groups share a common goal and set of norms which give direction and limits to their activity. They also develop a set of roles and a network of interpersonal attraction which serve to differentiate them from other groups.[2]

Individual preferences are made known through interaction. Each member of an interacting group may perceive products differently, may have different groups he wants to belong to, may have a different personality, and may vary to a degree in his physical needs. Actually, small, intimate groups such as the family do not require a great deal of time for consumer interaction. Knowing each other well, the members do not need constant reminders about individual preferences. Furthermore, there are many instances in which one member knows more than the others about a product, and the rest of the group depend on him. One would not expect the wife to argue about the kind of crankcase oil used in the car, nor would the husband tell his wife what brand of cosmetics to use (See Box 6-8). The children expect their parents to buy many items without their having any voice in the matter. The situation changes over time as the members mature or even as incomes, personalities, and life cycles change.

---

[2] A. Paul Hare, *Handbook of Small Group Research* (New York: 1962), Free Press of Glencoe, p. 10.

BOX 6-6

Advertisements Can Inform: 2075 Words in Seven-Point Bodoni Type

What should a good turntable do? Easy to put into words...move the record at the exact specified speed, without variation, and without inducing distortion. Here's how the Empire Troubador turntable achieves that goal: • Empire 208 belt-driven 3-speed "silent" turntable • There are only two moving parts in the 208, the motor and the turntable platter—precise bearing tolerances in those parts • Each motor and each turntable are individually adjusted to perfect dynamic balance • Complete rumble isolation is provided by the motor suspension, flexible belt drive and the resilient nylon "seat" which supports and cushions the thrust of the main bearing • Total vibration limited to less than 1/1,000,000th of an inch • 3 speeds, 33⅓, 45, 78 rpm • Constant speed, heavy duty hysteresis-synchronous motor operates independent of variations in current fluctuation • Continuous flexible belt—perfectly ground to constant thickness ±.0001 inch, couples turntable directly to the motor pulley—no intermediate idlers • Acoustic isolation motor suspension • Fine speed control • Push button power control with on-off light • Optimum distribution of turntable mass; 6 pound heavy machined aluminum, individually balanced to precise concentricity • Machined heavy aluminum base plate • Safety suspension rubber mat • Retractable 45 rpm adapter • Rumble better than −65 db • Wow and flutter less than .05% • Satin-chrome or satin-gold finish turntable, $110. (slightly higher west of the Rockies) • Handsome walnut base for 208 turntable, $15. • The "American Record Guide" (Larry Zide column) says of the Empire Troubador turntable: "I found speed variations—that is, flutter and wow—to be inaudible...vibration was extremely low... rumble figures have not been bettered by any turntable I have tested ...the heavy turntable is driven via a belt by a synchronous motor, thus assuring the user of constant speed, regardless of minor line variations" • Don Hambly, station manager of KRE AM/FM, Berkeley, Calif. said: "We have long realized that belt driven tables would be the best to use, but had not been impressed with those on the market ...the Empire tables, however, have all the basic requirements of design and simplicity of operation and maintenance that we have sought". • "Audio" magazine's "Equipment Profile" of the 208 said: "A massive turntable with precise performance...individually balanced...we tried to induce acoustic feedback by placing the turntable on top of our large speaker system and turning up the gain: we were unsuccessful". • (Still with us?) • "High Fidelity" magazine said of the 208: "Bold appearance which suggests massive and reliable construction—an impression which is quite borne out by its performance tests ...the various pieces of the turntable are carefully machined aluminum castings, thick enough to provide extreme rigidity...finely machined shaft... wow and flutter, with the Troubador', were completely undetectable by ear...rumble also was completely inaudible, even at high listening levels...the hum field above the platter was completely negligible...starting torque was good...speed accuracy very good" • What should a good arm do? It should hold the cartridge in place as the stylus follows the record in the groove...without detracting from the performance of the cartridge • Here's how the Empire 980 Arm achieves this objective: • Better dynamic balance achieved by locating the pivot points at the precise center of the arm's mass—equal mass on both sides of axis. Once in balance in one plane it is balanced in all planes. This permits the 980 arm to track at lowest levels, gives it its rock-like stability that will allow perfect tracking at any angle—even upside down • Lowest inertia achieved by critically calculated distribution of arm mass • Maximum compliance means it yields to the slightest impulse, responds and moves effortlessly, even with a tilted table, a badly warped record, or with the turntable turning upside down • Precision ball bearing suspensions—both the vertical and lateral pivot bearings of the 980 are suspended in precision steel-ball races, precision manufactured to instrument tolerances...vertical and lateral friction are both virtually unmeasurable, permitting high compliance and minimum hysteresis • Lowest fundamental resonance frequency; 6 cps (the lowest ever achieved in any arm), achieved by increasing the rigidity of the arm structure through weight distribution, and by making the cartridge shell an integral part of the arm • 5 wire circuit eliminates ground loops, hence eliminates the hum that gound loops induce • Easy plug-in installation...no wiring or soldering necessary • Self-latching arm rest...a slight push downward on the arm tube latches the arm in position. (Score yourself a fairly serious music lover) • Precise stylus force adjustment...calibrated knob dials any stylus force from 0 to 8 grams with an accuracy of 0.1 gram • Arm offset angle: 23.8° • Satin chrome or satin gold finish, $50. • Lowest tracking force possible, because of extreme compliance and low inertia • Counterweight zero balance adjustment for any cartridge from 2-25 grams • Maximum tracking error ±.650° • No acoustic feedback • Exact cartridge positioning, quick-release bracket-mount secures cartridge to arm shell. Stylus is aligned with front edge of cartridge mounting plate for exact overhang dimension • Dyna Lift (Patent Pending) lifts arm from record at play out • "High Fidelity" magazine's equipment report said: "The spring-loaded 12-inch 980 Arm moves exceptionally freely about its pivot points, indicating very well-made bearings" • "American Record Guide" (Larry Zide column) said: "One of the best available...substantial reduction in vertical mass...a cartridge of any dimensions can be aligned in the head for minimum tracking error...calibration is extremely accurate... Dyna Lift most useful...lateral and vertical friction is exceptionally low...exceptionally stable...steady even with shaky floors..." • "Audio" magazine's equipment profile said: "Much thicker walled tubing in the arm to reduce the fundamental resonant frequency, which is now below the lower limit of our test record" • (This settles it, score yourself a dedicated music-loving audiophile for reading this far) • What should a good cartridge do? It should translate mechanical energy into electrical energy without introducing distortion. And for maximum life of the stylus and your records (not to mention reduced distortion) it should perform this function at as slight a stylus force as possible • Here's how the Empire 880p cartridge achieves these objectives: • Lowest dynamic mass, less than .5 x 10^{-3} grams • Highest compliance, 30 x 10^{-6} cm/dyne ... Lower dynamic mass and higher compliance than any other cartridge made —eliminates distortion and makes possible many of the cartridge's other accomplishments • Performance range 6 to 30,000 cps, well beyond the range of human hearing • Channel separation more than 30 db—greater separation than any other cartridge means greater enjoyment of stereophonic sound • Tracking force as low as ¾ gram—lowest in the industry—at such low tracking force, the 880p not only eliminates record wear, but also eliminates distortion • Longest possible cartridge life insured by lightness of stylus and the low dynamic mass of the magnetic element. It's the last cartridge you're ever likely to buy • The amazing "Dyna-Life" Stylus (Patent Pending)—ultra-sophisticated hand-polished .6 mil diamond—world's lightest • Complete freedom from hum pickup: the Empire 880p incorporates a complete mu-metal shield to prevent stray hum in the cartridge • Fully compatible for stereo or mono • "Moving Magnet" principle • Balanced high output, 10 millivolts per channel ± ¼ db, etc. • Perfectly translates and responds to the intricate movements of the record groove • Stylus inertia approaches the irreducible minimum • Smooth, wide response • Inspected at each phase of its manufacture • The Empire 880p is so new, the country's hi fi magazines have not had an opportunity to test and publish their opinions ... in the meantime, here's what a happy new owner of the 880p wrote us recently: "Most musical, noise non-existent, the sound is transparent, spacious, airy, exceptionally musical, violins sound like violins not cellos or steel wires, in a class by itself" • The Empire 880p is the cartridge that renders every other cartridge on the market today obsolete • If you've read this far you are by all means a music lover most seriously interested in highest quality record playback equipment. Above you have read a "few" of the reasons why we believe the Empire Troubador is for you. You've got the facts about the Empire 208 turntable, the Empire 980 Arm, and the Empire 880p Cartridge. But what about the integration of these three components? Every Empire component was designed and built for maximum integration with the Troubador system ... no other manufacturer makes all three. • "High Fidelity" magazine said: "A precision-engineered product of the highest quality ... in sum, the parts of the 'Troubador'—taken separately—stand up as first-rate audio components. Taken together, they form one of the finest and handsomest record players available" • "Audio" magazine said: "Precise in appearance and performance ... as a system, the 'Troubador' Model 398 is not inexpensive [$222.50 including base], but it just reaffirms something we all know: higher quality means higher costs. The Model 398 is an excellent buy for those who want the quality" • To you determined readers we can only say that we rest our case. (sigh ... now you don't have to write for our brochure ... you've just read it).

Here are a few of the reasons why the EMPIRE TROUBADOR is called the "World's Most Perfect Record Playback System"

 EMPIRE

SCIENTIFIC CORP•845 STEWART AVE•GARDEN CITY, L.I.,N.Y.

EXPORT: CANADA Empire Scientific Corp., Ltd. Toronto, Canada • EXPORT EXCEPT CANADA EMEC, Plainview, L. I., N. Y.

Advertisement prepared by:
Katz, Jacobs & Co., Inc.

SOURCE: *Printers' Ink,* July 26, 1963, p. 16. Reprinted by permission of Katz, Jacobs & Co., Inc.

BOX 6-7

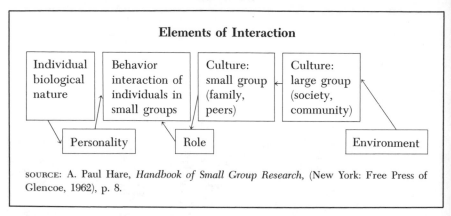

Elements of Interaction

SOURCE: A. Paul Hare, *Handbook of Small Group Research*, (New York: Free Press of Glencoe, 1962), p. 8.

In the wake of interaction, a kind of family power structure may develop. Little research has been done in this area, but it does appear possible that a family structure may be discerned with respect to buying behavior. In most families, responsibility for certain products may well exist among specific members. A similar structure exists in industry. A buying group may advise the purchasing agent of a company, but within this group one member may be more influential than the others. During the interaction, as the firm decides, for example, on an expensive item of machinery, the power structure undoubtedly emerges. Purchasing agents, production managers, and sales managers have to reconcile their points of view just as family members do with regard to buying decisions.

Buying groups have what Likert refers to as "interaction-influence systems." Drawing on Likert's discussion, we can note the interrelated and interdependent processes which characterize an organization, whether it is a purchasing department for a business firm, a procurement team for the government, or the family decision-making unit. Likert says of the organization:

It has a structure.
It has a communication process through which information flows.
It has decision-making processes.
It has action resources to carry out decisions.
It has influence processes.
It has attitudinal dimensions and motivational characteristics.

It has observational and measurement processes which collect information about the internal state of the organization, the environment in which the organization is functioning, and the relationship of the organization to this environment.[3]

[3] Renis Likert, *New Patterns of Management* (New York: McGraw-Hill Book Company, 1961), p. 178.

BOX 6-8

Husband's and Wife's Reports Regarding Decision-Making Patterns—Who in the Family Decides . . . ?

	When it's time to buy a car?		When it's time to buy household goods and furniture?	
	Husbands Say	Wives Say	Husbands Say	Wives Say
Wife only	3%	3%	24%	25%
Wife predominates	1	1	12	10
Both equally	31	23	53	51
Husband predominates	5	9	4	5
Husband only	51	54	4	6
Other answers	9	10	3	3
	100%	100%	100%	100%

SOURCE: Elizabeth H. Wolgast, "Do Husbands or Wives Make Purchasing Decisions?" *Journal of Marketing,* Vol. 23, No. 2, October 1958, p. 153.

Another kind of interaction should be mentioned, at least briefly. Consumers come into contact with salesmen, and the resulting exchange can be an important part of the decision-making process. This interaction takes place at every level of marketing: the manufacturer's agent calling on a manufacturer, the wholesaler calling on a retailer, the consumer walking into a retail store, and the house-to-house salesman calling on the consumer in her home. Frequently this interaction results in an immediate purchase. Of course, many times the consumer was in the final stages of the decision-making process before he had the discussion with the marketer, although this is not always true.

Accordingly, interaction serves a useful purpose throughout the decision-making process. Though not essential, it does take place often among different kinds of groups. It may involve the desirability of purchasing a certain product or brand, or of purchasing from a given source of supply. For most consumer decisions, some interaction is likely to have taken place prior to the actual decision.

A PICTURE OF THE DECISION-MAKING PROCESS

Pictures of the variegated process of consumer decision making at best produce an incomplete explanation. As already suggested, several sequential decisions may constitute one major decision, and any picture of the process should take this into account. Then, of course, we must consider the forces within and without—rational and emotional, irrelevant and relevant, strong and weak, and biological and psychological—which, along with their tendencies to change in relative importance over time, must be included in the decision process. In oversimplified manner, the consumer buying process may be portrayed as follows:

Forces $\longrightarrow$ Consumers $\longrightarrow$ Buying Action

Although this is essentially a correct model, it gives no details of the process.[4] We are well aware by now that forces of many kinds operate on the consumer; we know that consumers are of all types—industrial, household, and governmental; and we know that buying behavior represents the many individual decisions which are made by consumers. Let us now add some important details.

The time line which frequently exists in decision making has been suggested by Kornhauser and Lazarsfeld (Box 6-9). Along with the time line is the notion that individuals can change each time they come into contact

[4] Adapted from Vernon G. Lippitt, "Household Decision-Making," in Nelson N. Foote (ed.), *Household Decision-Making* (New York: New York University Press, 1961), p. 173.

BOX 6-9

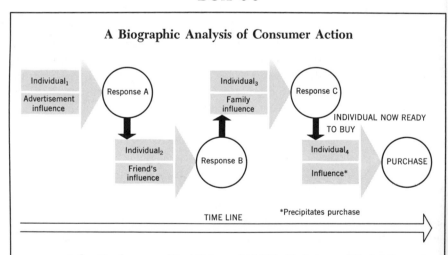

A Biographic Analysis of Consumer Action

SOURCE: Arthur Kornhauser and Paul F. Lazarsfeld, "The Techniques of Market Research from the Standpoint of a Psychologist," *Institute of Management*, No. 16, 1935, American Management Association.

with a force. This force, which may be an advertisement, a comment from a friend, or something else, moves the individual toward the "ready" position. Another way to think of this stage of the decision process is to consider the consumer's readiness-to-buy condition. In some decisions, this condition may be studied over a fairly long period of time (Box 6-10).

The readiness-to-buy condition does not always move slowly toward a positive decision. Frequently it moves back to a negative one and the purchase is not made, whereas at other times it almost explodes into action. This is understandable when we realize that the forces affecting purchase are precipitating forces. Given the right conditions, the consumer can suddenly make up his mind to buy, with the precipitating force acting as a buying trigger. The need to buy does not exist until something happens. Then an accident with the automobile or a burned-out motor on an appliance sets off a buying decision almost instantly. At other times the impetus can be analogous to a slow-burning fuse, as when an appliance gradually wears out. Usually it is possible to look back on a purchase and identify the precipitating factor(s).

BOX 6-10

Range of Consumers' Predisposition to Buy

Buying Continuum	Attitude Scale
I Firm and immediate intent to buy a specific brand.	"I am going to buy some right away." "I am going to buy some soon."
II Positive intention without definite buying plans.	"I am certain I will buy some sometime." "I probably buy some sometime."
III Neutrality: might buy, might not buy.	"I may buy some sometime." "I might buy some sometime, but I doubt it."
IV Inclined not to buy the brand, but not definite about it.	"I don't think I'm interested in buying any." "I probably willl never buy any."
V Firm intention not to buy the brand.	"I know I'm not interested in buying any." "If sombody gave some, I would give it away just to get rid of it."
VI Never considered buying.	"I have never heard of the brand."

SOURCE: William D. Wells, "Measuring Readiness to Buy," *Harvard Business Review*, Vol. 39, No. 4, July–August 1961, p. 82.

BOX 6-11

Attributes Involved in a Mattress Purchase

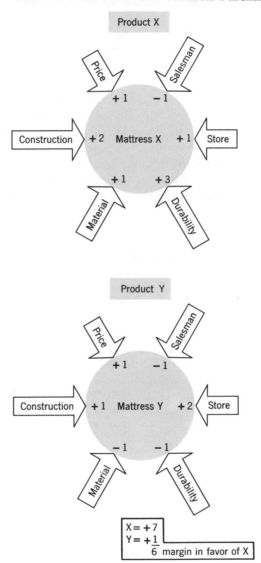

SOURCE: Adapted from Warren J. Bilkey, "A Psychological Approach to Consumer Behavior," *Journal of Marketing*, Vol. 18, No. 1, July 1953, p. 19.

The picture of a buying decision in Addendum 2 is not complete, nor is it typical of all purchases. For a rather deliberate purchase it is an attempt to include the important components of the decision-making process. The time line may be stretched out over years or it may be compressed into minutes, the immediacy of the situation often being all-important.

Each part of the decision process can be quite separate from the other parts, or all of them can merge into one. The difficult part may be the initial and basic decision to buy, or it may be the examination and evaluation of alternatives. One way to perceive this evaluation is to consider the various forces as psychic vectors. Thus, in the mattress illustration (Box 6-11), the consumers find some of the vectors negative and others positive as they choose between alternatives.

Each phase of the buying process has been analyzed by students of marketing. Some visualize the process from the economist's standpoint, others from the psychologist's, while others try to bring several disciplines to bear on the problem. Nicosia recently attempted to quantify the process. Carefully using defined variables (act of buying, consumer's motivation, attitude, advertising, and time), he developed a system of equations that describe various consumer activities and marketing operations.[5]

The decision-making process with all its ramifications cannot easily be pictured. It varies from product to product and person to person. There are interaction, internal and external forces, information, time factors, and the feed-back influence from one action to the next. The decision-making process does not end with the purchase. The purchase becomes vital feedback for the next decision. As a matter of fact, satisfaction with a product may be the most important factor in the next decision-making process. Thus, a decision to buy may be the culmination of one buying experience, but the experience from the product or service purchased becomes feedback for the next decision to buy. As one student of the consumer has concluded, "today's American consumer, although not rational and not fully logical, is conservative and sane. The much maligned, often misunderstood, and unorganized consumer is a stabilizing force in our economy."[6]

Questions

1. Develop fully the purchase of some durable goods which you have made. What factors influenced your decisions as to brand and source of supply? How many

[5]Francesco M. Nicosia, "Toward a Model of Consumer Decision-Making," in William S. Decker (ed.), *Emerging Concepts in Marketing* (Chicago: American Marketing Association, 1963), pp. 422–437.

[6]George Katona, *The Powerful Consumer* (New York; McGraw-Hill Book Company, 1960), p. 242.

decisions were actually made? Over what time span did you consider the purchase?

2. Make a list as best you can of all purchases you have made this year. Can you ascertain any decision-making generalizations from an examination of these purchases?

Statements to Consider

Unfortunately, the low-income groups which need to be the best buyers do the poorest job in making their buying decisions.

Although the husband may determine the scale of living by his income, the housewife probably determines the style of living.

Women tend to be different; men tend to be similar: or is it that men tend to be different; women tend to be similar?

Nonwhite consumers are more brand-conscious and loyal than white consumers.

People enjoy spending money. To learn how to be better spenders would remove much of life's satisfaction.

SELECTED REFERENCES

George Katona, *The Mass Consumption Society* (New York: McGraw-Hill Book Company, 1964).

George Katona, *The Powerful Consumer: Psychological Studies of the American Economy* (New York: McGraw-Hill Book Company, 1960).

James U. McNeal, *Dimensions of Consumer Behavior* (New York: Appleton-Century-Crofts, 1965).

National Industrial Conference Board, *A Graphic Guide to Consumer Markets* (New York: National Industrial Conference Board, 1966).

Joseph W. Newman (ed.), *On Knowing the Consumer* (New York: John Wiley and Sons, 1966).

Marcus Alexis, "The Changing Consumer Market: 1935–1959," *Journal of Marketing,* Vol. 26, No. 1, January 1962, pp. 42–46.

° Robert Ferber, "Our Changing Consumer Market," *Business Horizons,* Vol. 1, No. 2, Spring 1958, pp. 49–66.

° George Katona, "Economic Psychology," *Scientific American,* Vol. 191, No. 4, October 1954, pp. 31–35.

GENERALIZATIONS WERE TAKEN FROM:

Adaptations by students from general statements in a number of published sources.

Addendum 1. Personal Consumption Expenditures by Type of Product 1929 and 1962*

	Millions of Dollars		Percentage of Total	
	1929	1962	1929	1962
I. Food and tobacco	21,230	91,974	26.9	25.9
1. Food purchased for off-premise consumption (n.d.c.)	14,777	63,633	18.7	17.8
2. Purchased meals and beverages (n.d.c.)	2,911	18,236	3.7	5.1
3. Food furnished government (including military) and commercial employees (n.d.c.)	257	1,347	0.3	0.4
4. Food produced and consumed on farms (n.d.c.)	1,590	1,004	2.0	0.3
5. Tobacco products (n.d.c.)	1,695	7,754	2.1	2.2
II. Clothing, accessories, and jewelry	11,193	35,759	14.2	10.7
1. Shoes and other footwear (n.d.c.)	1,675	4,703	2.1	1.3
2. Shoe cleaning and repair (s.)	164	280	0.2	0.1
3. Clothing and accessories except footwear	7,682	24,983	9.7	7.0
4. Standard clothing issued to military personnel (n.d.c.)	12	68	0.02	0.02
5. Cleaning, dyeing, pressing, alteration, storage, and repair of garments including furs (in shops) not elsewhere classified (s.).	473	2,101	0.6	0.6

6. Laundering in establishments (s).	475	898	0.6	0.3
7. Jewelry and watches (d.c.)	560	2,160	0.7	0.6
8. Other (s.)	152	566	0.2	0.2
III. Personal care	1,116	6,213	1.4	1.8
1. Toilet articles and preparations (n.d.c.)	591	3,323	0.8	0.9
2. Barbershops, beauty parlors, and baths (s.)	525	2,890	0.7	0.3
IV. Housing	11,446	46,595	14.5	13.1
1. Owner-occupied nonfarm dwellings— space rental value (s.)	5,868	30,193	7.4	8.5
2. Tenant-occupied nonfarm dwellings (including lodging houses) space rent (s.)	4,500	12,914	5.7	3.6
3. Rental value of farm houses (s.)	829	2,064	1.1	0.6
4. Other (s.)	249	1,424	0.3	0.4
V. Household operation	10,735	49,638	13.6	14.0
1. Furniture (d.c.)	1,201	5,054	1.5	1.4
2. Kitchen and other household appliances (d.c.)	768	4,845	1.0	1.3
3. China, glassware, tableware, and utensils (d.c.)	628	2,316	0.8	0.7
4. Other durable house furnishings (d.c.)	1,148	3,977	1.5	1.1
5. Semidurable house furnishings (n.d.c.)	717	3,352	0.9	0.9
6. Cleaning and polishing preparations and miscellaneous household supplies and paper products (n.d.c.)	485	3,647	0.6	1.0
7. Stationery and writing supplies (n.d.c.)	143	1,199	0.2	0.3

8. Household utilities	3,044	14,047	3.9	4.0
9. Telephone, telegraph, cable, and wireless (s.)	569	4,989	0.7	1.4
10. Domestic service (s.)	1,716	3,838	2.2	1.0
11. Other (s.)	316	2,374	0.4	0.7
VI. Medical and death expenses	3,544	23,704	4.5	6.7
1. Drug preparations and sundries (n.d.c.)	604	4,157	0.8	1.2
2. Ophthalmic products and orthopedic appliances (d.c.)	131	1,372	0.2	0.4
3. Physicians (s.)	959	5,298	1.2	1.5
4. Dentists (s.)	482	2,189	0.6	0.6
5. Other professional services (s.)	250	975	0.3	0.3
6. Privately controlled hospitals and sanitariums (s.)	403	6,203	0.5	1.7
7. Medical care and hospitalization insurance (s.)	108	1,807	0.1	0.5
8. Funeral and burial expenses (s.)	607	1,703	0.8	0.5
VII. Personal business	5,086	22,115	6.4	6.2
1. Brokerage charges and interest, and investment counseling (s.)	1,707	1,077	2.2	0.3
2. Bank service charges, trust services, and safe-deposit box rental (s.)	76	953	0.1	0.3
3. Services furnished without payment by financial intermediaries except insurance companies (s.)	1,278	5,124	1.6	1.4
4. Expense of handling life insurance (s.)	874	4,834	1.1	1.4
5. Legal services (s.)	402	2,082	0.5	0.6

6. Interest on personal debt (s.)	584	6,950	0.7	2.0
7. Other (s.)	165	1,095	0.2	0.3
VIII. Transportation	7,612	44,082	9.6	12.4
1. User-operated transportation	5,960	40,389	7.5	11.4
2. Purchased local transportation	1,117	1,989	1.4	0.6
3. Purchased intercity transportation	535	1,704	0.7	0.5
IX. Recreation	4,331	21,555	5.5	6.0
1. Books and maps (d.c.)	309	1,677	0.4	0.5
2. Magazines, news-papers, and sheet music (n.d.c.)	538	2,645	0.7	0.7
3. Nondurable toys and sport supplies (n.d.c.)	336	2,786	0.4	0.8
4. Wheel goods, durable toys, sport equip-ment, boats, and pleasure aircraft (d.c.)	219	2,386	0.3	0.7
5. Radio and television receivers, records, and musical instru-ments (d.c.)	1,012	4,001	1.3	1.1
6. Radio and television repairs (s.)	26	950	0.03	0.3
7. Flowers, seeds, and potted plants (n.d.c.)	221	1,086	0.3	0.3
8. Admissions to specified spectator amusements	913	2,123	1.2	0.6
9. Clubs and fraternal organizations except insurance (s.)	302	798	0.4	0.2
10. Commercial partici-pant amusements (s.)	207	1,088	0.3	0.3
11. Pari-mutuel net receipts (s.)	8	588	0.01	0.2
12. Other (s.)	240	1,427	0.3	0.4

X. Private education and research	664	5,208	0.8	1.5
1. Higher education (s.)	219	2,461	0.3	0.7
2. Elementary and secondary schools (s.)	162	1,832	0.2	0.5
3. Other (s.)	283	915	0.3	0.3
XI. Religious and welfare activities (s.)	1,196	5,140	1.5	1.5
XII. Foreign travel and remittances-net	799	3,377	1.0	0.9
1. Foreign travel by United States residents (s.)	632	2,555	0.8	0.8
2. Expenditures abroad by United States Government personnel (military and civilian) (n.d.c.)	21	1,483	0.03	0.4
3. Personal cash remittances to foreign countries less personal cash remittances to the United States by foreigners (s.)	288	309	0.4	0.09
4. Less: expenditures in the United States by foreigners (s.)	142	970	0.2	0.3
Total personal consumption expenditures	78,952	355,360		
Durable commodities (d.c.)	9,212	48,236	11.7	13.6
Nondurable commodities (n.d.c.)	37,677	161,406	47.7	45.4
Services (s.)	32,063	145,718	40.6	41.0

Consumer durable commodities are designated (d.c.), nondurable commodities (n.d.c.) and services (s.) following group titles.

SOURCE: United States Department of Commerce.

ADDENDUM 2. *A Diagram of Consumer Decision Making*

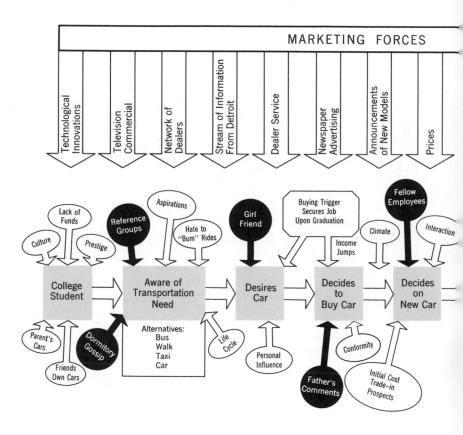

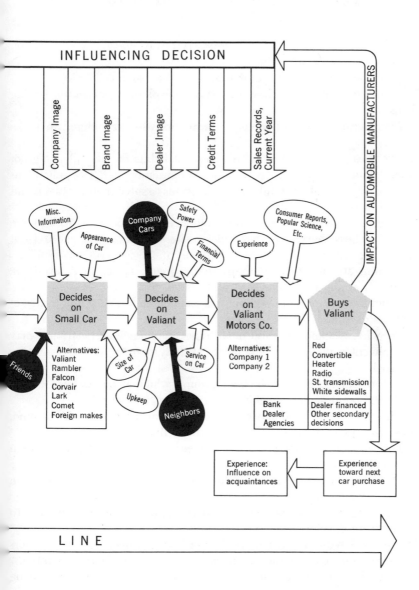

ADDENDUM 3.
Consumer Behavior Propositions

1. Advertisements for expensive items typically carry less information than those for low-priced products.
2. What our friends own we own also, or shall soon own.
3. As the size of the purchase increases, the planning period of buying lengthens.
4. Even with an affluent society, consumers still are obliged to make choices.
5. The idea that marketers simply implant habits or take advantage of consumer impulses in passive and befuddled consumers is not as reliable as the idea that buyers make careful buying decisions to solve their problems and to gain satisfaction.
6. Reference groups are powerful influences. Members are well aware what the members think and what the members would say if one did not conform to the norms.
7. Custom and habit are perhaps the strongest forces in determining specific wants at any particular time and place.
8. A fashion cannot be forced upon consumers unless they find it attractive and desire to adopt it.
9. Purchasing a known brand or a brand recommended by friends may be as intelligent a method of buying as carefully investigating the alternatives yourself.
10. Unfortunately, the low-income groups which need to be the best buyers do the poorest job in making their buying decisions.
11. Although the husband may determine the scale of living by his income, the housewife probably determines the style of living.
12. Fortunately, consumers desire and expect only slightly more than they presently have.
13. Most consumer buying is habitual buying: real problem solving is a rarity.
14. The longer a trend has been in existence, the more likely we are to see a new trend develop.
15. We have witnessed a change in marketing influence. The retailers have become more passive and our friends have become more influential.
16. A leveling process continues and in time consumers will be buying more and more like all others.
17. Consumers' attitudes toward products vary because of the lack of uniform information reaching them.

18. Market saturation may occur but it need not last very long. Consumers can simply change their desires for products and buy a second or a third or a fourth of the item which was once thought to have reached market saturation.

19. Cash customers are less quality-conscious than credit customers.

20. The husband makes the primary decision to buy the product and then the wife makes all the sequential decisions concerned with product details.

21. Most attitudes are formed early in life. Adult experience simply reinforces them.

22. Women tend to be different; men tend to be similar: or is it that men tend to be different; women tend to be similar?

23. Nonwhite consumers are more brand-conscious and loyal than white consumers.

24. The more effort one has to exert to attain something, the more value one places on that object. Higher prices *per se*, therefore, increase satisfaction.

25. People enjoy spending money. To learn how to be better spenders would remove much of life's satisfaction.

26. New products are almost always preferred to the old.

27. As we increase our ability to differentiate quality, our brand loyalty decreases.

28. Consumers pretend not to be influenced by remarks made by sellers because one does not like to let others know that one is easily persuaded.

29. Conformity is more important in advanced societies than in less developed societies.

30. Buying becomes more and more irrational as one proceeds from the subsistence scale of living to that of ample discretionary income.

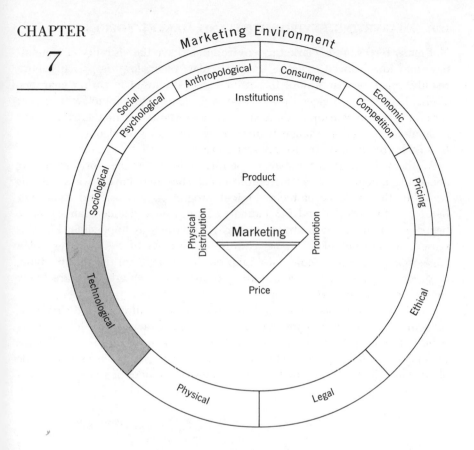

The Visible and Dynamic Force of Technology

A CLOSER LOOK AT TECHNOLOGY   *Primitive Societies   Advanced Societies   Management Goals* •   MARKETING THE TECHNOLOGY   *Goals* •   THE ROLE OF RESEARCH   •   THE LONG VIEW

Not many forces in the marketing environment have the visibility of technology, and in advanced societies, in particular, technology is perhaps more readily apparent than any of the other forces discussed in earlier chapters. Technology tends to electrify all those who come into contact with it; yet for all those who worship it, there are others to whom it is anathema. Because technology brings on change which many consider unwelcome, there are those who resent it or try to ignore its existence.

Without doubt great numbers of people believe that the world is forging ahead technologically at an incredible pace. They may have always felt this way, but the evidence of technological progress is now clearer than ever before, as Figures 7-1 and 7-2 indicate. Things once deemed fantasy have become so real that it is absurd to regard anything as impossible. For this reason, we are not likely to be astonished by news of the discovery of a cancer cure, or of the landing of a man on the moon, or of the routine flying of supersonic aircraft between municipal airports. Such advances are likely to be commonplace before long.

Marketers must take note of the tremendous outburst of technology, recognizing its enormous impact on the contemporary world, for a strong bond links the two. Indeed, in many instances marketers themselves influence technological development. The chemical industry has given us man-made fibers which have affected methods of production, modes of styling, advertis-

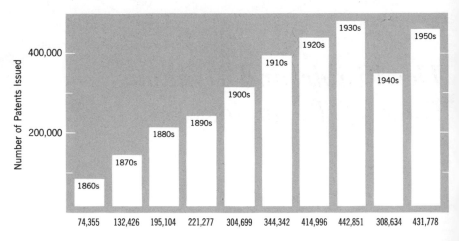

Figure 7-1. Number of patents issued by U. S. Government (shown as decade totals from 1860 to 1960).

SOURCE: United States Department of Commerce, Bureau of the Census, *Statistical Abstract of the United States, Colonial Times to 1957* (Washington D.C.: United States Department of Commerce, 1960), pp. 607–608, and *Statistical Abstract of the United States,* (Washington, D.C.: United States Department of Commerce, 1963), p. 548.

Figure 7-2. United States patents issued (inventions), 1790–1964

1790	3	1830	544	1870	12,137	1910	35,141	1950	43,040
1791	33	1831	573	1871	11,659	1911	32,856	1951	44,326
1792	11	1832	474	1872	12,180	1912	36,198	1952	43,616
1793	20	1833	586	1873	11,616	1913	33,917	1953	40,468
1794	22	1834	630	1874	12,230	1914	39,892	1954	33,809
1795	12	1835	752	1875	13,291	1915	43,118	1955	30,432
1796	44	1836	702	1876	14,169	1916	43,892	1956	46,817
1797	51	1837	426	1877	12,920	1917	40,935	1957	42,744
1798	28	1838	514	1878	12,345	1918	38,452	1958	48,330
1799	44	1839	404	1879	12,125	1919	36,797	1959	52,408
1800	41	1840	458	1880	12,903	1920	37,060	1960	47,170
1801	44	1841	490	1881	15,500	1921	37,798	1961	48,368
1802	65	1842	488	1882	18,091	1922	38,369	1962	55,691
1803	97	1843	493	1883	21,162	1923	38,616	1963	45,679
1804	84	1844	478	1884	19,118	1924	42,574	1964	47,376
1805	57	1845	473	1885	23,285	1925	46,432		
1806	63	1846	566	1886	21,767	1926	44,733		
1807	99	1847	495	1887	20,403	1927	41,717		
1808	158	1848	583	1888	19,551	1928	42,357		
1809	203	1849	984	1889	23,324	1929	45,267		
1810	223	1850	883	1890	25,313	1930	45,226		
1811	215	1851	752	1891	22,312	1931	51,756		
1812	238	1852	885	1892	22,647	1932	53,458		
1813	181	1853	844	1893	22,750	1933	48,774		
1814	210	1854	1,755	1894	19,855	1934	44,420		
1815	173	1855	1,881	1895	20,856	1935	40,618		
1816	206	1856	2,302	1896	21,822	1936	39,782		
1817	174	1857	2,674	1897	22,067	1937	37,683		
1818	222	1858	3,455	1898	20,377	1938	38,061		
1819	156	1859	4,160	1899	23,278	1939	43,073		
1820	155	1860	4,357	1900	24,644	1940	42,238		
1821	168	1861	3,020	1901	25,546	1941	41,109		
1822	200	1862	3,214	1902	27,119	1942	38,449		
1823	173	1863	3,773	1903	31,029	1943	31,054		
1824	228	1864	4,630	1904	30,258	1944	28,053		
1825	304	1865	6,088	1905	29,775	1945	25,695		
1826	323	1866	8,863	1906	31,170	1946	21,803		
1827	331	1867	12,277	1907	35,859	1947	20,139		
1828	368	1868	12,526	1908	32,735	1948	23,963		
1829	447	1869	12,931	1909	36,561	1949	35,131		

SOURCE: United States Department of Commerce, Bureau of the Census, *Statistical Abstract of the United States, 1965* (Washington, D.C.: United States Department of Commerce, 1965), pp. 552–608.

121

ing programs, and habits of consumption; in return consumers have indicated their likes and dislikes through their patterns of purchasing. These preferences of the consumer may be translated into instructions which guide the technical experts in their pursuit of further advances among the synthetics.

In a broad sense technological progress includes innovation and adaptation in many fields. Breakthroughs are not restricted to chemistry or medicine; no walk of life—communication, transportation, recreational facilities, or others —is immune. Even the academic disciplines have undergone a technological change of their own; new theories and research techniques have replaced old concepts with altered ones, and new instruments like the computer have been applied to a host of problems. Of course, not every technological advance attains ready acceptance. Frequently the potential user of a new device or new approach is reluctant to abandon his familiar technique, although, ironically, conformity can eventually initiate a bandwagon response to some innovation, despite any initial barrier to change. Acceptance of new technology is often blocked, in addition, by the many varieties of bureaucracy in government, industry, and education.

Nevertheless, technology and change are ever present in advanced societies. Research efforts reach out to distances never before approached as technological progress is nurtured, directed, and systematically and creatively developed. All this has had a profound effect on countries which have seen the fruits of technology. Certainly man lives in a most different world today from that of yesterday, even in the most literal sense.

A CLOSER LOOK AT TECHNOLOGY

We need not go back to the invention of the wheel to visualize the impact of technology. Consider the changes that have taken place in *transportation;* even individuals directly connected with the railroads, automobiles and trucks, ships, and aircraft have lacked adequate perspective of their own industries. Among household *appliances,* technology has had far-reaching effects; the "liberation" of the housewife, the changes in a family's consumption expenditures, and the creation of additional leisure time are only a few of the visible effects. Today's *food* is far different from the food of a few years ago; advances in chemistry, mechanics, breeding, and feeding have all played important roles in these changes, and along with food changes have come packaging developments. Consumers have enthusiastically accepted many of the new products and thus technological developments continue to flow in abundance from our production lines.

These technological changes wield great influence over the socio-economic system in which they occur. They can cause cities to grow up almost overnight or to diminish in importance. They even affect jobs; for example, the disappearance of an elevator operator from the scene is but a symbol of the problem of automation which confronts every modern nation. As jobs are affected so are income and the purchasing power it generates and, in turn, the standard of living which purchasing power determines. We tend to think of tomorrow in terms of *more*—more food, more clothing, more variety, more comfort, more convenience, more education, more pleasure. Aspirations change in the wake of attainment, and consumption expenditures follow.

Through scores of technological changes many economies have prospered. No western nation expects a GNP growth of less than three percent a year and, within each, individual companies have learned that research and development expenditures pay off; thus businesses hew to the path of technology. Yet technology has a disruptive aspect. It upsets work habits, modifies life expectancies, and creates new mobility patterns, greater leisure, and numerous new social norms. Sometimes it provokes serious upheavals to which few facets of life are immune, but man, resilient as he is, has adapted himself to these changes, as the following observation suggests.

Man is on the move, from the East to the West, from the South to the North, from town and country to the city, from the inner city to the suburbs, and from one suburb to another. . . . Man is also socially mobile in our technological world. . . . Families move across the country in search of new opportunities and new income. . . . Man is mechanized in a technological society. . . . The great god production is surrounded in the pantheon by the lesser deities of efficiency, competence, science, technical education, consumption, and advertising.[1]

In the United States many people accept change as a way of life. It is common to heap economic reward on the innovator and to rely on technology to help offset uncertainty (see Box 7-1). It is equally common in an environment that is favorable to innovation for a vigorous citizenry, growing in number, to attempt to reduce the work week and expand leisure time. Indeed, when stressing economic growth, political leaders include technological advances as integral parts of their programs.

The climate for technological change is excellent in many parts of the world and in the United States it has been favorable since colonial times. Looking to the future, we have emphasized the individual in our society and rewarded those who have made a practical contribution to the people.[2] This hospitable atmosphere has brought problems as well as progress. The impact on consumers is evident; the resulting impact on marketing should also be recognized.

---

[1] Alvin Pitcher, "The Importance of Being Human," *Harvard Business Review*, Vol. 39, 1961, p. 42.
[2] See Samuel A. Stouffer, "Sociological Factors Favoring Innovations," in Lincoln H. Clark, (ed.), *Consumer Behavior* (New York: Harper & Brothers, p. 52.

BOX 7-1

Pertinent Questions about Our Technological Progress

Is the independent inventor disappearing from the scene?

"The decline of the independent and the corresponding rise of the hired inventor probably reflect the same forces—the increased complexity of technology, the resulting rise in the scale of enterprise, and the growth of scientific and engineering knowledge." (p. 143)

Are patents all used commercially?

40 to 50 percent are used commercially (thought not necessarily profitably). "Thus, at a minimum, each year between 6,000 and 8,000 new products or processes created by independents are put to use." (p. 145)

What has created the environment for research and development in the United States?

Considerations of national survival in warfare, profits for business, our democratic ethos which made low-cost education available, strong interest in material things, and a consuming public sensitive to lower prices and new products. (p. 150)

Can Research be a social waste? Yes.

1. Making products worse (built-in deterioration)
2. Discovering what is already known
"The surest social defense is a competitive economy." (p. 155)

Is the patent system breaking down?

"The patent system, moreover, gives signs of breaking down. Firms expanded their RD activities greatly over the past two decades, but their patenting increased hardly at all. More and more, firms seem to patent only what they have little hope of keeping secret. Thus the objective of disclosure is poorly served. Their research is guided less by the possibility of patents than by the pressures of competition." (p. 157)

Do you agree with the above comments?

SOURCE: Jacob Schmookler, "Technological Progress and the Modern American Corporation," in Edward S. Mason (ed.), *The Corporation in Modern Society*, (Cambridge: Harvard University Press, 1959).

Primitive Societies

Marketing without technology reflects a primitive society. Here marketing plays a very minor role because there is lack of specialization of labor, there may be communal property, there is little separation of producer and consumer, and there is probably little contact with the outside trading world.

The Igorot country in the northern Philippines may illustrate such a society. Living in one of the most beautiful but most isolated spots in the world, the people of this region carry on their lives much as their ancestors did several thousand years ago. The rice terraces are communal, there is no industry, and the raising of sufficient quantities of rice and sweet potatoes to eat is the main productive effort. The people make their own clothing, repair their ancient huts, raise a few chickens and pigs, and make little effort to penetrate the outside world. It is a paradise for the anthropologist but not for the student of marketing. Any signs of contact with technology would seem wholly out of place. As a matter of fact, a steel corrugated building which was erected a few years ago stands out as a sore intrusion.

There is little marketing in the villages. Bare subsistence living is the rule, association with the outside is minimal, and little if any money changes hands. There is no marketing development work, no salesmen, no advertising; there are no supermarkets. Contact with technology would undoubtedly result in upheavals of various kinds. The introduction of fertilizer, farm implements, waterpower, and other technology could transform the way of life and alter all local attitudes and beliefs on religion, education, production, trading, and standards of living. Quite likely, marketing without technology probably means that marketing will at most be simple, if it exists at all. It is interesting to note that not many miles away from this isolated area are the modern cities of the Philippines which show the marks of technological progress and the visible signs of a marketing economy.

Advanced Societies

In more advanced societies, businessmen have learned that innovation pays handsome profits and that failure to keep pace can cause the downfall of a firm or even an industry (see Box 7-2). Industry and household consumers are fully aware of the impact of technology upon almost everything they do or see. Some technological developments force radical reorientations on the part of the consumer. Well-trained personnel can find themselves outmoded, capital investment can become obsolete, and industries and executives may have to sprint to keep up with the times. More often the changes are evolutionary, but their impact is recognizable. The simple box camera, for example, has gone through hundreds of changes so that a very elaborate mechanism is now available to the consumer, and the film used in the camera has gone through similar change. Although these changes have developed slowly, the current product sharply contrasts with the early model. Because the new products induced by technology make old ones obsolete, they require marketing personnel to develop new markets, persuade people to buy the improved item, and feed market information back to the producer.

The change is not always substantial—perhaps only a slight improvement in a wrapper or a new design for a package. Unfortunately changes are

BOX 7-2

Impact of new products in 1963 *

The hopes manufacturers have for new products are illustrated by this chart. Bars indicate percentages of sales that will be accounted for in 1963 by products that didn't exist four years ago, according to manufacturer estimates

New products: percent of sales

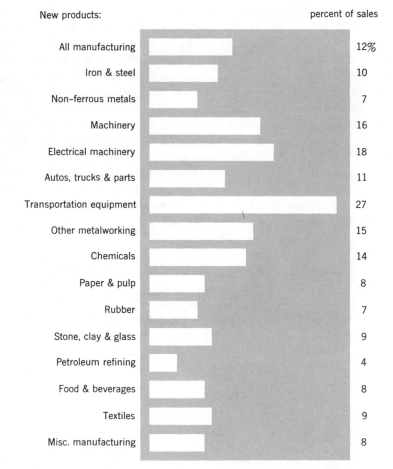

New products:	percent of sales
All manufacturing	12%
Iron & steel	10
Non-ferrous metals	7
Machinery	16
Electrical machinery	18
Autos, trucks & parts	11
Transportation equipment	27
Other metalworking	15
Chemicals	14
Paper & pulp	8
Rubber	7
Stone, clay & glass	9
Petroleum refining	4
Food & beverages	8
Textiles	9
Misc. manufacturing	8

SOURCE: *Printers' Ink*, February 1, 1963.

* New products are defined as products "not produced in 1959 or products sufficiently changed as to be reasonably considered as new products."

sometimes not even that substantial or worthwhile, and in these situations marketing is placed in an awkward position.

Changes in consumption caused by technology are interesting to follow. Many years ago radio was introduced to the household, and as hundreds of improvements were made and hundreds of styles added, multiple ownership of radio became common. Small radios, clock radios, car radios, console models, and others found wide acceptance. Later, when television invaded the home the same kind of pattern unfolded, the development of color television alone adding a new dimension to thousands of households. The impacts of radio and television belie description; in marketing they are evident in advertising, retailing, institutions, and living habits, with millions of people directly affected, and many more indirectly, as is shown by data on set ownership in Figure 7-3.

Technology has changed business operations more than the products we consume, affecting many of the ways in which marketing jobs are accomplished. Refrigerated trucks and rail cars, jet transports, money-changing machines, vending machines, and electronic data processing have made an

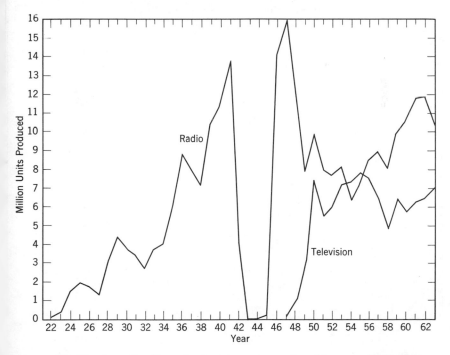

Figure 7-3. Number of radio and television sets produced by year 1926–1963.
SOURCE: *Electrical Merchandising Weekly.*

enormous impact; and banks, retailers, wholesalers, and producers have utilized new electronic equipment to revolutionize many of marketing's functions. Computers, new building concepts, material handling equipment, and
other developments have induced drastic changes in warehousing, and advertising and mail-order catalogs have changed in style and appearance as a
result of new printing processes.

Management

The impact of technology on marketing does not stop with improvement
of products and changes in operations, but goes farther into the managerial
aspects of marketing. Part III of this book deals in detail with these aspects.
At this point, it is only necessary to suggest how technology influences
decision making in marketing.

BOX 7-3

Comparison of Penicillin Production with Wholesale Price of 100,000—Unit Vial

Year	Production (b.i.u.)	Price per 100,000—Unit Vial
1943	1,000	$20.00
1944	1,600	1.20
1945	8,000	0.52
1946	27,000	0.38
1947	42,000	0.28
1948	92,947	0.20
1949	138,103	0.12
1950	219,903	0.12
1951	318,622	0.11
1952	342,326	0.10
1953	371,589	0.08
1954	476,658	0.07
1955	344,243	0.07
1956	478,259	0.05
1957	525,738	0.05
1958	391,574	0.05
1959	429,781	0.05

SOURCE: *Administered Prices in the Drug Industry (Antibiotics)*, Part 24, Washington,
D.C.: U.S. Government Printing Office, pp. 13840–13841.

The pricing of a product can be materially influenced by competition or by an existing or potential substitute product. Having to price a new product, a manufacturer of drugs has to consider not only present competition for the item but also possible new competition from drugs not yet on the market. Box 7-3 shows the effect of a substitute product on pricing.

The selling of electronic equipment requires more than a knowledge of selling techniques. It demands some knowledge both of equipment and of developments in application. To meet these needs, combined business and engineering training aids students to prepare for marketing careers in fields that require both business and engineering skills.

Managing the product line has become a major preoccupation of business. Product managers and committees for coordination of technical and marketing operations are essential for the firm and have grown rather common. Making the right product-line decision necessitates analysis of many factors, for technology has greatly complicated the product decision, which is a major area of marketing.

Historically, marketing institutions have adapted themselves to all kinds of change. This flexibility has been vital for them, because once they no longer serve a purpose they perish. If we examine the kinds of retailers in operation year by year, we see the impact of technological progress on retailing. Indeed, technology has played an important role in changing the character of both retailing and wholesaling through new products, developments in communications and transportation, and by such devices as the computer and material-handling equipment. Electrical supply houses, radio and television outlets and repair facilities, liquefied petroleum dealers, air conditioning dealers, electronic-parts suppliers, scientific equipment distributors, and merchandise vending-machine operators are illustrative of the way in which retailing and wholesaling adjust to technological change by specializing in newer areas.

A surprising proportion of a marketing manager's time is spent directly or indirectly with technology. Whether it involves reduction of costs, speedier handling of merchandise, determination of optimum inventory levels, or decisions on profitable product lines, the manager finds that technology plays an important role. At the same time, technology is influenced by other factors, including marketing.

MARKETING THE TECHNOLOGY

Much has been written in recent years about a new "marketing concept," the recognition of the consumer by the company. This new approach affords the consumer a dominant role in directing a firm's operations. The consumer view is deemed paramount, and research and development are geared to his wants with products fashioned, priced, and distributed according to them.

Thus technology becomes an obedient servant of the consumer, yet the relationship is neither that one-sided nor that simple. Although marketing certainly can and does influence technology, it is doubtful that the consumer would know in advance his acceptability of all products. Would complete consumer dominance have brought about development of the airplane, automatic transmissions, mail-order distribution, ball-point pens, or all the electric devices on an automobile as shown in Box 7-4? On the other hand, public demand for a polio vaccine generated public and private support of research which eventually developed the needed product. This is a good example of the interaction between the consumer and technician.

Companies frequently gamble on technology alone and ignore the marketing phase. The futility of this narrow view can be found in the failure record of business firms and new products. Few if any successful businessmen today would accept the "better-mousetrap" theory as their firm's philosophy and expect customers to seek out their superior product. Occasionally this happens, as in 1963 when an English firm introduced the new stainless steel razor blade. Fantastic prices were paid and unbelievable effort was expended to secure the new blades (Box 7-5), but it was only a matter of months before leading United States firms had mastered the technology necessary to produce their own stainless steel blades. The English firm had never attempted to dominate the United States market, probably because of the marketing task and the competition which it knew would be inevitable.

Prior to the Second World War, the Aluminum Company of America developed a superior sleeve bearing for diesel engines. Every test proved its superiority, yet the product failed to sell in satisfactory quantity. Aggressive marketing measures were necessary to gain market acceptance and this required salesmen and advertising; technology alone could not do the job.[3] The same company had a similar problem with aluminum windows. Lack of marketing effort from 1929 to 1945 played an important role in holding down consumer acceptance of the new type of window. After the Second World War, several small window manufacturers undertook production of the windows *and* the marketing task. Considerable consumer acceptance was immediately evident.[4] (Alcoa preferred in both cases to remain the producer of primary products.)

Millions of dollars are spent annually on research and development of new products and millions more on governmental research, some of which ultimately becomes useful to industry. The outpouring of these new products requires market development and distribution. If the technology is left at

---

[3] E. Raymond Corey, *Industrial Marketing* (Englewood Cliffs, N.J., Prentice-Hall, 1962), pp. 237–247.
[4] E. Raymond Corey, *The Development of Markets for New Materials* (Cambridge: Harvard University Press, 1956), pp. 36–38.

the production line it is worth little; to have value it must be converted into marketable products which must stimulate a demand among the appropriate consumers.

Industrial, governmental, institutional, and household consumers all have needs which can be satisfied by their particular resources. They make their wants known through the marketing process, encouraging some producers and discouraging others. The discouraged producers ascertain the reasons for consumer refusals to buy, and if the problem is one of product, they request technicians to remedy the situation. Marketing channels and marketing men then attempt to develop the market which has shown resistance. The "votes" cast by the buyers indeed influence technical decisions and can also influence the direction of research efforts for future products. When companies undertake market surveys to ascertain consumer wants, they are clearly asking for consumer guidance.

Retailing and wholesaling institutions play a role in feeding back information through marketing channels to the appropriate firms. The goal of all of them is the same: profit. Profit comes from sales and sales come from consumer acceptance of the products offered. In this connection marketing institutions play another role. Sales representatives educate or persuade many customers to buy a given new product, but a manufacturer cannot reach every consumer and so he relies on the marketing institutions for his development work. The manufacturer's agent, the drug contact man, and the retail clerk develop markets every day; more than the link between manufacturer and customer, they are the developers of the markets.

Suppose a firm develops a new portable typewriter. It cannot personally call on every college student. In order to develop the market, the firm will rely to some degree on advertising and it will rely on wholesalers to call on bookstores and other retailers who handle typewriters. Retail salesmen will distribute descriptive literature and demonstrate the new product to anyone who shows interest. If the technological and marketing efforts have been correctly performed, the firm experiences a successful product and the market becomes well penetrated.

"Missionary" salesman are frequently employed by companies to educate wholesalers, retailers, and industrial customers. Perhaps the assignment is to sell a new house paint, an electric drill, or a new air-conditioning unit. Regardless, the task is the same; it requires market development which is possible only through correct use of the available marketing institutions. In consequence, the importance of good information feedback from consumer to manufacturer becomes clearer. With accurately received information from the consumer, a firm may be able to produce a new product which requires relatively little marketing effort to sell in satisfactory quantities.

Much criticism is directed toward marketers because the emphasis is often

BOX 7-4

Technological Changes as Shown by Wiring Diagram of Chevrolet Automobile

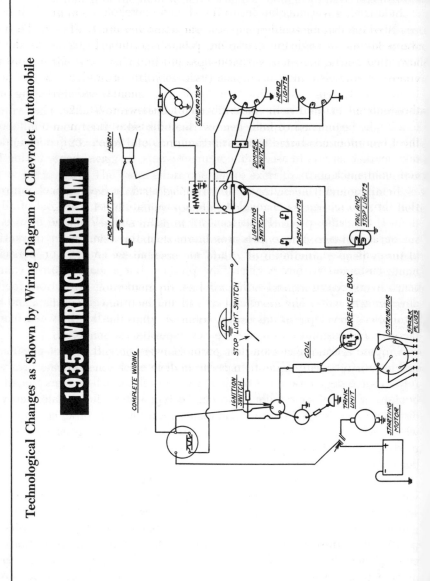

1935 WIRING DIAGRAM

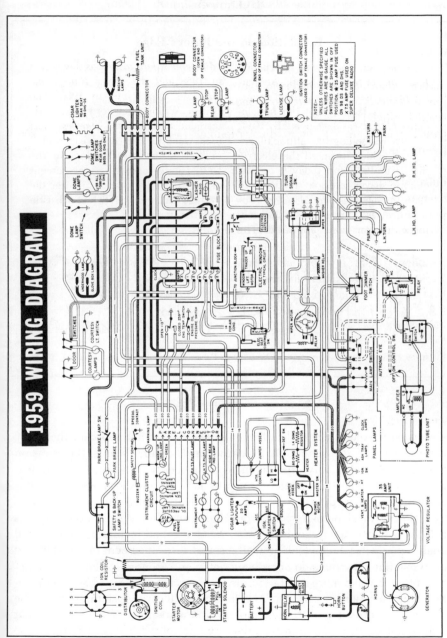

Reprinted by permission, General Motors Corporation.

133

BOX 7-5

Revolution on the Razor's Edge

Stone Age man used sharpened *flintstone* or a clam shell. Ancient Egyptians used *bronze straight razors*. 3000 years later (1890) the *hollow-ground blade* was developed! By 1917, Gillette was selling 120 million blades a year. Schick invented the electric shaver in 1923 and today 6 million electric shavers are sold annually. In 1938 the *one-piece double-edge razor* was invented and in 1941 the one-piece injector razor appeared. The *adjustable safety razor* was developed in 1958 and the *Super Blue Blade* made its appearance in 1960. The British Wilkinson Sword Co., Ltd., introduced the *coated stainless steel blade* and in the next year sold 7 million of the new product in the United States (one-fifth of one percent of the total U.S. market). Note: the average male grows 27½ feet of bristle in a lifetime.

SOURCE: Reprinted by permission *New York Times Magazine*, October 6, 1963, p. 58.

placed on frivolous and useless features. The fins on automobiles, the fancy details on washing machines, the narrow lapels on men's suits, the stress on fashion instead of quality, the "planned obsolescence," and other visible features probably merit the criticism of rational men. Furthermore, the tactics frequently employed to sell the many products turned out by companies become the focal point for additional criticism. Our system does have its deficiencies. Perhaps it would be wiser to channel all technology into useful quality products which would permit a sounder advancement of our standard of living. But consumers do not always act in an "economic" sense and sometimes they receive more satisfaction from a purchase decision based on emotion than on rational reasoning. And in a free-enterprise system, who is to be in charge of directing all the technology and marketing? Who is to say that a firm should not profit from manufacturing frivolity? It is largely up to the consumers.

Goals

Drucker has listed the innovation goals for a typical business.

1. New products or services that are needed to attain marketing objectives.
2. New products or services that will be needed because of technological changes that may make present products obsolete.
3. Product improvements needed both to attain market objectives and to anticipate expected technological changes.
4. New processes and improvements in old processes needed to satisfy market goals—for instance, manufacturing improvements to make possible the attainment of pricing objectives.
5. Innovations and improvements in all major areas of activity—in accounting or design, office management or labor relations—so as to keep up with the advances in knowledge and skill.[5]

It should be recognized that the marketing-technology relationship is generally satisfactory. It has accounted for unprecedented streams of desirable goods and has been responsible for standards of living that are clearly higher than ever before. Competition forces firms to push technology and marketing to the limits of their capacities. Both are needed for success. To be sure, there are examples of marketing and technology teaming up to develop and distribute worthless and even harmful goods, but there are many more examples of teamwork which has resulted in the development and marketing of desirable and beneficial products.

In the marketplace, technology is converted into profit. As Sumner Slichter stated, "Many of the most important technological advances are made in order to sell more goods—by the suppliers of the industry that experiences the gain in productivity."[6] Selling technological advances is the task of marketing.

THE ROLE OF RESEARCH

Research in industry is of several kinds, but notably it includes varieties of technical and marketing investigation. Millions of dollars are spent annually by firms on what may be called basic and applied research, and important contributions to society have resulted from both kinds of endeavors. Typically, as consumers, we are unaware of basic research and are not really much interested until the work has become "commercially feasible."

---

[5] Peter F. Drucker, The Practice of Management (New York: Harper & Brothers, 1954), p. 69.
[6] Sumner H. Slichter, "Technological Research as Related to the Growth and Stability of the Economy," Proceedings of a conference on research and development (Washington, D.C.: National Science Foundation, 1958), p. 116.

One may think of creative versus systematic research efforts or of the "flash" idea as opposed to the "plodding" variety of research. Both are profitable and both contribute a great deal.

An illustration may suffice to clarify some of this terminology. A number of years ago a young man developed a distaste for copying abstracts from periodicals. As a graduate student he had to write out many such abstracts and he thought of an idea (creative) which he figured had possibilities. His idea was based on a heat-transfer process similar to that which takes place when the sun shines on leaves which are on top of the snow. Later, as a company employee, he engaged in basic research work, systematically testing out various approaches to the copying problem. Following the basic stages, research was performed in the application stage and specific schemes for machines were tested. Ultimately the inventor was able to provide the company with one of the first successful copying machines, which eventually induced the company to establish a separate division to handle new office products.

The story does not stop there. Profit to a firm can come only from marketing its equipment. Salesmen, advertising, displays, and demonstrations must be used to develop the market for the new equipment. The question of marketing research enters the picture at a number of points. Marketing research would obviously be useful to the firm before it allocated any manpower resources to the technical research. If no market exists, no resources need be allocated. Frequently this information is not obtained from the market until the later stages of development, thus avoiding the release of information to the competition.

At some point, management needs an estimate of the size of the market in order to make an intelligent decision concerning resource allocations. Actually, technology is carried to the market under ideal conditions when the producer has studied the market to such an extent that he knows what buying motives to use in the advertising, what channels to use in the distribution, what price to charge, and what kind of a package to employ. Seldom does a producer have all the marketing answers, but as a rule he should certainly try to obtain them before committing himself to the new technology.

The research work performed by scientists and marketing investigators needs to be coordinated. Each group must in some way dovetail its activities with those of the other group. The many tasks involved in this coordination are summarized in Table 7-1.

THE LONG VIEW

Thus far we have presented the case for technology's influence on marketing and marketing's reciprocal influence on technology. The notion of an idea-

Table 7-1. Coordinating Technical and Marketing Research

Phase	Technical	Marketing
Ideas	Experimentation	Interpretation of sales, advertising and related marketing data
	Technical solution of existing problems	Outside sources
Investigation exploration	Technical possibilities	Thorough preliminary commercial evaluation
	Scientific problems	
	Technically practical	
Research and development	Product characteristic and design	Market potential
		Market requirements
	Performance	Share market goals
	Costs	Competition
Testing	Process development	Pilot marketing:
	Control methods	Panel tests
	Ingredient specifica- tions	Consumer tests
		Market tests
		Appraisal of sales potentials and market- ing plans
Initial sales and manufactur- ing	Aid to production in manufacturing	Thorough review with sales and advertising of:
	Product specifications for procurement	product potentials consumer reaction

SOURCE: B. F. Bowman, "Coordinating Technical and Marketing Research," *Cost and Profit Outlook*, Vol. 7, July 1954, pp. 2–3.

development and reward cycle has been suggested and it has been demonstrated that the impetus for technology can come at any point. Ideas originate from many sources.

The system is not perfect; failures occur frequently. Some failures are technical in nature, whereas others are the fault of poor marketing. For example, inadequate market estimates, whether they are too low or too high, create costly mistakes. Some products add little to society while others contribute substantially toward the improvement of our way of living. The system relies on financial reward, which is simply another way of saying that it relies on successful market development at a profit.

Besides technology and marketing, other aspects of a company's operations can be essential to success. Neither financing, production, nor other functions can be ignored and they, too, must be coordinated. In a free society, business firms employ different mixes of the functional skills required to operate an enterprise, which is as it should be. Undoubtedly each reader can identify firms that are research-oriented, marketing-oriented, finance-oriented, or production-oriented and point to successful ones in each category.

The product finally introduced to the market is a blend of many factors and a result of different business skills. These factors vary in their mixes and blends, which are partly summarized by the two-dimensional matrix in Box 7-6.

In the advanced societies, it is impossible not to be aware of the influence of technology. It surrounds us every day, as an important factor to be considered by anyone in business, and especially those in marketing. Taking its place alongside consumer behavior and the legal, ethical, and economic considerations, technology merges with these other forces to exert influence on marketing.

Marketing in turn exerts an influence on technology. Standards of living are improved, daily behavior is changed, and consumer goals are adjusted as technology is brought to the industrial, institutional, governmental, and ultimate consumer. Incentive is considerable, for the technology that best satisfies wants and needs will bring the highest monetary rewards to the firm. The results of our system of relating technology and marketing are visible to all. The question of our satisfaction with these results is an individual matter on which each passes his own judgment.

. . . Marketing is uniquely on the firing line where the impact of change is greatest for the business firm. Marketing is where the customer is, and it is the customer who in the end decides the fate of a business.[7]

The position of selling in relation to innovation and advancing technology can be briefly summarized:

(1) The extent of that application of existing machines and processes . . . will depend upon the extent of the potential demand and the degree to which that potential demand can be converted into actual buying actions. . . .

(2) . . . industrial scientific research must be paid for and is limited by sales income, actual and expected.

(3) New products can be developed and produced in low-cost, large-scale

[7] Theodore Levitt, *Innovation in Marketing* (New York: McGraw-Hill Book Company, 1962), p. 13.

BOX 7-6

Classification of New Products by Product Objective

|←——— Increasing technological newness ———→|

Product Objectives	No Technological Change	Improved Technology To utilize more fully the company's present scientific knowledge and production skills.	New Technology To acquire scientific knowledge and production skills new to the company.
No Market Change		*Reformulation* To maintain an optimum balance of cost quality, and availability in the formulas of present company products.	*Replacement* To seek new and better ingredients or formulation for present company products in technology not now employed by the company.
Strengthened Market To exploit more fully the existing markets for the present company products.	*Remerchandising* To increase sales to consumers of types now served by the company.	*Improved Product* To improve present products for greater utility and merchandisability to consumers.	*Product Line Extension* To broaden the line of products offered to present consumers through new technology.
New Market To increase the number types of consumers served by the company.	*New Use* To find new classes of consumers that can utilize present company products.	*Market Extension* To reach new classes of consumers by modifying present products.	*Diversification* To add to the classes of consumers served by development new technical knowledge.

Increasing market newness (vertical axis, left side)

SOURCE: Samuel C. Johnson and Conrad Jones, "How to Organize for New Products," *Harvard Business Review*, Vol. 35, No. 3, May–June 1957, p. 52.

quantities only because it is expected that they can be sold to produce income when needed to keep the firm alive and flourishing.

(4) . . . no research pays unless, sooner or later, it leads to production or improved products that can be sold to create income.

(5) New products are developed and produced for the public primarily because someone believed that people wanted them or would come to want them within a "reasonable" time.

In short, in our economy, selling determines the extent and rate of adoption of new consumer products and the rapidity with which development of new workers takes place and new processes are applied. Thus it determines the speed at which the results of innovation, research, and technical advances are brought into use for the benefit of all.[8]

Questions

1. What is marketing's responsibility in technological development within a firm?
2. Does marketing give indication that it gracefully accepts technological change? (This refers to the marketing processes, not product innovation.)
3. Is it up to the marketing people to foster the diffusion of innovation? How does the process take place?
4. Can you see any conflict between the technically oriented people in a firm and the marketing research staff?
5. Does a strong marketing-oriented firm need to rely on the patent system?
6. Describe the proper relationship between technology and marketing.

Statements to Consider

Demand creates its own supply.

The rate of diffusion tends to be higher for more profitable innovations and for those requiring relatively small investments.

Many radical technical advances have emerged outside the industry on which they had the most impact.

There is a social, economic, and industrial climate that often controls technological progress.

As a firm works on the frontiers of technology, greater risk is assumed and more failure will occur.

The fundamental impulse that sets and keeps the capitalist engine in motion comes from the new consumers' goods, the new methods of production or transportation, the new markets, the new forms of industrial organization that capitalist enterprise creates.

[8] Harry R. Tosdal, *Selling In Our Economy* (Homewood, Ill.: Richard B. Irwin, 1957), pp. 154–156.

Major inventions are normally made because particular economic problems have become more pressing or economic opportunities have been more inviting, and not because some scientific finding suddenly pushed them over the horizon.

An invention today is seldom a surprise.

The patent system performs a function in the marketing of inventions.

SELECTED REFERENCES

H. G. Barnett, *Innovation: The Basis of Cultural Change* (New York: McGraw-Hill Book Company, 1962).

Theodore Levitt, *Innovation in Marketing* (New York: McGraw-Hill Book Company, 1962).

Everett M. Rogers, *Diffusion of Innovations* (New York: Free Press of Glencoe, 1962).

° Theodore Levitt, "Marketing Myopia," in Edward C. Bursk and John F. Chapman (eds.), *Modern Marketing Strategy* (Cambridge: Harvard University Press, 1964), pp. 24–48.

° A. E. Reynolds, "Effects of Technology on Marketing," written expressly for Holloway and Hancock (eds.), *The Environment of Marketing Behavior*.

° W. B. Reynolds, "Research and the Marketing Concept," *Marketing Innovations*, Proceedings of the eighth Biennial Marketing Institute, American Marketing Association, Minnesota Chapter, November 1961, Part II, pp. 14–21.

Generalizations Were Taken From:

Jacob Schmookler, "Technological Change and Economic Theory," Speech before American Economic Association, December 29, 1964, Chicago, Illinois.

Edwin Mansfield, "Technical Change and the Management of Research and Development," in Floyd A. Bond (ed.), *Technological Change and Economic Growth* (Ann Arbor, Mich.: Bureau of Business Research, Graduate School of Business Administration, University of Michigan, 1965), pp. 19–31.

James R. Bright, "Management and Technological Innovation," in Floyd A. Bond (ed.), *op. cit*, pp. 32–46.

Joseph A. Schumpeter, *Capitalism, Socialism, and Democracy*, 2nd Ed. (New York: Harper & Brothers, 1947).

Wroe Alderson, Stanley J. Shapiro, and Vern Terpstra (eds.), *Patents and Progress: The Sources and Impact of Advancing Technology* (Homewood, Ill.: Richard D. Irwin, 1965).

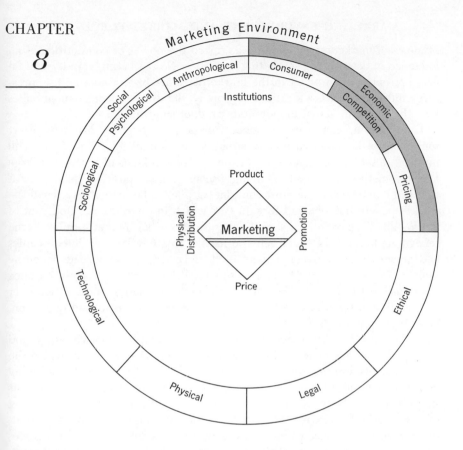

The Economic Environment
—Competition

'URE COMPETITION AND PURE MONOPOLY   *Monopoly* •   MONOPOLISTIC COMPETI-
'ION AND OLIGOPOLISTIC MARKET STRUCTURES   *The Concept of Differentiation   The
'asis of Differentiation   Pricing Under Monopolistic Competition   Pricing Under Oligopoly
'imitations of Theory* •   NONPRICE COMPETITION

Students of marketing have long recognized the power of competition as an influence in determining marketing activities. No marketing activity and no firm presenting its product in the marketplace are free of competitive pressures, unless the firm is a legalized monopoly. But even some legal monopolies face the threat of actual or potential product substitution.

Competition, moreover, is uncontrollable. Although a firm may exert some control in an actual market situation, its dominance is precarious and most often subject to change. By virtue of size and kinds of strategy, a large firm is sometimes regarded as having a secure market position, but competition can humble even the most complacent giant. The reader may recall the market penetration of small foreign cars which inspired the development of the so-called "compact" cars, or the demise of a major market supplier in the refrigerated-food field which left the market to a few large-scale companies and numerous smaller regionalized food processors, or the inroads made by Pepsi Cola, Royal Crown Cola, and other soft-beverage firms against a once impregnable Coca Cola. Thus, if a firm seems to exert its dominance over competition, it is perhaps well to conceive the situation as subject to erosion, or at best temporary.

A theoretical and practical knowledge of competition, its variables, and their probable influences is vital to a marketer. Economics has provided the basic concepts and theoretical descriptions of competition which are highly useful as a frame of reference and guide to orderly thinking. Economists simplify the problem of competition and price determination by limiting the assumptions necessary for their theoretical descriptions of market structures. Figure 8-1 indicates the market-structure models within which prices are determined. Pure competition and pure monopoly are the extreme conditions, whereas monopolistic competition and oligopoly are intermediate, representing a mixture of the elements of the extremes. The essential features embracing each market structure are of particular importance and these, also, are shown in the figure.

Any discussion of competition and market structure must of necessity be limited to the purpose at hand. In surveying the theoretical models of competition, it should be recognized that the real world is so complex that no brief discussion can do justice to the subject. The material which follows may fall short of giving a complete portrait of competition, but perhaps the reader can amplify the basic points.

PURE COMPETITION AND PURE MONOPOLY

The essence of *pure competition* is that no one seller has an appreciable influence on the market price. All participants sell an identical product, so that the buyer is indifferent as to whose output he buys. When there are

Figure 8-1. Market structures and their features

Features	Pure Competition	Monopolistic Competition	Oligopoly	Pure Monopoly
Number of sellers	Very large number	Substantial number	Few	One
Product	Undifferentiated perfect substitutes	Differentiated products with close substitutes°		No close substitute for unique good
Price	No control over price—seller must accept market price	Administered Prices		Much control over price—but can sell only what market will take at his price
		Some price competition can prevail. Price control depends much on degree of differentiation	Pricing in concert is strong tendency. Firms mutually interdependent	
Entry of new firms	Easy	Somewhat easy—but depends on technology and size of firms	Usually difficult because of size of firms and high costs	No entry as resource access is blocked
Marketing effort	None	Very large amount of nonprice competition with heavy emphasis on brands and product differentiation. Wide use of advertising and any marketing activity to build market share		Little, but can enjoy benefits if less product elasticity is created

°Except for undifferentiated oligopoly which is not common in actual market situations.

many sellers vending identical products and each is subject to sell at the market price, the producer must adapt his activities to market conditions. Given a producer's costs relative to the market price, he can decide the quantity to produce. Hence the volume which a seller will produce depends heavily on his costs. The individual producer will expand output so long as the additional cost (marginal cost) is less than the price he can charge for the additional unit. Of course, when marginal cost surpasses price, he will contract output.

Even though an individual seller acts as though he has no influence on the market price, the aggregate actions of all sellers exert a great influence on price. If costs relative to market price are high, this will cause restrictions of output by all sellers, thereby reducing supply, and other things remaining equal, market price will rise. Conversely, if costs are low relative to market price, an abundance of supply will be forthcoming and the price will fall. Thus, the quantity produced and sold, together with the market price, is automatically determined by impersonal forces of the market.

If any firm were operating under conditions of pure competition, marketing activities would be restrained. There would be no promotion, no incentive to improve the market offering, and no distinguishing characteristics of the sale. All such activities would only increase the firm's costs, placing it at a competitive disadvantage because no seller can command a price higher than the market price.

However, pure competition is virtually nonexistent. Agriculture—barring government controls, exchange regulations (that is, cotton, wheat, and other commodity exchange regulations), and grading—closely approximates the competitive model which has been an effective tool for analyzing the allocation of resources in a market-price system. Agriculture is often used as the norm against which competitive problems are measured, but this usage stirs controversy—particularly when public regulation of competition is at stake. From a marketing standpoint, agriculture lends a helping hand in studying the behavior of firms in certain sectors of the economy.

In some minor respects, retailing, wholesaling, service industries, and agricultural marketing institutions perform as though competition were pure. Certainly their offerings are not identical, and most of the sellers can exert control over price. However, competitive pressures are very strong, and if the price of any one among them is at all out of line he feels the loss of patronage and reacts as if the market were purely competitive.

Some observers, notably among the politicians, will on occasion imply that pure competition is the ideal for the American business scene. Perhaps this is done without a complete understanding of the long-run social impact of this form of competition. Essentially it means the survival of the most efficient, and the student can question for himself the desirability of a competitive system governed solely by costs and market prices.

Monopoly

The other extreme market structure shown in Figure 8-1 is monopoly, and it too is rare, except for monopolies sanctioned by public policy. The essential characteristic of a monopolist is that he is the sole seller of a product which does not have a close substitute. Local public utilities, aluminum prior to the Second World War, shoe machinery, and a few other industries are approximations of pure monopoly. But notwithstanding the complete control of an economic good, almost everything has a substitute. Gas and electricity are becoming more closely substitutable than before, and certainly aluminum has several substitutes. Whether pure monopoly exists is not of prime importance. The value of monopoly theory rests in its usefulness in analyzing real problems of pricing, output, and resource allocation, and its providing a clearer understanding of monopolistic competition and oligopolistic market structures.

In a purely monopolistic market the seller can set the price as he pleases and sell what the market will take *at that price*. Since he has complete control over price, the market demand will determine the number of units he sells. This contrasts with the seller in pure competition, who can sell any quantity, but at the market price. How then would a monopolist set price? Knowing that the number of units to be sold depends on the price, he would thus compare total costs and total revenues at each level of output and select that output which maximizes his profit. An alternate method of determining the same thing involves the use of marginal analysis. If marginal analysis is used, maximum total profit increases as long as the marginal revenue from producing the additional unit exceeds the marginal cost of producing the unit. Table 8-1 illustrates both methods, the last two columns comparing marginal costs with marginal revenues. Obviously the most profitable position is that output at which marginal cost equals marginal revenue.

Any monopolist can enjoy the rewards of marketing activities, whereas under pure competition there is nothing to be gained by marketing efforts.

Table 8-1. Revenue and Cost Data—Pure Monopolist

Output	Price	Total Revenue	Total Cost	Net Profit	Marginal Revenue	Marginal Cost
0	$25	$ 0	$ 0	$ 0	$ —	$ —
10	24	240	70	170	240	70
20	23	460	156	304	220	86
30	22	660	265	395	200	109
40	21	840	405	435	180	240
50	20	1000	583	417	160	178
60	19	1140	816	324	140	233
70	18	1260	1100	160	120	284

Any device that encourages the public to regard his product as highly desirable tends to reduce the elasticity of demand and also to shift the demand curve to the right. In real-life competitive situations, much marketing effort is designed to accomplish these ends. Of course, the use of marketing efforts (advertising and others) complicates the pricing process, and it then becomes necessary to estimate the additional revenue generated by the marketing effort.

MONOPOLISTIC COMPETITION
AND OLIGOPOLISTIC MARKET STRUCTURES

Somewhere on the continuum of Figure 8-1 between pure competition and pure monopoly most of the real world competes. Nobody in the United States either has a pure monopoly or competes in a purely competitive market. Almost all industries are a mixture of the two, with many having some partial monopoly. Some are in markets so heavily populated by competitors and containing very close substitutes, or having such weak partial monopolies that the market may be identified somewhere in the left extremity of the figure. If a firm (or industry) has a strong monopolistic element(s), such as fewness of competitors, it would fall in the right extremity of the continuum. Economists have identified these intermediate markets as *monopolistic competition* or, if fewness of sellers prevails, *oligopoly*.[1]

The question of the number of sellers in a given market causes some confusion. How *many* sellers must there be for monopolistic competition? How *few* sellers are required for oligopoly? There are no precise answers to these questions, but in general one can say that monopolistic competition prevails ". . . when the number of sellers is large enough so that the actions of any one have no perceptible effect upon the other sellers and their actions have no perceptible effect upon him. . . ."[2] An oligopoly, on the other hand, has so few participants that the actions of one of them do have an effect upon the others, who in turn react to offset repercussions. In other words, the individual oligopolistic seller is aware that his actions have repercussions—and when changing his price, output, product quality, sales promotion, and other marketing variables, he must take the probable reactions of the other few sellers into consideration.

Before discussing pricing under conditions of monopolistic competition and under oligopoly, it is desirable to apprise the reader of the dimensions

---

[1] Oligopoly theorists further distinguish between *pure oligopoly* and *differentiated oligopoly*. As a practical matter most sellers in oligopolistic industries differentiate their products. See Richard H. Leftwich, *The Price System and Resource Allocation* (3rd Edition, New York: Holt, Rinehart and Winston, 1966).

[2] *Ibid.*, p. 243.

and basis of the term "differentiation." Differentiation is the fundamental feature of monopolistic competition and is the characteristic upon which the theory rests. It is also the basis for those markets with few sellers of differentiated products, namely differentiated oligopoly.

The concept of differentiation

Differentiation is the essence of monopolistic competition and differentiated oligopoly. As a practical matter all sellers' offerings are differentiated from those of their competition. Two not widely understood aspects of differentiation have limited the appreciation of the theory of monopolistic competition. One of these is the myopic view that *product* differentiation *per se* is the full extent of the term, and the other is the failure to comprehend the basis of differentiation. An understanding of both points is essential to a clear conception of competition within a firm's environment.

The meaning of differentiation is much broader than mere product differentiation. Perhaps it would have been well for economists to have adopted the term *offering differentiation*, for this is what Chamberlin meant when he explored the concept in his classic volume. He wrote:

Differentiation may be based upon certain characteristics of the product itself, such as exclusive patented features; trade-marks; trade names; peculiarities of the package or container, if any; or singularly in quality, design, color, or style. It may also exist with respect to the conditions surrounding its sale. In retail trade to take only one instance, these conditions include such factors as the convenience of the seller's location, the general tone and character of his establishment, his way of doing business, his reputation for fair dealing, courtesy, efficiency, and all personal links which attach his customers either to himself or to those employed by him. In so far as these and other intangible factors vary from seller to seller, the "product" in each case is different, for buyers take them into account, more or less, and may be regarded as purchasing them along with the commodity itself. When these two aspects of differentiation are held in mind, it is evident that virtually all products offerings are differentiated, at least slightly, and that over a wide range of economic activity differentiation is of considerable importance.[3]

Any and all differentiation by a firm, then, gives it a partial monopoly and hence influences its price. For example, Coco Cola and Bayer Aspirin have partial monopolies; and A & P supermarket is convenient to the people in its vicinity and therefore enjoys a measure of monopoly; the small neighborhood dairy store can charge more for milk and ice cream by virtue of a location convenience, and hours-of-operation monopoly, or both. The student can undoubtedly expand on the factors that give firms partial monopolies besides

Edward Hastings Chamberlin, *The Theory of Monopolistic Competition*, (Cambridge: Harvard University Press, 1947), pp. 56–57.

the commonly cited product characteristics which also differentiate one firm from another.

The basis of differentiation

Because of the somewhat prevailing myopic view of the theorists' concepts of product differentiation, it has been common for students to regard differentiation as motivated by production. This is an easy but erroneous conclusion. It is wrong to regard differentiation as resulting solely from attempts to circumvent infringement on patents, from trade names, or from varying techniques of production. This is only a part of the basis of differentiation, and not a dominant one at that. The real source of differentiation rests in the nature of the consumer. Several earlier chapters have emphasized the economic and noneconomic aspects of consumer behavior. Tastes, preferences, and the various aspects of behavior discussed in these chapters form the bases for differentiation and hence the concept of monopolistic competition. Chamberlin recognized this in writing.

A general class of product is differentiated if any significant basis exists for distinguishing the goods [or services] of one seller from those of another. Such a basis may be real or fancied, so long as it is of any importance whatever to buyers, and leads to a preference for one variety of the product over another. Where such differentiation exists, even though it be slight, buyers will be paired with sellers, not by chance and at random (as in pure competition), but according to their preferences.[4]

The foundation upon which most American industry competes rests, then on differences in consumer tastes and preferences. The responses of firms to different consuming units is met by differentiating the offering. In this way "buyers are paired with sellers." This also helps to explain the constant development of new and improved products which are introduced to satisfy changing market demands. The basis for differentiation is the same whether the markets are monopolistically competitive or are characterized as oligopolistic.

Pricing under monopolistic competition

Of particular interest to students of marketing is the price-making process under conditions of monopolistic competition. Because the partial monopolist does not have to accept the market price, he will not have to produce at minimum possible cost. Although he is not entirely free from competitive pressures he has considerably more pricing freedom when competition is less active Returning to Figure 8-1, therefore, we can note that monopolistic competition comes within the area of administered prices. In other words, pricing under conditions of monopolistic competition and in oligopolistic industries will

[4] *Ibid.*, p. 56. Words in brackets inserted by the authors.

very likely be subject to management decisions. The prices set by managements will blend some aspects of pure competition with some aspects of monopoly.

Several factors help the manager to set a given price. First, he has a differentiated product, and every effort will be made to convince buyers that it is really different and that nothing else serves as a satisfactory substitute. The more successful he is in differentiating his product, the less elastic the demand curve will be. If the demand becomes relatively inelastic, a higher price may be commanded from the market without deterring trade. He thus sets himself apart from competition in a protected position.

Second, the manager will have a pretty good idea of how his competition will behave. Under most circumstances he will not have perfect knowledge about his rivals. But the more the firm knows about its competition, the more likely it will be that a more reasonable prediction of rival prices and retaliation can be made.

Third, the manager knows that if price is set high, and in turn high profits are forthcoming, new entrants into the field will likely upset existing price policies. In general, economic theory tells us that the larger the number of sellers competing, the more intense will be competition. This is particularly true if competition is on a price basis. But it should be recognized that market entry is a much more complex problem today than in the past. Advances in technology and the tendency for firms to grow to great size make entry more difficult. For these reasons, the withdrawal of a single firm from the market may have a marked effect on prices. Furthermore, the widespread use of nonprice competition to build market share is often so costly as to preclude market entry for some prospective rivals.

The main difficulty with maximizing revenue by pricing at that point where marginal cost equals marginal revenue is that even if the manager knew unit marginal cost and unit marginal revenue, he would not necessarily know where the most profitable output was. Most businessmen have never heard of these terms, but despite this they may act in a way which makes it seem as though they engaged in marginal analysis, equating marginal cost with marginal revenue.[5]

A somewhat reasonable and realistic alternative to marginal analysis is maximization of the difference between *total revenue* and *total cost*. Although total costs are seldom accurately stated for a given product, many business firms can reasonably approximate total costs. This device, also known as "break-even analysis," is a schedule of fixed costs and variable costs at varied levels of sales. From the schedule one can construct a graphic representation

[5] George Leland Bach, *Economics, An Introduction to Analysis and Policy*, 3rd Ed. (Englewood Cliffs, N.J.: Prentice-Hall, 1960), pp. 469–470.

of the break-even point and the point of maximum distance between total costs and total revenue, once the break-even point has been passed. The manager also knows that the demand for his product is a function of the total consumer demand for all similar but differentiated products and the firm's share of the total demand.

The success of a market entry will hinge on the firm's ability either to increase total demand for the product, to take customers away from competition, or both. Dial soap, for example, was introduced into the market at a price higher than most of the well-established brands, among them Lux, Palmolive, and Ivory. Yet Dial captured and has been able to retain a respectable market share. Did costs dictate a higher price for Dial? Was management trying to create the impression that Dial was a more highly differentiated soap and hence worthy of a higher price? In other words, does Dial have less price elasticity than its competition? Casual observation seems to indicate among other things, that, the answers to these questions are affirmative. In creating a strong brand identity for Dial, the tendency has been to diminish the appeal of substitutes and steepen the demand curve for Dial. Under monopolistic competition the relative elasticity, or relative inelasticity, of the firm's demand curve depends on how successful it is in creating a distinct differentiation and on what all other firms in the industry do.

In the long run, when there is monopolistic competition new firms will enter and old ones will leave the industries. Theory tells us that economic profits will attract new rivals and losses will cause firms to depart. These concepts need to be recast as statements of tendency, for real economic life often modifies theory. For example, a firm may have created such a measure of differentiation that new rivals do not enter, knowing that to penetrate the market would be either too costly or virtually impossible. Perhaps alternatives elsewhere are more attractive than meeting established firms in an industry head-on. Then there are always those in real life who accept less from their business than they could earn elsewhere. This is particularly true of small individual enterprises. These economic efforts continue for noneconomic reasons such as "It's a way of life," "It's all I know how to do," and other similar portrayals of reality.

Pricing under oligopoly

As noted earlier, the term *oligopoly* identifies those market structures populated by few sellers. Oligopolistic market structure characterizes several important industries in the United States. Table 8-2 shows some important markets which are dominated by as few as four firms. It goes without saying that vast size characterizes the firms in the oligopolistic industries listed in the table. It should also be noted that small firms in local markets have strong oligopolistic tendencies. Local markets when dominated by two, three, or

Table 8-2. *Market Domination by Leading Firms*

	Percent of Value of Shipments Accounted for By	
Industry	4 Largest Firms	8 Largest Firms
Aluminum	97	99
Electric lamps (bulbs)	92	97
Soap and glycerin	90	94
Chewing gum	88	95
Cereal breakfast foods	83	95
Tin cans and other tinware	80	89
Cigarettes	79	99
Typewriters	79	99
Computing and related machines	77	85
Flour mixes	75	86
Motor vehicles and parts	75	81
Tires and inner tubes	74	88
Domestic laundry equipment	71	90
Storage batteries	64	81

SOURCE: United States Senate Committee on the Judiciary, Subcommittee on Antitrust and Monopoly, *Economic Concentration*, Part I, 1964, p. 89.

even four suppliers seem to reflect some of the tendencies observed for large-scale national concerns. Building supply companies, a few local drug stores, or a few department stores often dominate a local market scene and exert oligopolistic tendencies described by the theory.

In discussing oligopolistic market structure, we must of necessity limit the extent of the analysis and hence deal only with the essential aspects of oligopoly. One paramount principle should guide the reader's analysis, however. This principle is that *when a market is dominated by few sellers it is both critical and imperative for each participating firm to weigh the reactions of the other firms in planning competitive and production policies.*

Prices under oligopoly are administered. The price, or cluster of prices, established must be fairly satisfactory to all sellers. In several oligopolistic industries a price leader can be identified. Price leadership may occur where an industry is populated by one or two large firms and several small firms, or in markets entirely dominated by large-scale enterprises. The price set by the leader permits the other firms a tolerable profit.[6]

[6] For the interested reader, a detailed theoretical analysis of oligopolistic pricing may be found in Richard H. Leftwich, *The Price System and Resource Allocation* (New York: Holt, Rinehart and Winston, 1966), Chapter 11, pp. 212–242.

Prices set by oligopolists are generally rigid and a persistent threat exists that price wars will erupt. The independent action of one oligopolist in lowering price may precipitate a disastrous price war. Because of this a live-and-let-live policy must prevail in the industry; otherwise the industry or some of its members face the threat of antitrust action if price decreases threaten the existence of some or one of the weaker sellers. Hence, nonprice competition is likely to be the principal form of competition. Another interesting aspect of oligopoly is that the market share of each seller is a critical measure of performance. A few percentage points increase or decrease in market share can readily be converted into revenue gained or lost.

The kinked demand curve in Figure 8-2 is an imprecise but adequate explanation of the aforementioned aspects of oligopoly. The curve helps us to visualize what may happen if one of the few sellers contemplates raising or lowering price. If one firm raises price within the range of *DP*, his sales will fall off and those maintaining price at *P* will gain in market share. Note that this portion of the demand curve is relatively elastic, which means that sales will decline by a greater proportion than the proportional increase in price. This is based on the assumption that the other sellers will not follow the newly established higher price. If, however, the industry is led to a higher price by a price leader, a new price is established almost in concert. No seller loses a share of market, for the industry merely reestablishes the kink at a point in some range above *P*. Clearly, if the new higher price takes some customers out of the market the new kink will be above and slightly to the left of point

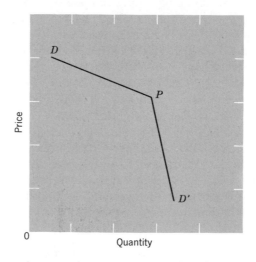

Figure 8-2. The kinked demand curve.

P. The student can easily redraw a number of possibilities which seem to reflect typical pricing behavior as price moves upward.

On the other hand, if one firm departs from the industry cluster of prices at *P* and lowers price along the range of *PD'*, the market shares of those retaining price *P* will decline and be distributed to the lower-priced rival. This portion of the demand curve is relatively inelastic. The lower-priced rival will thus increase his business, but relatively less than the proportional change in price. What is gained comes from the other firms in the industry. Chances are that the industry will not stand idly by and let its market shares erode. The other firms can also lower price.

There is no sense in pricing below the industry maverick. Rivals have only to lower price to the same level and the market shares redistribute, the market dividing in essentially the way it was before any action was precipitated. If this takes place, it will not be long before all participants in the oligopoly recognize the futility of price cutting. No one gains anything except the short spurts of sales volume achieved by the firm originating the price cut. Rather than risk these measures, the industry is likely to be most content at the higher price. Common sense will tell any participant that his price increases can be ignored by the other oligopolists and his price decreases met. This goes far to explain why price changes are infrequent and why firms are better off to avoid ruinous price wars. When and if price changes occur, they are likely to be mutually applicable and based on general cost adjustments.

Limitations of theory

Economic theory is often charged with falling short of analyzing real-life competition. It is true that theory leaves unexplained some of the practical and subtler aspects of real-life competitive behavior. Its purpose has a different end from the practice of market rivalry. The economist assumes one product, knowledge of its marginal cost and marginal revenue, and the decline or absence of competition as the number of sellers diminishes. These are essential to his goals, which are to analyze the behavior and performance of the whole economic system.

Despite its shortcomings the theory serves the marketing person by providing order and precision to one's thinking. For example, the discussion of oligopoly did not explain how *P* was originally arrived at in Figure 8–2. The price *P* is theoretically found by the equation of marginal cost and marginal revenue. This fact was not important to the discussion, but the oligopolist's view of the reaction of his rivals to price increases and decreases is most important. Certainly cigarette pricing, the clustering of auto prices (that is, model for model), the pricing of tires and gasoline, and pricing in a number of basic industries—all reflect the behavior described by portions of oligopoly theory. Although not all theory is of practical use to a marketer, certain aspects of economic theory lead to a clearer understanding of the basis of competitive behavior and of some rival reactions he is likely to encounter.

The limitations of economic theory in adequately explaining competitive behavior have many subtle and paradoxical arguments. Joel Dean is one well-known managerial economist who has taken a strong position in contrasting the economist's views of competition with those of businessmen. Of interest are his hallmarks of an intensely competitive situation in Box 8-1. Several of Dean's hallmarks have been held by theorists to be symptomatic of monopoly or at least strong monopolistic tendencies. Yet from a practical market point of view, they imply aggressive competitive activities.

Throughout the discussion of monopolistic competition and oliogopoly the implication has been that price *per se* does not function as the sole competitive variable in real-life rivalry. Some price competition is observable, but by and large much of American industry is very adept at nonprice competition. It is to this kind of competition that we now turn.

NONPRICE COMPETITION

Nonprice competition refers to all those activities designed to build trade except by means of price. Perhaps all commonly observed external marketing activities can be termed as nonprice-competitive variables. The designing of new and improved differentiated products, the selection of particular channels of distribution and exclusive dealerships, the use of advertising, premiums, and point-of-sale aids, and numerous other activities fall into the category of nonprice strategy.

The basic reason for the heavy emphasis on nonprice competition is found in the complexity of the market and the character of the demand. For example, the abundance of products and their increasing complexity tend to make comparisons difficult, and price differences are not as useful a yardstick as in a simpler economy. As one writer contends, "Our knowledge of machinery . . . is so limited that most of us cannot compare directly the relative merits of different refrigerators and of different automobiles. Our decisions to buy such products are more significantly influenced by the reputation of the seller or the effectiveness of his advertising rather than by differences in price."[7]

Any monopolistically competitive firm or oligopolist can gain a market edge by engaging in marketing efforts of the nonprice type. These firms use product differentiation, in the broad sense as explained by theory, to adapt the offering to consumer demand. As a counterpart to this effort, they use advertising and other means to bring consumer demand into correspondence

[7] Jules Backman, *Price Practices and Policies,* (New York: The Ronald Press Company, 1953), p. 89.

with their output. Competing on this basis, the rivals avoid destructive price wars and concentrate on building proficiency and expertise in the nonprice areas. This advantage is not trivial when we consider the social and economic costs of cutthroat or ruinous competition.

BOX 8-1

Hallmarks of Competition

1. *Price uniformity.* Close similarity of quoted prices of rivals, usually accompanied by undercover price shading.

2. *Price differentiation.* A structure of price discounts characterized by wide spreads between the lowest and the highest net price, e.g., the discount structure that is usual for suppliers of fairly standardized products to the automobile industry.

3. *Selling activities.* Substantial promotional outlays, i.e., much advertising, point-of-sale merchandising, and direct personal salesmanship.

4. *Product differentiation.* Preoccupation with the modernity, quality, and style of the company's products as compared with rivals' products and with "good service."

5. *Product research.* Large outlays on product research that is focused on creation of new products and continuous improvement in the firm's existing products.

6. *Selective distribution.* A strong dealer organization, i.e., rivalry through and for sponsored, franchised (and often exclusive) distributors.

7. *Market share.* Acute consciousness of the activities and position of competitors, and preoccupation with the company's market share and with the market occupancy of individual rivals.

8. *Market raiding.* Uninhibited efforts to detach big customers from rivals, often by price shading, or special concessions, business patronage, and "services." Sporadic penetration of the market by distant rivals, who frequently dump, so that their net-back is much lower than from sales in their own backyard territory. The converse is customer-freezing, i.e., the use of sewing-up devices such as requirements contracts, reciprocity, and lavish gifts, which make good customers hard to alienate.

9. *Customer sharing.* Widespread acceptance of the strike-born doctrine that for each important material or component the buyer needs the protection of having at least two suppliers.

SOURCE: Joel Dean, "Competition as Seen by the Businessman and by the Economist," in Harvey W. Huegy (ed.), *The Role and Nature of Competition in Our Marketing Economy* (Urbana: Bureau of Economic and Business Research, College of Commerce and Business Administration, University of Illinois, 1954), pp. 8–15.

Nonprice competition coupled with the ever-stimulated drive toward differentiation serves the American consumer well. It may be, as so often argued, that we pay more because of the absence of the purely competitive model in real life. As a practical matter most of us would not want to live in an economy based on pure competition. Monopolistic competition and oligopoly provide a vastly wider range of free choice to the consumer. Our tastes, whatever they may be, are most fully and satisfactorily met by *actual* competition rather than by the advantages claimed for the competitive model. If price, rather than nonprice, were the only variable we would indeed be in a peculiar position.

Questions

1. Can we rely on competition to shape the marketing processes as we would like to have it do?
2. Assume that you are the marketing manager of a commercial bank. One of your competitors increases the interest rate on savings by one percentage point. What are your alternatives?
3. How do you compete when prices are regulated by the government? (Airlines, for example, have their fares regulated.)
4. As a businessman, would you prefer to compete on a price basis or on a nonprice basis? Why?

Statements to Consider

Product innovation is largely an outgrowth of instability and uncertainty; instability of competitive position and instability, also, perhaps, unpredictability of consumer needs and desires.

In marketing, the excesses of competition are to be found primarily in the performance of the selling function; at least this is the area which is customarily criticized.

The severity of competition usually gives distributors strong incentive to stress selling, regardless of the presence of economies of scale.

Product competition supplements rather than supplants price competition.

SELECTED REFERENCES

Joel Dean, *Managerial Economics* (Englewood Cliffs, N.J.: Prentice-Hall, 1951).
Richard H. Leftwich, *The Price System and Resource Allocation,* 3rd Edition (New York: Holt, Rinehart and Winston, 1966).
° Joel Dean, "Competition as Seen by the Businessman and by the Economist," in Harvey W. Huegy (ed.), *The Role and Nature of Competition in Our Marketing*

Economy (Urbana: Bureau of Economic and Business Research, College of Commerce and Business Administration, University of Illinois, 1954), pp. 8–15.

° R. S. Meriam, "Bigness and the Economic Analysis of Competition," *Harvard Business Review*, Vol. 28, No. 2, March 1950, pp. 109–126.

Generalizations Were Taken From:

D. M. Phelps, "Comments on 'Consumer Product Acceptance Rates,' " in Lincoln H. Clark (ed.), *Consumer Behavior: Research on Consumer Reactions* (New York: Harper & Brothers, 1958), pp. 50–52.

Rayburn D. Tousley, Eugene Clark and Fred E. Clark, *Principles of Marketing* (New York: Macmillan Company, 1962).

Roland S. Vaile, E. T. Grether, and Reavis Cox, *Marketing in the American Economy* (New York: The Ronald Press Company, 1952).

Wroe Alderson, *Marketing Behavior and Executive Action* (Homewood, Ill.: Richard D. Irwin, 1957).

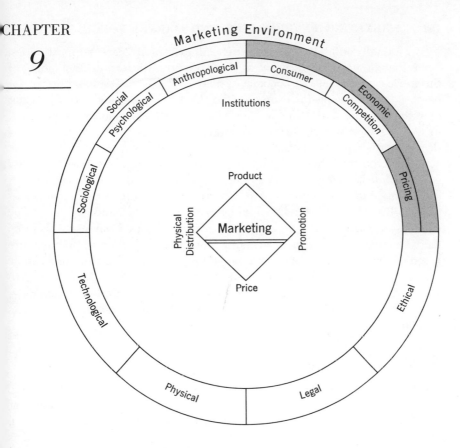

Demand Analysis

DETERMINANTS OF DEMAND • THE ABILITY TO BUY • THE WILLINGNESS TO
BUY • *The Tastes and Preferences of Consumers* *The Expectations of Consumers with Respect*
to Future Income and Future Prices *The Price of Related and Substitute Goods* • ELASTICITY
OF DEMAND • THE FIRM'S MARKETING COSTS

Either formally or informally, any firm needs to assess its market opportunities. Since the consumer is so central to these opportunities, an understanding of the intricacies of demand becomes essential. The term "demand" does not have precise meaning for everyone. To the layman demand usually means only the quantity sold. It might thus mean that the demand for automobiles in a given year was 8,500,000. The layman thus assesses the resultant of demand rather than a market opportunity implied by the term itself. The economist, on the other hand, has a precise definition of the term. *Demand is a schedule showing the various amounts of any product which consumers are willing and able to purchase at different prices during some stated period of time.* By definition a fundamental characteristic of demand is that as price declines the quantity of a specific good demanded rises. Conversely, as price increases the quantity demanded falls. Many actual marketing practices are based on this elementary but fundamental view of demand. Businessmen know that if their prices are set too high, consumers will shift their buying to substitute products or even withhold their spending. Similarly, bargain days, end-of-the-month sales, and the like are based on the theoretical constructs of demand.

DETERMINANTS OF DEMAND

All too often consumer income is used as the sole determinant of demand. Although it is true that no demand can be registered without income, economists have long recognized that consumer behavior also determines demand. It should be noted that the definition of demand implies that demand is influenced both by people's willingness and by their ability to buy. When a marketer estimates demand, it behooves him to consider those variables in addition to income which will more precisely determine the market demand. Many people may have the desire to own a Rolls Royce, which they regard as the ultimate in transportation; yet no willingness, apart from the ability to buy, will be forthcoming. Most consumers have whims, desires, and aspirations which may never materialize. Such mental processes do not constitute demand, but only mental exercises which most people can afford to enjoy.

On the other hand, in a capitalistic economy, consumer demand directs many noneconomic aspects of production. As consumers allocate their incomes among the numerous market offerings, they also register their demand for the asthetic and other noneconomic qualities found in goods and services If consumers want home appliances in colors other than white, then an array of colored appliances will be manufactured. If they want processed foods which emulate Italian, Spanish, or Far Eastern dishes, these too become available. Consumer demand thus directs not only what is produced and at what prices, but also the numerous ramifications appended to market offerings.

Economists recognized the determinants of demand as quite compatible with the factors a marketing person must take into consideration in assessing market opportunities. These factors are (1) the money incomes of consumers, (2) the tastes and preferences of consumers, (3) the expectations of consumers with respect to their future income and future prices, (4) the prices of related and substitute goods, and (5) the number of consumers in the market.[1] If one broadly interprets the demand determinants one finds, they correspond either to the *ability to buy* or to the *willingness to buy* as encompassed by the definition of demand.

THE ABILITY TO BUY

Businessmen and government officials are particularly sensitive to economic indicators which reveal tendencies toward increases and decreases in consumer demand. In the United States, as in other advanced economies, personal consumption expenditures made possible by the receipt of personal income are often watched closely. The relation of personal consumption expenditures, personal income, and other economic components to Gross National Product are shown in Figure 9-1.

It is obvious that income is fundamental to consumer demand. It is perhaps not as obvious to some of us that income is also fundamental to the expression of our social and psychological desires. Once a family or individual gains the position of being able to meet adequately the basic needs of life, remaining income may be used for the consumption of nonessential goods.

The potential purchasing power of consumers in the United States may be measured either by disposable personal income or by discretionary income. Disposable income is personal income less federal, state, and local taxes as shown in Figure 9-1. It is a measurement of the actual spending power in the hands of consumers. Normally, consumers do not spend all they earn, and hence personal outlays are the amounts received less the amounts saved. Of equal importance is the growth of disposable income. This may be seen in Figure 9-2. With such marked increases in disposable income, the consumption of practically all goods, except the most mundane necessities, has also increased in recent years. Clearly much of our abundance of new goods and services can be attributed to the basic fact that consumers continue to enjoy increasingly higher levels of disposable income.

Perhaps even more meaningful to the individual consumer and some marketing people is the magnitude of discretionary income. Discretionary income is found by subtracting from disposable income certain fixed or nondiscretionary expenditures. These are generally commitments to repay debts,

[1]Campbell R. McConnell, *Elementary Economics; Principles, Problems and Policies*, (New York: McGraw-Hill Book Company, 1960), p. 64.

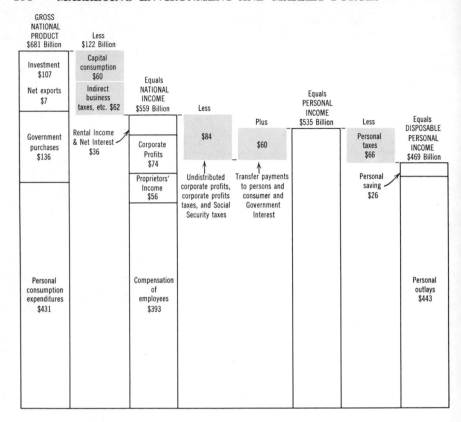

Figure 9-1. The relation of various components of gross national product, 1965.
SOURCE: *Survey of Current Business*, July 1966, p. 10.

obligations to pay real-estate taxes and rent, and amounts required for food, clothing, utilities, and other necessities. What is left is referred to as discretionary income because it may be spent or saved as the consumer desires. Figure 9-3 shows the marked increases in discretionary income enjoyed by American consumers. The consumer with such income has great latitude in how he spends it. He may acquire a more expensive home, club memberships for more status, trips abroad, and even a college education for his children. Since the holder of discretionary money incurs more long-term obligations, there is always the prospect of its diminishing unless his income (with other things remaining the same) periodically increases. Some middle- and higher-income consumers may have little discretionary money because of their greater obligations incurred by a more expensive way of living.

Durable-goods expenditures in particular are highly responsive to changes

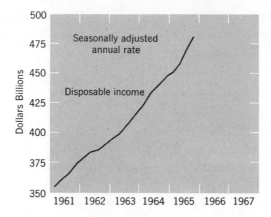

Figure 9-2. Disposable income, 1961-1965.
SOURCE: *A Graphic Guide to Consumer Markets,* (New York: National Industrial Conference Board, 1966), p. 27.

in discretionary income. This stems from the fact that consumers can postpone or speed up their purchases of durables in direct relation to their freely available funds. Automobiles, appliances, and new furniture can normally be postponed if income is eroded by prior fixed obligations, or by an increase in taxes or a decrease in income. Likewise, consumers are quite willing to speed up such purchases when more discretionary income becomes available. If the free funds are insufficient, the consumer is likely to extend his purchasing power by using installment credit. Lenders are also quite willing to accelerate

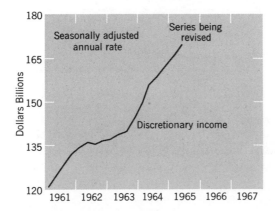

Figure 9-3. Discretionary income, 1961-1965.
SOURCE: *A Graphic Guide to Consumer Markets,* (New York: National Industrial Conference Board, 1966), p. 31.

debt creation during periods of rising incomes. Less postponable items such as most nondurable goods and services are not likely to react as strongly to changes in income.

Of course, an economy does not reflect high purchasing power unless income is rather equally distributed among the people. The fortunate financial position of most United States families results from the continuing decrease in the proportion of families in the lower income levels. Figure 9-4 shows projections of income distribution through 1975. These estimates are based on assumptions concerning wage rates, workweek, size of the labor force,

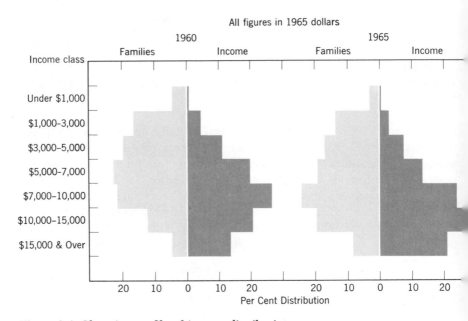

Figure 9-4. Changing profile of income distribution.
SOURCE: *A Graphic Guide to Consumer Markets*, (New York: The National Industrial Conference Board, 1966), p. 21.

and the further assumption that all segments of the population fare equally in the distribution of income. If these projections hold up, the American family will be in an even more improved financial position and the figures will indeed presage strengthened purchasing power.

THE WILLINGNESS TO BUY

Perhaps all students have heard of "the economic man" who can carefully evaluate each purchase and hence order his consumption toward maximum satisfaction. No one can compare oneself with this mythical person, and few of us will ever know whether we actually have allocated our incomes to the best possible advantage. About all we can do is hope that we have made wise purchase decisions. If one accepts the concept of the economic man, this would require that each consumer have complete information (particularly as regards the prices of all related or competitive goods) and be able to forecast his future satisfactions in order to make perfectly rational purchase decisions. Many economists are aware of the limitations of this concept and presumably would prefer to interpret the determinants of demand broadly rather than being guided by an analysis dominated by perfect rationality.

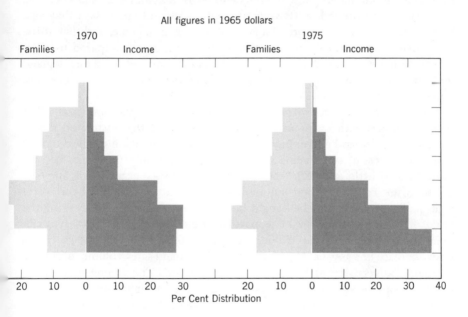

By broadly interpreting the concepts of (1) the tastes and preferences of consumers, (2) the expectations of consumers with respect to future income and future prices, and (3) the prices of related and substitute goods, the willingness to buy takes on reality. Some aspects of these determinants are economic, whereas other aspects are socio-psychological.

The Tastes and Preferences of Consumers

These may include a complex array of influences that tend to shift and stimulate demand. For example, much empirical evidence on the average annual expenditures for automobiles shows that higher-income families have substantially higher expenditures; it also shows that they are generally more educated, under fifty-five years of age, and hence more active, and that these families comprise three or more persons and live in metropolitan areas. The origin of demand for most things is not evenly distributed among all persons in a given income bracket. Each individual and family will spend its money income in different ways.

The tastes and preferences of consumers form the dominant influence in determining the specifics of a purchase once the decision to buy has been reached. In some instances consumers' tastes and preferences actually determine *what* may be purchased. Most students will recall that an individual's demand curve slopes downward. A downward-sloping demand curve says that at a lower price one can buy more of a good at any given income, and that at the lower price the good becomes relatively more attractive compared to other things. Although it may be true that as individuals we conceive our demand for particular goods along a negatively inclined demand curve, this does not explain consumer demand for a large number of things.

Brands, the characteristics of the point of sale, reputation, and other things combine with tastes and preferences to upset the postulated downward-sloping demand curve. Bayer aspirin is one of the leading sellers among aspirin products at $0.59 cents a hundred, yet many substitutes can be purchased for as little as $0.29 cents a hundred. Another exception is prestige goods. Mink coats, prestige automobiles, fine leather products, and very-high-quality watches may be bought because the price *is* high. Lowering the price of these products might jeopardize their "image" as status symbols. Even for such an everyday product as a cake mix, it is well known that a price increase of a few cents per package will expand sales volume, provided, of course, advertising of the product is intensified. This is one example of using a nonprice variable to advance sales even at a higher price. Nonprice variables often condition consumer tastes and preferences and hence may disrupt a strict theoretical model which is constructed on price, quantity, and given income. Much that was discussed in Chapters 4, 5, and 6 will be useful in considering consumer demand in light of a broadly interpreted concept of tastes and preferences.

The Expectations of Consumers with Respect to Future Income and Future Prices

These expectations have some bearing on present spending patterns. For a number of years the Survey Research Center of the University of Michigan has conducted studies of consumer buying intentions. More recently the Federal Reserve Board and the National Industrial Conference Board have also investigated consumer expectations and buying plans. In general, these studies attempt to identify expectative aspects of spending behavior and saving. Apparently the central hypothesis of these studies is that consumer spending on homes, automobiles, appliances, furniture, and other durable goods is directly influenced by future expectations regarding income. If such expectations are favorable, optimism prevails and plans to purchase become realities in the near future. Pessimism prevails if expectations are negative.

George Katona, of the Survey Research Center, is regarded as the originator of studies of this nature, and he views economic psychology as having a marked influence on market demand. In recognizing demand as being determined by the interaction of economic and psychological variables, he states:

> Psychological factors, such as motives, attitudes, expectations, and group belonging, are intervening variables operating between the stimuli of market conditions and the responses to them in the form of economic decisions. The psychological factors do not alone determine the final decision, but under certain conditions they are powerful enough to alter individual as well as mass reactions and thereby influence the entire economy.[2]

Most marketing professionals accept Katona's thesis, and it appears that the surveys have borne out the contention that willingness to buy cannot be analyzed in strictly economic terms.

The Price of Related and Substitute Goods

The price of related and substitute goods has long been regarded as a realistic determinant of demand by both economists and marketing students. In essence, this is a common-sense principle which says that consumer demand is affected not only by changes in price of a given product, but also by changes in prices of related and substitute goods. As the price increases for a good demanded by consumers, it results in a decline in the consumers' real income. This presumably tends to shift consumers to other lower-priced goods. The classic elementary textbook example is "the amount of oleomargarine purchased will depend on the price of butter." As the price of butter increases, consumers will redirect their consumption to the product substitute, oleomargarine. When the prices of two or more goods are directly related, they are referred to as substitute or competing goods. In setting the prices of their wares businessmen seldom ignore this basic principle.

One other aspect of this concept concerns *complementary* goods. Here again, as the price of a complementary good falls, it may set off expanded consumption. For example, several years ago the price of long-playing records was lowered and, as a result, the purchase of record players increased. Of course, one must be careful in attributing a shift of demand solely to price changes; the variables affecting purchasing behavior are so numerous and

[2] George Katona, *The Powerful Consumer*, (New York: McGraw-Hill Book Company, 1960), pp. 5–6.

complex that they muddy cause-and-effect relationships. Empirical evidence during periods of strong price increases lends support to the shifting of consumer demand to related or substitute goods, and vice versa.

A remaining determinant of demand is *the number of buyers in the market.* As the number of buyers increases, the demand curve shifts to the right. More buyers may be a reflection of population increases, wider acceptance of a good once sold to the elite few, or even new or adjusted channels of distribution and marketing strategies. An example is the much greater quantity of toys marketed each year in the United States. This is due not only to an increase in the number of children, but also to the increased number of parents and grandparents who actually buy the toys. Further expansion of the toy market was achieved by offering toys at an increased number of outlets and by marked changes in the distribution policies of toy manufacturers. All of these factors and more contribute to the increased willingness to buy toys at each possible price.

ELASTICITY OF DEMAND

One of the more important and useful economic concepts for the businessman is the elasticity of demand. Unless businessmen, and marketing people in particular, can measure the responsiveness of consumers to changes in price, they are likely to make major price-policy blunders. The law of demand tells us that consumers will buy more of a given product as price declines. Even though this is not always true, one must be careful not to generalize from specific cases. Noneconomic factors often create special circumstances in which price changes generate little responsiveness, or even tend to bolster demand if higher prices are equated with high quality and status. Consumers also tend to be affected by the quantities of a good held, and may have reached a point of diminishing marginal utility for further goods of like kind. Here, too, responsiveness to lower prices may be offset by this factor which influences buying behavior. Despite the exceptions to the law of demand, the businessman should have some idea of the *degree* of responsiveness to price change. If this is known, the firm can estimate to what extent price changes will expand consumption, restrain it, or have little or no effect.

Figure 9-5 depicts three hypothetical demand curves. Curve *a* is an inelastic demand curve, curve *b* an elastic one, and curve *c* a unitary demand curve. To measure the degree of elasticity or inelasticity, economists use the following formula:

$$\text{Elasticity} = \frac{\% \text{ change in quantity demanded}}{\% \text{ change in price}}$$

Hence the elasticity of demand is the ratio between the relative change in quantity demanded and the relative change in price. Demand is said to be

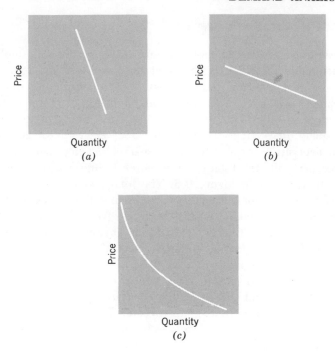

Figure 9-5. Hypothetical demand curves.

elastic if the percentage of change in price brings about a larger percentage of change in quantity demanded. When demand is elastic the elasticity co-efficient will be greater than 1. Demand is said to be inelastic when the percentage of change in price results in a relatively smaller change in the quantity demanded. In this case the elasticity coefficient will be less than 1. Unit elasticity, or a unitary demand curve, occurs when the percentage of change in price is equal to the percentage of change in the quantity demanded.

From a marketer's standpoint, the real importance of the elasticity concept rests in the fact that a company's total revenue is affected by the prices it sets and the quantity sold at those prices. If the firm's demand curve is inelastic (a in Figure 9-5), price changes will result in less than proportional changes in the quantity sold. In this case price increases may not seriously erode total revenue, and price decreases will not generate the same proportion of total revenue. Clearly the converse is true if the demand curve looks more like b. A unitary demand curve says that price changes will be exactly offset by changes in quantity; hence total revenue either expands or contracts by the same proportion. The student can examine the demand curves in Figure 9-5 and hypothesize a number of real marketing situations.

THE FIRM'S MARKETING COSTS

The discussion of demand elasticity and other matters has implied that businessmen prefer to think in terms of total revenue and total cost. In consequence, break-even analysis is a useful tool to businessmen in analyzing their marketing expenditures at various levels of output. Total costs at any level of output (or sales) comprise total fixed costs and total variable costs. As sales expand, marketing costs increase, since each additional increment of volume necessitates expenditures for market development. Assuming a given price per unit, the total-revenue curve is linear and slopes upward starting at point O, as in Figure 9-6. The total-cost curve originates at a point above O because some fixed costs arise even without output and at zero sales. Maximum profits obtain where the total-revenue curve is farthest removed from the total-cost curve. This occurs at sales volume Y and is also the point at which marginal cost equals marginal revenue. However, most firms do not possess marginal-cost and marginal-revenue data, whereas they often have total-cost and total-revenue information.

If market development activities carry the firm beyond point Y, total costs will mount at a more rapid rate than revenue. The chart also suggests that if the firm is not careful it can make sales but lose money as it passes P'—the second break-even point where total costs for each increment of volume become greater than total revenue. Within a substantial range, marketing

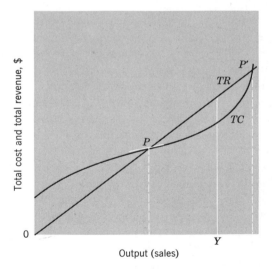

Figure 9-6. Break-even chart.

BOX 9-1

Year End Results: Earnings Up; Sales Down

General Mills expects net profits for the fiscal year ended May 29, 1966, to reach a new high of $23.3 million. This represents earnings per share of $3.07, also an improvement over last year.

While earnings figures rose, total sales figures recorded a decline as the result of the closing of nine of the company's 17 flour mills. Total sales of $524.7 million were about six percent less than last year's $559 million. However, sales of all products exclusive of bakery flour increased about nine percent. Profits per sales dollar represented an increase over the 3.6 cents earned last year.

Chairman Charles H. Bell and President Edwin W. Rawlings attributed the improving earnings picture primarily to a continuing strong demand for the company's established brands, a high level of consumer acceptance of some of its newer products and streamlining of the company's milling operations in low profit areas.

In releasing the preliminary figures, the company emphasized that they are subject to adjustments after the public accountants have finished their review. The company's annual report will be mailed to reach stockholders by August 1, 1966.

SOURCE: *The Modern Millwheel,* General Mills, Inc., Minneapolis, Minn., Vol. 30, No. 7, 1966.

costs are variable. Thus, when market expansion efforts are not deployed with some awareness of their results, a firm could conceivably be better off to retrench and move back to the area closest to point Y. Figure 9-6 provides a lesson for those who try to expand sales at *all costs*. Box 9-1 illustrates retrenchment in a famous company which reports that it is enjoying more by doing less.

Questions

1. A foreign person asks you to describe the needs and demands of a typical American consumer. What does a consumer demand during a year?
2. Do you consider demand to be a stable force in the economy? What forces affect demand for any given product?
3. Select a product and trace the demand for that product over a period of ten years.

4. If you were marketing a consumer product, what kind of an existing demand situation would you prefer?

Statements to Consider

The theory of diminishing marginal utility says that the more an individual has of some object, the less will his satisfaction increase by obtaining an additional unit.

Expenditures for clothing do not remain a constant percentage of total expenditures as claimed in the so-called Engel's laws.

During the contraction and recovery phases of the four postwar business cycles, consumer incomes have followed strikingly similar patterns. Typically, purchases of nondurable goods have declined only slightly during recessions, and purchases of services have continued to advance, but less rapidly than during expansions.

The willingness to purchase durable goods may decline at a time of relatively high and stable incomes and may usher in a recession.

Stimulating, altering, and directing consumer demand is accomplished largely through advertising and personal salesmanship.

The starting point of any analysis of consumer demand must be the enabling conditions represented by income, assets, and debts, as well as by such demographic facts as population growth and the age distribution of the population.

SELECTED REFERENCES

George Leland Bach, *Economics, An Introduction To Analysis and Policy*, 3rd Ed. (Englewood Cliffs, N.J.: Prentice-Hall, 1960).

H. S. Houthakker and Lester D. Taylor, *Consumer Demand in the United States, 1929–1970*, (Cambridge: Harvard University Press, 1966).

Robert H. Haverman and Kenyon A. Knopf, *The Market System* (New York: John Wiley and Sons, 1966).

John A. Howard, *Marketing Management*, Revised Ed. (Homewood, Ill.: Richard D. Irwin, 1963).

George Katona, *The Powerful Consumer* (New York: McGraw-Hill Book Co., 1960).

Richard H. Leftwich, *The Price System and Resource Allocation*, 3rd Ed. (New York: Holt, Rinehart and Winston, 1966).

Vernon G. Lippitt, *Determinants of Consumer Demand for House Furnishings and Equipment* (Cambridge: Harvard University Press, 1959).

Richard R. Still and Edward W. Cundiff, *Essentials of Marketing* (Englewood Cliffs, N.J.: Prentice-Hall, 1966).

Paul H. Nystrom, "The Significance of Fashion," in *Fashion Merchandising* (New York: The Ronald Press Company, 1932).

Elmer J. Working, "What Do 'Statistical Demand' Curves Show?" *Quarterly Journal of Economics*, Vol. 41, 1927, pp. 212–235.

Generalizations Were Taken From:

George Katona, *The Powerful Consumer* (New York: McGraw-Hill Book Company, 1960).
Theodore N. Beckman, Nathaniel H. Engle, and Robert D. Buzzell, *Wholesaling* (New York: The Ronald Press Company, 1959).
"Patterns of Consumer Spending," *Federal Reserve Bulletin*, April 1962, pp. 389–395.

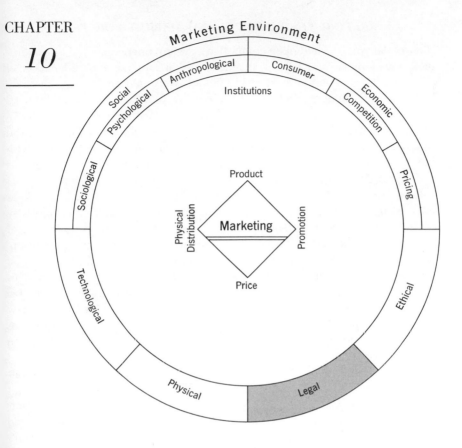

Marketing and the Law

he Demand for and Origin of Legislation • THE ANTITRUST LAWS *The Sherman Act
he Federal Trade Commission Act The Clayton Act The Robinson-Patman Act The Cel-
er-Kefauver Act* • FEDERAL LAWS AGAINST DECEPTIVE PRACTICES *The Origin and
)emand for Consumer Protection* • LEGISLATION IN THE STATES *Resale Price Main-
enance An Evaluation of the Legal Framework*

Theoretically, a free and open competitive system unencumbered by government interference and legal restraint would assure the best allocation of resources. Thus, if self-interest of individuals were given free play, the only curb on their actions would be rival competition and the most desirable social ends would follow. In general, this theory favors the efficient and powerful firm at the expense of the inefficient and less powerful, which would tend to disappear from the market. It not only forces businessmen to compete with their rivals, but also encourages them to restrain competition so as to ensure profits and their own survival.

Restraint of trade can be accomplished by several devices. Price-fixing schemes, the division of markets among conspiring competitors, discriminatory pricing practices, and vertical restraints on institutions within a channel of distribution are some of the practices which tend to restrain competition. Such practices preclude firms from equal opportunity to compete and also diminish the freedom of entry of potential competitors. For these reasons antitrust laws are designed to check those who would attempt to monopolize an already imperfect market condition. In a basic sense, the intent of the law is to perpetuate a free and open competitive system, protect all businesses from acts which would destroy their ability to compete, and provide freedom of entry to markets.

Not only is business conduct restrained and in turn protected, but consumers are protected against false and deceptive practices. Consumers are not always well informed, and it is possible for a business to capitalize on their ignorance. False and deceptive advertising and mislabeling; the unrevealed presence of used, reprocessed, and substitute materials; the use of impure materials and substances harmful to the human body; and the practice of misleading the public as to the true retail price of an item (automobiles, in particular) represent the bases for some laws enacted to protect the public. False and deceptive practices do not tend to create monopolistic conditions, but are regarded as unfair to competitors and detrimental to public welfare. Hence the intent of the law is to keep competition on a fair basis and thus protect the ethical seller while guarding consumer interests.

The Demand for and Origin of Legislation

The public demand for control of American business enterprise has its roots in the industrial revolution. Whereas industrialization began to evolve early in the nineteenth century, it was not until the end of the Civil War that rapid economic growth and expansion occurred. From the end of the Civil War to the turn of the century, the social and economic structure of the nation underwent rapid change. Large-scale business enterprises and the concentration of economic power became realities of the era. These important developments were paralleled by the following:

1. The growing demand for capital created by the higher investment require-ments of specialization. This was fed by the corporate device for raising capital and was widely adopted.
2. Pressures for larger and larger volumes of sales to compensate for the high costs of industrialization which meant that firms could no longer survive on local product demand.
3. The expanding network of railroads providing the means of market expansion. The railroads stood out as the corporate giants of the day.
4. The opportunities for skilled and unskilled labor in the cities, especially northern cities, precipitated a migration from rural areas to the industrial centers.

As market opportunities grew, enterprises that had once enjoyed a virtual local monopoly were threatened by competition. The now widely separated business rivals became intense and even bitter competitors. Vast personal fortunes were to be made, and this encouraged numerous new businesses to engage in an even more competitive search for customers. Cutthroat tactics and business failures characterized the marketplace. Under such conditions a natural tendency is to attempt to reduce the rivalry. Hence, monopolistic devices which insulated a firm from the inroads of competition were common. Businesses which failed to enter into monopolistic agreements and combina-tions were at the mercy of the ruthless, underhanded power of the giant trusts.

The corporate form of business and the problems of the era leading to combinations have been concisely presented by Clair Wilcox.

The corporate form of organization, in turn, facilitated industrial consolidation and made for increasing concentration of control. In this situation the growth of monopoly was stimulated by a steady decline in the general level of prices, accom-panied by recurring periods of business depression. Concerns with large invest-ments, entailing heavy fixed charges were impelled successively to slash their prices in an effort to cover some portion of their costs. Competition, on this basis, threatened to become mutually destructive, and business sought refuge in monopolistic agree-ments and in the combination of competing firms. This movement was stimulated, too, by the prospect of profits that were to be obtained in the process of promoting corporate reorganizations and those that were to be realized through the exercise of monopoly power. In consequence, during the 1880's, many of the country's major industries were brought under some form of concentrated control. In petroleum, cottonseed oil, linseed oil, meat packing, cordage, sugar, lead, coal, whiskey, tobacco, matches, gunpowder, and elsewhere, power over markets was attained through the devices of monopoly.[1]

A case in point was the vast productive and market power of the Standard Oil Company. Through acquisition of competitors, pricing policies which

[1] Clair Wilcox, *Public Policies Toward Business*, (Homewood, Ill.: Richard D. Irwin, 1960) p. 52.

destroyed the competively weak, and other practices which included a system of railroad rebates, the company had amassed control of about ninety percent of the country's refining capacity and almost as much control over the oil pipelines. This phenomenal degree of domination was accomplished in the brief period from 1870 to 1882.

It became evident that the public and the economy would have to be protected from the growth of corporate concentration and its resulting threats to the competitive system. Discontent with "trusts" and combinations rapidly became widespread. Farmers who were subjected to a decline in farm prices, but high prices for manufactured goods; small businessmen and others who were threatened with extinction if the competitive system of the time prevailed; raw-material suppliers who found themselves competitively weak against one or a few giant buyers in monopolized industries; and labor which relied on industrial jobs—all gave strong support to the antitrust movement. This organized discontent was instrumental in fostering the development of state and national third-party reform platforms. As the antitrust movement spread, all political parties professed opposition to monopoly. By 1888, each of the nation's four principal political parties included an antitrust plank in its platform. The issue had thus become central in the political arena and the movement soon achieved its goals. In 1890 the Sherman Act was enacted at the federal level, whereas eighteen states enacted antitrust laws between 1889 and 1891.[2]

THE ANTITRUST LAWS

Commencing with the movement just described and the subsequent demands by business and other interests, a body of federal laws known as the "anti-trust laws" were enacted. During the 60 years from 1890 to 1950 the following federal acts became law:

> Sherman Act—1890
> Federal Trade Commission Act—1914
> Clayton Act—1914
> Robinson-Patman Act—1936
> Wheeler-Lea Act—1938
> Celler Antimerger Act—1950

The Sherman Act

The Sherman Antitrust Act of 1890 is the hallmark of public policy toward restraint of trade and monopoly. Though brief, it is a general statement of intent to preserve freedom of entry and the maintenance of competition.

[2] *Ibid.*, pp. 52–54.

Section 1 declares that "every contract, combination in the form of a trust or otherwise, or conspiracy, in restraint of trade or commerce among the several states, or with foreign nations, is hereby declared to be illegal. . . ." Section 2 declares that "every person who shall monopolize, or attempt to monopolize, or combine or conspire with any other person or persons, to monopolize any part of the trade or commerce among the several states, or with foreign nations, shall be guilty of a misdemeanor. . . . " Thus Section 1 of the Act applies to agreements of two or more persons which restrain trade. The second section has broader application and applies also to individual activities that monopolize.

Many years of judicial interpretation of the Sherman Act have set forth a number of business practices as illegal *per se*. All vertical and horizontal price agreements,[3] restriction of production as a device of price fixing, division of markets by competitors and group boycotts are illegal *per se*. Such practices violate Section 1 of the Act, and the law has generally been enforced against them without investigation or regard for their effects.

Section 2 of the Sherman Act provides no *per se* illegality. Cases brought under Section 2 require that all circumstances be examined and in particular that their effect on competition always be part of the inquiry.

The use of the word *every* in the Sherman Act implies that all contracts and agreements among firms are illegal. This was not the intent of Congress, but not until 1911 was the famous "rule of reason" applied. Two historically important cases—Standard Oil Co. versus United States and American Tobacco Company versus United States—were decided by the United States Supreme Court and these gave rise to the rule of reason with respect to restraint of trade.[4] As a result every contract or agreement among businesses is *not* illegal. Only unreasonable agreements that restrain trade are now held illegal; reasonable agreements do not involve restraint. The acceptance of the rule-of-reason doctrine has compounded much of the confusion and controversy which have characterized the Act since its inception.

Examples of recent violations of the Sherman Act are summarized in Boxes 10-1 and 10-2. Perhaps the most shocking recent violation of Section 1 of the Sherman Act is what has become known as the "electrical conspiracy." American industry was apprised of one of the most clandestine antitrust violations as the facts and devices of the conspiracy were exposed in the press. Box 10-1 summarizes the essential aspects of the case.[5]

---

[3] Except vertical price agreements permitted by the Miller-Tydings Act and McGuire Act in those states with resale price maintenance laws. These agreements are commonly referred to as "fair trade" agreements. See pp. 196–197.

[4] Standard Oil Company of New Jersey Versus United States (1911), and American Tobacco Company Versus United States 221 U.S. 106, (1911).

[5] For a detailed account, see Richard Austin Smith, "The Incredible Electrical Conspiracy," *Fortune*, Part I, April 1961; Part II, May 1961.

BOX 10-1

The Electrical Conspiracy, a Violation of Section 1, Sherman Act

In February 1960 a federal grand jury in Philadelphia indicted 14 electrical equipment manufacturers and 18 individuals on charges of price fixing. Later in the year additional indictments brought the total number of companies charged to 29 firms and 53 individuals. In effect, this represented virtually the entire electrical equipment industry.

Among the indicted companies were: Westinghouse Electric Corp., General Electric Co., Allis-Chalmers Manufacturing Co., I-T-E Circuit Breaker Co., Ohio Brass Co., McGraw-Edison Co., and other firms representing every type of power generation and distribution equipment.The indictments grew out of government charges that the industry rigged prices and doled out market shares among the 29 companies involved. General Electric, Westinghouse and Allis-Chalmers Manufacturing Corp. had by far the largest at stake in settlement of the government's charges. They along with others agreed to either plead guilty or nolo contendere (no contest) to almost all of the Justice Department's charges.[a]

The cost of being guilty of conspiracy charges can be high. Fines totaling about $2 million were imposed on the 29 companies and 45 of the individuals originally indicted. Individual executives paid fines of $2000 to $3000, but one defendant was fined $12,500. Judge Ganey, for the first time in the history of the Sherman Act, imposed prison sentences of thirty days on seven corporate officials. Additionally, the defendant companies faced more than 1800 damage suits brought by customers. The guilty pleas by defendants opened the way for damages three times the value of the overcharge. It was estimated that for General Electric alone the settlements with customers would exceed $160 million.[b]

[a] SOURCE: *Business Week*, December 3, 1960, pp. 32–34 and January 28, 1961, p. 35.
[b] SOURCE: *The Wall Street Journal*, April 30, 1964, p. 4.

Box 10-2 reveals a conspiracy of a different nature. This case arose from one of the more complex and subtle problems in marketing which has to do with manufacturer-distributor relations. Because of the value of good relations with distributors, there is a strong temptation to go to their aid when they request help. In many situations, however, the manufacturer places itself in legal jeopardy by doing so. This was the result in *United States versus General Motors,* in which the Supreme Court found a *per se* violation of the Sherman Act where General Motors cooperated with three Chevrolet dealer associations in stopping discount houses from selling new Chevrolets

BOX 10-2

United States versus General Motors Corporation et al.,
a Violation of Sec. 1 Sherman Act

*Boycott—Manufacturer and Dealer Cooperation—Automobile
Sales Through Discount Houses.*

An automobile manufacturer and three dealer associations unlawfully conspired to eliminate sales of cars through discount houses in the Los Angeles area and thereby eliminate discount houses as a class of competitors, in view of evidence that one association complained to the manufacturer about sales through discount houses, the manufacturer discussed the matter with every dealer and obtained from each a promise not to do business with discounters, the three associations created a joint investigating committee and jointly policed such promises, the associations supplied information to the manufacturer at its request so that it could bring dealers into line, and several dealers were induced to repurchase cars they had sold through discount houses and promised not to sell cars through discounters in the future. The elimination, by joint collaborative action, of the discount houses from access to the car market was a *per se* violation of the Sherman Act.

Findings of Conspiracy

These findings include the essentials of a conspiracy within § 1 of the Sherman Act: That in the summer of 1960 the Losor Chevrolet Dealers Association, "through some of its members," complained to General Motors personnel about sales through discounters (Finding 34); that at a Losor meeting in November 1960 the dealers there present agreed to embark on a letter-writing campaign directed at enlisting the aid of General Motors (Finding 35); that in December and January General Motors personnel discussed the matter with every Chevrolet dealer in the Los Angeles area and elicited from each a promise not to do business with the discounters (Finding 39); that representatives of the three associations of Chevrolet dealers met on December 15, 1960, and created a joint investigating committee (Finding 40); that the three associations then undertook jointly to police the agreements obtained from each of the dealers by General Motors; that the associations supplied information to General Motors for use by it in bringing wayward dealers into line, and that Chevrolet's O'Connor asked the associations to do so (Findings 41 and 42); that as a result of this collaborative effort, a number of Chevrolet dealers were induced to repurchase cars they had sold through discounters and to promise to abjure such sales in [the] future.

These findings by the trial judge compel the conclusion that a conspiracy to restrain trade was proved.

SOURCE: Reproduced by permission, Commerce Clearing House, Inc., Trade Regulation Reporter, 1966, p. 82,470, par. 71,750.

in the Los Angeles area. The Court referred to this case as a "classic conspiracy" and found it was a group boycott to protect GM franchised dealers from apparent price competition. One of the charges and the bases upon which the court concluded conspiracy are reproduced in Box 10-2.

The Federal Trade Commission Act

Passage of the Sherman Act did not end dissatisfaction with trusts, discriminatory practices, and other devices of monopolistic character. Before 1914 it became evident that the Sherman Act needed strengthening and improved enforcement. Powerful new combinations arose in steel, farm machinery, tin containers, and several other industries. In the national political campaign of 1912, trusts and monopoly again became a central issue. It was recognized that some agency would have to be established to strengthen enforcement of the law and adherence to it. In 1914 the Federal Trade Commission Act established a specialized administrative agency known as the Federal Trade Commission (FTC). The Commission was given broad powers over the enforcement of Section 5 of the Act, which declared "unfair methods of competition" illegal. Since its establishment the duties of the Commission have been broadened by amendments and subsequent legislation.

An important amendment to the Federal Trade Commission Act came in 1938 with passage of the Wheeler-Lea Act. Before, Section 5 of the FTC Act was concerned with the somewhat limiting and ambiguous phrase "unfair methods of competition." Adverse court rulings made it apparent that this phrase needed broader and more inclusive language to deal with the problem. The Wheeler-Lea Act thus amended Section 5, which now outlaws "unfair or deceptive acts or practices in commerce." The Commission was also given jurisdiction over false advertising of foods, drugs, cosmetics, and curative devices. The Wheeler-Lea Act further provides the Commission with power to restrain the dissemination of false advertising by means of injunctive proceedings.

Today the duties of the FTC are:

1. To promote free and fair competition in interstate commerce in the interest of the public through prevention of price-fixing agreements, boycotts, combinations in restraint of trade, other unfair methods of competition, and unfair or deceptive acts or practices (Federal Trade Commission Act, Section 5).

2. To safeguard the consuming public by preventing the dissemination of false or deceptive advertisements of food, drugs, cosmetics, and devices (Federal Trade Commission Act, Sections 12 to 15).

3. To prevent certain unlawful price and other discriminations, exclusive-dealing and tying contracts and arrangements, acquisitions of the stock of competitors, and interlocking directorates (Clayton Act, Sections 2, 3, 7, and 8).

4. To protect producers, manufacturers, distributors, and consumers from the unrevealed presence of substitutes and mixtures in manufactured wool products (Wool Products Labeling Act of 1939).

5. To supervise the registration and operation of associations of American exporters engaged solely in export trade (Export Trade Act).

6. To petition for the cancellation of the registrations of trademarks which were illegally registered or which have been used for purposes contrary to the intent of the Trade-Mark Act of 1946 (Lanham Trade-Mark Act).

7. To gather and make available to the Congress, the President, and the public, factual data concerning economic and business conditions as a basis for remedial legislation where needed, and for guidance and protection of the public (Federal Trade Commission Act, Section 6).

From the above it should be noted that the Commission is concerned not only with restraints of trade but also with deceptive practices which may injure competitors and mislead consumers. Insofar as marketing is concerned, the first four duties noted are of major significance.

The Clayton Act

To strengthen the Sherman Act further and strike down certain restraints of trade which persisted, the Clayton Act was passed in 1914. This Act attempted to make the law more specific with respect to restraints of trade and also sought to bar at incipiency the creation of trusts, conspiracies, and monopolies. The original Act outlawed price discrimination (Section 2), agreements by buyers not to deal in goods of other sellers (Section 3), intercorporate stockholdings (Section 7), and interlocking directorates. None of these provisions of the law was absolute, but they were forbidden where the effect "may be to substantially lessen competition or tend to create a monopoly in any line of commerce."

Section 2 of the original Act (later amended by the Robinson-Patman Act in 1936) forbade sellers to discriminate in price between different purchasers of commodities . . . where the effect of such discrimination may be to substantially lessen competition or tend to create a monopoly in any line of commerce: *Provided,* That nothing herein . . . shall prevent discrimination in price . . . on account of differences in the grade, quality, or quantity of the commodity sold, or that makes only due allowance for difference in the cost of selling or transportation, or discrimination in price in the same or different communities made in good faith to meet competition.[6]

Section 3 stands unamended and declares that "it shall be unlawful . . . to lease or make for sale or contract for sale of goods, wares, . . . supplies or other commodities . . . on the condition, agreement or understanding that the leasee or purchaser thereof shall not use or deal in the goods . . . of a competitor. . . ."[7]

Section 7 (later amended by the Celler-Kefauver Act of 1950) originally declared "that no corporation . . . shall acquire . . . the whole or any part

[6] 38 Stat. 730.
[7] *Ibid.*

of the stock or other share capital of another corporation . . . where the effect of such acquisition may be to substantially lessen competition . . . or tend to create a monopoly in any line of commerce."[8]

With passage of the Clayton Act the more general foundation established by the Sherman Act was supplemented and some of its shortcomings were overcome. The general terms of the Sherman Act led to problems of interpretation and dealt with monopoly after the fact. The more explicit Clayton Act was concerned with the *methods* through which monopoly was reached. Hence, the latter Act and its subsequent amendments, which will be seen in the discussion of the Robinson-Patman Act and the Celler-Kefauver Act, are designed to curb those activities which may tend to restrain trade, create monopoly, or both.

It should be noted that tying contracts and exclusive dealer arrangements, dealt with in Section 3, may enhance competition but may also be harmful to it. The reasoning behind this contention takes the following form:

> Modern production may necessitate the use of certain commodities in conjunction with others and may, as a means of protecting the manufacturer, justify the imposition of restrictions or conditions upon sale. As a consequence, tying contracts may even enhance competition. Similarly, exclusive-dealer arrangements may lead to economies of production or marketing, when they bring about a concentration of distribution that results in greater marketing efficiency. On the other hand, both devices may be used effectively to restrain competition or maintain monopoly. The purpose of the law was not to outlaw these business practices but only to prevent their use when the result would be substantially to lessen competition or to tend to create a monopoly in any line of commerce. It is the difficulty of drawing the line between the desirable and undesirable aspects that has rendered the enforcement of the law halting and uncertain.[9]

The Robinson-Patman Act

The Robinson-Patman Act completely revised Section 2 of the Clayton Act. The original section was intended to curb large manufacturers from price cutting in selected areas while leaving other market prices unaffected. This was a notorious practice of some of the early trusts and often resulted in elimination of smaller competitors. The attempts of the Clayton Act to deal adequately with this problem were disappointing. The courts had ruled against the Federal Trade Commission in a number of price-discrimination cases, and clarification of the law was needed.

Perhaps more influential in generating the need for additional antitrust legislation was the rapid growth of the corporate chain during the era from

---

[8] *Ibid.*
[9] Dudley F. Pegrum, *Public Regulation of Business*, (Homewood, Ill.: Richard D. Irwin, 1965, Revised Edition) p. 286.

the end of the First World War to the mid-1930s. Wholesalers and retailers across the nation faced powerful competition and lower prices. The lower prices of the mass distributors were in part attributed to the lower prices paid to manufacturers and other market suppliers. The power of the large chains further enabled them to bargain for and receive concessions not usually granted to smaller independent buyers. Brokerage allowances, even where a broker was not employed, were demanded, and there were bargaining for advertising and other concessions out of proportion to the quantities purchased. Because of the substantial proportion of a manufacturer's output sold by chain stores, manufacturers were placed in a vunerable position if they refused to yield to these demands.

The Robinson-Patman Act was designed to provide equality of opportunity for buyers. In attempting to accomplish this end, Section 2 of the Act amended Section 2 of the Clayton Act. It now reads in part "that it shall be unlawful for any person engaged in commerce . . . to discriminate in price between different purchasers of commodities of like grade and quality . . . where the effect of such discrimination may be substantially to lessen competition or tend to create a monopoly in any line of commerce, or to injure, destroy, or prevent competition with any person who either grants or knowingly receives the benefit of such discrimination, or with customers of cither of them. . . ." The broadening of the Act was achieved by inclusion of the words "prevent competition with any person."

The same section permits price differentials, as did the Clayton Act, provided the differences are made for "only due allowance in the cost of manufacture, sale or delivery resulting from differing methods or quantities." The Federal Trade Commission is empowered to fix and establish quantity limits, and to adjust them where purchasers of greater quantities are so few as to discriminate unjustly or promote monopoly. In other words, quantity discounts, even though allowable by the seller's cost savings, could be limited if large-scale marketers were given an undue advantage. Section 2 further provides for "price changes from time to time . . . in response to changing conditions affecting the market."[10]

The amount of leeway a seller has to adapt prices to changing market conditions is most difficult to determine. The burden of proof that there has been no discrimination rests with the seller charged with violating the Act. Of course, a seller may argue that a price was lowered in good faith to meet competition. Whether this is an adequate defense remains for the FTC and the courts to decide. Much controversy about the Act revolves around this unsettled issue.

The law also forbids other concessions which often have been used to cloak

[10] 49 Stat. 1526

price discrimination. It outlaws brokerage and other compensations by stating, "It shall be unlawful . . . to pay or grant, or to receive or accept, anything of value as a commission, brokerage, or other compensation . . . except for services rendered in connection with the sale or purchase of goods, wares, or merchandise." If a seller offers anything of value to a customer, such payment or compensation must be "available on proportionally equal terms to all other customers competing in the distribution of such products or commodities."[11]

Section 3 of the Robinson-Patman Act forbids any transaction which discriminates against the buyer's competitors by means of any discount, rebate, allowance, or advertising benefit which is greater than that available to them. This section also forbids sales in one locality at prices lower than those in other localities when the purpose is to destroy competition. Finally, it forbids prices at unreasonably low levels for the purpose of ending competition or eliminating a competitor.

From a marketing standpoint the Robinson-Patman Act is perhaps the most important single piece of legislation of its type. It should be noted that it endeavors only to establish standards of competition. Any attempt to measure discrimination or the lack of it by cost standards is extremely difficult. The Act has been criticized for failing to do so, since it can be argued that it imposes restrictions on large-scale producers at the expense of consumers. This, of course, assumes that economies of scale which produce lower costs are passed on to the consumer through the distributive process.

Of interest is a recent ruling of the Supreme Court of the United States in the case of the Federal Trade Commission versus the Borden Company. The decision summarized in Box 10-3 was originally brought by the FTC on a charge of price discrimination between customers of the Borden national brand and the company's private brand.

The Celler-Kefauver Act

Section 7 of the Clayton Act was amended in 1950 by the Celler-Kefauver Act.[12] The inability of the original law to meet competitive problems stemming from mergers and acquisitions led to its passage. The now broader Section 7 reads in part: "That no corporation engaged in commerce shall acquire directly or indirectly, the whole or any part of the stock or other share capital and no corporation subject to the jurisdiction of the Federal Trade Commission shall acquire the whole or any part of the assets of another corporation engaged also in commerce, where in any line of commerce in any section of the country, the effect of such acquisition may be substantially to lessen competition, or to tend to create a monopoly."

[11] Ibid.
[12] 64 Stat. 1125

BOX 10-3

Federal Trade Commission versus the Borden Company,
a Violation of Section 2, Robinson-Patman Act

The United States Supreme Court has reversed a 5th Circuit Court of Appeals decision (which, in turn, had reversed a Federal Trade Commission ruling) to the effect that a product marketed under an extensively advertised and well-known brand of its manufacturer is not "of like grade and quality" with a physically identical commodity when packaged under a private brand.

In this case, involving national and private brands of evaporated milk, Borden was charged under section 2(a) of the Robinson-Patman Act with unlawfully discriminating in price between customers of its house brand and customers of its private label goods. In defense of the difference in price between the two classes of goods, Borden asserted that they were not "of like grade and quality" (a requirement under section 2(a) before discrimination can be found) because of the greater consumer demand that had been created for the house brand by extensive advertising. This argument was rejected by the Supreme Court on the ground that Congress intended that only chemical and physical properties of products be taken into consideration in determining "like grade and quality".

Unanswered by the decision is whether the difference in prices between the national and private brands was justified by cost differentials, and whether the price difference was potentially injurious to competition. These questions were referred back to the Court of Appeals for decision. In a dissenting opinion, two of the Supreme Court Justices stated that they thought it unlikely that economic differences could reasonably be taken into account in answering the remaining questions. Assuming that the cost justification and "injury to competition" questions would be answered unfavorably to The Borden Company, the dissenting Justices said that the result of the decision would be that: ". . . Borden must now make private label milk available to all customers of its premium brand [or] To avoid supplying a private label brand to a premium brand customer, Borden need only forego further sales of its premium brand to that customer."

source: Legal Bulletin, Association of National Advertisers Inc., New York, April 1966.

This legislation is much more restrictive than the original Section 7. It has a wider objective in that it applies to the lessening of competition in any line of commerce in any section of the country as well as between the corporation acquiring the stock and the one whose stock is acquired. It also was intended that mergers tending to lessen competition would be halted at incipiency.

Companies often seek to merge with other companies or acquire them outright for sound marketing reasons. The most common reason for merging appears to be for the purpose of diversifying product line or expanding existing lines with compatible products. The much discussed attempt of Proctor and Gamble to acquire the Clorox Chemical Company (maker of Clorox bleach) is related in Box 10-4. This case is unusual in that the merger was illegal by virtue of Proctor and Gamble's market power and the efficiency with which it develops markets.

BOX 10-4

Federal Trade Commission versus Procter and Gamble Company, a Violation of Section 7, Clayton Act and the Celler-Kefauver Act

[¶ 15,773] The Procter & Gamble Co.—Second initial order to cease and desist, Dkt. 6901.

For the second time, a Commission hearing examiner has ruled that the acquisition of The Clorox Chemical Co., Oakland, Calif., by The Procter & Gamble Co., Cincinnati, Ohio, is illegal, and issued an order which would require P & G to sell Clorox so as to restore it as a going concern.

P & G, the nation's leading producer of soap and detergent products, acquired Clorox, maker of "Clorox," the dominant brand of household liquid bleach, on August 1, 1957 through an exchange of stock valued at approximately $30 million. The FTC's complaint challenging the acquisition was filed on September 30 of that year. In an initial decision of June 17, 1960, the examiner had held the acquisition violates Section 7 of the Clayton Act, the Celler-Kefauver antimerger law, and issued an order of divestiture. The Commission subsequently remanded the case to the examiner for receipt of further evidence concerning the competitive impact of the acquisition, and further hearings were held before him last December 1 and 12 in Washington, D.C. [¶ 15,245, TRADE REGULATION REPORTER].

In this decision, the examiner again found that the acquisition is unlawful because its result "probably will be the substantial lessening of competition between the respondent-owned Clorox and the smaller manufacturers and distributors of household liquid bleach, in the United States, and the definite tendency to create a monopoly in" P & G in this industry.

This finding was based on the following factors, among others:

Clorox's dominant market position was increased as a result of the acquisition and the various advertising campaigns, sales promotion programs and devices subsequently employed by P & G;

P & G's financial and economic strength and advertising and promotional experience as compared with its competitors in the liquid bleach industry;

Its ability to command consumer acceptance of its products and to acquire and retain valuable shelf space in grocery stores because of its advertising and promotional experience and financial resources;

The increasing tendency of concentration of competitors in the industry;

FEDERAL LAWS AGAINST DECEPTIVE PRACTICES

Antitrust laws serve the public interest by maintaining competition. If competition is maintained, access to markets is open to all, prices reflect more closely the actual competitive and demand conditions of the market, and consumer welfare is indirectly served. It is not enough for the government to preclude restraints on competition, price fixing, and other unfair market

---

Clorox's ability, through aggressive P & G-inspired advertising and promotional methods, to prevent the entry of additional competitors into the industry, and to prevent existing competitors from expanding by normal methods of competition.

In addition, the examiner pointed out, according to the testimony of competitors, "there is an apparently well-founded fear on their part that the aggressive advertising and sales promotion methods of respondent P & G used by Clorox in the household liquid bleach industry will result in serious injury to their business. The evidence introduced at the recent hearings showing a decline in the market share of some of Clorox's smaller competitors, since the acquisition, indicates that such fear expressed by at least some of these competitors was, in fact, well-founded. . . . [T]he record indicates that it was not the policy of the Clorox Chemical Company, the acquired corporation, to meet the sales promotions or test marketing of its smaller competitors with aggressive counter-promotions and retaliatory tactics. It had attained its leading position in the household liquid bleach industry mainly by national advertising. However, the evidence indicates that it has been the policy of Clorox, since its acquisition by P & G, to meet, and meet vigorously, the promotions and test marketing of its competitors. . . . [T]hese retaliatory tactics have been used especially against Purex and Roman Cleanser, the second and third largest household liquid bleach manufacturers in the industry."

The deciding factor in concluding that the acquisition may substantially lessen competition and tend toward monopoly, the examiner said, is the ability of P & G's "conglomerate organization to shift financial resources and competitive strength through a broad front of different products and markets and its ability to strategically alter the selected point of greatest impact as time, place and market conditions require. It is not necessary that the conglomerate enjoy a predominate position in any industry or market, although in this particular case Procter & Gamble does enjoy such a position in the soap and detergent industry. The test of conglomerate power is whether a corporation is able to concentrate its competitive efforts at one point by shifting its financial resources and competitive strength from one industry or market to another. Procter & Gamble possesses this power and ability."

SOURCE: Reproduced by permission, Commerce Clearing House, Inc., Trade Regulation Reporter, 1962, p. 20,582, par. 15,773.

practices. It must do more. Fraud and deception in the marketplace have always been practiced by the unscrupulous few to the disadvantage of the consumer. Business and industrial buyers are in a much better position than the consumer to avoid deception; skilled purchasing agents who have objective information, set specifications on quality and performance, and test products in their laboratories can make sure that a product meets the business or industrial need. Consumers, on the other hand, do not have the skills of purchasing agents and more often than not cannot develop them in view of the variety, complexity, and abundance of things in the market. It is only the rare individual who feels that he can judge quality and performance to say nothing of meeting his socio-psychological needs with the purchase of a product. Hence, the government must protect the consumer against deception.

The purpose of the federal laws designed to prevent fraud and deception is twofold. First, the laws protect the scrupulous businessman from unscrupulous rivals. Fraud and deception do not usually create monopolistic conditions, but they are dangerous in that an entire industry may be forced into the worst forms of competition rather than being able to attain the most ethical. Second, the laws protect the consumer from the unscrupulous behavior of businessmen. They protect him in part from the following practices.

1. False and deceptive advertising.
2. Unfair methods of competition.
3. Deceptive product contents in alcohol, fur, wool, and textile products.
4. Contaminated, unclean, and injurious products produced for human consumption.
5. Hazardous substances which without warning may cause personal injury or death.

In addition, standard weights and measures and standardized container sizes serve the public interest. In some instances standard grades of products have been established by law. Whereas the Constitution gives Congress the power to establish standard weights and measures, the Congress has not taken full responsibility for them. The states have been active in enacting and enforcing laws and in supervising established specifications. For example, gasoline pumps, scales, and dispensers of food and drink are usually inspected by state agencies.

The Origin and Demand for Consumer Protection

For almost a century the federal government has undertaken laws to protect the consumer. Since 1872, the use of the mails to defraud has been unlawful. Much of the need for laws stemmed originally from the development of canned foods, the growth of the patent medicine field, and the lack of standards in the processing of meat products and other consumable items.

By 1880 it became apparent that some laws would have to be enacted to guard the public against harmful substances used to preserve canned food, habit-forming and dangerous drugs used in medicines, and the filth found in meat-packing plants. The public became aroused by Upton Sinclair's book *The Jungle*, which described the conditions and diseased meat products in Chicago packing plants. Government scientists took the initiative in uncovering contaminated food and substances used in products which were harmful to the person if used on his body or consumed. A series of articles in *Collier's* magazine exposed the drug business. Women's clubs, political groups, and others became aroused and organized drives for legislation. As a result the Pure Food and Drug Act of 1906 was passed. In 1927, much impetus for additional and stronger legislation came from the publication of *Your Money's Worth* by Stuart Chase and F. J. Schlink. During this century numerous bills have been proposed calling for regulation.[13] Among those which have been passed are the following.

1. The Pure Food and Drug Act, 1906, which outlawed adulterated and misbranded foods and drugs sold in interstate commerce.

2. The Federal Trade Commission Act of 1914, amended and strengthened by the Wheeler-Lea Act in 1938 which outlawed unfair methods of competition and unfair or deceptive practices. The latter Act also forbids the dissemination of false advertising of foods, drugs, cosmetics, and devices.

3. The Tariff Act of 1930, which requires that imported articles or their containers clearly indicate the country of origin.

4. The Federal Alcohol Administration Act of 1935, which forbids commercial bribery, misleading advertising, and deceptive labeling of alcoholic beverages.

5. The Food, Drug, and Cosmetic Act of 1938, which strengthened and broadened the Pure Food and Drug Act of 1906. This Act gave the Food and Drug Administration authority over problems of contamination, filth, and those compounds and preparatory substances which might be injurious to health. The Administration was enpowered to set standards for canned foods in respect to quality, conditions of the contents, and fill. The law extended the scope of products to include cosmetics and therapeutic devices. It forbade cosmetics that may be injurious, false and misleading labels, and deceptive containers. It also provided that labels of such products must give adequate warnings of irritation and injury.

6. The Wool Products Labeling Act of 1939, which requires full disclosure of the percentages of new wool, reprocessed wool, and other fibers or fillers used. Such information must be shown on the labels of products containing wool, except carpets, rugs, and some other textile items.

7. The Fur Products Labeling Act of 1951, which requires labels that fully disclose whether the fur is new or used, from what part of the animal the fur derives, and whether the fur is bleached or dyed. The FTC, after hearings concerning the confusion and problems of the trade, issued a Fur Products Name Guide.

---

[3]For a more detailed account see Clair Wilcox, *Public Policies Toward Business.* Homewood, Ill.: Richard D. Irwin, 1966) Chapter 24, pp. 579–609.

8. The Federal Aviation Act of 1958, which forbids carriers to enter into unfair or deceptive practices including misleading advertising.

9. The Automobile Information Disclosure Act of 1958, which requires auto manufacturers to post the suggested retail price, detailing the price of all extra equipment and transportation charges on all new passenger vehicles. This law was designed to stop dealers from inflating the price of a new auto so as to misrepresent the true value of the customer's trade-in. (Few people had any idea as to the suggested retail price of new autos prior to the passage of this law.)

10. The Hazardous Substances Labeling Act of 1960, which empowered the Food and Drug Administration to require all household products which contain hazardous substances to give warnings on the labels. Products such as household cleaning agents, paint and varnish removers, and pressurized containers are a few of the products which may cause injury because of toxic, corrosive, or highly flammable substances.

From the listing it is apparent that several government agencies are assigned the task of protecting the consumer. The Food and Drug Administration has been empowered with a comprehensive set of responsibilities which range from problems of mislabeling to the use of agents which chemically may cause injury or even death. The FDA cooperates with the Department of Agriculture, the Public Health Service, and any other agency which can be of assistance in examining business claims, product composition, and any additives which might be harmful to the user. In recent years the use of pesticides has come under attack with the publication of Rachel Carson's book *The Silent Spring*. The FDA and the Department of Agriculture have been watchful of the long-run effects of the use of pesticides and herbicides, and unquestionably there will be tighter controls on their use in the future. Fish kills and the loss of wildlife by mass spraying is of major concern of the Public Health Service, the Department of Interior, the Department of Agriculture, and the FDA.

With few exceptions public health and safety are the direct responsibility of the agencies noted and in particular the Food and Drug Administration. On the other hand, the Federal Trade Commission concerns itself with protecting the public and business firms from false and deceptive practices and unfair methods of competition. Some idea of the work load which the Bureau of Deceptive Practices in the FTC faces may be obtained from noting its activities in the course of a year. The bureau reports more than 5000 outside complaints, more than 800 investigations, the review of 250,000 printed advertisements, and more than 500,000 radio and television commercials. Of the advertisements, it questions about 40,000, of which 500 may lead to some action. The range of practices attacked by the FTC is quite broad. The catalog of some actual FTC proceedings enumerated in Box 10-5 indicates the kinds of business practice that are suspect.

BOX 10-5

Selected Federal Trade Commission Proceedings Against Deceptive Practices

1. Misrepresentation in connection with the sale of vending machines.

2. Misrepresentations in the sale of a correspondence course in motel management.

3. Composition of candles misrepresentation.

4. Misrepresenting of a free-trial offer of vitamin capsules and refusal to concel orders for undelivered merchandise.

5. Fictitious representation of earnings from servicing candy vending machines.

6. Misrepresentation in the interstate sale of photographs and photographic albums.

7. Fictitious pricing of waterproof coatings and paint.

8. Selling and distributing lottery devices.

9. Misrepresentations in connection with the sale of encyclopedias.

10. Deceptive use of oriental names to describe domestic rugs.

11. Deception in the claimed therapeutic value of a drug preparation.

12. Price misrepresentations in the sale of prefabricated houses.

SOURCE: Annual Report of the Federal Trade Commission (Washington, D.C.: United States Government Printing Office, 1956), pp. 61–62.

LECISLATION IN THE STATES

In conjunction with the antitrust movement which brought about federal legislation, about one half of the states enacted their own laws against monopolies and trusts. These laws vary in detail, but in general they can be said to outlaw price discrimination, price fixing, division of markets, and other devices which may restrain trade. Although some states have enforced their antitrust laws, the overall assessment is that states have not engaged actively in attempting to prevent monopolistic practices. For all practical purposes antitrust has been a federal concern.

Some legislation, rather than being primarily directed toward maintaining competition, has often had the effect of limiting it. Most of the states have legalized resale price maintenance, as we shall see presently, and more than half of them have statutes prohibiting sales below cost which have the effect of assuring wholesalers and retailers a margin of profit. Certain products such as milk (especially in dairy states), gasoline, cigarettes, and alcoholic beverages are sold at prices regulated by some states. The purpose of this legislation has been the protection of the small independent retailer from the pricing tactics of the large integrated chain. Some products are also singled out and their sale is forbidden because of some special-interest group. The once widespread ban in the midwestern states on the sale of yellow oleomargarine is a case in point. Wisconsin, until 1967, discriminated against the sale of yellow oleomargarine by outright prohibition of its sale, whereas Minnesota has a per-pound tax on the product. The tax is earmarked for enhancement of the dairy industry. When, as some have done, states regulate the resale price of selected products (that is, by restricting the number and specifying the location of establishments), a true geographical monopoly exists. This results in an artificially high price paid by the consumer and a diminishment of his real income.

Resale-price Maintenance

Perhaps the most widespread and controversial kind of legislation adopted by the states is resale-price maintenance, or so-called fair trade. These laws permit manufacturers to set the resale price of branded products throughout their channels of distribution. Obviously, this is a vertical pricing arrangement and a circumvention of the Sherman Antitrust Act. For such activities to be legal, a federal statute amending the Sherman Act was enacted. The Miller-Tyding Act of 1937 became the first Act to amend the antitrust law directly so as to permit vertical price agreements. The Act simply legalized resale-price maintenance in interstate commerce and hence permitted manufacturers to enter into such agreements.

Resale-price maintenance had its origin during the Great Depression of the 1930s. Manufacturers sought to maintain their resale prices because some retailers were using well-known branded products as "price leaders" to build customer traffic. Manufacturers feared that many retailers would fail to "push" their products or that the distribution of their goods would become unprofitable if something was not done to stem the "price leader" tide. Some branded goods, particularly dentifrice goods, were commonly used in this way which tended to destroy retailer loyalty or even encouraged retailers to drop the item from their stocks. Manufacturers of well-known brands along with small independent retailers vigorously supported fair-trade legislation. To this day the retail druggists through their association (National Association of Retail Druggists) are perhaps most adamant in their support of such legislation.

The first of the resale-price-maintenance laws was passed in California in 1931. It soon became apparent that some device which bound all resellers to the stipulated price was necessary because those who did not sign price agreements undercut the price of those who had signed. Hence, the nonsigner clause was incorporated into state fair-trade statutes. The nonsigner clause bound those not party to a contract to the contract price. As a result the manufacturer would need only the signature of one retailer and one distributor in any state with a price-maintenance statute in order to fix the resale price, and this would then be binding on all resellers.

The need for amendment to the Sherman Act arose because most manufacturers do not sell their products solely in intrastate commerce. Because of the interstate implications and the fact that such agreements violated the Sherman Act, Congress enacted the Miller-Tydings Act which, as noted, provides for resale-price maintenance to be an exception to the antitrust law. As the states enacted their own fair-trade laws, they copied a model statute drafted by the National Association of Retail Druggists. In all, forty-six states adopted the essentials of the NARD model statute.

The nonsigner provision of the statutes ran into trouble in 1951 when the Supreme Court ruled in the cases of Schwegmann Brothers versus Calvert Corporation and Schwegmann Brothers versus Seagram Distillers Corporation. Schwegmann, a price-cutting nonsigner to a fair-trade contract in Louisana, had been sued by Calvert and Seagram. The case went to the Supreme Court, which ruled in favor of Schwegmann. The response to this decision was dramatic as nonsigners reduced prices on many branded goods in fair-trade states. This brought enactment of the McGuire Act in 1952, which extended the basic antitrust exemption and went farther to sanction nonsigner's clauses. The Federal Trade Commission, the Department of Justice, the American Bar Association, and organizations of labor and agriculture opposed the bill. It was enacted, however, with the help of the NARD and the American Fair Trade Council. Since passage of the McGuire Act the Supreme Court has either refused to review lower court decisions or has found the nonsigner clause in conformity with the Act.

Fair Trade has nevertheless been dealt some death blows in state courts. In all but about 22 states (of the original 46) resale price maintenance has been nullified either by rulings of unconstitutionality or by ruling the nonsigner's clause null and void. The fate of the state laws encouraged then Senator H. H. Humphrey (Minn.) and Senator William Proxmire (Wis.) to propose a Quality Stabilization Bill which in effect would be a federal fair-trade act. At this writing the bill has not had enough support to move beyond the confines of committee despite attempts to bring it to the Senate floor during several sessions of Congress.

An Evaluation of the Legal Framework

The federal and state laws pose a complex and often bewildering environment in which marketing operates. Some of the laws, it should be noted, came into being by virtue of either an assumed or a real impact of marketing behavior. That is, the antitrust laws resulted from observable competition and the injurious long-run effects of particular kinds of competitive behavior. Other laws, particularly those concerned with public health and safety, are the result of carelessness and disregard by some businesses of the consuming public.

Most economists agree that the antitrust laws have made important contributions to the maintenance of competition. Simon N. Whitney has stated that the laws have prevented cartelization of American industry along European lines; they have barred consolidations intended to enable firms to dominate their industries; and they have helped preserve freedom of entry and equality of opportunity.[14]

Edward S. Mason, another authority, views the antitrust laws as affecting business decisions; he states that "the consideration of whether a particular course of business action may or may not be in violation of the antitrust laws is a persistent factor affecting business judgment."[15]

Criticism of the antitrust laws does not usually ignore the laws as a positive force for maintaining competition; rather, it is directed at problems of interpretation, the apparent view of the courts that bigness is evil *per se*, and the inability of the laws to reflect adequately a changing competitive structure and the attendant competitive devices.

At this writing, protection of the consumer from fraud, deception, and misrepresentation is by no means a dead issue. Commencing with the late President Kennedy's administration, a Consumer-Advisory Council was established for the purpose of promoting consumer interest. The council has been urging the President and Congress to extend consumer protection further by enacting the Hart Truth-in-Packaging Bill (S. 387) and the Douglas Truth-in-Lending Bill (S. 750). A modified bill was enacted in 1966. There is no question that government interest in the consumer will take on increased dimensions. One might question, however, whether existing federal and state statutes are not adequate, if enforced.

Questions

1. Discuss the tie-in between operation of the marketing system and some laws which are essentially nonmarketing laws.
2. How far should government go in regulating marketing? Who should decide? Who does decide?

[14] Simon N. Whitney, *Antitrust Policies*, (New York: Twentieth Century Fund, 1958), Vol. II, p. 429.
[15] Edward S. Mason "The Effectiveness of the Federal Antitrust Laws: A Symposium", *American Economic Review*, Vol. 39 (1949), p. 713.

3. What kinds of legal issues can you visualize will become important issues in the next decade? Can these be detected ahead of time? What should marketing do about legal trends?
4. What kind of competition is government trying to preserve?
5. Does Adam Smith's "invisible hand" no longer function in the United States?

Statements to Consider

Trade regulation is a necessary concomitant of the free-enterprise system, to assure the maintenance of free and effective competition.

Where certain conditions of demand and supply are present, business firms realize that unless they act to try to control prices, their profits are likely to suffer.

The fact that prices are identical in itself proves nothing about price fixing.

In general, the law remains a secondary consideration as compared with demand, competition, cost and the structure of distribution.

The large body of law affecting marketing decisions has been enacted to insure that company behavior is consistent with "public interest," which is identified with protecting the buyer from the seller, the seller from the buyer, and one competitor from another.

Too much competition may not be good for the consumer.

SELECTED REFERENCES

Marshall C. Howard, *Legal Aspects of Marketing* (New York: McGraw-Hill Book Company, 1964).

Dudley F. Pegrum, *Public Regulation of Business* (Homewood, Ill.: Richard D. Irwin, 1965).

Charles F. Phillips, Jr., *The Economics of Regulation* (Homewood, Ill.: Richard D. Irwin, 1965).

Irwin M. Stelzer, *Selected Antitrust Cases: Landmark Decisions*, Rev. Ed. (Homewood, Ill.: Richard D. Irwin, 1966).

Clair Wilcox *Public Policies Toward Business*, Rev. Ed. (Homewood, Ill.: Richard D. Irwin, 1966).

M. A. Adelman, "Effective Competition and the Antitrust Laws," *Harvard Law Review*, Vol. 61, No. 8, September 1948, pp. 1289–1350.

° William F. Brown, "The Protection of the Consumer and Competition, Some Fundamental Issues," in George L. Baker, Jr., (ed.), *Effective Marketing Coordination*, Proceedings of the 44th National Conference of the American Marketing Association, June 1961, pp. 426–438.

° Earl W. Kintner, "How Much Control Can Business Endure?" *Journal of Marketing*, Vol. 25, No. 5, July 1961, pp. 1–6.

° W. David Robbins, "A Marketing Appraisal of the Robinson-Patman Act," *Journal of Marketing*, Vol. 24, No. 1, July 1959, pp. 15–21.

° Select Committee on Small Business, "The Nature and Background of the Fair Trade Problem," Report of the Select Committee on Small Business, United States Congress, House Report No. 1292, 82nd Congress, 2nd Session, 1952, pp. 3–15.

° Small Business Administration, "Trade Regulation and Small Business," from *Small Marketers Aids* (Washington, D.C.: Small Business Administration, June 1961), No. 67.

Generalizations Were Taken From:

Marshall C. Howard, *Legal Aspects of Marketing* (New York: McGraw-Hill Book Company, 1964).

John A. Howard, *Marketing Management: Analysis and Planning* (Homewood, Ill.: Richard D. Irwin, 1963).

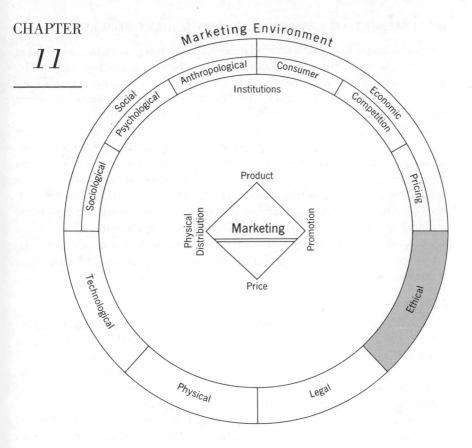

The Ethical Dimension in Marketing

The Issues   *Ethics Today—A Gray Area* • CONTEMPORARY ATTACKS ON MARKETING
A Criticism of the Economic Order   *Criticisms of Advertising and Selling*   *Criticisms of Products*
Criticisms of Price • PRESSURES TOWARD UNETHICAL BEHAVIOR • CODES OF ETHICS

Ethical behavior in business is by no means a new topic; the ethical awakening and the developments since the mid-1950s are, however, another matter. The ethical and moral responsibilities of businessmen have become a major concern in many corners of business life. Hardly a major corporation, an active trade association, or a professional society has avoided either consideration or detailed exploration of the subject. Academicians from several disciplines have paid great attention to ethics in business, with the philosopher, sociologist, economist and, not the least, the marketing people all contributing much thought to the issue. The impetus for an examination of business ethics has not always come from within. Two opposing efforts operating almost simultaneously have exerted considerable influence. One has been the search for a moral philosophy by those engaged in business endeavor and the other has been the age-old attacks on business, regenerated by critics of the American scene who have been examining the practices, policies, and judgments of the business community.

The issues

What, if anything, is the relationship of marketing to ethics in business? No comprehensive discussion of ethics in business can avoid an evaluation of American marketing methods and, more specifically, the ethics of certain marketing practices. Much marketing activity occurs before the eye of the public. It is directed to masses of people with the result that it is openly judged, sometimes harshly, by numerous thinking persons.

Some argue that marketing influences and even creates social values. If this argument holds, it follows that it is desirable for business to take into account the kinds of social values created and those violated. There are those, however, who take the opposite position. They maintain that business is not the guardian of social values and that marketing plays little part in shaping them. Some marketing scholars, along with some businessmen, support this concept and contend that American marketing activity merely reflects society's norms. Carried to the extreme, this posture would seem to support the thesis that we should be free to employ *any* marketing technique which the public will accept in buying goods.

A somewhat subtler point concerns the fact that human beings spend most of their waking hours in some form of economic endeavor. Professor J. M. Clark said many years ago, "The individual is so molded in body, mind, and character by his economic activities and relations, stimuli and disabilities, freedoms and servitudes, that industry can truly be said to make the men and women who work in it, no less truly than the commodities it turns out for the market."[1] The products of our system, therefore, are not only goods and

---

[1] J. M. Clark, *Social Control of Business*, 1st Ed. (Chicago: University of Chicago Press, 1926), p. 47.

services but also the character of the people working in it. Marketing, like all other forms of economic activity, requires human endeavor. Every activity of marketing is designed and operated by someone. It goes without saying that what a person is asked to do may either contribute to or detract from his character. The marketing person guilty of false or misleading statements to his customers is a very different person from the one who honestly represents his products. Professor Clark's statement requires that businessmen not corrupt the integrity of the individual by asking him to perpetrate falsehoods.

There are perhaps few persons who on occasion have not found something objectionable about a product, marketing effort, or tactic. This is the basis for the oft-heard statement, "There ought to be a law." As noted in Chapter 10, legislation and legal remedy have frequently stemmed from some form of unscrupulous behavior which ignored its effects on competition or consumer welfare. The alternative to ethical behavior is unquestionably legal restraint. If businesses, and especially marketers, value freedom, as they so often protest, it behooves them to consider the ethical aspects of their operation.

The following, then, are the central issues as to why marketing ethics are worthy of consideration.

1. In all likelihood, the dominant belief is that marketing does influence social values.
2. The individual's character and integrity are influenced by the nature and character of his economic endeavor.
3. The alternative to ethical marketing behavior has been public policies which restrain the unscrupulous. Existing marketing practices which may be unethical or even obnoxious are likely to be eyed by government agencies and Congressional committees with an aim toward more public control of business.

Ethics Today—A Gray Area

Ethical problems are often compounded by the uncertainty and vagueness which surround ethical versus unethical activity. Ethics, in contrast to law, has no norms, and ethical values are not clearly set forth. Those of us who may judge an activity as ethical or unethical will find little agreement on some of today's specific issues. The origin, nature, and strength of our personal values are so diverse that it is difficult to discover what constitutes agreement.

Years ago, the problem of what was ethical and what was unethical was less complex and indeterminate. The issues that led to enactment of the antitrust laws and laws that protect society from fraud, deception, and impurities in products are no longer of cardinal concern insofar as ethics are concerned. Business in support of legislation, Better Business Bureaus, industry codes, self-policing, and the like have diminished the occurrences of the inhumane, the vulgar, the dishonest, and injurious devices. Howard R. Bowen (now President, University of Iowa) enumerated a host of accomplishments of American business, all of which testify to the businessman's keener sense of ethical behavior and awareness of social responsibility.[2] These are in part itemized in Box 11-1. In addition to that itemization, Bowen noted accomplishments in discrimination among workers, the recognition of unions, the respect for workers, and other important ethical and social gains. Even advertising, which receives the brunt of much criticism, is not perpetrating outright falsehoods as it once did. A not entirely isolated example of a nineteenth-century advertisement read:

I CURE FITS

When I say cure, I do not mean merely to stop them for a time and then have them return again. I mean a radical cure. I have made the disease of FITS, EPILEPSY or FALLING SICKNESS a life-long study. I warrant my remedy to cure the worst cases. Because others have failed is no reason for not now receiving a cure. Send at once for a treatise and a Free Bottle of my infallible remedy. Give Express and Post Office. H. G. Root, M. C., 183 Pearl St., New York.[3]

[2] Howard R. Bowen, *Social Responsibilities of Businessmen*, (New York: Harper & Brothers, 1953), pp. 69–70.
[3] S. Watson Dunn, *Advertising, Its Role in Modern Marketing*, (New York: Holt, Rinehart and Winston, 1961), p. 74.

BOX 11-1

Ethical and Social Accomplishments of American Business

1. Many companies have deliberately held prices below the market level during the postwar inflation . . . .

2. Many businesses have worked out effective codes of ethics designed to improve their business practices . . . .

3. Great progress has occurred in overcoming misrepresentation and adulteration of products, short weights . . . . Better Business Bureaus, Chambers of Commerce, and other voluntary agencies have carried on effective work in this field.

4. Secrecy in business has given way to fuller reporting and accounting to workers and the public.

5. Companies have tried to avoid speculative accumulation of inventories.

6. Practices in the field of consumer credit, insurance . . . have been greatly improved.

SOURCE: Howard R. Bowen, *Social Responsibilities of Businessmen*, (New York: Harper & Brothers, 1953), pp. 69–70.

The great strides that have been made in improving the ethical and moral plane of business contribute vagueness to the right and wrong of an issue. Whereas the nineteenth-century problems were clearly black and white or right and wrong, contemporary ethical problems are much subtler. The subtlety of issues, then, makes it even more difficult to reach agreement among those debating the ethics and moral responsibility in marketing activity.

CONTEMPORARY ATTACKS ON MARKETING

If marketing were no more than the selling of goods and services, it would not receive attention from those in other disciplines. Because its impact has broad social, political, economic, and philosophic importance, it has attracted attention and criticism from many sources. Traders and merchandisers have never been held in high esteem. Many early philosophers, religious leaders, and economists leveled attacks against business in general and marketing activities in particular. The content of early criticisms is not wholly germane to contemporary problems except to note a long tradition of charges against business activity.

Any modern marketing system populated by millions of manufacturers, wholesalers, and retailers and supplying millions of customers is certain to generate criticism. The attacks on marketing range from the kind of economic order it creates to specific charges against advertising, pricing, and product characteristics. The critics of the critics sometimes reply that the attacks lack logic, are highly emotional and hence unsound, or that the originator of the attack (that is, from a nonbusiness discipline) does not understand the complex ramifications of business life. Another common method of dealing with a critic is to contend that the ends justify the means. For example, many advertising men defend themselves on the grounds that they are promoting economic growth. Whatever the approach, defenses have done little to still critical voices.

Evidence that something is *wrong* and that some marketing is not conducted on a high ethical plane was gathered from business executives themselves in a recent study. The study, conducted at the Harvard Graduate School of Business Administration, among other things included a question concerning practices which the respondents would like to see eliminated. Figure 11-1 summarizes these practices. It is clearly evident that items 1 through 6 involve marketing. The same respondents felt that industry self-regulation would contribute to the elimination of such practices.[4] In the long run, of

---

[4] Raymond C. Baumhart, "How Ethical Are Businessmen?" *Harvard Business Review*, Vol. 39 No. 4, July–August 1961, p. 160.

Figure 11-1. The business practices executives would like to see eliminated

Unethical Practices Executives Want to Eliminate	Percent of Total Specifying the Practice
1. Gifts, gratuities, bribes, and "call girls"	23
2. Price discrimination, unfair pricing	18
3. Dishonest advertising	14
4. Miscellaneous unfair competitive practices	10
5. Cheating customers, unfair credit practices, overselling	9
6. Price collusion by competitors	8
7. Dishonesty in making or keeping a contract	7
8. Unfairness to employees, prejudice in hiring	6
9. Other	5
	100 $n = 1531$

SOURCE: Raymond C. Baumhart, "How Ethical Are Businessmen?" *Harvard Business Review*, Vol. 39, No. 4, July–August 1961, p. 160.

course, if industries are not effective in policing themselves public policy will.

A Criticism of the Economic Order

Perhaps the best-known contemporary criticism of our economy's excesses is John Kenneth Galbraith's book, *The Affluent Society*. Galbraith sees a social imbalance in our system because the wealth of privately produced goods has caused a crisis in the supply of public services. One of his more caustic comments is the following.

The family which takes its mauve and cerise, air-conditioned, power-steered, and power-braked automobile out for a tour passes through cities that are badly paved, made hideous by litter, blighted buildings, billboards, and posts for wires that should long since have been put underground. They pass on into a countryside that has been rendered largely invisible by commercial art. (The goods which the latter advertise have an absolute priority in our value system. Such aesthetic considerations as a view of the countryside accordingly come second. On such matters we are consistent.) They picnic on exquisitely packaged food from a portable icebox by a polluted stream and go on to spend the night at a park which is a menace to public health and morals. Just before dozing off on an air mattress, beneath a nylon tent, amid the stench of decaying refuse, they may reflect vaguely on the curious unevenness of their blessings. Is this, indeed, the American genius?[5]

[5] John Kenneth Galbraith, *The Affluent Society* (Boston: Houghton Mifflin Co., 1958), pp. 199–200.

Rather than concentrate our resources on private satisfactions, Galbraith argues that a society would be as well regarded by allocating more resources to schools, better parks, and other public service. This, he contends, would maximize our satisfactions more readily than the buying of bigger automobiles.[6]

Critics of excessive materialism have generally argued that industrial civilization is not good because it inverts social values. As a consequence the only values of prime order are materialistic and in turn, material gain rather than moral values becomes the sole motivating force. J. P. Marquand's *Point of No Return*, R. H. Towney's *The Acquisitive Society*, Aldous Huxley's *Brave New World*, and a host of other books were forerunners of Galbraith, and they all developed a thesis concerned with excessive materialism. Not so impressive nor scholarly a critic is Vance Packard, whose well-known works carry the theme that society subverts moral values for social approval. His attacks, especially directed toward advertising, are regarded as gross exaggerations of isolated instances.

Criticisms of Advertising and Selling

The most widespread and persistent attacks are made against advertising. To a lesser degree, personal selling is also a target. One of the subtlest criticisms of advertising and selling was developed by Howard R. Bowen in his book, *Social Responsibilities of the Businessman*. Rather than pass judgment on a series of delicate issues, he merely asked some relevant questions about whether the businessman ought to engage in specified kinds of advertising and selling. Some of the questions he raised are the following.[7]

1. Should he conduct selling in ways that intrude on the privacy of people . . . ?
2. Should he employ "high pressure" tactics in persuading people to buy?
3. Should he try . . . to make people dissatisfied with what they have?
4. Should he emphasize sex in his advertising appeals?
5. Should he attempt to set himself up as the arbiter of good taste and "proper" living standards through his advertising and selling activities?

The reader will find these questions difficult to reconcile and, of course, responses will differ depending on the role assumed for businessmen in shaping or responding to consumer demand.

Vance Packard,[8] although he seems to attribute too much power to advertising, is the angriest of contemporary critics. A few of his selected remarks provide a perspective of his position.

[6] *Ibid.* See pp. 200–204 for a more complete discussion.
[7] Howard R. Bowen, *op. cit.*, pp. 214–215.
[8] Author of *The Hidden Persuaders*, *The Status Seekers*, and *The Waste Makers*.

They [admen] have . . . become major wielders of social control in America . . . .
About 40 percent of the things we buy . . . are unnecessary . . . .
We [are] persuaded that the old product has become hopelessly inadequate to meet our needs . . . . Advertising men call this "creating psychological obsolescence."[9]

Among other practices he abhors are "appeals designed to play upon our hidden weaknesses. Strategies involving the manipulation of children. The deliberate sale of products for their status enhancement values" and "the exploitation of our deepest sexual sensitivities."

A quite different criticism of advertising is that it damages the concept of consumer sovereignty and hence destroys the theoretical basis of the free-enterprise system. For example, one critic says:

Practitioners of advertising have eaten the fruit of a new tree of knowledge. Many today openly proclaim their objective to be appeals to the irrational or the irrelevant. Even those who have paid out the highest fees to motivational researchers, though, have not actually intended thereby to destroy the theoretical basis of a free enterprise system. These very same advertisers who hold that sales appeals must be irrational point in the next breath to those sales as "votes for advertised goods"—as public acclaim of their efforts. They cannot have it both ways. If sales must be achieved through irrational means, then those sales are the empty votes of a disenfranchised electorate and merely represent consumer manipulation. . . . In the absence of rationality in purchase, consumer sovereignty becomes a meaningless concept.[10]

Another area closely allied to advertising and selling is packaging. The problem of subtle deception and misrepresentation in packaging has occupied the attention of a United States Senate subcommittee headed by Senator Philip Hart. Hearings since 1960 have exposed what is purported to be widespread defrauding of the American housewife. At this writing Congress had under consideration and after much debate passed a truth-in-packaging bill. Some of the practices which the bill will either outlaw or modify are the following.

1. Inconspicuous, hard-to-read statements of quantity.
2. Manufacturers' "cents-off" promotions when there is no assurance that the savings will be passed on to the shopper.
3. Designations such as "giant pint" and "king size."
4. Fractional ounces which make it difficult if not impossible for the shopper to compare.

---

[9] Vance Packard, "The Growing Power of Admen," *Atlantic*, Vol. 200, No. 3, September 1957, pp. 55–59. Bracketed material inserted by the authors.
[10] Colston E. Warne, "Advertising—A Critic's View," *Journal of Marketing*, Vol. 26, No. 4, October 1962, pp. 11–12.

5. Boxes far larger than the food they contain.
6. Designations of how many servings are contained in the package.
7. Failure to list ingredients when this information is important.

Illustrative of at least one of these practices is Figure 11-2, which is based on an actual shopping trip. The data compare package sizes as to per-ounce cost. It is interesting to note that the largest sizes are not always the "best buy." Information of this kind has been responsible for much criticism of American packaging practices.

That there is irresponsibility in advertising and selling cannot be denied. Whether the irresponsibility is greater or less than in other sectors of industry is not ascertainable. Defenders of the critics point out that few American families would have any difficulty finding ways to spend their money whether advertising were increased or not. Some of advertising's supporters believe, however, that the attacks on advertising are based on a false assumption, namely, the assumed *power* of advertising. One of them contends: "This sense

Figure 11-2. The "best buy" (in terms of lowest cost per quart or ounce)

Product	Container Designation	Quantity	Price
Wisk	(none)	1 gal.	$2.69
		½ gal.	1.19— best buy
		1 qt.	0.69
Cheer	King size	5 lbs., 11 oz.	1.31
	Giant size	3 lbs., 5½ oz.	0.69—best buy
	Regular size	1 lb., 5¾ oz.	0.33
Ad	Home laundry size	20 lbs.	4.14
	Jumbo size	9 lbs., 13 oz.	1.99—best buy
	Giant size	3 lbs., 2 oz.	0.79
Dash	Home laundry size	20 lbs.	4.79—best buy
	Jumbo size	9 lbs., 13 oz.	2.39
	Giant size	3 lbs., 2½ oz.	0.79
Tide	Home laundry size	16 lbs., 1 oz.	3.98—best buy
	King size	5 lbs., 3¾ oz.	1.31
	Giant size	3 lbs., 1¼ oz.	0.79
	Regular size	1 lb., 4 oz.	0.33

of power is overdrawn. A more realistic view suggests that advertising is akin to casting in a stream when the fish are biting. It does not lure fish into hitherto uninhabited waters."[11] If one considers the realities of life, the proportion of luxury goods purchased by the average family is indeed small, and hence the actual influence of advertising may not be as great as generally believed.

As noted in Chapter 10, the unethical aspects of packaging could well be eliminated by the Federal Trade Commission or other responsible agencies under existing laws. United States Representative Catherine May (Washington) contends that only eleven complaints prompted the provisions of the Truth-in-Packaging bill.[12] On the other hand, it is a widely held belief that consumers are exploited. The AFL-CIO has given many pages in support of this belief in its publication *Agenda,* and the prospect is that more legislation will be forthcoming.

Criticisms of Products

The most persistent charge against products is "planned obsolescence." Planned obsolescence refers to frequent model changes as typified by the appliance and auto industries, and the frequency with which "new" and "improved" products displace the old.

One argument against product model changes is the increased costs which result from the retooling and other necessary technology. This in turn increases the price of the product, and the critic would argue that fewer people are afforded the opportunity to buy. Volkswagen, Maytag, and Rolls Royce exemplify products that permit several years of ownership without the owner feeling his possession is obsolete. Some manufacturers have built their advertising around consistent styling (Volkswagen and Maytag among them) with a message that tells of "hidden" product improvement. New features, product deficiencies, and more satisfactory performance are the implied advantages of the consistently styled product. Planned obsolescence is purported to be nothing more than a superficial redesign of products for the sole purpose of sales. The social and economic critic questions the motives of marketing men who would perpetuate this waste.

Vance Packard, in his third and most successful book, *The Waste Makers,* makes a broadside attack on what he terms "consumption for consumption's sake." The theme of his attack is summarized on the dust jacket. It reads in part:

---

[11]Clarence C. Walton, "Ethical Theory, Societal Expectations, and Marketing Practices," *The Social Responsibilities of Marketing,* Proceedings of the American Marketing Association, December 1961, ed. William D. Stevens.

[12]"Washington Consumer Aid is Deceptive Packaging," *Nation's Business,* Vol. 54, No. 5, May 1966, p. 54.

Consumption for consumption's sake—with no real relevance to the needs and desires of the citizens—is rapidly being exalted into a virtue in its own right, says Packard, one transcending those values that have been revered in the Western world throughout the ages. This is coming about, says Mr. Packard, through the capacity of America's productive system to produce more goods than we need, resulting in the increasingly frantic effort of industry, its promoters, marketers, and merchandisers, to persuade the buyer to waste more and more.

In *The Waste Makers*, Mr. Packard now demonstrates that persuasion and a desire for social upgrading are no longer enough to sell the surplus of products industry produces. Productivity is now being maintained by such strategies as "planned obsolescence," and in startling—and to many horrifying—detail, Packard now shows how *waste* has become a virtue and "product death" a watchword in American industry.

Though Mr. Packard has no quarrel with legitimate technological advancement, he seriously questions the morality and economic validity of a system that in order to exist depends upon artificially shortening the useful life of products. In his searching analysis and thorough airing of this hush-hush phase of industrial design and marketing, Mr. Packard gets to the heart of this new "philosophy of waste," tells who the waste makers are, and how they operate, what they do to us.[13]

One should recognize that Packard and other critics imply alternatives which are difficult to reconcile, let alone except. They also imply that all of us should be "economic man." This is an old, obsolete concept which was never known to exist. The serious reader may ask: Are we disposed to accept a lower standard of living given the diminishment of product change if there were less technological advancement? Is the apparent waste of resources more socially undesirable than unemployment? Is a centrally directed economy more acceptable than one which is market directed even though excesses do occur? Some readers may find the alternatives wholly unacceptable, others may not.[14]

Criticisms of Price

Price and price practices are perhaps the most esoteric of the several marketing functions. As a consequence, critics of pricing are less vocal and numerous than critics of other marketing activities. Business executives have, however, named price discrimination, unfair pricing, and price collusion as practices they would most like to see eliminated (see Box 11-1). The electrical conspiracy, referred to in Chapter 10, was not only illegal, it also represented

---

[13] Vance Packard, *The Waste Makers* (New York: David McKay Company, 1960).
[14] Adapted from J. Howard Westing and Gerald Albaum, *Modern Marketing Thought* (New York: The Macmillan Company, 1964).

a gross ethical violation. One of the defendants was reported to have rationalized the conspiracy as follows:

"One of the problems of business is what is normal practice, not what is the law," he said. "If it's normal practice, it's ethical—not legal, but ethical."

Bolstered by his own brand of ethics, this executive, even in the aftermath, felt no sense of guilt. His only reservation was that the conspiracy, once embarked upon, had gone too far; it was wrong to allocate business, he felt, but he still found nothing wrong about rigging prices because "the customer buys total value in which price is only one significant factor."[15]

Consumer criticism of price is generally leveled at rising prices during periods of apparent abundance. The housewife will usually charge that food prices rise because "those middlemen are raising prices for their own profit." Few realize that the pricing of food items is complex and often based on the scarcities or abundances which must be forecast by the price maker. The prices of canned food items, for example, fluctuate with estimates of the *quantity* and *quality* of the next crop. Too much rain, too little rain, hail, wind, and numerous other variables influence the quality of crops. Yet the housewife often reacts as though a single variable, the middlemen, influenced retail prices.

PRESSURES TOWARD UNETHICAL BEHAVIOR

For the casual observer the ability of a businessman to act ethically appears a simple matter. This is not the case. The whole system of American enterprise is geared to impel businessmen to greater efficiency and higher profits. Men themselves are measured in quantitative terms on "how much" the firm or activity grows with their actions. Men are not measured on the basis of their moral contributions to the business enterprise. Hence, they become caught up in a system which is characterized by an ethic foreign to and often lower than the ethics of man. There is always the temptation for the businessman to push harder even though there are infractions of the "rules of the game."

The character of competition and the degree of its intensity are keenly felt by every businessman. Generally, the more ethical competitors are placed in a position of electing lower profits or lower ethics. A case in point was reported before a Senate subcommittee in which one candy manufacturer had deceived his customers but increased his profits by redesigning the candy package. The new package, although of the same size, held less candy while

---

[15] Fred J. Cook, "The Corrupt Society," *The Nation*, Vol. 196, No. 22, June 1–8, 1963, p. 458.

selling for the same price. The unethical business was followed by its two closest competitors, who soon resorted to the same deception.

Advertising copy and television and radio commercials serve as similar examples of how the "super-superlatives," ballyhoo, bad taste, and emphasis on sex soon encompass an entire industry. Admen are also caught up in a competitive system in which, if they are to "succeed" quantitatively, they must excel the ad power of their competitors. It is no wonder that "jumbo size" impels "giant size," which in turn forces "king size," thence "economy size," and so on *ad nauseam*.

One other problem precludes complete honesty among businessmen. Although noted earlier, it deserves repeating. It is that the boundary between truth and deception is not easy to establish. For example, does ethical behavior require a marketer to tell about the bad as well as the good features of a product? This is a question that can be raised about any product which might cause injury or even death—for instance, power tools, electrical devices, automobiles, and power mowers. Is it ethical to perpetuate the belief that price denotes quality? In many instances this is a truism, but with aspirin it is well known to be a falsehood. Should a product be featured as superior when in fact it holds no superiority? These and numerous other questions cannot easily be resolved. They need careful consideration, perhaps even by each industry.

CODES OF ETHICS

Ethical codes are often mentioned as devices which will heighten the standard of conduct. Many individual businesses have formulated codes of good business practice. Industry groups and professional associations have given much time and effort to developing codes (see Box 11-2). The American Marketing Association has a Marketing Research Code of Ethics. The American Management Association has a Business Ethics Advisory Service which has gathered a large number of existing codes for use by businessmen. Box 11-3 is illustrative of a code in a somewhat controversial marketing area. Whether a code will enhance behavior is contingent on its content and the methods of enforcement. A few essentials appear necessary for an effective code. First, it must be specific and concrete rather than general. Second, the code should formulate standards which should be revised as economic, social, and marketing conditions change. Finally, for a code to be honored, some method of self-policing is needed.

Codes which incorporate the foregoing requisites can be helpful to a businessman. From such a code the traditions and accepted practices are recognized. They will often provide statements which are for the general good of the field of endeavor, and this can be in the public interest. A well-

BOX 11-2

Principles and Standards
of Purchasing Practice

ADVOCATED BY

National Association of
Purchasing Agents

LOYALTY TO HIS COMPANY

JUSTICE TO THOSE WITH WHOM HE DEALS

FAITH IN HIS PROFESSION

From these principles are derived the N. A. P. A.
standards of purchasing practice.

[1] To consider, first, the interests of his company in all transactions and to carry out and believe in its established policies.

[2] To be receptive to competent counsel from his colleagues and to be guided by such counsel without impairing the dignity and responsibility of his office.

[3] To buy without prejudice, seeking to obtain the maximum ultimate value for each dollar of expenditure.

[4] To strive consistently for knowledge of the materials and processes of manufacture, and to establish practical methods for the conduct of his office.

[5] To subscribe to and work for honesty and truth in buying and selling, and to denounce all forms and manifestations of commerical bribery.

[6] To accord a prompt and courteous reception, so far as conditions will permit, to all who call on a legitimate business mission.

[7] To respect his obligations and to require that obligations to him and to his concern be respected, consistent with good business practice.

[8] To avoid sharp practice.

[9] To counsel and assist fellow purchasing agents in the performance of their duties, whenever occasion permits.

[10] To co-operate with all organizations and individuals engaged in activities designed to enhance the development and standing of purchasing.

WE SUBSCRIBE TO THESE STANDARDS

built code provides guidance for new employees and especially young people entering the field. And, finally, if an enforcement measure is provided, the code provides the basis for remedial or disciplinary action.[16]

[16]Adapted and modified from Philip W. Van Vlack, *Management Ethics Guide* (Brookings: Economics Department, Agricultural Experiment Station, South Dakota State University, 1965), p. 97.

BOX 11-3

General Television Advertising Standards[*]

1. This Code establishes basic standards for all television broadcasting. The principles of acceptability and good taste within the Program Standards section govern the presentation of advertising where applicable. In addition, the Code establishes in this section special standards which apply to television advertising.

2. A commercial television broadcaster makes his facilities available for the advertising of products and services and accepts commercial presentations for such advertising. However, a television broadcaster should, in recognition of his responsibility to the public, refuse the facilities of his station to an advertiser where he has good reason to doubt the integrity of the advertiser, the truth of the advertising representations, or the compliance of the advertiser with the spirit and purpose of all applicable legal requirements.

3. Identification of sponsorship must be made in all sponsored programs in accordance with the requirements of the Communications Act of 1934, as amended, and the Rules and Regulations of the Federal Communications Commission.

4. In consideration of the customs and attitudes of the communities served, each television broadcaster should refuse his facilities to the advertisement of products and services, or the use of advertising scripts, which the station has good reason to believe would be objectionable to a substantial and responsible segment of the community. These standards should be applied with judgment and flexibility, taking into consideration the characteristics of the medium, its home and family audience, and the form and content of the particular presentation.

5. The advertising of hard liquor (distilled spirits) is not acceptable.

6. The advertising of beer and wines is acceptable only when presented in the best of good taste and discretion, and is acceptable only subject to Federal and local laws. (*See Television Code Interpretation No. 6*)

7. The advertising of cigarettes should not be presented in a manner to convey the impression that cigarette smoking promotes health or is important to personal development of the youth of our country.

8. Advertising by institutions or enterprises which in their offers of instruction imply promises of employment or make exaggerated claims for the opportunities awaiting those who enroll for courses is generally unacceptable.

9. The advertising of firearms and fireworks is acceptable only subject to Federal and local laws.

10. The advertising of fortune-telling, occultism, astrology, phrenology, palm-reading, numerology, mind-reading, character reading or subjects of a like nature is not permitted.

11. Because all products of a personal nature create special problems, such products, when accepted, should be treated with especial emphasis on ethics and the canons of good taste. Such advertising of personal products as is accepted must be presented in a restrained and obviously inoffensive manner. The advertising of particularly intimate products which ordinarily are not freely mentioned or discussed is not acceptable. (*See Television Code Interpretation No. 3*)

12. The advertising of tip sheets, race track publications, or organizations seeking to advertise for the purpose of giving odds or promoting betting or lotteries is unacceptable.

13. An advertiser who markets more than one product should not be permitted to use advertising copy devoted to an acceptable product for purposes of publicizing the brand name or other identification of a product which is not acceptable.

14. "Bait-switch" advertising, whereby goods or services which the advertiser has no intention of selling are offered merely to lure the customer into purchasing higher-priced substitutes, is not acceptable.

15. Personal endorsements (testimonials) shall be genuine and reflect personal experience. They shall contain no statement that cannot be supported if presented in the advertiser's own words.

SOURCE: National Association of Broadcasters, *The Television Code* (Washington, D.C., 11th Ed. National Association of Broadcasters, August, 1966), Section IX, pp. 13–15.

° The interested student should refer to *The Television Code* for interpretation and greater detail of the code.

Questions

1. What is there about the marketing process that makes it so controversial?

2. Comment on the following statements:

"The heart of the matter . . . is that the seller always has an advantage over the buyer. . . ." (p. 30)

"Here's the rule for bargains: Do other men, for they would do you. That's the true business precept." (Dickens' cynical observation) (p. 26)

"In the jungle of the market place, indeed, the intelligent buyer must be alert to every commercial sound, to every snapping of a selling twig, to every rustle that may signal the uprising arm holding the knife pointed toward the jugular vein." (p. 21)

From Dexter Masters, *The Intelligent Buyer's Guide to Sellers* (Mount Vernon, N.Y.: Consumers Union, 1965).

3. Can we rely on marketing codes which are devised by businessmen?

Statements to Consider

The problems of ethics in marketing are no more numerous or difficult than those in medicine, law, teaching, or any other field.

Marketing is by nature a more visible and conspicuous activity than most fields and, therefore, more likely to be noted and criticized.

The law is not an adequate guideline for ethics in the business community because it can be interpreted in many different ways.

Competition forces business decisions in a "gray area" in which what is right or wrong, ethical or unethical, is not clearly defined.

We cannot arrive at a rule of choice which will always give us the best personal ethic by a process involving pure logic, without reference to the world of experience.

In every culture or subculture there is an ethical system which both creates it and is created by it.

Managers cannot assume that what is good for their company is automatically in the best interests of the nation.

Dishonesty is bred by incompetence, cowardice, and myopia.

SELECTED REFERENCES

Howard R. Bowen, *Social Responsibilities of Businessmen* (New York: Harper & Bros., 1953).

Joseph W. McGuire, *Business and Society* (New York: McGraw-Hill Book Company, 1963).

° Eugene J. Kelley, "Marketing and Moral Values in an Acquisitive Society," in *Marketing: A Maturing Discipline*, Proceedings of the American Marketing Association, December 1960, pp. 195–203.

° Arnold Toynbee and William Berenback, "Is Advertising Morally Defensible?" *Yale Daily News*, Special Issues 1963, p. 2.

Generalizations Were Taken From:

Eugene J. Kelley, "Marketing and Moral Values in an Acquisitive Society," in Robert J. Holloway and Robert S. Hancock, *The Environment of Marketing Behavior* (New York: John Wiley and Sons, 1964), pp. 130–134.

Joseph W. McGuire, "Business Ethics, with Special Reference to Marketing," in J. Russell Nelson and Aubrey Strickland (eds.), *Ethics and Marketing* (Minneapolis,: Graduate School of Business Administration, University of Minnesota, 1966), pp. 3–12.

Earl A. Clasen, "Controlling Market Behavior in the Large Firm," in Nelson and Strickland, *op. cit.*, pp. 13–23.

Ethics and Business (University Park: College of Business Administration of the Pennsylvania State University, 1962).

Thomas M. Garrett, S. J., *Ethics in Business* (New York: Sheed and Ward, 1963).

Market Development

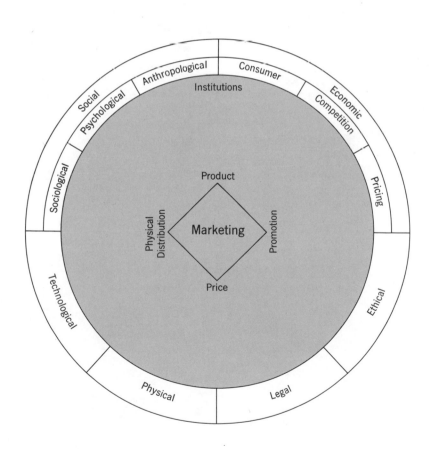

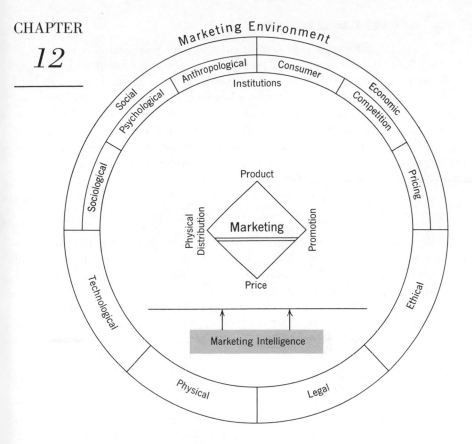

Marketing Intelligence—I

A WAY OF LIFE   *Value   Environment   Information* •   MARKETING DECISIONS   *Basic* Marketing Decisions   Competitive Decisions   Routine Decisions •   METHODS OF GATHER- ING INFORMATION

The term "intelligence" has several meanings, each of which is relevant to marketing. Intelligence is the "power to meet a novel situation by proper behavior adjustments." Certainly the marketer looks to intelligence to help him meet many new and different situations. Intelligence is also "information, news, and advice." The term further refers to the "obtaining of information, especially secret information." Even more descriptive, intelligence is "the ability to comprehend interrelationships of presented facts in such a way to guide action toward a desired goal." Intelligence includes all these meanings in a marketing context.

A WAY OF LIFE

It would be difficult for any of us even to imagine what life would be like without information. We admire good scouting of a college football team. Professional golfers carefully note distances and terrain features as they gather intelligence during preliminary rounds. Generals and admirals make military decisions using the best available intelligence. Senators take trips to various places in order to gain first-hand information about diverse trouble spots. A United Nations agency sends its observers for close and objective examinations of critical situations. Information comes so naturally that we almost forget its importance, at least until we need it.

Business executives obviously must rely on intelligence as they make hundreds of decisions in the face of competition and uncertainties. Major and minor problems are solved in accordance with information supplied to the problem solver, the decision makers. This chapter and the following indicate the role of information in market development endeavors, stress the importance of reliable information, and discuss the ways in which market intelligence may be gathered.

Intelligence is everywhere. So is the need for business intelligence. Regardless of the type or size of industry, the need for information is present; regardless of the level of operation—manufacturer, retailer, or wholesaler—intelligence serves as a basis for judgment; regardless of location, executives require information. The awareness of this need is universally evident in marketing circles. In Europe, the Organization for Economic Cooperation and Development strongly encourages the gathering of marketing data, and ESOMAR (European Society for Opinion Surveys and Market Research) was created especially for the improvement of marketing and marketing research as was the International Marketing Federation (IMF). Information reaches those engaged in marketing in the Philippines through the periodical, *Marketing Horizons,* in England, through *Scientific Marketing,* and so forth.

The search for marketing information is not unique to the free-enterprise nations. The USSR employs vast amounts of market information in its economic planning. Recently, Soviet retail institutions have instituted modest programs of research, and new food stores are often located as a result of voluntary write-in statements from persons who feel the need for a new store.

Value

The stakes in modern business are high. To launch a new product may require a firm to invest millions of dollars, and for a product doomed to failure the consequence may be more than an embarrassing withdrawal from the market. Intelligence is therefore intended to save business from disaster in the same manner that an aerial reconnaissance serves the military. The success of a business program is usually measured in dollars, although we recognize that successful ventures have a broader impact than an attractive financial statement for the firm.

Intelligence can serve as a most important factor in company *growth*. As shown in Box 12-1, growth is attributed to several factors, all of them based on intelligence.

Intelligence plays an important role in increasing a firm's *profits* in a variety of ways. Supply schedules, for example, can be adjusted more accurately with knowledge of demand. Through the use of intelligence, budgeting improves, pricing schedules better fit the situation, advertisements are more efficient, and procurement of materials is more precise. In short, a firm's marketing program is going to be more efficient when it is based on intelligence. In one study of small business firms, specific benefits from marketing research were cited by the owners. These included the following.

"We were able to prune down our product line."
"Product decisions are vastly improved."
"We revised our sales territories on the basis of the collected data."

BOX 12-1

Why Companies Grow

The study indicates that companies with high rates of sales growth usually have:

1. An affinity for growth products or fields,

2. Organized programs to seek and promote new business opportunities,

3. Proven competitive abilities in their present lines of business, and

4. Courageous and energetic management, willing to take carefully studied risks.

SOURCE: N. R. Maines, *Why Companies Grow* (Menlo Park, Cal.: Stanford Research Institute, 1955), p. 1.

"Research helped us get product acceptance."
"We believe our marketing information stopped a downturn in sales."[1]

Information helps to eliminate waste and waste motion. Some of this can be accomplished in time-study fashion, but other improvements require scrutiny of a variety of marketing figures on costs. As early as 1915, Arch W. Shaw lamented:

> They [businessmen] guess at the most effective sales ideas which analysis of their product discloses, guess at the most forceful forms of expressing these, and guess at the most efficient agencies and mediums for transmitting them to prospective purchasers. . . . The need of a search study of all the activities of distribution . . . is emphasized by the appalling waste of money, effort and merchandise due to this general lack of standardization in the materials of demand creation as well as all the other factors bearing on the efficiency of our marketing system.[2]

We may not always learn of the products, retailers, advertising, salesmen, packages, and other facets of marketing that fail each year. The vacant service station on the corner starkly testifies to the mistakes made in allocating marketing resources. Money is spent by some of our largest firms on products that have no market potential. How could the Edsel, with the backing of the Ford Motor Company, have failed? It may surprise the reader to learn that approximately 2500 other brands of automobiles have been withdrawn from the United States automobile market since the turn of the century.

A recent study of 71 firms representing 55 industries and $57 billion of sales indicates that over half of the marketing managers believe that market research has a "great deal" of influence on marketing decisions. Thirty-nine percent replied "some influence," and only six percent replied "very little." An overwhelming percentage of the replies indicated that this influence had increased during the past five years.[3] Clearly, business firms rely heavily on market information.

The value of marketing research spreads farther than among businessmen. The consumer gains from proper use of quality information on his part as well as on the firm's part. Products are more properly geared to the consumer as a result of the use of information, and they are more efficiently distributed. Indeed, the improvement in the directing of marketing resources aids the consumer just as it aids the business firm.

---

[1] Robert J. Holloway, "Marketing Research and Market Planning for the Small Manufacturer," *Small Business Management Research Reports,* University of Minnesota, 1961, p. 16.
[2] Arch W. Shaw, *Some Problems in Market Distribution,* (Cambridge, Harvard University Press, 1915), p. 16. Since Shaw's time, literally hundreds of marketing innovations have been introduced. The search for improvement, nevertheless, continues.
[3] Victor P. Buell, "Take Market Research Out of Its Ivory Tower," *Sales Management,* June 7, 1963, p. 45.

Manifestly the economy benefits from intelligence. Market information permits governments to anticipate needs in various areas, thereby improving allocation of resources. One can consider almost every government program and immediately note the important role played by information. Often the information is routinely collected but at other times it is the result of a formal research project. A study performed for the Post Office Department on the effects of a postage rate increase is an example of the latter. As Ferber and Verdoorn point out, there is first the investigation of economic structure (continual compilation of facts), then the diagnosis, and finally the prognosis.[4] The results of these phases of collecting information are clearly evident in many governmental marketing and economic programs.

Although ours is an affluent society, there remains the need for elimination of waste and for improvement in the allocation of national and private resources. There is no need for mistakes resulting from the failure to collect and use information. The imperfections of our economic system can be eliminated in part, certainly minimized, through the proper use of quality information.

Environment Information

Vast amounts of information come to the marketer from the environment in which he performs his tasks. Most of it accrues with little effort on the part of the marketer, but much of the accessible information is irrelevant or even unreliable. Nevertheless, the environment is the source of much information, whether it be unsolicited or formally collected. The marketer's task is to sort the data and use those that fit the occasion. His response to all this information is, of course, a product offering complete with price, promotion, package, and all other marketing activities.

One of the rich environmental sources of information is government. Some of this information is contained in printed booklets, some is available in various records, and some appears in the form of news releases or comes from personal contacts with officials. Statements concerning grain-buying programs, a nuclear power development, a State Department crisis in some part of the world, a change in the Consumer Price Index, or the Federal Reserve Board's buying plans all illustrate the kind of governmental information which is useful to the marketer.

Legal developments become known from a number of sources. A firm's lawyer, news media, and trade publications contribute to the dissemination of legal information which can be vital to business activity. A slight change in a law or in its interpretation by the courts can make a great deal of dif-

---

[4] Robert Ferber and P. J. Verdoorn, *Research Methods in Economics and Business*, (New York: The Macmillan Company, 1962), pp. 3–7.

ference to the firm. For many years the *Journal of Marketing* has carried a legal section designed to keep marketing people up to date on legal matters.

Since economic information is everyday news, it is unbelievable that a businessman could isolate himself from information concerning the economy. A powerful source of information is the sales force because its intelligence is in the form of dollars of business lost or gained. The suppliers' salesmen also gather a certain amount of economic information.

Technological information is announced through the press, trade publications, and company sources. Marketing people serve as a kind of ears for the firm in learning of technological innovations or those still in the development stage. A marketer cannot wait to learn of technological developments from his customer; if he does so, he will be too late. A company producing equipment for the care of golf-course greens most certainly should be aware of the development of a product which would replace the grass green, thereby requiring no care.

Information about competition can come from printed sources, advertisements, customers, or in other ways. Corporate spies may provide some information, but this channel is fortunately condemned by many managers. Competitive information is often in the nature of rumor which is difficult to evaluate. Some firms deliberately mislead their competitors, while others leave a fairly easy trail to follow. A few years ago one of the chemical companies placed a new brand of antifreeze on the market with the purpose of concealing the market developments of a genuine new product. The decoy product was carried for a number of years, since it was purchased by a sizable number of car owners!

Much environmental marketing information descends upon us without any effort on our part. If we are at all receptive to the environmental forces, we cannot help but learn of many marketing developments. Usually, this kind of information is inadequate and the marketing manager is forced to undertake a more formal program for collecting data. This formal method is known as marketing research and is discussed in the next chapter. In view of the great supply of information, the task of the marketer is not an easy one of collecting, sorting, evaluating, and using the data to make decisions. Figure 12-1 depicts the anatomy of management information.

MARKETING DECISIONS

Marketing decisions range from the trivial to the most vital matters. They include basic management problems, market development activities, and the details of packing a product for shipment. Most of these decisions have to be made over and over again. Each year advertising programs have to be devised, each quarter the sales quotas may be adjusted, and perhaps each day inventories are examined.

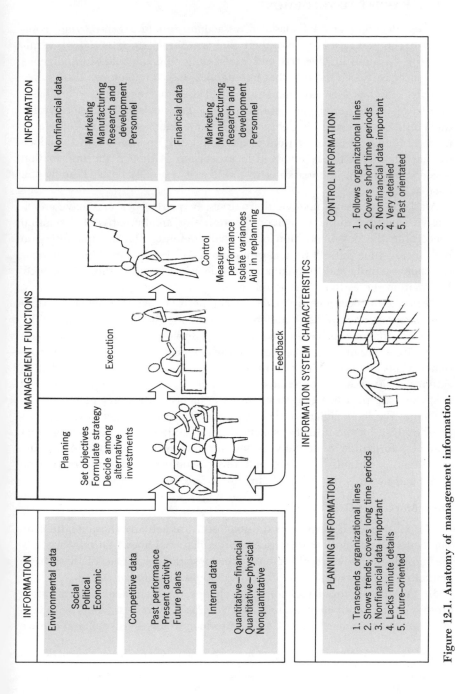

Figure 12-1. Anatomy of management information.

SOURCES: D. Ronald David, "Management Information Crisis," *Harvard Business Review*, Vol. 39, No. 5 (September–October, 1961), p. 114.

These decisions are not made in a vacuum, but in a fast-moving, competitive, complex business atmosphere that is exciting but potentially frustrating. The decisions involve risk and uncertainty, and this makes intelligence indispensable. Recall the role that intelligence played in October 1962, when the late President Kennedy made a critical decision regarding Soviet bases located in Cuba. Aerial photographs provided the essential information for the President to make his decision. The same kind of development takes place in business time after time as marketing information serves to reduce the uncertainity and risk involved in a decision. Although the information is seldom as good as the marketer would like, it is usually better than having none at all.

Marketing decisions involve alternatives. A quarterback may have an extensive repertoire of plays, each one representing an alternative. Information concerning the down, position of the ball, defense, player capabilities on both teams, time left, score, and other pieces of data permit him to narrow the choice rapidly and to make a logical decision based on this intelligence. Information serves the same useful function in marketing.

As marketing decisions are made in a competitive society, reliable information concerning competitive action can be among the most valuable intelligence a marketer can obtain. Cassady has observed: "The key to intelligent competitive activity is market research which seeks information about consumer wants and behavior patterns to serve as a basis for effective marketing activity."[5] Knowledge of competitive plans relative to these wants and behavior patterns can have considerable influence on a firm's plans.

One of the most difficult tasks is to forecast certain market developments (see Box 12-2 for the futurity aspects of automobile production), and a great deal of information is actually useless for forecasting purposes. Since the marketer is constantly thinking in terms of tomorrow, the information he wants and needs is that which helps him improve his predictions.

Basic Marketing Decisions

The most basic decisions for the marketer are actually those of the firm. These are the decisions that transcend organizational lines. Not only are they the most basic, they are also among the most difficult.[6] One of these basic marketing decisions is: What product(s) should my company sell?

In this day of rapid technological change, mergers, and diversification programs, the problem is almost overwhelming. What products will sell? What do the customers want? Can we produce what we can sell and can we

---

[5] Ralph Cassady, Jr., "Market Measurement in a Free Society," *California Management Review*, Vol. II, No. 2, Winter 1960, p. 57.
[6] An excellent discussion of these basic decisions is to be found in D. M. Phelps, "Marketing Research," *Michigan Business Studies*, Vol. 8, No. 2, Ann Arbor, 1937.

BOX 12-2

When It Comes to Predicting, Automen Look to These Factors:

In General Business

Gross national product	Growing 3½% a year
Industrial production	Up seven points this year
Personal income	Increasing
Wholesale prices	Firm
Consumer prices	Rising slowly
Manufacturing inventory-sales ratio	Low by historical standards

In Their Own Business

Prices: autos versus industrial	Auto prices positioned well, rising at slower rate than industrial
Prices: used cars versus new cars	Strong
Car sales share of disposable income	About the same as 10-year average
New car registrations as percent of cars on the road	In line, about 12½%
Car-buying population	Will grow by 13% over next 8 years, compared to only 8% over past 8 years
Installment debt repayments as percent of disposable income	Approaching 14%
Percent of spending units with installment debt	Rising to 50%

SOURCE: "Another Big Year Ahead," *Business Week*, September 14, 1963, p. 24.

sell what we are capable of producing? If we are established in consumer goods, should we enter the industrial market? Management examines many kinds of information during the product-decision process (see Box 12-3).

Many varieties of check lists for new products exist, and basic to all of them is the extremely difficult question—How much can be sold? The many decisions based on the answer to this question are also significant. Product,

BOX 12-3

Factors Considered in Management Review
of New Products

The Market Opportunity

1. Is there a new or current need for the product?
2. How big is the total market?
   a. What types of consumers or industries will buy the product?
   b. How many potential customers are there? How is this group broken down by industry, price class, geographically, etc.?
   c. How big is the market in dollars and units?
3. Is the market growing or declining? Stable or temporary?
4. How much of the market can we sell?
5. Is the amount we can sell enough to offer attractive volume?
6. Is our product the "best of its kind" for the market?
7. What is the attitude of consumers toward our product?
8. What consumer buying habits affect the product?

Competition

1. Is the field overcrowded?
2. What are current competitive products, prices?
3. Are competitive marketing methods deteriorating or improving?
4. Can our product compete successfully with products already on the market?
5. Can present competitive products be improved? Can a competitor bring out a seriously competitive item quickly? Is it likely that other manufacturers will enter the field with a product similar to ours?
6. Does our product have features that will meet and overcome current or anticipated competition?

Distribution

1. Does the product fit our regular distribution pattern and organization?
2. Can the product be sold through our regular channels of distribution?
3. Can our present sales force handle the new product without neglecting sales of our regular product? If not, what modifications are necessary?
4. What opinion of the product is held by jobbers and dealers?
5. How much advertising and promotion will be required to introduce the product?

SOURCE: National Industrial Conference Board, Studies in Business Policy, No. 69, "New Product Development," (New York: National Industrial Conference Board, 1954).

plant, promotion, and other decisions follow logically from the prediction of sales volume. Information does not provide the magic necessary to produce precise forecasts but it does narrow the range of error.

Management makes a number of decisions based on the answers to the question—*When* will the customers buy? For staple items, this may not be difficult, but for many other products, demand may fluctuate a great deal. Predicting purchases for hydraulic presses is far more difficult than for table salt or industrial lubricants.

Another basic decision concerns the *price* to charge. Every product and service sold has a price, and information will influence the basic pricing decision. The impact of market information is seen most vividly in a futures pit of a grain exchange, where extremely small bits of information can provoke a change in price. In a competitive economy, these decisions are made primarily by business executives who study data on competition, demand, supply, and other factors. During times of emergency, government takes on the enormous task, and in planned economies, government assumes the task in its entirety. Since the decision involving price is common to all market situations, both the businessman and the government seek information which will enable them to price correctly the many industrial and consumer goods.

Still another basic decision for the marketer involves *where* the company should sell. The territorial decision rests on information of shipping rates, competition, market potentials, and other factors. Expansion decisions may at times simply confirm a natural tendency to spread beyond the original territory, but at other times they may reflect substantial changes of company policy. For example, a firm may decide after examining the appropriate information to invade foreign markets. When Standard Oil of California after many years decided to invade the eastern markets, both legal and market information was of paramount importance in the company's decision.

How to sell is obviously another basic marketing decision. The entire plan for developing the market constitutes an answer to this question. Since this topic will receive emphasis in the coming chapters, little need be said at this point except to suggest that information plays a significant role in arriving at questions of distribution, promotion, and other facets of the market development task.

These basic questions are applicable to all firms and involve analyses of the market, anticipations of demand, and an appreciation of the immediate situations. Before settling on basic market questions, information is collected and then used as an aid to managerial judgment. As White pointed out long long ago:

A market may be compared to a sponge, which absorbs the output of business. It is necessary to determine how much this sponge will absorb, how fast it will absorb it, and many other facts, before it is possible to understand and reckon intelligently with the possibilities and limitations of that market.[7]

Competitive decisions

At some point the basic decisions must be implemented in the market-place. Subsequent and sequential decisions adjust the basic decisions to the immediate situation. Market development plans are most certainly competitive in nature. Sometimes the marketer makes the decisions these plans require according to intuitive type of judgment, but where possible he prefers to base his decisions on a careful analysis of market information.

Though they may be unwritten, firms typically have goals which may be in terms of gross sales, profit, share of the market, quality of product, customer service, or any of a number of other aspirations. Regardless, the marketing manager must make his plans for the market development of his product, and this means reaching competitive decisions which will best achieve the goals of the firm. Goals are not easy to achieve; competitors frequently have the same ones. Over the years the mouse-trap theory has proven unsatisfactory, and today it is expected that the marketer will develop the "pathway to the door" in terms of a selling policy. Intelligence, obviously, should play an important role.

Following the basic decisions of pricing, producing, selecting a territory, and methods of selling, detailed, subsidiary decisions must be made. A firm deciding to enter the razor-blade market must spell out quality, price, packaging, promotion, and other decisions to the letter. The name, even the color of the wrapper, and the television series must be carefully decided. The exact appeal must be ascertained, information on buying motives obtained, and commercials worked out precisely to take advantage of this information. Once television habits are determined, the commercials are scheduled for optimum hours of viewing. Gillette's sponsorship of the World Series is a good example of a promotional decision of this kind.

The package for a laundry soap is developed after preferences from housewives are ascertained, or a name for a new shampoo is announced following a study of a thousand alternatives. Which is best remembered? Which is most pleasing? Which is easiest to pronounce? What meanings do the design and names convey? A company examines a competitor's lines and then fills in gaps in its own lines. Rival automobiles are taken apart, piece by piece, in order to determine manufacturing processes, materials, and features incorporated in the automobile. Or an appliance manufacturer may gather information on returned merchandise on the basis of which it inaugurates a new repair service for its small motors on washing machines, driers, and dishwashers. A manufacturer of high-fidelity equipment learns from its

---

[7]Percival White, *Market Analysis*, (New York: McGraw-Hill Book Company, 1925), p. 1.

dealers that warranty stations must be decentralized if the concern is to remain competitive.

Information of this kind from the market tells the marketer a good deal about his competitive situation. He learns that his product has some special appeal to a particular occupational class, to a certain income, or to one life-cycle group of consumers. Information may help him to define the market segment which he can then exploit, in lieu of broadcasting his appeal to everyone in general and to no one in particular.

Trade circles may provide advance information on some technological breakthrough. This intelligence could possibly permit a firm to speed its own research and development along given lines in order to prevent the competitor from securing a market lead of months or even years.

Marketing information frequently reveals facts about the market which were not at all recognized by the seller. For instance, a breakfast-food manufacturer became cognizant of a large institutional market (hotels, schools, and hospitals) when his market analyst attempted to reconcile discrepancies in two sets of sales data.

These are only samples of marketing decisions which are made over and over again in any firm. Each of these decisions is based on some amount of information and probably each can be improved as a result of better intelligence. Ideally, competitive decisions would be made only after all the facts were in, but since the marketplace does not wait for anyone, competitive decisions must frequently be made on the basis of insufficient information. The naval commander in the Second World War often made crucial decisions when he could not ascertain the position of his own ships, let alone those of the enemy. The same kind of situation frequently exists in business when rumors, confusion, and various pressures force action prior to a careful analysis of the circumstances. Nevertheless, whenever possible, the decision maker prefers to have the facts before him.   .

Routine decisions

Many marketing decisions require much less effort to solve than the foregoing. It is not that the decisions are unimportant but that the decision itself is easier to make. Furthermore, some data are collected routinely and these simplify some managerial problems. For example, the method of shipment is important to the buyer and hence to the seller. Sometimes the buyer makes the shipping decision for the seller; often he accepts the seller's suggestions. Much of the shipping data is fairly easy to gather (rates, insurance, shipping time, and packaging requirements) and this enables the seller to make routine decisions which become standard procedure. Recently, linear programming has supplied the seller with useful data which contribute to better efficiency for the entire physical distribution program.

Customer billings are handled routinely. Underlying them are the terms of the sale which have been agreed upon, and in making the sale, information regarding competitors' terms is useful. Once the basic policies have been determined, the more routine tasks of billing the customer are almost forgotten. Compensation of the sales force can also be routine or can be exaggerated in importance. Either way, the marketing manager requires certain information in order to determine a compensation schedule which blends incentive with security and missionary work with selling effort.

The problem of identifying customers is aided in some instances by the simple expedient of having buyers return warranty cards. The marketer who sells indirectly can at least ascertain who is buying his product. Usually the warranty card includes certain vital statistics about the customer and the distributor involved in the sale. This routine method of handling information aids the firm in making a number of marketing decisions relative to market development.

The minimum size of a profitable order is another routine decision which is relatively easy to handle from cost data. Similarly, cost-of-distribution studies can yield significant data for the manufacturer or distributor without an expenditure of large sums of money.

The feedback of information from salesmen is often handled routinely during weekly sales meetings or in salesmen's reports. A tip from a salesman concerning a new use of one of the firm's products can be parlayed into many new orders simply by notifying the other salesmen. Although feedback is important, little is generally done in the way of systematizing the information flow, perhaps because of the reluctance of salesmen to file reports of this kind.

Information collected routinely can often serve several roles. Reported for tax and various other purposes such as lease arrangements and personnel compensation, gasoline gallonage sold can also provide market information which aids in location, demand analysis, pricing, and other kinds of developmental decisions. Changes in gallonage may be checked against new advertising campaigns, new pumps, gasoline additives, and competition, and vital marketing decisions arise from that one figure collected simply by reading the dials on the pumps.

It is hoped that the use of marketing information by all kinds of marketing institutions and manufacturers is now more clearly appreciated. Major marketing decisions, such as plant acquisition or the introduction of a new product, are usually based on as much reliable information as one can acquire. The vigorous competitive actions of a marketing executive also derive to some degree from the combining of marketing information with judgment.

Intelligence has generally been instrumental in improving the status of marketing and marketing executives within industry. Decision making has improved, leading to the growth of many firms. Long-range growth plans and short-range operating plans have been better conceived by virtue of the information provided. Selling strategies increase their probabilities of success when based on reliable marketing information. Performing descriptive duties for the executive, information explains what has happened in the marketplace and aids the predictions which must be made. Profitable marketing is likely to follow when decisions are based on such intelligence.

Newman has pointed out that the marketing executive should regard the use of information as a "continuous program designed to help management set its objectives, plan for their accomplishment, implement the plans successfully, and evaluate the outcome so that better programs may be undertaken in the future."[8] There is nothing fleeting, superficial, or perishable in this statement. It is true that researchers and decision makers occasionally lose perspective, but few would deny the important role which information plays in business today. Perhaps a fitting conclusion to this section is a quotation from one of the pioneers of marketing research, C. S. Duncan. Five of his propositions underlying marketing research appear in Box 12-4.

METHODS OF GATHERING INFORMATION

The systematic gathering of marketing information will be discussed in the next chapter. Here, we allude only to the casual or informal gathering of information. This is the information that accumulates with little effort on

[8]Joseph W. Newman, "Put Research Into Marketing Decisions," *Harvard Business Review,* Vol. 40, March–April 1962, p. 180.

BOX 12-4

A Series of Propositions

1. The immediate and primary need of business today is intelligent direction and control . . . .

2. Intelligent direction and control can be had only by a better knowledge of business principles.

3. A better knowledge of business principles can be derived only from a careful and comprehensive survey of business facts.

4. To secure a careful and comprehensive survey of business facts is a problem for business research.

5. Therefore, the immediate and primary need of business today can be met only by business research.

SOURCE: C. S. Duncan, *Commercial Research,* (New York: The MacMillan Company, 1921), p. *v.*

our part. Environmental in its source, it is the kind of information of which we are barely cognizant at times. It can be misleading or it can be vital. It cannot be dismissed but must be examined and checked as to reliability.

During any given day, a marketing executive probably receives several thousand bits of information. He is exposed to hearsay, gossip, and newspapers (several), periodicals, books, salesmen, buyers, radio, television, and other disseminators of information. He is constantly sending "feelers" to the market. These feelers are his product offering, changes in pricing, or promotion, and so on. Each of them provokes some kind of market response which in turn is in some way fed back to the marketing executive. The sum total of all of the marketing man's daily contacts helps him to develop attitudes, biases, and intuition. Though not subjected to a formal testing program, his intuition is tested by the market time and again. Exposures to information combined with his experience assist him to develop sound judgment which is not eliminated by any amount of information, but rather aided by it.

Businessmen should train themselves to be observant because in this way they can acquire additional information. An executive of an oil company observes competitive practices as he drives to and from his suburban home each day. Seldom can anyone report a competitive development which he has not already noted.

Informal information is being communicated all the time, perhaps in fragments, perhaps distorted, but the marketer finds himself always listening and looking for clues. He examines all the clues he can, rejects many, and permits some to have influence on his decisions. Because he has learned that he cannot operate solely on intuition and informal intelligence, the marketing executive resorts to more formal methods of gathering and examining marketing information.

The following anecdote illustrates the conclusion that marketing can stand formal research. Sales of a new product soared beyond expectations and each advertising campaign which was directed to the housewife and her need for the product brought in huge new orders. Things went well until some formal research was attempted. It was found that sales were highest where low readership of ads and low population density coexisted. The product intended to aid the housewife in the care of hair and fingernails was being used with baby chicks and suckling pigs. And two competitors were imitating the company with similar advertising appeals because they chose to follow the leader without checking the facts.

Questions

1. What do you think are the real purposes of marketing research?
2. Suggest the basic information essential to the intelligent operation of a consumer-goods manufacturer insofar as marketing is concerned.

3. Is marketing research overrated or underrated? Can marketing research handle basic questions or is it restricted to simple and superficial marketing questions?
4. Do you know of any firms which have relied heavily on marketing research? In what way has marketing research helped them develop a growth pattern?
5. Does the dynamic characteristic of marketing render the job of the researcher useless?

Statements to Consider

Systematically applied, market diagnosis provides, in principle, the opportunity of judging the efficiency of each act of management after some time has elapsed, of analyzing operating results in relation to market developments, and of expressing the quantitative influence of business policy on this result.

A sales forecast is impossible without a price estimate, which is, in turn, impossible without a product quality estimate.

Perhaps the most important potential contribution of "research" in marketing comes from the relatively objective viewpoint that research encourages even those who do not directly execute it.

Research is probably more effective in unearthing new possibilities for action than in predicting the response to existing possibilities.

The single most useful step in fitting research into marketing management would be greater recognition of the fact that the essence of research is neither surveys nor samples, but the evolution and testing of hypotheses about marketing by testing the predictions to which they lead.

SELECTED REFERENCES

Harper W. Boyd, Jr., and Ralph Weftfall, *Marketing Research: Text and Cases*, Rev. Ed. (Homewood, Ill.: Richard D. Irwin, 1964).
° Ralph Cassady, Jr., "Market Measurement in a Free Society," *California Management Review*, Vol. 2, No. 2, Winter 1960.
° D. Maynard Phelps, "The Place of Marketing Research in Economic Activity," *Marketing Research* (Ann Arbor: Bureau of Business and Economic Research, Graduate School of Business Administration, University of Michigan, 1937), pp. 69–74.
Alfred R. Oxenfeldt, "Scientific Marketing: Ideal and Ordeal," *Harvard Business Review*, Vol. 39, No. 2, March–April 1961, pp. 51–64.

Generalizations Were Taken From:

Robert Ferber and P. J. Verdoorn, *Research Methods in Economics and Business* (New York: The Macmillan Company, 1962).
Harry V. Roberts, "The Role of Research in Marketing Management," in Parker Holmes, *Marketing Research: Principles and Readings* (Cincinnati: South-Western Publishing Company, 1960), pp. 5–16.

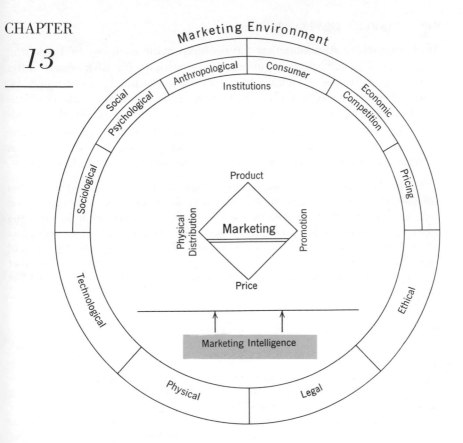

Marketing Intelligence—II

MARKETING RESEARCH   *Characteristics   Trends* •   MARKETING RESEARCH IN OPERA-
TION   *The Researchers   Collection of the Data* •   TECHNIQUES EMPLOYED BY THE
MARKETING RESEARCHER   *Statistical Techniques   Surveys   Panel   Operations Research
Motivational Research   Cost Analyses   Media Analysis   Experimental Design* •   CONCLUD-
ING COMMENTS

ADDENDA: 1. MARKETING   RESEARCH   POSITION   DESCRIPTIONS •   2. A   CASE
STUDY IN MARKETING RESEARCH •   3. MARKETING RESEARCH CODE OF ETHICS

239

Marketing information underlies the decisions made each day by marketing executives. The sources of this information are many, for each corner of the marketing environment yields some clues for operational and planning decisions. It is the marketer's job to look at the information and make decisions that will determine the success of the product or service involved. The advertising, selling, pricing, distributive, and other marketing plans are those that will result in the development of the market. Essential for the soundness of these plans is a well-organized program of marketing research. In summary,

Market research is not magic. It takes time. It costs money. It performs no miracles. How much it can increase your profits and reduce your risks depends on you. Nobody else affects the results you get. You hire your research director. You appropriate his budget. You set the terms and conditions under which he works. You establish the general lines of inquiry he pursues. You get the results. You file and forget them or you use them. . . . If you do not give him the tools he needs, that is your fault. If you do not put him to work on major problems, you will not get major results.[1]

MARKETING RESEARCH

Marketing research may be defined as:

The systematic gathering, recording, and analyzing of data about problems relating to the marketing of goods and services. Such research may be undertaken by impartial agencies or by business firms or their agents for the solution of their marketing problems. . . . Marketing Research is the inclusive term which embraces all research activities carried on in connection with the management of marketing work. . . .[2]

Characteristics

Marketing research is a means to an end. Marketing managers use it to improve their decisions in the marketplace. Its desirable characteristics may be considered from the standpoint of the researcher, the user, or both. For instance, the user wants his information as soon, as inexpensive, and as accurate as possible. The researcher customarily presses for more time, more money, and more accuracy. The marketing executive can be more specific about his research needs. After all, he utilizes a great amount of marketing information every day as he handles a wide range of marketing problems. For research to be most helpful to him, it should be:

[1] Willard M. Fox, *How to Use Market Research for Profit*, (Englewood Cliffs, N.J.: Prentice-Hall, 1950), p. 327.
[2] Committee on Definitions of the American Marketing Association, *Marketing Definitions* (Chicago: American Marketing Association, 1960), pp. 16–17.

Geared to the marketing problem; designed to answer the query; tailor-made to the situation.

Objective; free of bias from any source, from problem formulation to interpretation of results.

Deliberate; hurried research involves too many short-cuts and opens possibilities for errors.

Capable of making predictions; the marketer is concerned more about next month than last year.

Accurate to a sensible degree; well within the user's margin-of-error restrictions.

Presented in a report which is understandable, uncluttered, and free from difficult research terminology.

Common sense in its approach and direction; not divorced from the realities of the company and the marketplace.

Applied to the important problems; limited resources prohibit lavish expenditures for research.

The best possible information within the financial and personnel limitations of the firm.

Marketing research should provide the executive with evidence which will help him decide on the plant acquisition, the coming television production, the number of price lines, the size of the sales force, and the corporate symbol. The researcher occupies a staff job and must integrate his results with his company's operations. His *raison d'être* is to provide useful information to the manager.

Trends

Marketing researchers over the years have created a genuine respect for themselves among business executives. Fortunately, their efforts have slowly and carefully developed into an occupational endeavor which is now recognized as essential by most sizable firms and many small establishments. Marketing research has benefited from many disciplines (see Box 13-1). Sampling, interviewing, and other phases of the problem-solving and research processes have improved as a result of the lessons taught by other disciplines. In addition, marketing researchers have developed techniques and procedures of their own which are designed to find answers to the manager's problems.

The growth of marketing research has reached the point where some firms each spend several hundred thousand dollars annually for such services. Surveys of marketing research activities indicate that a substantial range remains insofar as expenditures are concerned. Growth of the marketing research function can be detected through a number of criteria: dollar volume of research services, number of employees, number of firms engaged in research, number of firms using marketing research services, number and kind of

BOX 13-1

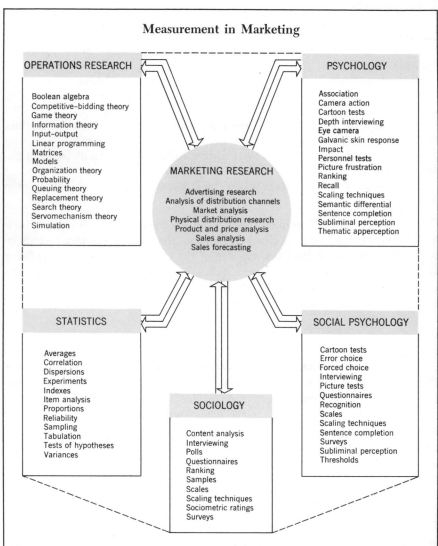

Measurement in Marketing

OPERATIONS RESEARCH

Boolean algebra
Competitive-bidding theory
Game theory
Information theory
Input-output
Linear programming
Matrices
Models
Organization theory
Probability
Queuing theory
Replacement theory
Search theory
Servomechanism theory
Simulation

MARKETING RESEARCH

Advertising research
Analysis of distribution channels
Market analysis
Physical distribution research
Product and price analysis
Sales analysis
Sales forecasting

PSYCHOLOGY

Association
Camera action
Cartoon tests
Depth interviewing
Eye camera
Galvanic skin response
Impact
Personnel tests
Picture frustration
Ranking
Recall
Scaling techniques
Semantic differential
Sentence completion
Subliminal perception
Thematic apperception

STATISTICS

Averages
Correlation
Dispersions
Experiments
Indexes
Item analysis
Proportions
Reliability
Sampling
Tabulation
Tests of hypotheses
Variances

SOCIOLOGY

Content analysis
Interviewing
Polls
Questionnaires
Ranking
Samples
Scales
Scaling techniques
Sociometric ratings
Surveys

SOCIAL PSYCHOLOGY

Cartoon tests
Error choice
Forced choice
Interviewing
Picture tests
Questionnaires
Recognition
Scales
Scaling techniques
Sentence completion
Surveys
Subliminal perception
Thresholds

SOURCE: William Lazer and Eugene J. Kelley, "Interdisciplinary Contributions to Marketing Management," *Marketing and Transportation Paper No. 5* (East Lansing: Bureau of Business and Economic Research, Michigan State University, 1959), p. 18.

problems to which research is applied, reliance upon the results, and sources of information such as books, periodicals, meetings, and university publications. By all these standards, marketing research has grown steadily over the past generation.

Informal marketing research has, of course, been conducted for many years. Formal marketing research probably had its beginning just before the turn of the century when an advertising agency (probably by accident) made an application of marketing research to marketing and advertising.[3] As the years went by, other men began to use the idea. Harlow Gale (University of Minnesota), Walter Dill Scott (Agate Club of Chicago), J. George Frederick (The Business Bourse), R. O. Eastman (Kellogg Company), A. W. Shaw (Harvard), Charles Parlin (Curtis Publishing Company), and Paul Nystrom (United States Rubber Company) were among the pioneers. Their standards were high and the start they gave the industry was a good one.

Some believe that marketing research is becoming scientific. There is a lot of debate over what is and what is not scientific in nature. In many ways, the argument is not very important. Much more to the point is that researchers are constantly trying to improve their methods and are studying the methods of the more exact sciences in order to learn everything they can. This is indeed a healthy trend.

That marketing research is here on a permanent basis has been attested to by many, including the successor to Charles Parlin, Donald M. Hobart.

Because efficient distribution and marketing will be vital to the producing of profits, business generally is being driven to a quest for facts as a sound basis for solving its urgent problems. . . . Armed with a knowledge of his own business, or his customers and his dealer's reactions, of the trend of general business conditions, the businessman is in a position to meet competition and make a profit. . . . For these reasons marketing research will increase in importance until almost every company of any size will be engaged in it.[4]

MARKETING RESEARCH IN OPERATION

Marketing research is continuously serving all other functions of marketing. It is a process of gathering, analyzing, and interpreting information for marketing executives. The diagram in Figure 13-1 illustrates the flow of marketing research. The research commences with the formulation of the problem and is completed upon its solution and implementation of the decision.

[3] Lawrence C. Lockley, "Notes on the History of Marketing Research," *Journal of Marketing*, Vol. 14, No. 5, April 1950, p. 733.
[4] David M. Hobart, *Marketing Research Practice*, (New York: The Ronald Press Company, 1950), p. 9.

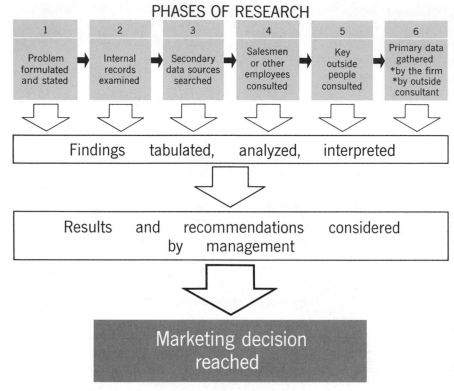

Figure 13-1. The phases and flow of marketing research.

The Researchers

Many persons engage in marketing research of one kind or another. These include marketers, advertisers, statisticians, psychologists, sociologists, anthropologists, and others. Some are highly specialized in their handling of marketing problems. An anthropologist, for example, may concentrate on names for new products, utilizing his knowledge of the meaning of language. Other researchers are generalists who delve into an assortment of marketing problems. In common, they all examine data which they hope can improve the decision-making process. Their training should include at least a college education, but preferably they should have a properly programmed master's degree. A number of them are now Ph.D's, usually specialists in some kind of methodology. Ideally, the researcher has talent, training, perspective, and a desire to initiate, plan, and carry out investigatory activities.

Diversity characterizes a researcher's training and interests. A small marketing research department needs a generalist to handle its many problems, whereas the larger firm can afford the luxury of its own specialists.

By hiring consultants for short periods of time, the small marketing research department can avail itself of the specialists. This suggests that several kinds of organizations for research exist. Most often the company has its own marketing research department which ranges in size from a one-man affair to a fairly large one of perhaps fifty people. Independent marketing research firms service companies that lack their own staffs or that want to supplement their staff's work. Again, size varies from the small independent consultant firm to a far-flung international agency such as the A. C. Nielsen Co.

Many advertising agencies perform research functions for their clients and for their own edification; several of them are noted for fine research work but a number still lack this distinction. Trade associations collect information for their members and sometimes go further to suggest or even perform certain problem-centered research activities. Marketing research is also performed by various governmental agencies which have published hundreds of research reports. Agricultural reports are probably most numerous, although the commerce and labor departments have also published many research reports. If one includes census data, the Department of Commerce, of course, dominates.

Universities frequently have research bureaus which handle certain research functions. With or without these bureaus, faculty members engage in substantial marketing research activities of their own choosing and their findings are published in a wide variety of books and periodicals.

It is rather difficult to generalize on market researchers. Their backgrounds, interests, organizations, tasks, budgets, and other resources differ significantly from one to the next. The diversity in backgrounds is healthy for the profession. The highly skilled psychologist, for example, learns from the statistician who, in turn, learns from the marketing management staff, and so on. Diversity probably helps to create and maintain an atmosphere in which researchers continually strive for new information, try new techniques, and submit themselves to educational devices such as journals, meetings, and books as well as discussions inside and outside the firm.

Collection of the data

The marketing researcher finds his data located in many places. One is not surprised, therefore, to learn that researchers have to be resourceful individuals. Since the only source for information concerning pharmaceutical products may be the busy medical doctors, the problem for the researcher is evident: how does he get doctors to provide valuable information about certain drugs and treatments? Or if the desired information is income, how does the researcher extract it from people who do not like to provide such data?

A good rule in collecting data is to exhaust what is readily available before reaching out for additional information. The data generated by the researcher's own firm are seldom fully utilized by management. Government data are greatly underutilized, yet these are inexpensive and reliable. If a department-store manager wishes to learn why customers return items, he does not have to commit himself to an expensive personal-interview type of survey. It is far easier, less expensive, faster, and more reliable to record systematically the actual returns of the firm's customers. Furthermore, unless one needs current information on population, the census data offer the researcher a true bonanza.

Data collection is part of the research task. However, the process should be closely related to the problem-solving sequence, for often it is possible to solve the problem with data collected from company records or from secondary sources. The point is that the researcher should collect only essential data. When it appears that the problem can be solved with the data at hand, that is the time to solve it. The reason for belaboring this point is that data collectors become involved in problems and seemingly dislike to stop the collection process. This is a real temptation for the researcher who wants to do his job thoroughly. One lead may turn up another, and so on, until he has opened up vistas of information which he did not know existed.

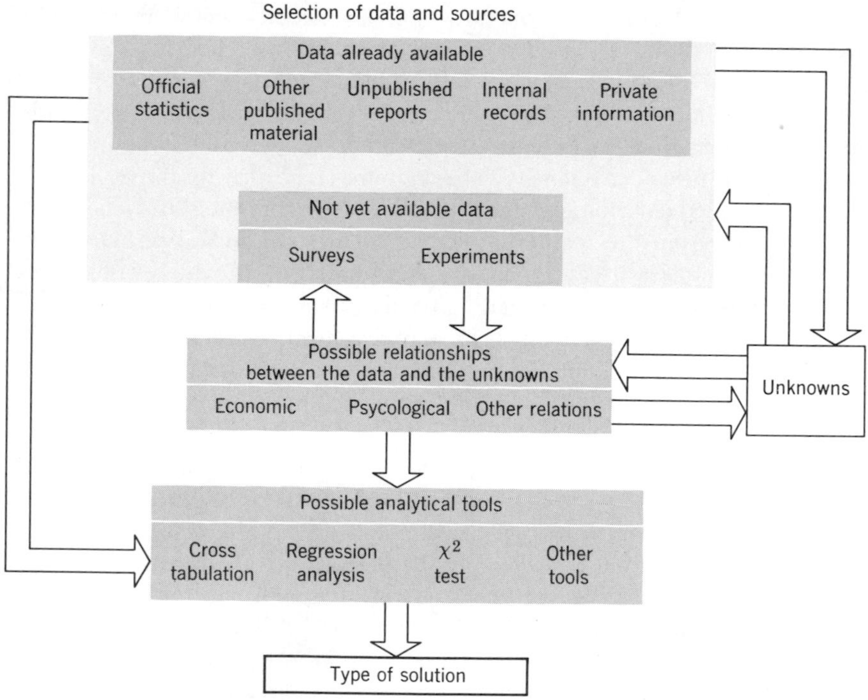

Figure 13-2. The relationship between printed data and primary sources.
SOURCE: Robert Ferber and P. J. Verdoorn, *Research Methods in Economics and Business* (New York: The Macmillan Company, 1962), p. 41.

What can happen then is that other phases of the research (for example, analysis and interpretation) have to be shortened because of the time limit on the problem.

Sources of information continue to multiply. The researcher must learn to locate the pertinent information in an efficient way and not to digress from the problem. Figure 13-2 shows some of the relationships between printed data and primary information.

Students will find that a rather small number of journals provide a great deal of information about almost any marketing problem.

MARKETING

Journal of Marketing	*Journal of Marketing Research*
Journal of Advertising Research	*Industrial Marketing*
Printers' Ink	*Sales Management*
Survey of Current Business	*Harvard Business Review*
Business Horizons	*California Management Review*
Journal of Business	

ECONOMICS

American Economic Review	*Quarterly Journal of Economics*

STATISTICS

Journal of American Statistical Association	*Review of Economics and Statistics*

PSYCHOLOGY

Journal of Applied Psychology	*Journal of Abnormal and Social Psychology*
Public Opinion Quarterly	

SOCIOLOGY

American Sociological Review

Trade publications such as the following provide additional information.

Progressive Grocer	*Iron Age*
Motor Age	*Women's Wear Daily*
Electrical Wholesaling	*Purchasing*

The following organizations publish a great deal of pertinent material for the marketing researcher.

American Marketing Association	Survey Research Center
Opinion Research Center	American Management Association
National Industrial Conference Board	

The United States Department of Commerce disseminates vast quantities of marketing information including the censuses of population, housing, retailing, wholesaling, manufacturing, services, and distribution. The Departments of Labor and Agriculture and the Federal Reserve Board also assist the marketer.

The foregoing citations of information sources barely suggest the storehouses of information available to the researcher. But with all of the company, government, association, and other printed data, many marketing problems would remain unsolved unless the marketer could collect information from other sources. The consumer represents one of the most researched persons alive today. Business executives, television viewers, new car buyers, and the "man in the street" are important sources of information, and the researcher constantly improves his techniques in securing intelligence from these sources. It makes sense for him to exhaust the company and printed sources first. Usually he does this and then turns to a more formal type of research to tap the remainder of the information.

TECHNIQUES EMPLOYED BY THE MARKETING RESEARCHER

When you leave your residence in the morning, you have a number of alternatives for securing information about weather conditions. You may observe from the window, walk outside for a moment, listen to a late weather report, ask someone nearby, look at the change in barometric pressure, read the newspaper report, or call the weather station. Similarly the researcher has a number of sources of information and a number of alternative techniques for obtaining it.

Statistical techniques

There was a time when marketing researchers were adding very little statistical finesse to their research operations. In recent years, however, statisticians have literally exploded with new techniques which most marketers have not yet absorbed. Time-series analyses, correlation, index numbers, and other devices were widely used in the past. To this have been added linear programming, Markov chains, Monte Carlo methods, Heuristic programming, and many other techniques and theories falling under such broader topics as operations research, probability, and quantitative analysis. Each one of these new techniques will improve the researcher's ability to examine data and to arrive at operational conclusions. Boxes 13-2 and 13-3 depict extremes of statistical techniques: the simple device of using standard scores and the development of a mathematical model. The literature now provides the reader with ample information on the newer research techniques.

Surveys

Surveys take many forms. Widely used and widely misused, they are deceptively simple; their quality depends on each and every link involved—

BOX 13-2

Estimate of Trade Potential

In an effort to determine which cities could be served economically by airline companies, standard scores were calculated for per capita wholesale sales and the percentage of persons employed in mining and manufacturing. Studies of established air traffic patterns indicate that potentials diminish as one goes from trade centers to trade institutionals to institutionals to balanced and finally to industrials.

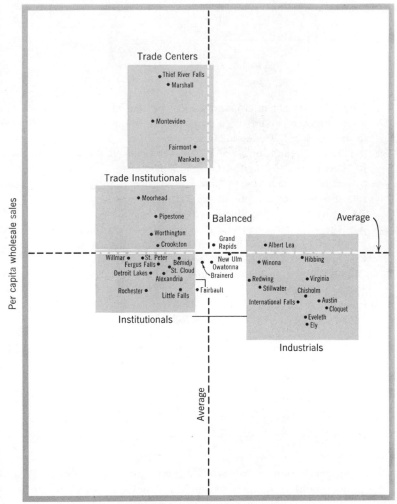

SOURCE: Robert J. Holloway, "Which Cities Can Support Airline Service," *Journal of Marketing*, Vol. 17, No. 2, October 1953, p. 178.

BOX 13-3

Model of Consumer Brand Shifting

The optimal advertising expenditure for brand (i) can be computed as shown below. The potential brand shifters for all brands $(A_{i,T})$ is defined as proportional to the product of the advertising expenditures $(C_{i,T})$ for each brand and its effectiveness $(E_{i,T})$, where $\Sigma A_{i,T} = 1$.

$$C_{i,T} = \left(\frac{C_{c,T}E_{c,T}}{E_{i,T}} \right) \left(\frac{1 - \sqrt{\dfrac{C_{c,T}E_{c,T}(1 - \rho re)}{m_i I_o E_{i,T}(\rho k)^L k^{(T-1)}(k - re)}}}{\sqrt{\dfrac{C_{c,T}E_{c,T}(1 - \rho re)}{m_i I_o E_{i,T}(\rho k)^L k^{(T-1)}(k - re)}}} \right)$$

where:

$A_{i,T}$ = Probability of "potential brand shifter" or new customer of the product being drawn to brand (i) in time period t as a result of advertising in time period T. The distinction between i and T takes cognizance of the fact that there may be a time lag between the advertising and its effect upon consumer purchasing behavior.

$C_{k,T}$ = Advertising expenditure by brand (i) at time T; in the above decision rule, it represents the optimal expenditure,

$C_{c,T}$ = Total advertising expenditures by competitors in time period T,

$E_{c,T}$ = Average weighted effectiveness of advertising in behalf of competitive brands at time T, the effectiveness of each brand's advertising being weighted by its dollar expenditures,

ρ = Discount factor applied to future dollar receipts and expenditures = $1/(1 + \text{rate of interest})$,

m_i = Profit margin on sales of brand (i) apart from advertising costs,

I_o = Total industry sales in the base period $(i = g)$,

$k = e + g$ = the net growth of industry sales per period, and

L = the lag (number of time periods) between the advertising expenditures and its influence upon new and shifting customers.

SOURCE: Alfred A. Kuehn, "Mathematical Models and Marketing Theory," *Proceedings, Conference of Marketing Teachers for Western States,* ed. Delbert J. Duncan (Berkeley: University of California Press, 1958), pp. 51–52.

design, sample, questionnaire, interviewing, and analysis. Surveys may solicit facts or opinions, and frequently both. Many persons consider the survey technique to be synonymous with marketing research, but surveys represent only one alternative which may be used by the market researcher. The term "survey" has been applied to most any data gathering by pollsters, marketing researchers, sociologists, and others.

The marketing researcher thinks of the survey as a device to collect information from a sample of people. He may want to make it a motivational type of study or he may wish to gather facts: "To which television program are you listening right now?" A number of techniques, such as projective techniques (to be discussed later), are combined with survey methods. The information may be gathered by mail, telephone, or personal interviewers. The sample may be some variety of a random sample or it may be arbitrarily drawn and not submissible to mathematical checks for reliability. The most expensive type of survey, that of personal interviewing of a randomly selected audience, is considered most reliable. Because of the expense involved, researchers have had to develop more efficient sampling methods (stratified sampling, for example), mail or telephone interviewing, and shorter lists of questions. As pointed out earlier, the design rests not only on the problem but also on the financial and personnel resources and the time permitted to gather the data. Box 13-4 illustrates a survey.

Panel

A panel resembles a survey but in the case of the panel, the respondents are interviewed over and over again. Respondents may be included in the panel for several weeks or indefinitely. The panel provides the researcher with data quickly through comparison of its responses with the company's own sales records which include a long time lag between the producer-wholesaler-retailer-consumer. The panel, on the other hand, supplies consumer information immediately after purchase. The panel operation further enables the researcher to measure the impact of a price change, a new advertising appeal, a new product, or a competitor's strategy. Analysts must be aware of any tendency for a respondent to become an "expert" through serving on the panel, and if this happens the panel member loses her effectiveness as a "typical housewife." Box 13-5 describes one panel operation.

There are variations of the panel technique. The Market Research Corporation of America maintains a 15,000-consumer panel which has value for many firms. The A. C. Nielsen Co. has a number of operations, one of which gathers some of the same kind of information obtained in a consumer panel operation except that the Nielsen panel consists of food and drug stores. Periodic checks of these stores are made by Nielsen employees in order to secure information on purchases, inventories, sales, and store promotion. (The consumer panel acquires buying information directly from the consumer.) Some of the information obtained by the *store audit* operation is shown in Box 13-6.

Operations research

A rather broad assortment of studies have been classified as operations research. The studies are usually characterized by team research, quantitative

BOX 13-4

A Survey: Will Minnesotans Support Major League Baseball

QUESTION: An American league baseball club will be playing its home games in Minnesota this year. Do you happen to know the name of this team?

Replies from people who had previously stated that they had a great deal of interest in baseball:

Minnesota Twins	40%
"Twins"	25
Incorrect answers	9
Don't know	26
	100%

QUESTION: Do you plan to attend any of the home games of the new baseball club? If Yes, about how many times do you think you will be going to a major league baseball game in the Twin Cities?

Replies:

Plan to attend	
1 time	9%
2 times	9
3 times	4
4 times	2
5 times	2
6 times or more	6
Not sure	4
	36%
Do not plan to attend, not sure	64
	100%

Prediction of attendance based on the survey: 1,200,000

Note: The attendance for the actual games have been as follows:

1962—1,433,216	1965—1,463,268
1963—1,406,652	1966—1,259,374
1964—1,217,514	

Undoubtedly the Minnesota Poll intended this survey to reflect public opinion throughout the state rather than for it to serve as a precise forecast of attendance. The accuracy exhibited, therefore, is even more surprising.

SOURCE: *Minnesota Poll,* "1,200,000 Plan to See Twins Play," *Minneapolis Sunday Tribune,* April 2, 1961.

BOX 13-5

A Description of the National Family Opinion Panel

90,000 consumers who can answer any questions on ownership, use, brand preference, purchase expectations; or test any product requested.

Serves business firms and advertising agencies.

All data is treated as confidential.

40 separate on-going panels of 1000 families each, drawn from pool of 90,000.

Quota sample used—each panel consists of 189 strata, balanced against the latest projected census statistics.

The maintenance of a perfectly balanced panel is maintained. The costs must be amortized over many assignments.

SOURCE: *Marketing Knowledge from Consumer Facts*, National Family Opinion, Inc., Toledo 2, Ohio.

---

methods, emphasis on operations, and attempts to broaden the problem as in a model (see Box 13-7).

Motivational research

Marketing researchers continue to search for the key that will open up the answer to "Why" questions. The most recent strides toward the goal have been made through motivational research. An array of techniques endeavors to ascertain the motivations behind the purchase, the reading of

BOX 13-6

Selected Information Secured Every 60 Days in Food Stores

1. Sales to consumers
2. Special factory packs
3. Dealer support (displays, etc.)
4. Retail inventories
5. Prices (wholesale and retail)
6. Average order size
7. Retail distribution
8. Out-of-stock
9. Total food store sales

Broken Down By

BRANDS   TERRITORIES   COUNTY SIZES   STORE TYPES
PACKAGE SIZES   PRODUCT TYPES

SOURCE: Arthur C. Nielsen, "The Responsibilities of Marketing Research," Speech Given at Lucurne, Switzerland, September 20, 1966, p. 40.

BOX 13-7

Operations Research in Marketing

A method for choosing between alternative procedures on the basis of numerical evaluations is illustrated with a merchandising handling problem.

Problem: Should a price tag be placed on ladies' dresses?

Alternatives illustrated: (1) 100 percent tagging
(2) 10 percent tagging
(3) no tagging at all

Objectives: (1) merchandise control for inventory and
cost purposes;   *(0.8)*
(2) customer satisfaction with identi-
fication of items;   *(0.2)*
(3) reduction in handling costs;   *(0.6)*
(4) control over non-legitimate returns;   *(0.1)*

Steps: 1st Weigh the objectives according to their importance. (See figures in parentheses above.)

2nd Compare and evaluate the three alternatives according to the degree to which each satisfies each objective and the importance of each objective.

100% Tagging: $(0.9)(0.8) + (1.0)(0.2) +$
$(0.9)(0.1) + (0.0)(0.6) = 1.01$

10% Tagging: $(0.6)(0.8) + (0.6)(0.2) +$
$(0.4)(0.1) + (0.4)(0.6) = 0.88$

0 Tagging: $(0.4)(0.8) + (0.0)(0.2) +$
$(0.4)(0.1) + (1.0)   = 0.96$

Divide each sum by 0.0101 so that the best procedure corresponds to 100 percent efficiency:

Alternative	Efficiency in Percent
100% Tagging	100
10% Tagging	87
0 Tagging	95

SOURCE: Earl Lamm, "Operations Research Applied to Marketing," *Case Institute of Technology*, Proceedings of the Conference on Operations Research in Marketing, January 1953, p. 49.

an advertisement, or a reaction to a brand name. Examples of some of these techniques are shown in Box 13-8.

Cost Analyses

Cost studies are performed both inside and outside the marketing research department. Cost analysis is intended to reduce various operating costs, and thus its direction is slightly different from marketing research, which is typically involved in expanding sales. Nevertheless, both are expected to improve marketing and profits. Calculations which prove helpful to management include profit related to size of order, selling cost per customer, costs related to product lines, and shipping costs for orders. Internal data are usually relied upon, although outside statistics frequently enable the researcher to compare his company's costs with an industry "standard."

Media Analysis

The effectiveness of all kinds of selling and advertising continues to be elusive. Many hours and much money are invested in evaluation techniques for all kinds of persuasive devices. Most people are familiar with radio and television ratings which may be based on telephone surveys, mechanical devices placed on the set, diaries, or other techniques including personal interviewing. Magazines and newspapers have their own species of marketing research to help advertisers evaluate many kinds of printed media. The task of establishing the number of readers, listeners, or viewers is difficult enough, even for the purpose of defining a reader or a viewer. More difficult is the task of ascertaining the effectiveness of an advertisement on the reader. Evidence such as the following is frequently examined.

	1000 Viewers	1000 Nonviewers
Number of Buyers	400	50
Number of Nonbuyers	600	950

The results of a readership study are shown in Box 13-9.

Experimental Design

This technique has been a difficult one for the researcher. Usually the variables in a marketing situation are extremely difficult to control, and for that reason experimentation has not been used by many marketing research men. In more recent years, however, social psychologists and others have shown that the experimental design method is possible for the study of human behavior and as a consequence there has been additional activity built around this technique. Changes in attitude, recency-primacy studies, effort as related to satisfaction, conformity, and other types of studies have been carried out successfully. The authors of this text believe that the technique has a most

BOX 13-8

Determining Motivation—A Study of Automobiles

(Selected Motivation Research Techniques)

Depth Interviewing: "I'd like you to think of the most satisfying things about owning and driving a car. What would you say they are?"

Thematic Apperception Test:

"The boy has asked Dad for advice about getting a car.
Imagine that you are the parent; what would you tell him?"

Incomplete Sentences: "People who drive convertibles . . . ."

Role Playing: "Pick out a car from this list (on card) that goes with each person the best."

"He's a young guy, just starting out, bright and hopeful."

Attitude Study: "What is the best thing and the worst thing about each of the following cars?"

Descriptions: "Below are some descriptions of automobiles. Which car-make do you think fits closest to each description?"

"A quality car. Expensive, impressive but not flashy.
It's built to last."

SOURCE: *Automobiles—What They Mean to Americans,* Social Research, Inc., Chicago, pp. 6–14.

BOX 13-9

Readership of Business Week

Definition of Qualified Reader: One who can identify more of the published than the unpublished items reproduced in the qualifying kit. The qualifying kit consisted of pages from an actual issue and pages from an issue that had never been published.

Readership of Business Week's pages for April 22, 1950. Of the 112 pages in the issue, 89 had some advertising, 75 had editorial matter, and 40 had editorial illustrations. The percent of readers ranged from 13 for page 96 to 87 for page 9.

Readership of
Business Week's pages
continues
at a high level
throughout the issue

April 22, 1950 Issue
112 Pages Plus Covers

Editorial reading matter appeared on 75 pages in the surveyed issue of Business Week. Forty pages had editorial illustrations.

Advertising appeared on 89 pages, including covers. The issue contained 101 display advertisements and two columns of classified advertising.

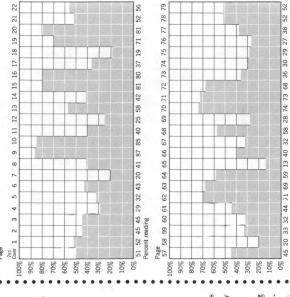

SOURCE: "The Audience and Readership of Business Week," based on the First Advertising Research Foundation Study of an Executive Management Publication, *Business Week*, New York, 1950.

significant potential and that it will be used to a much greater extent in the future.

One type of experiment is that conducted in the laboratory. This may be a pilot test for an experiment which later may be taken to the field, or it may be a basic type of experiment which does not lend itself to direct application. Marketing scholars should probably place more emphasis on the laboratory experiment as they seek answers to such questions as those involving brand loyalty, use of information, advertising stimuli, and personal influence. Box 13-10 illustrates the design of a laboratory experiment.

Field experiments may prove more useful to marketing practitioners than they were in the past. A number of them have been completed with adequate results. Conditions are more difficult to control in the field, but the technique offers a wide variety of opportunities for studying the merchandising of products, especially consumer goods. Box 13-11 provides an example of a field experiment.

BOX 13-10

Effort, Expectation and Satisfaction

Hypotheses: When customers expend little effort to obtain a product, those who receive a product less valuable than they expected will rate that product lower than will those who expected to receive, and do receive, the same product.

As effort expended increases, this effect decreases.

Design:

	Expectation (X)	
Effort (F)	low (l)	high (h)
Low (l)	A	B
High (h)	C	D

Selected Results: Index of mean product evaluation scores (Maximum $= 100$)

	Expectation (X)	
Effort (F)	low (l)	high (h)
Low (l)	51	35
High (h)	54	44

Hypotheses 1 and 2 were supported by the data.

SOURCE: Richard N. Cardozo, "An Experimental Study of Customer Effort, Expectation, and Satisfaction," *Journal of Marketing Research*, Vol. 2, No. 3, August 1965, pages 244–249.

BOX 13-11

Do Consumers Prefer Even or Odd Prices?

Many believe that psychological or odd pricing is more effective than even pricing. By this they mean that $.49, $.98, $19.99, etc., are considerably more attractive to the consumer than prices rounded off at $.50, $1.00, etc. There is little evidence to support this. One such experimental technique provided a means to evaluate the two systems of pricing. Some catalogs of a mail order company were sent out with psychological pricing for selected items: other catalogs were distributed with even pricing for those same items.

The results were interesting and perplexing. For certain items, the two systems were equally effective; for others, even prices resulted in larger sales; for still others, psychological prices proved superior. The results were inconclusive. Further experiments were not attempted when management realized that a change of one cent a yard led to a loss of $50,000!

A modification of this experiment would be depicted in the following design.

	Before Measure	Experimental Variable	After Measure
Group I	Purchases from regular catalog	Catalog with selected even prices	Purchases from even price catalog
Group II	Purchases from regular catalog	Catalog with selected psycho-logical prices	Purchases from psychological price catalog
Group III (Control)	Purchases from regular catalog	Regular catalog	Purchases from regular catalog

SOURCE: Eli Ginsberg, "Customary Prices," *American Economic Review*, Vol. 26, No. 2, March 1936, p. 296.

CONCLUDING COMMENTS

The task of the marketing researcher is not an easy one. He must know research methodology and the role research information plays for his company. Serving all of marketing, he operates under budgetary constraints. His job is continuous, since the need for information never ceases. He wants to provide the most accurate answers at all times but recognizes that accuracy carried to an extreme can be prohibitive in cost. His is a vital staff job, offering techniques which make him a valuable intelligence arm of the company.

Under the best of circumstances, a researcher is going to make mistakes which can mislead management. These instances will be few in number if the researcher and his superiors understand the role of research. The research must not get "lost" in techniques and terminology. Management, on the other hand, must not demand the impossible in terms of quick results, nor should it suggest or compel the researcher to bias his results in any manner.

With the value of marketing information well accepted, the task becomes to improve the information obtainable and the decisions based on it. As Fox has summarized:

Marketing research is an orderly way of finding out:

$$
\begin{Bmatrix} \text{Where} \\ \text{When} \\ \text{How} \\ \text{Why} \\ \text{By Whom} \end{Bmatrix} \quad \begin{Bmatrix} \text{competitive} \\ \text{alternative} \\ \text{our own} \end{Bmatrix} \quad \begin{Bmatrix} \text{products} \\ \text{services} \end{Bmatrix} \quad \text{are} \quad \begin{Bmatrix} \text{sold} \\ \text{bought} \\ \text{used} \end{Bmatrix} \quad \text{and}
$$

WHAT CAN WE DO ABOUT THESE FACTS TO INCREASE PROFITS?[5]

A number of basic, competitive, and routine problems facing the marketer were mentioned in the last chapter. In this chapter, the techniques employed by the researcher as he solves these problems have been briefly discussed. By way of summary, we bring these problems and techniques together in matrix fashion so that the reader has a convenient picture of marketing research. Figure 13-3 serves this purpose.

Questions

1. With what kind of marketing problems can you foresee increased usage of quantitative methods of research?
2. Describe a marketing research program for a firm of your choice. What kinds of people would you hire? What kinds of problems would you assign them?
3. How does a knowledge of the marketing environment relate to the task of the researcher?
4. Apply or suggest techniques of the marketing researcher that would be applicable to the solving of a problem which involves the estimation of demand for a new food product.

---

[5] Fox, *Loc. Cit.*

Marketing Problems	Internal Record Analysis	Census Type Data	Statistical Analysis	Observation	Survey	Motivational Research	Panel Type	Depth Interviewing	Experimental Design	Test Marketing	Experience
Determining market potential	X	X	X				X				X
Delineation sales Territories	X	X	X								X
Images—product, brand, company					X	X		X			
Attitudes					X	X		X			
Attitude changes						X	X	X	X		
Advertising methods and media	X				X	X					X
Store location	X		X	X	X		X			X	X
Packaging						X	X		X	X	X
Product design						X			X	X	X
Brand loyalty					X	X	X	X	X	X	
Channel of distribution	X										X
Pricing	X		X				X		X	X	X
Competitive actions				X			X	X		X	X
Buying habits					X	X	X	X			
Family interaction				X					X		
Product names					X	X	X		X	X	
Demand structure	X		X				X	X		X	
Forecasting	X		X							X	
Selling methods	X			X				X	X		X
Costs of distribution	X										
Uses of products				X	X		X			X	
Returned goods analysis	X										
Consumption expenditures		X			X		X				
Buying attitudes and expectations					X	X		X			
Economic research		X	X								
Product acceptance	X				X		X	X	X	X	
Characteristics of market	X				X		X		X		
Merchandising techniques				X					X	X	X

X = Useful technique for the problem solving

261

Statements to Consider

Market research does not relieve management from the responsibility for making decisions.

Customer analysis is best adapted and most widely used in the marketing of industrial goods, since the number of buyers or customers is small.

To the extent that the services involved in the collection, communication, and interpretation of market information are perfected, accurate forecasting is more likely to occur with respect to selling and buying activities.

Motivation research practitioners are not capable of discovering people's hidden fears and desires.

SELECTED REFERENCES

Robert Ferber and P. J. Verdoorn, *Research Methods in Economics and Business* (New York: The Macmillan Company, 1962).

Paul E. Green and Donald S. Tull, *Research for Marketing Decisions* (Englewood Cliffs, N.J.: Prentice-Hall, 1966).

Melvin Anshen, "Management Science in Marketing: Status and Prospects," *Management Science,* Vol. 2, No. 3, April 1959, pp. 222–231.

° Leo Bogart, "Inside Marketing Research," *Public Opinion Quarterly,* Vol. 27, No. 4, Winter 1963, pp. 562–577.

° Ernest Dichter, "Psychology in Market Research," *Harvard Business Review,* Vol. 25, No. 4, Summer 1947, pp. 432–443.

Paul E. Green, "Bayesian Statistics and Product Decisions," *Business Horizons,* Vol. 5, No. 9, Fall 1962, pp. 101–110.

Generalizations Were Taken From:

Roland S. Vaile, E. T. Grether, and Reavis Cox, *Marketing in the American Economy* (New York: The Ronald Press Company, 1952).

Rayburn D. Tousley, Eugene Clark, and Fred E. Clark, *Principles of Marketing* (New York: The Macmillian Company, 1962).

George Katona, *The Powerful Consumer* (New York: McGraw-Hill Book Company, 1960).

ADDENDUM 1.

Marketing Research Position Descriptions

GREEN GIANT COMPANY: DIRECTOR—MARKET RESEARCH,
JOB DESCRIPTION

Responsible to the Vice President—Marketing for administering the Company's market research activity.

Responsibility and Authority

A. Operational
   1. Formulate and recommend investigations of marketing policies, programs, and procedures of the Company and other companies.
   2. Direct and supervise approved investigations of marketing activities.
   3. Direct the performance of tests:
      (a) To determine the relative market standing of Company products and competitive products, both overall and by individual marketing area.
      (b) To measure consumer reaction to proposed new products and new product ideas or actual new products.
      (c) To measure the impact of Company and competitive advertising.
      (d) To study consumer attitudes and feelings toward Company and competitive brands and products.
   4. Compile and maintain files concerning the marketing of Company products.
   5. Analyze and interpret such data so as to bring to management's attention various factors which may have immediate or long-term influence on the marketing of Company products.
   6. Initiate with aid of Brand Marketing Directors and Corporate Planning short and long-term Company sales forecasts.
   7. Recommend to the Director of Sales the purchase of canned goods when necessary.

B. Organizational
   1. Train and maintain a market research organization adequate for the needs of the Company.
   2. Direct and supervise the activities of: Two Market Research Analysts and Sales Research Analyst.

Relationships

A. Within the Company
   1. Coordinate his activities in obtaining shipping information from Controller's Department.

2. Cooperate with Product Development Department by coordinating his activities in investigating consumer reaction to new products or new product ideas.
3. Cooperate with other departments of the Company in developing and executing market research plans.
4. Coordinate Market Research activities of Green Giant of Canada and the International Division.

B. Outside the Company
   1. Conduct such relationships with outside research service agencies, government agencies, industrial and professional organizations as are necessary to accomplish his function.
   2. Maintain liaison with the Market Research Department of the advertising agency.

LINCOLN-MERCURY DIVISION, FORD MOTOR COMPANY

Responsibilities of Marketing Research Department

1. Develop, interpret and report survey information concerning the characteristics, motivations, attitudes and behavior of automobile consumers, dealers and salesmen as they relate to the plans and activities of the Division.

2. Report on and interpret estimates of basic economic factors and trends affecting automobile demand as developed by consultants and economic research groups outside the Division.

3. Develop effective and economical survey and analysis procedures and conduct marketing research studies consistent with approved organization procedures.

4. Ascertain consumer reaction to proposed styling concepts, designs, or product features.

5. Ascertain consumer reaction to proposed advertising, solicitation, and promotional programs.

6. Develop basic, continuing measurements of the effectiveness of Division and competitors' advertising; dealer sales solicitation and service; and product design, features, and quality.

7. Develop basic, continuing information on consumer motivations, characteristics, preferences, and shopping behavior.

8. Ascertain dealer and salesman attitudes toward the Division's product and merchandising practices.

9. Ascertain prices being asked by dealers for Divisional and competitive products.

ADDENDUM 2. A Case Study in Marketing Research

Company: Archer Daniels Midland Company, a 61-year-old, diversified producer of industrial products made primarily from agricultural commodities and from chemicals.

The company operates approximately 80 plants, mines, and elevators in the United States and has production facilities in 10 other countries.

Customers are located in over 100 industries.

1963 sales—$271,000,000

The Problem: Lack of public identification—"What is ADM?" Management agreed that something had to be done about the corporate image if the company were to achieve its very ambitious growth objectives. New products meant marketing to new industries and more intensive marketing to some industries where ADM did not have extensive penetration.

Procedure: (1) Define the present ADM identification.
(2) Develop a set of corporate objectives.
(3) Study the complete product line.
(4) Develop an identity system.
 (a) Name
 (b) Symbol and corporate signature

Selected Findings: (1) A variety of names and trademarks were being used.
(2) Many products had no identification except for a number or technical marking, e.g. many of the 19 million bags, cartons, cans, and drums carried no identification.
(3) Buildings and rolling stock were remarked or marked inconsistently.
(4) Profile studies revealed differences between what people thought the company was and what they thought it should be.

Use of Marketing Research: The data gathered through surveys and other devices enabled management to program for a new identity system.

Final Result: The adoption of a distinctive symbol which identified the company, its strong interest in agriculture and chemicals and its research. The symbol implied a progressive firm with a "new look."

Implementation: Letterheads, invoices, advertising, buildings, containers, rolling stock, company literature, displays, and all other visual instruments received the new look.

Comment: Subsequent research has indicated that the corporation is solving its problem of identification.

ADDENDUM 3. *Marketing Research Code of Ethics*

The American Marketing Association, in furtherance of its central objective of the advancement of science in marketing and in recognition of its obligation to the public, has established these principles of ethical practice of marketing research for the guidance of its members. In an increasingly complex society, marketing management is more and more dependent upon marketing information intelligently and systematically obtained. The consumer is the source of much of this information. Seeking the cooperation of the consumer in the development of information, marketing management must acknowledge its obligation to protect the public from misrepresentation and exploitation under the guise of research.

Similarly the research practitioner has an obligation to the discipline he practices and to those who provide support for his practice—an obligation to adhere to basic and commonly accepted standards of scientific investigation as they apply to the domain of marketing research.

It is the intent of this code to define ethical standards required of marketing research in satisfying these obligations.

Adherence to this code will assure the users of marketing research that the research was done in accordance with acceptable ethical practices. Those engaged in research will find in this code an affirmation of sound and honest basic principles which have developed over the years as the profession has grown. The field interviewers who are the point of contact between the profession and the consumer will also find guidance in fulfilling their vitally important role.

For Research Users, Practitioners and Interviewers

1. No individual or organization will undertake any activity which is directly or indirectly represented to be marketing research, but which has as its real purpose the attempted sale of merchandise or services to some or all of the respondents interviewed in the course of the research.

2. If a respondent has been led to believe, directly or indirectly, that he is participating in a marketing research survey and that his anonymity will be protected, his name shall not be made known to anyone outside the research organization or research department, or used for other than research purposes.

For Research Practitioners

1. There will be no intentional or deliberate misrepresentation of research methods or re-

sults. An adequate description of methods employed will be made available upon request to the sponsor of the research. Evidence that field work has been completed according to specifications will, upon request, be made available to buyers of research.

2. The identity of the survey sponsor and/or the ultimate client for whom a survey is being done will be held in confidence at all times, unless this identity is to be revealed as part of the research design. Research information shall be held in confidence by the research organization or department and not used for personal gain or made available to any outside party unless the client specifically authorizes such release.

3. A research organization shall not undertake marketing studies for competitive clients when such studies would jeopardize the confidential nature of client-agency relationships.

For Users of Marketing Research

1. A user of research shall not knowingly disseminate conclusions from a given research project or service that are inconsistent with or not warranted by the data.

2. To the extent that there is involved in a research project a unique design involving techniques, approaches or concepts not commonly available to research practitioners, the prospective user of research shall not solicit such a design from one practitioner and deliver it to another for execution without the approval of the design originator.

For Field Interviewers

1. Research assignments and materials received, as well as information obtained from respondents, shall be held in confidence by the interviewer and revealed to no one except the research organization conducting the marketing study.

2. No information gained through a marketing research activity shall be used directly or indirectly, for the personal gain or advantage of the interviewer.

3. Interviews shall be conducted in strict accordance with specifications and instructions received.

4. An interviewer shall not carry out two or more interviewing assignments simultaneously unless authorized by all contractors or employers concerned.

Members of the American Marketing Association will be expected to conduct themselves in accordance with the provisions of this Code in all of their marketing research activities.

SOURCE: American Marketing Association.

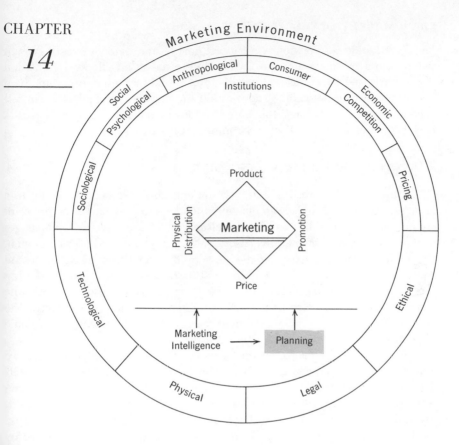

Planning for Marketing Development

MARKETING DEVELOPMENT AND DECISION MAKING · THE NATURE OF MARKET-
ING DEVELOPMENT · SETTING MARKETING OBJECTIVES · THE PLAN FOR MAR-
KETING DEVELOPMENT   *Kinds of Plans   Elements of the Plan* · AN OVERALL VIEW OF
PLANNING · AN ILLUSTRATION OF PLANNING · ADDENDUM—GENERALIZATIONS
ON MARKETING PLANNING

Since marketing is so obviously a natural part of our society's overall growth patterns and the marketer is primarily interested in an effective allocation of his marketing effort, his real need is for a sound marketing program. Such a program has the sole aim of developing the market. Its objective is to sell products, and in achieving this end it allocates marketing effort against a background of many kinds of environmental forces and restrictions.

MARKETING DEVELOPMENT AND DECISION MAKING

At this point the broad and almost impersonal statements about the role of marketing take on added significance. Blended into the marketing program are myriads of individual marketing decisions which are made by top management, middle management, advertisers, salesmen, clerks, and warehousemen. These many decisions concern the development of the market; successful development reflects proper implementation of a well-conceived marketing program. The broad program must become precisely targeted when the actual marketing development work commences. Box 14-1 illustrates the merging of broad environmental and narrower company forces into one important aspect of marketing, the sales forecast.

It is clear that the marketer must perform his functions in an atmosphere of simultaneously and constantly occurring problems and influences. Marketing-development operations are competitive and difficult, requiring the marketer's decisions to anticipate changes in a host of economic and even psychological indicators. These decisions, one by one, should be made on the basis of a company marketing program. A desultory change in price by even one cent may be translated into a loss of thousands of dollars; a well-conceived advertising program may mean the difference between profit and loss; a well-timed change in product design may win accolades and brand loyalty from consumers; a strengthened network of distributors can result in adequate physical supply as needed. These are the marketing decisions made by all marketers. They are not made in a vacuum, but are simultaneously arrived at in the often cyclonic marketplace. Sometimes marketing decisions are routine, other times they are once-in-a-lifetime decisions. Some are easy, others difficult. Presumably they are based on fact, although some decisions will utilize tenuous or flimsy evidence. It is not surprising to find that marketers are criticized in their marketing-development effort for attempts to persuade consumers.

The marketer's task can be depicted rather simply. He views the product as a bundle of features. These features include price, package, style, and other ingredients that represent a company's best interpretation of its ability to match its resources to the needs of the market place through the product bundle.

BOX 14-1

Sales Forecasting: a Focus for Integrative Planning

Noncontrollable and Partially Controllable External factors

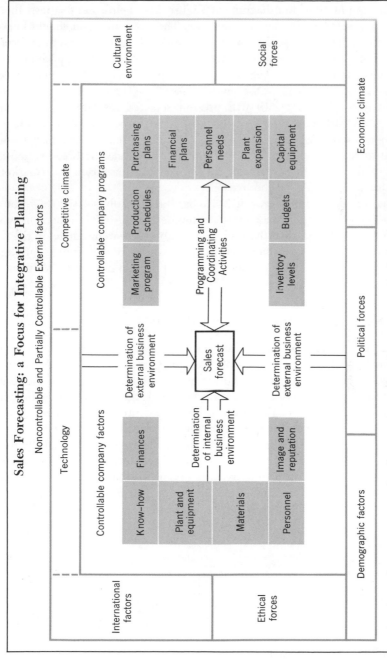

The above figure portrays sales forecasting as an aid to integrative planning. It indicates the controllable, partially controllable, and noncontrollable factors that management should integrate and take into account in making effective sales forecasting.

SOURCE: William Lazar, "Sales Forecasting: Key to Integrated Management," *Business Horizons*, Vol. 2, Fall 1959, p. 65.

The simplicity of the diagram in Figure 14-1 helps one to grasp the job of the marketer, or marketing manager. The basic function should be kept in mind as the reader pursues some of the details of the marketing-development task. One should also be aware of the complexity of the problem, since each facet of the job can become most involved. Box 14-2 depicts this complexity for one segment of the market plan—the media plan.

Chapters 15 through 19 will present selected marketing development tasks, with particular reference to determining product policy, pricing the product, persuading people to buy, and deciding upon the channels through which to sell the product. This chapter, in presenting the broader ramifications of the marketing program, emphasizes the formation of a marketing plan for development of the market.

The order of material in this book has intentionally set the stage for the marketing-development task by first considering the environment in which marketing functions, then the role of marketing research. Partly on the basis of the marketing research information, the marketer conceives of an intelligent program and on the basis of the marketing program he will actively engage in an efficient development task.

THE NATURE OF MARKETING DEVELOPMENT

The activity in the marketplace may be roughly comparable to the play on the football field. Each coach has given resources which he matches against those of the opponent, the teams have similar though not necessarily identical objectives, and scouting reports provide the information upon which the game plan is based. Elaborate preparations precede the game. As each man learns to execute his responsibilities, timing improves. New plays are developed in order to employ the various team weapons effectively and to achieve surprise. After the whistle blows, the quarterback is in a situation of calling plays, one at a time, usually under less-than-favorable conditions, from his standpoint. Simultaneously the game's elements converge upon the team. A bouncing ball, a penalty, an injury, a lucky break, a missed block, a

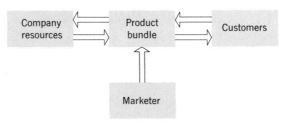

Figure 14-1. A view of marketing management.
SOURCE: Conversations with William F. Ogden, General Electric Corporation.

grasping hand, or an extra burst of energy may make the difference between the team's meeting its objective or missing it.

A game is certainly similar to a business situation. We think of managers instead of coaches and quarterbacks, competitors instead of opponents. Poor game decisions are analogous to misallocation of resources, fumbles resemble poor selling efforts, and a favorable wind is comparable to favorable buying attitudes. Companies, like teams, can fumble, be penalized, make their objectives, or punt when the going becomes too difficult. Time-outs and half-time intermissions are matched in business by lulls and periods of inactivity. Basically, the game and the market activity are built upon intelligence, planning, and developmental effort.

The marketer must be prepared to move his plan forward into an uncertain situation in which many different kinds of forces operate simultaneously. New product introductions, changes in buying attitudes, changes in styles, new legislation, competition added to or subtracted from the scene, advertising campaigns, and price wars are only some of the visible activities which confront the marketing manager. Emphasis in recent years has been on a *total plan* which encompasses all phases of marketing. In this light, the marketer can grasp and plan for any kind of contingency, and he runs less risk of overlooking an integral part of the overall program.

The decision-making task of the marketer is a key one. Decisions concerning the development of the market represent much of what we recognize to be marketing. Development of the market must be done under conditions which are almost less than ideal. The marketer gathers pertinent information, builds his program, and executes his development task with systematic direction. Marketing is "heard" the loudest during development, for it is in this stage that plans collide with actual market conditions.

SETTING MARKETING OBJECTIVES

Many, perhaps most, firms operate without explicit and written statements of objectives. The objectives are likely to be implicit, however, although it is apparent that some firms have little understanding of where they are attempting to "go." General as it may be, the profit objective certainly serves as a guiding force. Recently one of the authors met with a group of middle-management personnel from a large firm and asked each to indicate the company's objectives. Answers were varied: "Make money," "Sell more each year," "Be number one," "Increase our share of the market," among others. It was clear that all had assumed profit to be important, although only a few explicitly mentioned it. Drucker (see Box 14-3) suggests that most businesses have seven distinct marketing goals.

Actually, a corporation has objectives which must respond to pressures

BOX 14-2

Factors and People Influencing Media Selection

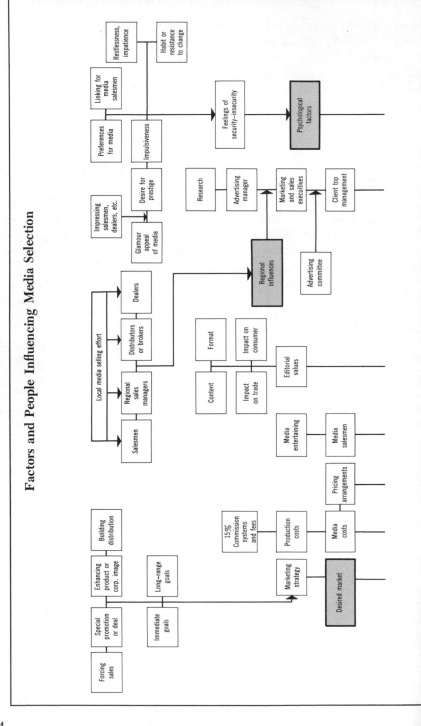

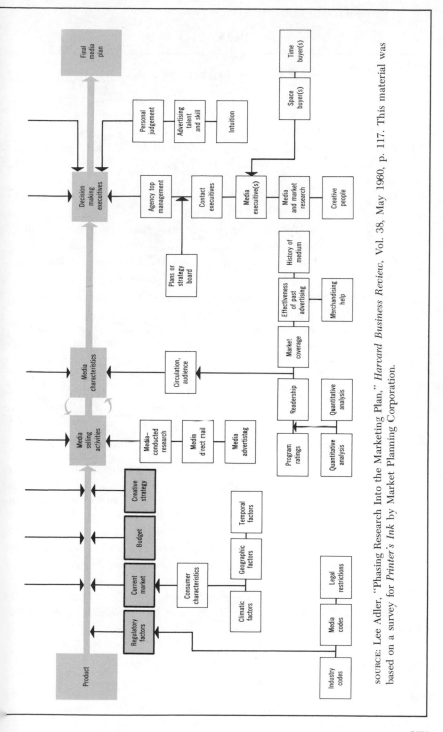

SOURCE: Lee Adler, "Phasing Research Into the Marketing Plan," *Harvard Business Review*, Vol. 38, May 1960, p. 117. This material was based on a survey for *Printer's Ink* by Market Planning Corporation.

BOX 14-3

The Seven Marketing Goals

1. The desired standing of existing products in their present market, expressed in dollars as well as in percentage of the market, measured against both direct and indirect competition.

2. The desired standing of existing products in new markets set both in dollars and percentage points, and measured against direct and indirect competition.

3. The existing products that should be abandoned—technology, market trend, improved product mix, change in objectives.

4. New products needed in existing markets—number, properties, dollar volume, market share for each.

5. The new markets that new products should develop—dollars and percentages.

6. Distributive organization needed to accomplish the marketing goals and the pricing policy appropriate to them.

7. A service objective measuring how well the customer should be supplied with what he considers value by the company, its products, its sales and service organization.

SOURCE: Peter F. Drucker, *The Practice of Management* (New York: Harper & Brothers, 1954), pp. 67–68.

from both insiders and outsiders. Drucker's objectives are the firm's marketing objectives but, of course, the marketer has to be aware also of broader corporate objectives. Not all firms can have the same objectives, since one type of pressure group may be dominant in one firm and subordinate in another. For example, a company locating today in a small city must be more civic-conscious than the firm locating in an already developed industrial complex. The objectives developed by one corporation are reproduced in Box 14-4.

These objectives have been developed in some detail. The objective of "adequate return" includes new ventures, and the criteria for judging such ventures have been listed.

1. Offer a substantial growth potential.
2. Be in an industry which is at the early stage of its growth cycle.
3. Offer an attractive return on investment.
4. Provide a relatively quick payout period.

BOX 14-4

OBJECTIVES

of the

Archer Daniels Midland Company

ADM aims to be a vigorous, responsible and growing customer-and-profit oriented enterprise. Guided by market research and planning and supported by technical research, we intend to fill the needs and wants of specific industries with products developed and produced by ADM'S specialized know-how and experience.

Utilizing selected materials derived from farm, sea, mine and laboratory, efficiently purchased, stored, transported and processed, chemically or mechanically upgraded, and professionally marketed, it is our purpose to be leaders in carefully chosen fields of growth and opportunity on an international scale.

OUR OBJECTIVES ARE TO:

... Achieve leadership and growth in selected fields by efficiently serving the needs and wants of present and future CUSTOMERS.

... Produce earnings sufficient to pay SHAREHOLDERS an adequate return and to provide for long-term growth and stability.

... Provide opportunity and incentive for EMPLOYEES.

... Conduct our relationships with SUPPLIERS honestly and fairly and expect from them maximum value in goods and services.

... Take our place as good citizens in the COMMUNITY and to earn and keep the good will of the public.

SOURCE: "Corporate Objectives," Archer Daniels Midland Company, Minneapolis, undated.

5. Be an industry in which the company is qualified by know-how, capital, and experience to offer equal or better service, performance, and economy than competitors.
6. Serve industrial markets.

It is difficult to spell out all details related to objectives, and it may be unwise to go to an extreme position which could conceivably eliminate the firm's maneuverability. General statements of objectives usually serve as sufficient guidelines for marketers.

THE PLAN FOR MARKETING DEVELOPMENT

Marketers have a variety of tasks to perform. Planning these tasks represents one of the more important responsibilities of the marketing manager. He investigates the market, forecasts demand, proposes the product bundle, and plans for marketing-development work. Investigation (marketing research) is the basis for planning; corporate objectives serve as guidelines. Planning follows analyses and precedes the actual development task. The plan need not sacrifice flexibility, for its purpose is not to introduce rigidity. As a quarterback frequently changes signals after he reaches the line of scrimmage, so the marketer adjusts his efforts in the development process.

Urwick has carefully set forth his views about planning. Since these ideas are relevant and since they summarize the role of planning, excerpts from one of his works may be appropriate.

The basic principle underlying planning is Order. That is why we plan, so that action may follow in a systematic, orderly way and not be checked or confused because this essential item has not been supplied or because that preliminary process has not been completed in time. Planning is essentially the analysis and measurement of materials and processes in advance of the event and the perfection of the records so that we may know exactly where we are at any given moment. . . .

The principle underlying all planning is policy: planning must be the expression of policy or it is meaningless. . . .

The effect of separating planning from performance is that you get calculation. . . .

The principle underlying separation of planning from performance is Simplification. . . .

The principle underlying all planning calculations should be balance. . . .

The purpose of all planning is order. It is possible to think logically and comprehensively about the process of management as a whole, to arrange our knowledge about grouping and correlating tasks and about directing and motivating groups, in some kind of pattern which includes almost everything that anyone in a position of authority has said about it. . . .[1]

[1] Lyndall F. Urwick, *The Pattern of Management* (Minneapolis: University of Minnesota Press, 1956), pp. 85–88.

Kinds of plans

Any study made of corporate planning will doubtless uncover a wide assortment of plans. Some companies place their plans in writing whereas others follow a practice of forming only oral ones. Some plans are general and others are detailed and specific. Some are for the short run but others cover a planning period of a decade. Plans are formed from the top management group downward and from the lower echelons upward. Both total and partial marketing plans exist. Regardless of form or kind, the plans are all devised for the purpose of helping the firm proceed from its present position to some future goal.

The diversity present in the kinds of plans should not be looked upon disparagingly. Companies have different planning needs, and the same company can have several kinds of plans. Both long- and short-term plans are common within the same company, as are general and specific plans. The reasons for planning, the procedure, the period covered, and the totality of the plan may all vary from firm to firm, but the important point is that many firms now recognize the value of planning their marketing procedures. It has become axiomatic that the effect of planning marketing decisions is to increase efficiency in allocating marketing resources, that is, in matching resources with markets.

Elements of the plan

The elements of a marketing plan differ a good deal from one another. Nevertheless, it is useful to enumerate some of the elements which may appear in a marketing plan. Box 14-5 presents one set of elements which illustrates the ramifications of a marketing program. These elements must be examined in the light of pertinent and reliable marketing information. If company policy is made clear to the marketers, a realistic and flexible marketing plan can then evolve, one which takes the elements into consideration.

A close examination of the marketing plan suggests that a marketing-development program is quite all-inclusive and that the marketing-development process itself represents a formidable effort. Planning does not complicate the process, although planning itself is no easy task. Planning serves to simplify and put order into the development program so that resources are efficiently utilized.

The ideal marketing plan, then, is one which permits the firm to market its products in an orderly, efficient, and profitable manner. To be more specific, a plan should have a number of characteristics in order for the plan itself to accomplish anything. The following characteristics should be kept

BOX 14-5

Elements of Market Planning

SALES GOALS
> *Measuring Opportunity*
> Sales forecasts
> Market potentials
> Consumer behavior and motivation
> Market testing
> Industrial markets

MARKETING
PROGRAMS
> *Allocating Effort*
> Product line
> Marketing channels
> Prices and discounts
> Sales budgets
> Marketing mix
> Advertising media
> Advertising appeals
> Sales compensation
> Production scheduling
> Quality control

ORGANIZATION
> *Mobilizing Capacity*
> Organization structure
> Internal communication
> Standards and supervision
> Training and executive development
> Inventory policy
> Production and procurement base
> Investment planning
> Financing market expansion

SOURCE: "The Challenge of Marketing Management," *Cost and Profit Outlook*, Vol. 10, No. 1, January 1957, p. 1.

in mind as one plans one's marketing effort. It can be seen quite readily that "violation" of one of these can render a plan unworkable. For example, a plan which is not communicated to all pertinent personnel is one which hardly has an opportunity to be put into effect. Or a plan which is not objective or which is not based on intelligence may be unrealistic and so biased that it is far wide of the mark.

Characteristics of an Ideal Marketing Plan

Objective	Balanced
Well timed	Allocates resources efficiently
Simple	Developed through participation
Based on clearly defined objectives	of several layers of management
Acceptable to both top	Comprehensive
and lower management	Integrated with all operations
Based on marketing intelligence	Accompanied by a schedule
Flexible	Controlled by periodic examination
Communicated to all concerned	Realistic

It is highly unlikely that any marketing plan would fulfill all these pre-requisites. On the other hand, management should strive for these characteristics, compromising only when necessary. In the business world these compromises are forced upon the firm because of lack of agreement among management, lack of intelligence data, inadequate resources, and perhaps because of uncontrollable factors such as war or depression.

AN OVERALL VIEW OF PLANNING

In order to gain perspective, let us first review the firm's management tasks, which are both important and interrelated. Planning fits naturally into the scheme. Diagrammatically, one might represent management's tasks as in Figure 14-2. The end result of the process is, of course, the product bundle of the firm and the elements of the marketing-development task. The actions

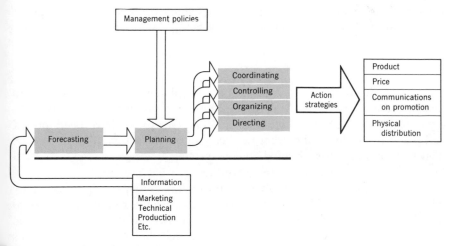

Figure 14-2. The tasks of management.
SOURCE: Urwick, *op. cit.*, p. 52.

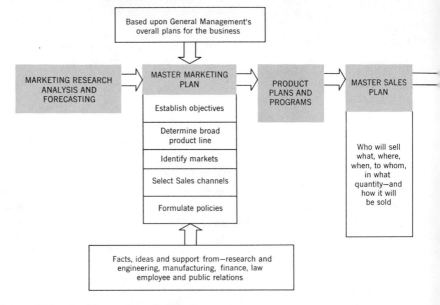

Figure 14-3. An illustration of planning.
SOURCE: Adapted from Edward S. McKay, "How to Plan and Set up Your Marketing Program," *Marketing Series No. 91*, American Management Association, January, 1954, pp. 16–17.

taken by salesmen, advertisers, clerks, warehousemen, buyers, and others are based on the management activities. Although the typical consumer thinks only of the development process when he thinks of marketing, it becomes clear that the planning and programming which precede the development task are an integral part of successful marketing by any firm.

AN ILLUSTRATION OF PLANNING

Perhaps the best way to summarize the planning for marketing is to illustrate the entire process. For example, assume that we are affiliated with a company which produces outboard motors. Our profits have been modest and our share of the total market has been an unsatisfactory 10 percent. The Board of Directors has directed that marketing management take steps to improve the firm's market share as well as its profit picture.

Marketing research will supply the information. Perhaps a consumer survey will show unquestionable evidence that many customers desire an outboard motor which provides approximately 30 horsepower while at the same time being light in weight. The engineers may find that they can meet consumer's desires through use of new materials and new techniques. Thus, marketing and technical research forces can dovetail their activities.

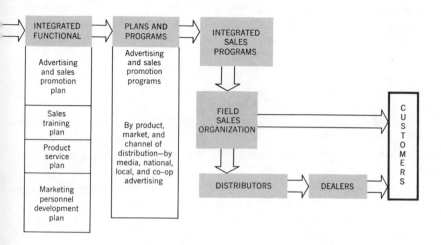

A master marketing plan will be drawn with objectives established, a product line decided upon, markets identified, sales channels determined, and sales policies formulated. Later, a detailed sales plan will evolve and the marketing-development tasks and responsibilities will be made known to those involved. The advertising manager will devise a promotion plan to handle some of the development, the sales manager will map out the training necessary for his sales forces, product repair services will be examined, and a policy for handling it will be decided.

Ultimately, distributors will be brought into the picture, and will be trained for the new product-development work. Television, magazines, and local newspapers will finally announce the new outboard motor to the public, and the marketing plan can be considered to be in operation. This entire planning program is summarized in Figure 14-3, which depicts the marketing planning process from start to finish. Based on marketing intelligence, the marketer devises a plan to employ his resources, making decisions which involve each fragment of his resources, and considering each facet of the development process.

Questions

1. Flexibility is a constraint on planning. Explain.
2. In setting long-range market objectives and plans, *completeness* does not mean a detailed program. What does completeness mean in this setting?

3. Assume that you are the marketing manager of a United States airline. Your company is faced with a decision concerning the purchase of a new plane which will be ready for delivery in six years. In what ways can you help your firm decide on the purchase?
4. Describe how the marketing-research department can provide help to those who are in charge of corporate planning.

Statements to Consider

All marketing decisions, to bear any relation to reality, must be based on a forecast of what the future holds.

The purpose of marketing planning is to take advantage of existing preferences in such a way that business can profit.

Tactical surprise is usually the reward of the daring, the imaginative, and the ingenious. It will rarely be gained by recourse to the obvious.

Decisions will have to be made regardless of the fact that the situation may be vague, abnormal, or illogical. Each event that occurs, each bit of information received, will cause the manager to ask himself, "Shall I continue with my present plan and operations, or is it now necessary for me to give a new order?" Whatever the answer to this question, it involves a decision on the part of the manager.

A simple, workable plan is important; a clear, understandable order is important; but supervision to see that the policies of management are followed is all-important.

Rapid changes in a situation often require rapid changes in decisions. Therefore changes in plans will be frequent and should be accepted as normal incidents of competition.

In business a large safety factor should be included in all time and space calculations.

SELECTED REFERENCES

Steuart Henderson Britt and Harper W. Boyd, Jr., *Marketing Management and Administrative Action* (New York: McGraw-Hill Book Company, 1964).

William Lazer and Eugene J. Kelley, *Managerial Marketing: Perspectives and Viewpoints*, Rev. Ed. (Homewood, Ill.: Richard D. Irwin, 1962).

Martin Zober, *Marketing Management* (New York: John Wiley and Sons, 1964).

° Henry C. Baker, "Sales and Marketing Planning of the Edsel," in *Marketing's Role in Scientific Management*, Proceedings of the 39th National Conference of the American Marketing Association, June 1957, pp. 128–144.

° Victor P. Buell, "Long-Range Planning in a Decentralized Company," in *Effective Marketing Coordination*, Proceedings of the 44th National Conference of the American Marketing Association, June 1961, pp. 255–262.

° Robert J. Keith, "The Marketing Revolution," *Journal of Marketing*, Vol. 24, No. 3, January 1960, pp. 35–38.

° Wendell R. Smith, "Product Differentiation and Market Segmentation as Alternative Marketing Strategies," *Journal of Marketing*, Vol. 21, No. 1, July 1957, pp. 3–8.

Generalizations Were Adapted From:

Infantry in Battle (Washington, D.C.: The Infantry Journal Incorporated, 1939).

ADDENDUM. *Generalizations on Marketing Planning—For Discussion Purposes*

1. All sound marketing planning starts with research.

2. Planning is not an end in itself.

3. Planning is fundamentally an intellectual process, a mental predisposition to do things in an orderly way.

4. Planning does not superimpose any new authority.

5. In business, obscurity and confusion are normal. Late, exaggerated, or misleading information, surprise situations, and counter-orders are to be expected.

6. The manager must not permit himself to be paralyzed by chronic obscurity. He must be prepared to take prompt and decisive action in spite of the scarcity or total absence of reliable information. He must learn that in business the abnormal is normal and that uncertainty is certain.

7. In business the simplest way is usually the best way. Direct, simple plans, clear, concise orders, and operations that facilitate control will smooth the way for subordinates, minimize the confusion of business, and ordinarily increase the chances of success.

8. In business, time always presses; therefore, managers should be quick to seize upon any time-saving expedient.

9. Surprise is a master key to success.

10. No rule can tell us how to time decisions correctly. All we can say is that the decision must be made early enough for action based upon it to be

effective. On the other hand, it must not be taken prematurely, lest it fail to meet a changing situation.

11. We consider it axiomatic that in business there will always be a plan. But history is replete with instances where organizations have drifted into competition for no particular reason and with no particular plan. It is true that the manager's plan may, and frequently will, change with changes in the situation, but the motivating idea behind it must remain.

12. Tenacity does not necessarily mean dogged persistence in a given course of action. A change of methods may be desirable. The will must be powerful without being pigheaded and stupid; it must have suppleness and the spirit of adaptation.

13. Superior mobility must be achieved if we are to surprise our competitor, select the grounds on which we are to compete, and gain the initiative. There is no alternative.[2]

[2] Many of the above have been adapted from *Infantry in Battle* (Washington, D.C.: The Infantry Journal, Incorporated, 1939).

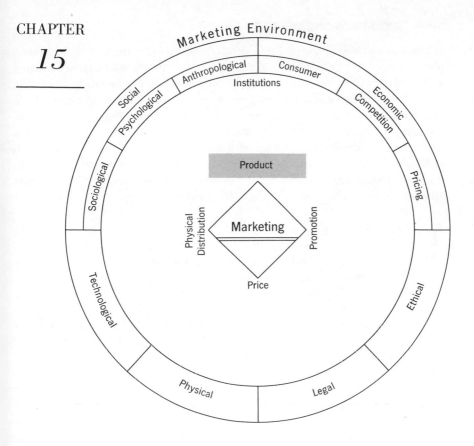

Market Development: The Product

The Product Focus   A Product   Product Life Cycles • **THE PRODUCT IN THE MARKETING ENVIRONMENT**   *Competition   The Consumer   Technology and the Product   Ethics and the Product   The Law and the Product* • **DEVELOPING THE MARKET FOR THE PRODUCT**   *Plans and Strategies   Research   Pricing   Physical Distribution   Persuasion* • ADDENDA: 1. WAYS A PRODUCT CAN BE NEW • 2. DROPOUT BRANDS OF AUTO-MOBILES SINCE 1920

When money is exchanged for a product or service, marketing has taken place, matter has been placed in motion, and a product has been matched with a market. The buyer anticipates that the product will satisfy his needs, the seller that the transaction will result in some amount of profit. Millions of products and services are offered for sale, some having been on the market for many years and others being relative newcomers. Millions of products successfully "deliver the standard of living," whereas millions of others fail in some way to satisfy buyers or sellers or both, and are removed from the market. In each instance, the seller hopes to develop a niche in the market into which he can successfully place his product.

The product focus

The product is the focus of marketing. Enormous human and capital resources are concentrated on the development of products and the development of markets for them. The product is produced, distributed, stored, financed, bought and sold, promoted, and ultimately consumed. Most marketing tasks are directed in some way toward the product. Aggregate data such as Gross National Product provide some indication of the vast number of products placed in motion, but perhaps a little reflection on the goods and services we consume each day provides a better notion of the marketing task.

Management decisions to produce and distribute a given product are decisions of resource allocation. The resources involved are more than those of production, since they include the resources of marketing, finance, and other business operations. Many factors influence these decisions, and the ensuing products reflect the dynamics of the environment in which the decisions are made.

Product alterations may cause changes in the firm's marketing processes and, conversely, changes in marketing influence a company's considerations of its products. Adding an industrial film product to a line of consumer camera film products obviously will mean changes in channels, packaging, pricing, promotion, and selling. Likewise, the development of a new frozen or dehydrated process for foods can bring about the introduction of a new line of products. Or vending machine distribution may affect a firm's product line. These examples illustrate the focal point of the product in the affluent society of today. Marketers play vital roles in matching company resources (through products) with a wide variety of consumer needs. Marketers help to make decisions which enable the firm to concentrate on the opportunities afforded by the marketplace. Outstanding performance comes only when resources are well matched to niches of the market.

A product

We have used the term "product" in a broad sense. Any bundle of features from toothpicks to watch repair may be thought of as a product. Products can be classified in many ways. Peter Drucker sees eight categories of products and services:

1. Today's breadwinner—a product at or near its zenith.
2. Yesterday's breadwinner—frequently confused with today's.
3. Tomorrow's breadwinner—both a reality and a promise.
4. The repair job—suffers from one major and definable defect.
5. The unnecessary specialty—needs standardization.
6. The unjustified specialty—fills no economic function.
7. Investment in managerial ego—the Edsel, for example.
8. Cinderella—lacks the support of the management.[1]

Drucker's classification is management-oriented, and anyone can see immediate examples of products which fall into each of the categories.

A behavioral scientist may argue that a product includes everything that a person perceives about it. A product "image," then, could include color, taste, reputation, ingredients, and so on. For our purposes, a product may be a bundle of ingredients put together for sale as something useful to a consumer —an automobile, for example. The product may also be a service, for developing a market for a service differs only in detail from doing so for a tangible product.

Product life cycles

The typical notion of a product life cycle may be seen in Figure 15-1. Time is a relative matter on the chart, for a product's life cycle may vary from a matter of hours to decades. Marketing's task is to build the market toward the saturation point and to "hold" it at that place for as long as possible. Replacements can account for many sales, depending on the item. For many products, however, replacements cannot account for a large enough sales volume and the product slowly disappears from the market. It is no easy matter to estimate how long a product will be in each phase of the life cycle. Indeed, it is difficult to know at any given time exactly where the product is. For example, one economist wrote in 1926:

The automobile industry has proceeded through its introductory stage, in which sales to new users were difficult. . . . The sale of cars at the present rate for a few years more will bring the number of cars in use to such a level that the replace-

[1] Peter F. Drucker, "Care and Feeding of the Profitable Product," *Fortune*, March 1964, pp. 133–135.

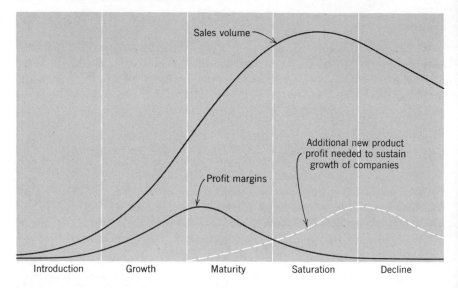

Figure 15-1. The basic life cycle of new products.
SOURCE: Booz, Allen, and Hamilton, *Management of New Products*, New York, 1960.

ment of those cars from year to year will demand a production about equal to the present output of the industry. . . . In other words, the industry will have come to maturity and will take its place beside the iron and steel industry, the agricultural implement industry, shoe manufacturing, and other established, stable industries of the country.[2]

This analysis was an excellent one. Griffin saw that families might own more than one car. Yet, even with a quarter of a century of data at hand, it was extremely difficult to place the automobile exactly in a life or growth cycle. In the year when Griffin wrote, 3,692,317 passenger cars were produced. In the years after the Second World War, passenger-car production has ranged from a low of 3,558,178 in 1947 to 7,920,186 in 1955 and 7,554,100 in 1966.

The timing of the introduction of a product may be crucial to its success. Frequently a product fails at one time and then succeeds at another. (Cake mixes were unsuccessfully introduced in the 1920s.) Sometimes the product slowly makes its way into acceptance. In other words, products are introduced to the market in very different ways, and their timing and speed of introduction and acceptance also show vast differences.

The tracing of a product's life cycle may be a difficult task. For one thing, there is the matter of product modification. Richard Trevithick's horseless carriage, introduced in 1801, bears little resemblance to today's powerful automobiles. Altering a product in some way can give it "nine lives." The

[2]Clare Elmer Griffin, "The Evolution of the Automobile Market," *Harvard Business Review*, Vol. 4, July 1926, p. 416.

radio is a good example. The number of sets sold increased until the market appeared to have taken about as many sets as it could absorb except for replacements and new families. Radio manufacturers learned early, however, that consoles and table radios had different markets. They also learned that the radio could be packaged in a variety of ways. By selling different radio products, manufacturers have prolonged or extended radio's life cycle for many years. Auto, FM, stereophonic, clock, and transistor radios are some of the "new" products. Figure 7-3 shows radio production in the United States during its early days and during recent years.

Television is similar to radio in many respects. The growth of the industry was rapid, there was a tapering off of sales, and then the product was modified. Larger screens, portables, and later colored television altered the original product life cycle for television. Furthermore, families found need for a second television set as they had previously found need for a second, third, or even thirteenth radio set (see Figure 15-2). Perhaps product life cycles are

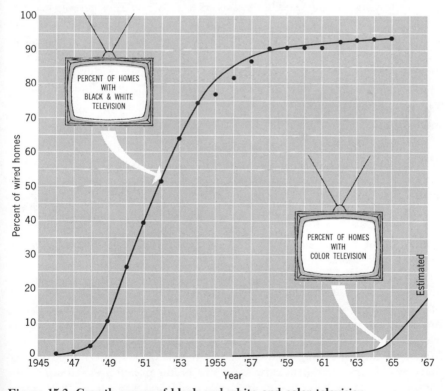

Figure 15-2. Growth curves of black and white and color television.

SOURCES: *The Economic Almanac, 1964*, (New York: National Industrial Conference Board, 1964), p. 414; *Electrical Industries Yearbook 1966*, (Washington: Electronic Industries Association), p. 6; *Financial World*, August 24, 1966, p. 6. Figures derived by R. C. Goldstein.

really many small sequential life cycles which, put together, form the smooth basic life cycle most frequently discussed.

The assignment of prognosticating product sales far into the future is more difficult. (More candles are sold today than at any time in our history!) The forecaster needs to be able to weigh probable technological changes, changes in the wants and needs of consumers, and many diverse factors which enter into market acceptance initially as well as later. At each sequence, it is marketing's job to develop the market for the "first new product in years" or for a major change in the basic product.

THE PRODUCT IN THE MARKETING ENVIRONMENT

A product is placed in motion because a seller believes it is vendible. He hopes that a need exists and that a profitable market can be developed. Each product is offered for sale within the marketing environment. Competition, technology, buying power, ethics, laws, and other facets of the environment help to determine vendibility. Buyers usually give considerable thought before they exchange their money resources for products and services. The ultimate consumer does not examine the exchange as systematically and as carefully as does the industrial buyer or the retail store buyer (see Box 15-1). Nevertheless, there is some consideration of the product within the confines imposed on the buyer. The following are some of the environmental forces which influence product acceptance in the market.

Competition

Milling Company A introduces a new type of flour. Before many weeks pass, Companies B, C, and others introduce similar products. A new low-calorie beverage is introduced and is followed by several competitors before many consumers are even aware of the first new product. One airline introduces movies. The second airline introduces movies and also television. The third airline offers both television and movies and adds pictures taken from a camera in the nose of the plane. Our competitive system is relentless in its press for new things.

Among some products, differences are easily detected. With others, product differentiation is more difficult. Still, marketing has the task of developing product differentiation in order to cultivate a competitive advantage for a product. Brand names, packaging, color, advertising, and slight differences go a long way in creating product differences. Blindfold tests show that consumers cannot distinguish among brands of cigarettes or beverages despite the fact that these same consumers express strong brand preferences. Competitors constantly strive to find the bundle of product features which will give their brands some advantage in the marketplace. Some of these features have little to do with the quality of the product, whereas others have a great deal to do with the inherent nature of the product itself.

BOX 15-1

Product Information Form

To all Sales Representatives:

Gentlemen:
Date

This form is made available to you so that you may provide us with the complete details concerning your product. Use a separate form for each product. Make sure all information is complete and accurate. If NEW PRODUCT PLEASE ATTACH COPY OF COOPERATIVE ADVERTISING CONTRACT AND PRODUCT LIABILITY INSURANCE POLICY.

1. Name of Product _____
2. Manufactured by _____
3. Address _____
   City & State _____
4. Telephone Number _____

5. Represented by _____
6. Address _____
   City & State _____
7. Telephone Number _____

8. Size _____
9. Price ____ ____ Per doz.
10. Price ____ Per case
11. Packed ____ Per case
12. Weight ____ Per case
13. F.O.B. Point _____
14. Freight Cost ____ Per case
15. Freight Rate _____
16. Price Protection Policy
    Yes ____ No ____
17. Suggested Retail Price _____
18. Fair Traded   Yes ____ No ____
19. Sale Guaranteed Yes ____ No ____
20. Quantity Discount _____
21. Trade Discount _____
22. Cash Discount _____
23. Free Goods _____
24. Advertising Allow. _____
25. Label Allowance _____

26. Swell Allowance _____
27. Special Promotions
    Yes ____ No ____
    A. Newspapers _____
    B. Radio _____
    C. Television _____
    D. Demonstration _____
28. Length of Proposed Advertising
    Campaign _____
29. Product Liability Insurance
    Yes ____ No ____
    A. Amount _____
30. Store Handling Considerations
    A. Spot for Pricing:
    Yes ____ No ____
    B. Shelf Stacking:
    Good ____ Fair ____ Poor ____
    C. Tear Strip Case:
    Yes ____ No ____

General Information

SOURCE: "Progress," *Progressive Grocer*, September 1959, p. 2.

Any product or service must meet the market test. It must find acceptability in a competitive environment. The total product, complete with price, package, and promotion, will be the company's best estimate of how the product should be developed for the market niche in sight. Each company and each product have certain competitive advantages and disadvantages. It is largely up to the marketing staff to develop the market on the basis of these recognized limitations and advantages.

The Consumer

Much has been said about the consumer. Added together, consumers *are* the market. Each group represents a market niche awaiting the products best suited to it. In addition to the economic, psychological, and sociological aspects of consumption, there is need to stress the dynamics of consumer wants. There exists a feeling that consumers prefer the new to the old. They demand change; they demand modifications and improvements of existing products. On the other hand, they like reliability. Much too little is known about the way consumers arrive at many of their buying decisions.

Because demand for a product can rise suddenly and exceed all expectations, companies continue to search for the pot of gold at the end of the rainbow. Each new product launched has the opportunity of being accepted by millions and of being repurchased over and over again by millions of consumers. Thus companies expand their product lines, diversify into new fields, acquire other existing plants, and constantly seek to improve their resource allocations. By doing these things the businessman hopes to acquire and maintain a satisfactory market acceptance for his products. Although he may not grant that the consumer is king, he recognizes that the consumer has the power or at least the alternative to accept or reject any market offering.

Technology and the product

Technology's influence in the marketing environment was discussed in Chapter 7. Technology, like marketing, focuses upon the product. Product improvements and new products are most frequently the result of technology. Along with the changes in products, changes in the marketing mechanism come about in part through technology. Also, as previously noted, marketing directs some of the technological research. Technology must go hand in hand with marketing, for any technological development needs marketing development in order for it to find its niche or acceptance in the marketplace. New products often originate by virtue of either a technological objective or a marketing objective. This helps to account for the need of a strong technological-marketing perspective. Table 15-1 shows the classification of new products by one or the other objective.

One of the best ways to picture the impact of technology on marketing is to examine the history of a business firm. Box 15-2 depicts a product growth list of the Minnesota Mining and Manufacturing Company from 1902 to 1948. From the humble beginnings in 1902–1904 the firm today has over 27,000 products.

The relationship between technological and market development is clearly illustrated by the history of the microfilm type of product. In the late 1880s, René-Prudent-Dragon of France learned to photograph 1000 telegrams on a filmstrip small enough to be banded to the leg of a pigeon. Microfilm was thus born, but relatively little utilization was made of it for many years; that is, not much of a market was developed for this new technology.

During the Second World War, transport planes carried up to 9,600,000 letters apiece on microfilm reels. Later the aperture card (microfilm mounted in a standard business-machine card), microfilm cartridge, microfiche, microform, and other microproducts were developed for the marketplace.

The market potential for microfilm products is enormous owing to the information explosion upon us, but development of the market is rather slow and difficult. However, through persuasion and education (selling) and because they are technically well developed, microform products are experiencing acceptance today.

Ethics and the product

Probably the most visible kind of unethical business activity is the product which in some way deceives the consumer. The promotion concerned with that product is another visible activity. The decision to market a product which is in some way fraudulent is not, of course, the sole responsibility of the marketing personnel. It is ultimately the responsibility of top management. Yet marketing shares in the responsibility as it distributes and promotes the product. Since marketing is visible to all concerned, it frequently takes the brunt of an attack on a product.

Fortunately most products are honestly conceived and promoted. Failures certainly come not so much from dishonesty as from the failure of a product to gain acceptance. Consumers place a good deal of trust in products distributed by certain companies (see Box 15-3). Industrial buyers also place trust in their suppliers with whom they have dealt for many years.

Millions upon millions of marketing transactions take place each year and only a few of them involve products which in some way cheat the buyer. It is probably true that the promotion, selling, pricing, and packaging practices receive more complaints than the product ingredients, but these are all closely related to the product. At least this would be the case for consumer products, whereas it may not be so for industrial and governmental purchases, where more attention is given to product specifications. Regardless, anyone in marketing should recognize that he is the company's contact with the public. He is the person responsible for distribution of the product. There

Table 15-1. Classification of New Products by Product Objective

→ INCREASING TECHNOLOGICAL NEWNESS →

PRODUCT OBJECTIVES	NO TECHNOLOGICAL CHANGE	IMPROVED TECHNOLOGY To utilize more fully the company's present scientific knowledge and production skills.	NEW TECHNOLOGY To acquire scientific knowledge and production skills new to the company.
NO MARKET CHANGE		Reformulation To maintain an optimum balance of cost, quality, and availability in the formulas of present company products. Example: use of oxidized microcrystalline waxes in Glo-Coat (1946).	Replacement To seek new and better ingredients or formulation for present company products in technology not now employed by the company. Example: development of synthetic resin as a replacement for shellac in Glo-Coat (1950).

INCREASING MARKET NEWNESS →		Remerchandising	Improved Product	Product Line Extension
STRENGTHENED MARKET To exploit more fully the existing markets for the present company products.		To increase sales to consumers of types now served by the company. Example: use of dripless spout can for emulsion waxes (1955).	To improve present products for greater utility and merchandisability to consumers. Example: combination of auto paste wax and cleaner into one-step "J-Wax" (1956).	To broaden the line of products offered to present consumers through new technology. Example: development of a general purpose floor cleaner "Emerel" in maintenance product line (1953).
		New Use	Market Extension	Diversification
NEW MARKET To increase the number of types of consumers served by the company.		To find new classes of consumers that can utilize present company products. Example: sale of paste wax to furniture manufacturers for Caul Board wax (1946).	To reach new classes of consumers by modifying present products. Example: wax-based coolants and drawing compounds for industrial machining operations (1951).	To add to the classes of consumers served by developing new technical knowledge. Example: development of "Raid"—dual purpose insecticide (1955).

SOURCE: Samuel C. Johnson and Conrad Jones, "How to Organize for New Products," *Harvard Business Review*, Vol. 35, No. 3, May–June 1957, p. 52.

BOX 15-2

New Products of the Minnesota Mining and Manufacturing Co., 1902–1948

Pressure-sensitive
adhesive tapes
Masking tape

1902–1904

Abrasive grain
Mining & crushing

1905–1910

Coated abrasives
• *Sandpaper*

1911–1924

Coated abrasives
Sandpaper
• *Waterproof
sandpapers*
• Special varnishes
• Wax & polish

1925–1929

Coated abrasives
Sandpaper
*Waterproof
sandpapers*
Special varnishes
Wax & polish
• Commercial sands

SOURCE: "Minnesota Mining in Motion," *Fortune*, March 1949, p. 95.

298

Upper section:

1930–1934	1935–1939	1940–1945	1946–1948
			• Tile & construction adhesives & compounds
			• Marine adhesives & calking compounds
			• Non-woven synthetic fabrics
			• Sound-recording tape
			Gummed paper products (Mid-States Gummed Paper Co.)
		• Gummed paper products (Mid-States Gummed Paper Co.)	Tires, etc. (Inland Rubber Corp.)
		• Tires, etc. (Inland Rubber Corp.)	Industrial adhesives
	• Industrial adhesives	Industrial adhesives	Sandblast stencil
	Sandblast stencil	Sandblast stencil	Automotive adhesives
	Automotive adhesives	Automotive adhesives	Pressure-sensitive adhesive tapes
	Pressure-sensitive adhesive tapes	Pressure-sensitive adhesive tapes	• *Filament tape*
Sandblast stencil			• *Plastic tape*
Automotive adhesives	• *Special tapes*	*Special tapes*	• *Printed cellophane tape*
Pressure-sensitive adhesive tapes	• *Cellophane tape*	*Cellophane tape*	*Special tapes*
Acetate tape	*Acetate & acetate fiber tape*	*Acetate & acetate fiber tape*	*Cellophane tape*
Electrical tape	*Electrical tape*	*Electrical tape*	*Acetate & acetate fiber tape*
Shoe tape	*Shoe tape*	*Shoe tape*	*Electrical tape*
Masking tape	*Masking tape*	*Masking tape*	*Shoe tape*
			Masking tape

1930–1934	1935–1939	1940–1945	1946–1948
Coated abrasives	Coated abrasives	Coated abrasives	Coated abrasives
Sandpaper	*Sandpaper*	*Sandpaper*	*Sandpaper*
Waterproof sandpapers	*Waterproof sandpapers*	*Waterproof sandpapers*	*Waterproof sandpapers*
Special varnishes	• *Waterproof abrasive cloth*	*Waterproof abrasive cloth*	*Waterproof abrasive cloth*
Wax & polish	Special varnishes	Special varnishes	Special varnishes
Commercial sands	Wax & polish	Wax & polish	Wax & polish
Fiber packing	Commercial sands	Commercial sands	Commercial sands
Roofing granules	Fiber packing	Fiber packing	Fiber packing
	Roofing granules	Roofing granules	Roofing granules
	• Pigments—chrome & iron oxides	Pigments—chrome & iron oxides	Pigments—Krox, K series & C series, iron oxides & chrome oxides
		• Sulfuric acid	Sulfuric acid
		• Special synthetic resins	Special synthetic resins
		• Non-slip cleats & strips	Non-slip cleats & strips
		• Scotchlite reflective sheeting	Scotchlite reflective sheeting
		• Centerlite reflective compound	Centerlite reflective compound
		• Tympan papers	Tympan papers
			• Scotchlite advertising
			• Special abrasives
			• Premix highway blacktop
			• Special welding fluxes

BOX 15-3

Marketing Values

There is an increasing emphasis within the American economy upon the marketing of goods and services. This is indigenous to the nation's advanced standard of living and a reflection of the material well-being of the American people.

The several functions of the marketing process, in first determining the needs and wants of the consumer and then in delivering the products at the time and place, and in the form and quantity of his choice, all are integral parts of our productive process. Thus, the economic value of the two processes of fabrication and marketing are indistinguishable. Each lends worth to the product of our labor and each contributes its share of benefits to the ultimate satisfaction of the buyer.

o   o   o   o   o

. . . Industry, therefore, believes in and advocates national policies reflecting the following principles:

Under our system of intensely competitive marketing, the quality of American-made goods seeks continuously higher levels of excellence. The best values of quality, utility, convenience or esthetics are preserved to suit the varying tastes of the consuming public, and the shoddy and meretricious tend to disappear from the market as producers and sellers vie for the favor of consumers. The proliferation of government boards and tribunals arbitrarily to evaluate, test or control the production and marketing of products is a costly and dangerous imposition upon the free market.

Products of industry are conceived, developed, manufactured and marketed in a variety of sizes, shapes, quantities, qualities and prices to meet the myriad desires of a diverse population. The phenomenon of such product diversification is observable within the economy because each form possesses a meaningful value and appeal to individual consumer tastes. Thus, aggressive competition within the market place is assured not by price alone, but by a diversity of product values and the freedom of consumers to choose, whether it be a price or a non-price value. However, there is only one significant kind of competition, and that is to satisfy the consumer's individualistic sense of value, whatever it may be. Monopoly cannot exist under such a competitive force.

SOURCE: Reprinted in part from a statement of the National Association of Manufacturers, February 12, 1964.

is an obligation on the part of the marketer to handle only those products which, in his estimation, are honest values and free of misrepresentation.

The law and the product

Today many legal restrictions exist on the marketing of goods and services. Laws pertaining to the distribution of liquor or drugs receive a good deal of attention, but there are literally thousands of other laws at the federal, state, and local levels which regulate products and their distribution. These laws must be understood by those in business. The ingredients, labeling, pricing, and even retailing may all be regulated by legislation. Some of the pertinent legal aspects were discussed in Chapter 10.

There are several groups in need of legal protection. Consumers, obviously, should be protected in some way from the unscrupulous entrepreneur. Business needs to be protected from unfair competition. A product containing alcohol and which could be sold without a physician's prescription is an example of a product that could harm both the consumer and the honest drug manufacturer.

Patent protection is another important type of legislation. It protects the patent holder and restricts the person who would like to copy the idea.

The legal side of our environment can be most important, and any consideration of products must certainly include the legal aspects. Actually each part of the marketing environment must be examined. The product is going to be sold eventually to those in the marketplace, and it follows logically that environmental considerations are quite germane to most all product decisions.

DEVELOPING THE MARKET FOR THE PRODUCT

It is through the product that companies match their resources to the needs and wants of various markets. The entire effort of developing a product must take place with the total marketing environment in mind. Eventually the product is taken to the market where the producer hopes that a profitable segment can be located and expanded through a strong program of market development. Plans, strategies, and research are worked into the many marketing decisions relating to size, color, design, price, promotion, channels, and package. This kind of effort ties in closely with the material of the last chapter, in which the problems of developing the market plans were discussed in some detail.

Plans and strategies

Product planning and strategy today receive a great deal of attention. Actually, product strategy involves pricing, promotion, and other marketing activities.

Company policies are implemented through product introduction and product continuation (see Box 15-4).

Many basic questions concerning products need to be answered. What kinds of products should be produced or distributed? Does each product fit logically into the existing line(s) of products? How large is the market? Who will buy? Are present channels of distribution adequate for the products handled? What is the nature of the competition? What is the predicted life cycle? Is there patent protection? Will additional plant facilities be needed?

BOX 15-4

A Product Planning Statement

PRODUCT PLANNING——— is the continuous process of fully integrating the planning,

Here are those dynamic customer oriented considerations! $\longmapsto$ the timing, the pricing, and the servicing required to add the

They control the product line! new, discontinue the undesired, and maintain, modify, and improve the existing products, so as most profitably to meet marketing

Here's the Planning part! $\rightarrow$ needs and to justify the manufacture of these products by the Company. This process is carried out by analyzing, organizing, and combining relevant facts as to the product and related company-wide interests (including every functional component)

And here is the Programing! $\longmapsto$ to obtain operating agreements and management decision for required

Teamwork is essential! product programs and each product's total composition. This process embraces the business and requires understanding and cooperation of all functional components.

Piloting the process is the Product Planning Manager's responsibility! $\longmapsto$ Accountability for it rests with the general manager while integrating responsibility is vested in the marketing component.

SOURCE: *Product Planning Course, Marketing Services* (New York: General Electric Company, 1956).

Why do people buy the item? Can it be priced competitively and profitably? Can it be shipped efficiently? Answers to such questions help each firm to establish formal or informal product policies.

Decisions regarding the breadth and depth of a product line, price, private branding, channels, warranties, promotion, foreign market possibilities, and other factors have to be made at some time during the product planning and distributing stages. Obviously, a plan for the product is desirable. Frequently, experience in the marketplace will dictate changes in earlier policies. Flexibility becomes an important quality for the firm after the product is launched.

With new products, some have a much higher risk factor than others. Figure 15-3 illustrates the relationship between risk and profit. Although the illustration is generally correct, a product with very little cost involved and very little risk attached can sometimes become a "pot of gold."

Research

Risk can better be ascertained and ways of mitigating it better developed through a research program geared to product and marketing development. This is especially true with products, for they represent the judgment of the firm that some particular product line is the best way to allocate the firm's resources. Judgment can be materially aided by a good intelligence program. Production is expected to answer the question, "Can we produce it?" whereas

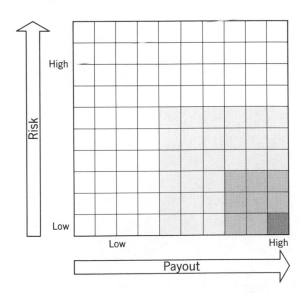

Figure 15-3. Objective of new product selection.
SOURCE: Booz, Allen, and Hamilton, *Op. Cit.*

marketing research is expected to shed light on design, pricing, and other important decisions to be made. For example, buyer attitudes are important in the early stages as well as later on. Actually, all along the spectrum of product development, marketing research should be undertaken, from the preproduction to the postintroduction stage. Research provides information essential to the actual marketing activities involved through testing markets and providing a continuing fact-finding process for the product as it is launched in the market. Figure 15-4 reveals some of the steps in product evolution. At each stage, one can see some of the marketing research activities which should be carried on. Research, however, should not stifle creativity. Rather, in all aspects of marketing both should go hand in hand.

Pricing

This important product ingredient will be discussed in the next chapter. At this point, however, a few comments will endeavor to relate the role of pricing to the market development for a product.

When Ford Motor Company introduced the Mustang in 1964, price was given more attention in the promotion than it had had for almost any other automobile during postwar years. By contrast, price may be of no consideration to the user of a new and badly needed drug product. Companies are also cognizant of their price lines. The Edsel was created to fill a gap in the Ford price lines. Automobiles provide a good example of price lining as do many other products such as men's hats and shirts. For example, see Box 15-5.

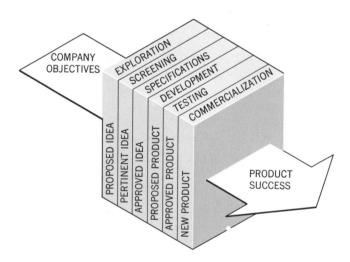

Figure 15-4. Stages of new Product evolution.
SOURCE: Booz, Allen, and Hamilton, *Op. Cit.*

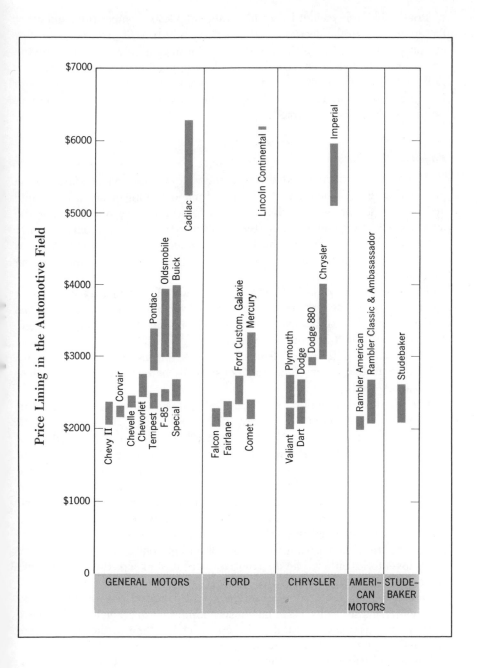

Price Lining in the Automotive Field

Prices obviously cannot be set in a vacuum. Costs, competition, and other factors enter into the decision, and this is equally true of price changes. For our purposes here, it is only necessary to point out the role of pricing and the important influence pricing can have in developing a market for the product. Different prices can cultivate different segments of a market. A firm can aim for a small, high-priced segment or, at the opposite end of the continuum, the larger, lower-price market.

Physical distribution

Market development is aided substantially though not spectacularly by the physical handling of the product. The need for a marketing mechanism capable of handling the product has been known for centuries, which explains the development of the middleman system existing in most nations today. Recently the potential of the mechanism has been better understood and new techniques such as linear programming have permitted improvements in the physical handling of goods.

The question is considerably more than one of finding a channel for a good or service. The costs and efficiencies of various systems differ, and the firm must find the optimum system of distribution for the product concerned. This results in adjustments in the functions performed by middlemen at both the wholesale and the retail levels. It means improved inventory control systems; it further means that transportation is better matched to product and market needs.

The physical distribution of a product, then, does affect the development of a market. To develop the market for a food product, for example, calls for an efficient network of institutions to handle the item. By way of illustrating this point, a bakery has need for effective distributing points for its inflow of ingredients. An effective distributive mechanism can do much in the way of developing markets. Good distribution which has supply ready when needed and at a competitive cost can mean satisfactory market shares and profits for the seller and much satisfaction for the buyer. Almost all buyers (but especially industrial buyers) are "between the devil and the deep blue sea" in that they do not want to run out of an item but do not want to carry heavy inventories either. The distributive mechanism keeps them from being overcome by either threat.

Vending machines provide an efficient and effective way of distributing some merchandise. Self-service has been adopted by many fields of business. Mail-order houses have streamlined their order handling to the point where time-and-motion experts cannot squeeze much more out of the process.

Physical distribution is another link in the chain of good market development.

Persuasion

Marketers utilize a wide variety of techniques of persuasion in varying quantities for the many products they sell. One product may receive little or no attention and another may become part of a television extravaganza. Buyers are the targets of these persuasive attempts, industrial, governmental, and household consumers all receiving market-development treatment.

Persuasion in some way focuses on the product. This is not to say that all advertising concentrates on the attributes of the product, but rather that directly or indirectly the seller attempts to persuade the buyer to order his product. The creation of a favorable company image is planned in order to sell products. Featuring personal service may sell more gasoline for a service station than featuring the product itself. The point is that markets are developed in part by good promotion and selling. These persuasion attempts have something in common. Their goals are to gain product acceptability for the firm, and to persuade buyers to try the product and continue buying it.

The ebb and flow of products continue from year to year. Old products are pruned from the company line and new products are added for reasons of diversification or competition or for some other reason. In a sense the marketer straddles the gap between the firm and the consumer. It is his task to match the product with the buyer who has a wide variety of needs and wants. Every firm hopes that its product decisions will prove profitable and that any new product will have a long life cycle. Regardless of the outcome, it is marketing's task to develop the market for the product. Trying to ready the market, persuade consumers to buy, gain acceptance for the product, and distribute the product to the buyer, marketing's job is big and difficult. Certainly part of the success and failure of many products can be traced to the job performed by the firm's marketing force.

Note: There are two addenda to this chapter. The first is a list of ways a product can be "new," the second is a summary of the dropout brands of automobiles since 1920.

Questions

1. How secure is a producer whose brand is synonymous with its generic product class (for example Kleenex)? How do such situations arise?
2. Is there anything more important to the business firm than its product?
3. Does a consumer differentiate between brand and product?
4. What causes a product to lose its share of the market?
5. What signals can be detected in the marketplace insofar as a product's acceptance is concerned?

Statements to Consider

Time and timing—the most valuable raw material and the most valuable industrial skill—are the major determining factors of a successful product-range development program.

If a new product under consideration by consumers is a more or less direct replacement for something previously known, the item being replaced may serve as a yardstick for evaluating the new one.

The difference between the new product offered and the established product must be discernible, identifiable, and reproducible.

Rarely, if ever, would any single product possess all the intrinsic and production characteristics, as well as those of use, purchase, and demand, which are favorable for brand promotion.

Products are initially purchased and tried on the basis of conceptual appeal; they are repurchased or discarded on the basis of tangible satisfaction.

SELECTED REFERENCES

Thomas L. Berg and Abraham Shuchman, *Product Strategy and Management* (New York: Holt, Rinehart and Winston, 1963).

Purnell H. Benson, and F. Pilgrim, "Testing Less Desirable Product Possibilities," *Journal of Marketing*, Vol. 25, No. 5, July 1961, pp. 56–69.

° Herta Herzog, "Behavioral Science Concepts for Analyzing the Consumer," in *Proceedings of the Conference of Marketing Teachers from Far Western States* Berkeley, University of California.: September 1958, pp. 32–41

° Chester R. Wasson, "What Is 'New' About a New Product?" *Journal of Marketing*, Vol. 25, No. 1, July 1960, pp. 52–56.

Generalizations Were Taken From:

Graham Leman, "New Product Development and the Development of a Product Range," *Commentary*, Summer 1962, pp. 7–12.

Wroe Alderson, *Marketing Behavior and Executive Action* (Homewood, Ill.: Richard D. Irwin, 1957).

Wroe Alderson, "Consumer Reaction to Product Innovation," in Lincoln H. Clark, (ed.), *Consumer Behavior: Research on Consumer Reactions* (New York: Harper & Brothers, 1958), pp. 3–9.

Roland S. Vaile, E. T. Grether, and Reavis Cox, *Marketing in the American Economy* (New York: The Ronald Press Company, 1952).

Steuart Henderson Britt, *Consumer Behavior and the Behavioral Sciences: Theories and Applications* (New York: John Wiley and Sons, 1966).

ADDENDUM 1.   Ways a Product Can Be New

A. Six novel attributes are positive, in the sense that they ease the job of introduction:

1. New cost—or, better yet, price—if lower.
2. New convenience in use—if greater.
3. New performance—if better, more dependable and in the range of experience of the prospect—if believable.
4. New availability, in place, or time, or both (including antiseasonality).
5. Conspicuous-consumption (status symbol) possibilities.
6. Easy credibility of benefits.

B. At least four characteristics make the job more difficult, slow up market development, and usually make it costlier:

7. New methods of use (unless obviously simpler).
8. Unfamiliar patterns of use (any necessity for learning new habits in connection with performance of a task associated with the new product).
9. Unfamiliar benefit (in terms of the prospect's understanding).
10. Costliness, fancied or real, of a possible error in use.

C. Three others are ambivalent in their effect—that is, the effect on market development probably depends not only on their exact nature, but also on the cultural climate at the moment. However, extreme unfamiliarity would probably be negative in effect:

11. New appearance, or other sensed difference (style or texture, for example).
12. Different accompanying or implied services.
13. New market (including different channels of sale).

SOURCE: Chester R. Wasson, "What is 'New' About a New Product?" *Journal of Marketing,* Vol. 25, No. 1, July 1960, p. 54.

Addendum 2. Dropout Brands of
Automobiles since 1920

	1922	1923	1924	1925	1926
(+)	Bay State	Flint	Chrysler	Ajax	Pontiac
	Jewett	Yellow			Erskine
	Gray	Rollen			Falcon Knight
	Rickenbacker				Diana
	Star				
(−)	Elgin		Bay State	Ajax	Rickenbacker
	Grant		Chalmers	Gray	H.C.S.
	National		Dart	King	Wills St. Claire
	Saxon		Earl	Liberty	Overland
			Mitchell	Mercer	
			R & V Knight	Rollen	
			Stephens	Yellow	
			Winton	Anderson	
			Lafayette	Apperson	
				Cleveland	
				Cole	
				Columbia	
				Haynes	
				Maxwell	
				Westcott	

	1927	1928	1929	1930	1931	1932
(+)	Wolverine Whippet LaSalle	Moon-Diana Plymouth DeSoto Grahm Paige	Cord Marquette	Willys-Overland Graham Austin	Rockne	Terraplane
(−)	Wolverine Flint Case Diana Paige	Moon-Diana Star Jewett Davis Lexington Falcon Knight Chandler Durant	Erskine Locomobile Velie Grahm Paige	Kissel Elcar Moon Stearns-Knight Marquette	Jordan Oakland	Whippet Peerless Rockne Willys-Knight

	1933	1934	1935	1936	1937	1938	1939
(+)	Continental	LaFayette				Mercury	
(−)	Marmon	Austin Continental Franklin		Gardner Stutz LaFayette Reo	Cord Auburn Pierce Arrow	Terraplane	Essex

311

World War II Years (1941–1945)

	1940	1941	1942	1943	1944	1945	1946	1947	1948	1949	1950	1951
(+)							Kaiser Frazer Crosley				Henry J Rambler	
(−)	LaSalle Graham Hupmobile											Frazer

	1952	1953	1954	1955	1956	1957	1958	1959
(+)	Allstate	Corvette		Thunderbird		Imperial Edsel		Lark
(−)	Crosley	Allstate	Henry J	Willys-Overland Kaiser		Nash Hudson	Packard	Edsel

	1960	1961	1962	1963	1964	1965	1966	1967
(+)	Dart Valiant Comet Corvair Falcon	Tempest Olds F-85 Buick Special Lancer	Meteor Chevy II	Riviera Avanti	Barracuda Chevelle Mustang		Charger Marlin Toronado	Camero Cugar Firebird Javelin
(−)	DeSoto					Avanti° Studebaker°		

° now manufactured in Canada only.

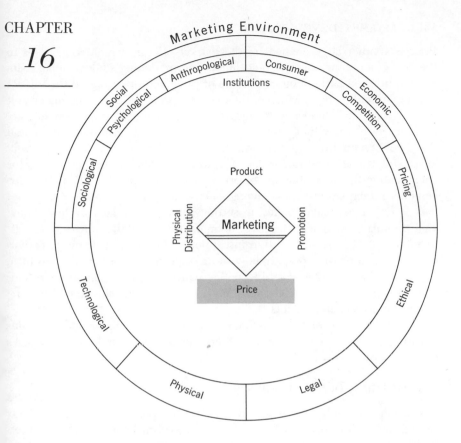

Market Development:
The Price

THE MEANING OF PRICE POLICIES • THE INTERRELATIONSHIP OF PRICES • MAJOR INFLUENCES ON PRICE POLICIES *Character of Product   Product Differentiation   Costs and Prices   New versus Mature Products   Other Price Considerations* • PRICING POLICIES • PRICING PRACTICES *One Price to All Buyers   Price Lining   Odd-Even Pricing   Psychological Pricing   Prestige Pricing* • GEOGRAPHICAL PRICING PRACTICES

Price is another large element of the market offering which contributes to the firm's success or failure. Practitioners and marketing students alike seem to have little understanding of the role of price and often regard the subject as complex and esoteric. Much of the misconception about pricing may result from the common tendency to equate *price theory with price practice:* accounting emphasizes that costs play a major role in determining prices, and the purely competitive market structure model tells us that at successively lower prices, increased quantities of a good are demanded. Another factor complicating the understanding of price policies and practices is that no discernible pricing pattern exists among American companies. Some companies may follow a particular policy in setting prices, but relatively few follow well-formulated policies. Moreover, manufacturers follow policies quite different from those of distributive institutions. Unless the pricing objectives of a manufacturer are compatible with those of its distributors, there is little likelihood that a single workable policy can be applied. Finally, one finds that the pricing of industrial goods has a very different character from the pricing of consumer products.

Despite the lack of a generalized statement of principles and the complicating aspects noted, a survey of pricing activity should sharpen one's total view of marketing.

THE MEANING OF PRICE POLICIES

Price decisions play an integral part in business policies. Prices of products and services are rarely determined by the impersonal forces of the market. Rather, the seller has the freedom to engage directly in the price-making process and, in general, he can quote the price at which the goods may be sold. When prices are established through action of the seller, a price policy emerges. Under conditions of pure competition the seller has no alternative to electing to sell at the market price; he has a production policy but not a price policy. Because market structures more closely correspond to monopolistic competition and oligopoly than to pure competition, the seller can by his marketing policies exercise an influence over the market to his own advantage. Thus the producer has both production and marketing policies, which include price policy.

THE INTERRELATIONSHIP OF PRICES

The contention that prices cannot be determined independently means that price interrelationships take many forms and play a major role in the establishment of specific prices. For our purposes it is necessary to recognize that price is related (1) to many other prices, and (2) to the objectives of a firm.

Our economy functions through the delicate balance of prices. Any breakdown in the mechanism is likely to affect a whole series of economic events. Jules Backman likens the interrelationship of prices between industries to the ripples in a lake:[1]

This interrelationship can be symbolized by the series of ripples that spread out when a stone is thrown into a lake. The ripples flow in every direction. A similar tendency is found in our economy. The prices of one industry are the costs of another, and the prices of the latter industry are the costs of a third industry, and so on until the ultimate consumer is reached. Thus, actions which cause prices to rise will be felt in many directions and may set in motion forces having results entirely different from those anticipated or desired.

Thus most prices in our economy are influenced by many other prices. Prices constitute a system of many parts and the system is responsive to many factors. For example, the general level of prices determines the real value of incomes. If the general level is rising, the rise can lead to demands for higher incomes to offset the diminishing value of incomes. Any person who commences a study and analysis of a given price soon learns that he invokes other prices and even the prices of a whole industry.

The very nature of the price system causes one to expect that the prices of goods on the shelves of wholesalers and retailers are closely related to the prices of goods in the hands of manufacturers. In turn, these prices are related to the prices of producers' goods such as raw materials, capital goods, parts, supplies, and so on. All of these prices have some relationship to the prices in any trade, the prices of securities, and even the prices of services. Figure 16-1 illustrates a rough parallelism of some prices. Unquestionably some of these prices are affected by the same basic factors. For example, if passenger cars and household appliances indicate a downward trend and steel mill products move upward, factors other than the price of steel are perhaps of more dominant influence. Steel prices often influence the price of automobiles but seldom influence appliances, because of the relatively lower quantity of steel used in them.

Just as prices in the economy are closely related to other prices and other economic factors, the prices set by a firm are related to its other prices, which are related to administrative policies. Hence most firms would be unwilling to delegate the formation of price formulas to members of the sales force, for instance. The determination of price formulas or the setting of prices on key items is too sensitive an activity to delegate below the policy-making level. In a large firm, overall price policy is usually determined by the executives of the several major departments such as marketing,

---

[1] Jules Backman, *Price Practices and Price Policies* (New York: The Ronald Press Company, 1953), p. 14.

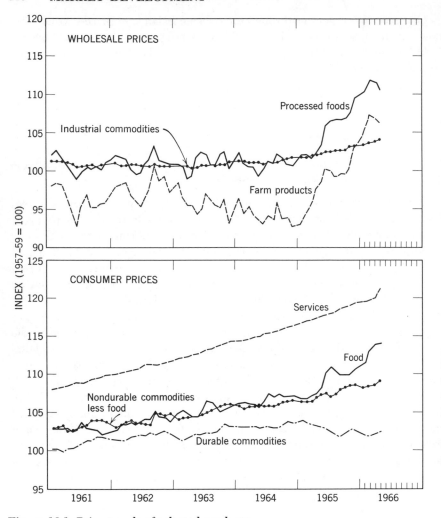

Figure 16-1. Price trends of selected products.
SOURCE: *Price Trends*, Bulletin No. 1510, March 1966, United States Department of Labor, Washington, D. C.

manufacturing, engineering, and financial or accounting. It is at this level that other major policies take shape, and because pricing influences the accomplishment of other objectives it must be decided here. For example, if a company wanting to be a growth company has determined its dividend policy as some percentage of net earnings and desires to acquire its major financing from retained earnings, it will have to establish some "rules of the game." Perhaps top management has set the growth rate at *X* percent of

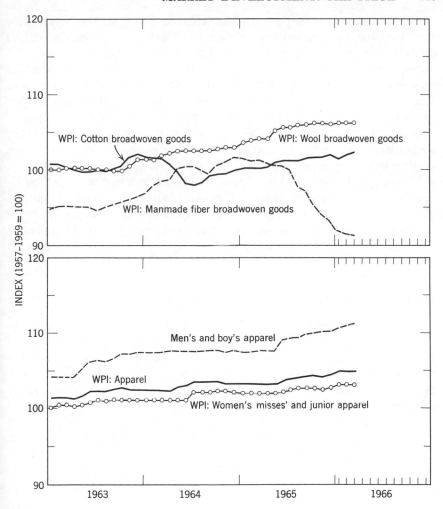

INDEX (1957–1959 = 100)

WPI: Cotton broadwoven goods

WPI: Wool broadwoven goods

WPI: Manmade fiber broadwoven goods

Men's and boy's apparel

WPI: Apparel

WPI: Women's misses' junior apparel

1963   1964   1965   1966

Figure 16-1—(*Continued*)

sales each year and knows that growth will require continuous investment; to achieve this objective requires a profit margin of Y amount. One "rule of the game" will be the setting of prices which are in accord with the stated policies of the firm. In large corporations where there are many thousands of items to price, the overall price guidelines are developed at conferences of the major responsible executives. Once pricing policies that are compatible with the corporate objectives have been determined, the price structure for specific items, discounts, and geographic pricing problems can be worked out by employees at lower echelons.

One further aspect of pricing is its rationing function. The firm's price tends to determine what will be produced, the amount to be produced, and the way in which the good is to be distributed. If price is too low, the claimants for the revenue received may be too great to warrant production and distribution. Price obviously influences the income of producers and hence serves to allocate the firm's resources. Likewise, prices that are too low relative to demand fail to induce the required capacity expansion needed to supply the demand. Thus resources that might flow to an industry are pulled elsewhere by more attractive prices. Conversely, when prices are too high they tend to cut off some of the demand, and a firm may not dispose of its output. This invites new entrants, usually at a lower price, which increases the quantities in the market. If an abundant supply appears unsalable, one or more firms in the industry may lower price to avoid an inventory accumulation. This glut, of course, discourages entry into the industry. Although prices are not a wholly sensitive regulator and rationer, they do operate within these broad limits.[2]

MAJOR INFLUENCES ON PRICE POLICIES

Whereas much might be said about the desirability of developing well-formulated *price policies* and *price objectives*, conditioning factors that influence these policies must be recognized. It may be possible to develop policies that cannot be disrupted, but this would be the exception rather than the rule. The influences on price and price policies are unquestionably numerous. Some idea of their number and complexity may be attained from study of Box 16-1.[3] These influences are not of equal importance to all companies and industries. Differences in management, legacies of the past, character of the particular firm and its products, to mention a few, either diminish or magnify the factors of influence. Rather than discuss each factor in the box, we shall dwell only on some major influences which have more or less universal applicability.

Character of the Product

For most firms the starting place in developing a price policy is the character of the product. The boundaries of price policy are set by the item's physical and market attributes, its production aspects, its degree of differentiation, and whether it is new or mature.

With perishable products, little opportunity exists for the seller to adopt

---

[2] *Ibid.*, pp. 8–9.

[3] This listing developed by Jules Backman in his book *Price Practices and Price Policies* was originally intended to explain price behavior and price inflexibility. With few exceptions the listing is also useful in categorizing the major influences on price policies.

BOX 16-1

Factors Affecting Price Behavior

I. Characteristics of the product or industry
   A. In terms of factors affecting demand
      1. Durability. 2. Producers' or consumers' goods. 3. Degree of processing—finished or semifinished goods or raw materials. 4. Joint demand. 5. Availability of substitutes. 6. Luxury or style goods or necessaries. 7. Standardized, unique, or differentiated. 8. Number of buyers. 9. Seasonality.
   B. In terms of factors affecting costs
      1. Rigidity of wage rates. 2. Price rigidity of materials. 3. Non-postponable overhead.
   C. In terms of factors affecting physical supplies
      1. Ease of entry for new producers. 2. Number of sellers. 3. Time required to expand capacity and output. 4. Perishability of product. 5. Seasonality.

II. Law or administrative degree
   A. Governmental agencies—telephone, gas, railroad, electric, and water rates
   B. Minimum wage and maximum hour legislation
   C. Tariff
   D. Direct price control
   E. Indirect price control
      1. Production control. 2. Loan programs. 3. Marketing agreements.
   F. Making it possible for private interests to control prices
      1. Patents and copyrights. 2. Resale price fixing—Fair Trade Acts. 3. Limitations on sales below cost—Unfair Practices Acts.

III. Concentration of control
   A. Monopoly or oligopoly
      1. Producers. 2. Labor unions.
   B. Collusion—to restrict output, allocate production, share markets, etc.
   C. Price Leadership
   D. Central sales agencies
   E. Trade association activities

IV. Marketing techniques
   A. Suggested prices on packages
   B. Advertising of standard prices
   C. One-price policy
   D. Product differentiation
   E. "In between" prices

BOX 16-1—(*Continued*)

V. Structure of the market
  A. Organized or "unorganized" markets
  B. Scope of market area
  C. Marketing channels used

VI. Habits and customs
  A. Price of professional services
  B. Price lining
  C. Coinage system

VII. Contractual arrangements—long-term

SOURCE: Jules Backman, *Price Practices and Price Policies*, (New York: The Ronald Press Company, 1953) pp. 59–60.

a price policy that is insensitive to market demand. The unpredictability of the supply and the fact that there is storage limitation mean that selling prices, both wholesale and retail, are dominated by approximations of supply and demand. Unless these prices are administered by a pricing authority or some established formula (for example, milk prices), the seller can expect prices to be imposed by the perishable character of the product.

Durable goods which lend themselves to storage, postponment of purchase, and some control over raw material are much more amenable to pricing that accomplishes some company policy. Durable industrial goods are likely to be purchased in order to produce some other goods or services. The demand for such goods is said to be a "derived" demand. That is, their purchase is based on the market opportunities for the goods and services *to be* marketed. In this situation, the price of the good may play little or no part in the decision to purchase. Even the seller's lowering of the price produces sales if the demand forecast for the ultimate market is dismal.

The concept of "joint" demand is also useful in determining prices of industrial goods. When numerous goods make up the overall cost of a product, individual prices are less likely to be responsive to demand. The construction industry is often cited as an example of joint demand. The cost and demand for construction cannot be altered by a marked increase or decrease in the price of one of the component materials. The lowering of the price of insulation, for example, will not seriously affect the total cost of construction, because it accounts for a very small proportion of the total materials cost. The seller well knows that a reduction in his price of insulation would only result in a loss of revenue and not in an increase in sales. If, however, the cost of all construction materials were either increased or lowered, the total cost of construction would be affected. Yet it should be recognized that some construction costs are seriously influenced by the price of a single product. Steel prices, for example, contribute heavily to the cost of construction when the proportion of steel used is high relative to other materials. Clearly this is not a joint-demand situation, but one where the importance of a single industrial material to the end product predominates.

Industrial goods are purchased because the buyer forecasts a market opportunity for goods or services produced by the industrial goods. When the demand for goods derives from another market, they are said to have a "derived" demand. The purchase of most industrial goods hinges on the opportunities in another market. For example, the automobile manufacturer's demand for automobile tires and parts is conditioned by the forecasts of the quantity of automobiles demanded. If automobile demand is sluggish this will be reflected in the demand for tires. The demand for all other components is similarly influenced. Price generally cannot play an incentive role in industrial goods when the ultimate demand for the goods to be produced is sluggish. Hence, when derived demand is present, price *per se* is not likely to be the dominant factor that determines whether a sale is made.

Consumer goods are sometimes identified as *convenience goods, shopping goods*, and *specialty goods*. This classification, used in most traditional marketing literature, is based on the shopping effort and buying patterns of consumers. Despite definite limitations, it has an application to the development of price guidelines and the selection of channels of distribution. Convenience goods are low in unit price and are purchased frequently and in small quantities. Shopping goods are higher in unit price and are compared with the close substitutes offered; the buyer will expend some effort in seeking out the "best buy" among them. Specialty goods are often high in unit price and the buyer will go to considerable length before making the purchase; they are purchased only infrequently. The buyer of a specialty good is not as likely as a shopping goods' buyer to make comparisons with other goods.

From a price standpoint, producers of convenience goods have little leeway in setting price. Their items have weak brand loyalty and are so slightly differentiated that their prices must fall within a narrow range of possibilities. If the price of a convenience good such as cigarettes, gasoline, or bread is out of line, the possibility of substitution is likely to occur.

Shopping goods open the door to price differentials. Because consumers can exercise strong brand preferences and are susceptible to uniqueness of features, styling, and the like, price differentials between competing products become possible. The price of a shopping good often results in a major money outlay, but the time span between such expenditures is often long. If a firm creates strong product differentiation it can usually command a somewhat higher price; consumers are quite adept at associating price with quality. Consumers are also believed to be less sensitive to the price of shopping goods because a substantial portion of them are purchased through installment credit. Hence, it is presumed that the amount of the installment payment is the critical factor.

Specialty goods permit the seller a large amount of discretion in setting price. Since consumers will exert much effort to acquire them and they fulfill a particular need, these goods are not purchased because of their price. High prices are in fact desirable for most specialty goods, particularly if the goods meet a prestige or status need. Fur coats, antiques, custom-tailored items, and rare jewelry are best priced high rather than low. Low prices on these and similar products would likely cause them to lose much of their exclusive appeal. Another aspect of specialty goods is that they are usually sold in few outlets. The dealer who is significant to the buyer must convey the same kind of exclusive character as the product. For all of this the consumer *expects* to pay a price.

Product Differentiation

Product differentiation can be a significant aspect of price policy for both industrial-goods and consumer-goods sellers. The fullest advantage of differentiation can be exploited when a company's product line has a distinct advantage over more standard competing products. If products do not offer this possibility, companies can develop differentiation in other aspects of the sale such as delivery terms, service, credit conditions, and others.

Market strategists recognize that for a clearly differentiated product, price is subordinated in the purchase decision. Because of this, they feature actual and psychological differences in their marketing effort. Advertising claims, package designs, distribution methods, and pricing build the concept of differentiation and hence strong brand or company preferences.

When the offering of a firm or the product itself is difficult to differentiate, attempts can be made to distinguish the firm. This often occurs among whole-sale and retail firms which may exploit an advantage in their location, their array of services or lack of them, and the breadth and depth of lines of merchandise carried. Retail firms appear to have distinct possibilities to develop strong differentiation by virtue of their location, decor, price lines, and other assets. As noted in Chapter 8, differentiation lends to the steepening of the demand curve. This is the basic reasoning behind the fact that differentiation and price are so closely related. Businessmen seem to practice differentiation even though they may not recognize its influence on the demand for their products.

Costs and Prices[4]

Perhaps the most widespread idea concerning pricing is that costs determine prices. This is a gross oversimplification of the issue and in most instances is erroneous. Certainly prices must cover all costs, but it is wrong to assume that every product price must cover its own individual costs. There are too many concepts of cost and too many variables influencing price to permit cost to be the sole determinant of price (for example, see Box 16-1).

Economic theory teaches that in the long run price tends to equal the cost of production. This theoretical construction may itself be one of the reasons for much misunderstanding. Although the economist does include a profit in his concept of cost of production, this element is often overlooked. Perhaps the greatest drawback to the attitude that costs determine prices is that it completely ignores demand considerations.

Cost is more important in the long run than the short run. Economic doctrine is correct in telling us that when costs of production are above the market price, the firm will be forced, in the long run, to cease operations. And, if price is so high above the cost of production that it brings in large profits, new entrants will be drawn into the industry with ensuing pressure on existing prices. Thus, in the long run, effective competition tends to make prices equal the cost of production.

There are many instances in our economy where *costs are determined by prices*. Numerous products have their prices (or at least a range of possible prices) set by market forces. This puts the firm in the position of having to determine the price it can reasonably expect and then working from that figure to see if it can profitably produce the item. When prices are determined by the market, manufacturers must seek cost-reduction measures through substituting raw materials, finding a lower cost technology, and attempting to reduce distribution costs when profits shrink because of lower prices or inflated costs. In short, when market prices move downward, this leads to pressures on costs and the firm attempts to reduce those items of cost that are controllable. When business is enjoying the reverse situation, rising costs exert pressures on prices. Prices will rise, but only to the limits permitted by market forces. The five-cent or ten-cent price of a candy bar, for example, is what is known as a customary market price—and the manufacturer meets rising costs by reducing the quantity of the product. Other and more complex measures are faced by most other manufacturers.

Backman summarizes the complexity of the interrelationship of business conditions, costs, and prices in the following passage:

---

[4]For a somewhat detailed discussion of the relationship of costs to prices, see Jules Backman, *Price Practices and Price Policies*, pp. 119–148; or a brief but excellent discussion by Donald V. Harper, *Price Policy and Procedure*, pp. 49–59.

In periods of rapidly changing business conditions, the importance of the psychology of a market situation should not be minimized, since the point of view of businessmen obviously exerts a very important influence upon market trends. In such situations it cannot be too strongly emphasized that the relation between costs and prices is not direct, mechanical, or exact. The cost structure of a concern and the condition of its market establish certain limits within which decisions must be made, but within these boundaries there may be a broad field for the exercise of individual judgment. . . .[5]

Thus costs should be regarded as setting the lower limits on price, whereas the upper limit is the value of the product to buyer. The decision to be made by the price maker is to select a price somewhere between these extremes.[6]

New Products versus Mature Products

Perhaps of greatest interest is the pricing of new products. The approach to pricing a new product varies depending on whether the product is completely new or similar to existing products. If a new product has existing substitutes, the frame of reference for pricing is, of course, the price range of the existing substitutes. Unless influenced heavily by other factors, price will fall somewhere in the known price range of the other products.

If the product is completely new, then the problem is complicated by the lack of any experience or any reasonable price range. Several attempts have been made to develop pricing approaches for new products. Perhaps the best known is Joel Dean's *skimming price* and *penetration price*.[7] A skimming price, in Dean's view, is a high price accompanied by heavy promotional expenditures during the early phases of market development, followed by lower prices during later phases. This is a widely practiced approach and has been successful in numerous instances. The reasons for the success of this approach are cited by Dean as follows:

1. Demand is likely to be more elastic with respect to price in the early stages than it is when the product is full grown. . . . Consumers are still ignorant about its value as compared with the value of conventional alternatives. . . . At least in the early stages, the product has so few close rivals that cross-elasticity of demand is low.

2. [An initial] high price is an efficient device for breaking the market up into segments that differ in price elasticity of demand. The initial high price serves to skim the cream of the market that is relatively insensitive to price. Subsequent price reductions tap successively more elastic sectors of the market. . . .

---

[5] Jules Backman, *Price Practices and Price Policies*, p. 127.
[6] Donald V. Harper, *Price Policy and Procedure*, p. 53.
[7] Joel Dean, "Pricing Policies for New Products," *Harvard Business Review*, Vol. 28, No.6 November 1950, pp. 49–53.

3. . . . Facing an unknown elasticity of demand, a high initial price serves as a "refusal" price during the stage of exploration. How much costs can be reduced as the market expands and as design of the product is improved by increasing production efficiency with new techniques is difficult to predict.

4. Many companies are not in a position to finance the product flotation out of distant future revenues. High cash outlays in the early stages result from heavy costs of production and distributor organizing. . . . High prices are a reasonable financing technique for shouldering these burdens in the light of the many uncertainties about the future.[8]

The reader can undoubtedly cite instances where the foregoing approach has been useful to specific firms or for specified goods. Firms find a high initial price, with subsequent price reductions, much easier to live with because it is obviously easier to justify lowering price than raising it.

A penetration price is a low price designed to capture mass markets early in the new product stages. This policy has the advantage of encouraging sales to a wider segment of the market. Whereas a skimming policy may preclude the purchase by those with low incomes, the lower penetration price has broad appeal to the lower-income groups. Dean believes that a penetration price policy is worthy of consideration at various stages in the product's life cycle. The thought behind this view is that new markets may be developed by examining price from product inception to its maturity. An often cited example is the pricing policies of airlines, which have cut fares by instituting coach rates and more recently the 12-21 half-fares. Each policy sharply appealed to new market segments. Dean cites the following conditions which are compatible with a penetration price:

1. . . . A high-price elasticity of demand in the short run, i.e., a high degree of responsiveness of sales to reductions in price . . . .

2. . . . A substantial savings in production costs as the result of greater volume . . . .

3. . . . Product characteristics such that it will not seem bizarre when it is first fitted into the consumers' expenditure pattern. . . .

4. . . . A strong threat of potential competition.[9]

The term "mature product" identifies the market and competitive conditions as a product progresses through its life cycle. Price practices at this stage are vastly different from the earlier situation, and the firm needs to identify the condition before it can act on price. The symptoms of maturity are:

1. A deterioration of brand preferences caused by the close similarity of substitutes. Premium prices which once could be commanded are now not possible without losing market position.

[8] Ibid., brackets are the authors'.
[9] Ibid.

2. The physical differences among competing products, disappear and the better designs become standardized.

3. Private-label competition emerges.

4. The market is saturated and replacement sales represent a major proportion of all sales.

5. Production methods are stabilized; that is, technological innovation which may reduce costs may upset the stability enjoyed by an oligopolistic market condition.[10]

Although it is difficult to state categorically the price action to be taken when the preceding conditions are observable, some generalized remarks may be helpful in deciding on a course of action. Most firms facing product maturity can exercise little discretion in their price because only minor product differentiation exists. If price is higher than comparable substitutes, market position is jeopardized. Price reductions can be easily met by competition, but this may also precipitate a lower level of prices for the industry with nothing but a reduced total revenue for the firm (unless, of course, market position improves, which is unlikely). Perhaps the best course of action, as suggested by Dean, is to meet the situation by reducing *real* prices. This means, rather than open price warfare, that the manufacturer can strengthen his position by giving more at the same price. Such an approach can mean product improvement, product refinements, better service, and other upgrading of the market offering.

Other Price Considerations

Many firms face numerous other price considerations. The pricing of a product line, for example, raises a number of questions. How should differences in size be priced? What is the industry custom in pricing product lines?—and so on. In general, a pattern of prices for the line should exist so as to ease the entry of new additions to the line. From the established pattern other variations of product can be fitted into the company's line without serious price disruptions.

The number of buyers may also influence pricing practices and policies. In some instances thousands of buyers are in the market, while in others there may be only a few or even one buyer. In general, where the number of buyers is large, the influence of any one buyer on price is nil or at least small. However, when the market is populated by only a few they have a greater opportunity to exert influence on the firm's price and price structure.

Finally, whether firms are large or small and sellers are many or few, all are influenced by legal considerations. In particular, the antitrust laws provide the legal environment within which all parties must operate. The

[10] *Ibid.*

student is referred to Chapter 10 for a complete discussion of this aspect of pricing.

PRICING POLICIES

There is apparently some confusion between price policies and price practices. Certain literature on pricing identifies practices such as customary prices, odd pricing, psychological pricing, and the like as price policies. Actually these are price practices adopted more or less by the convention of an industry and these are discussed in the next section. One of the few well-known and highly authentic statements of actual company price policies resulted from a research study conducted some years ago. Table 16-1 is one result of this study, whereas much of the interview material may be found in *Pricing in Big Business*, by A. D. H. Kaplan, Joel B. Dirlam, and Robert F. Lanzillotti. In this volume the authors isolate and identify the five most frequently encountered pricing policies which are as follows:

1. Pricing to achieve target return on investment.
2. Stabilization of price and margin.
3. Pricing to maintain or improve market position.
4. Pricing to meet or follow competition.
5. Pricing subordinated to product differentiation.[11]

Among these policies, target return on investment was the most commonly cited. This obviously refers to a percentage return on the investment required for the product or product line. The policy is sometimes modified to establish a target return on sales. The du Pont company, which cites target return on investment as its policy (see Table 16-1), states:

Our price is based upon the obvious elements of conducting business. The probable factory cost of manufacture is calculated. Expected sales and distribution charges are added. We then consider what return on investment is desirable, appropriate and consistent with our own long-term risk and tax exposure, and finally, we make an appraisal of the use value of the product to the consumer, as well as of its worth in relation to competitive counterpart or alternate materials. The end result is usually a compromise of these various factors. On occasion, I have even relied upon my . . . intuition to establish a price for a new article.[12]

Stabilization of price and margin is a policy sometimes practiced by firms faced by wide fluctuations in demand. Instability of prices can seriously upset production, marketing, and financial planning, and if the firm is successful in implementing this policy it reduces the risk of disturb-

[1]A. D. H. Kaplan, Joel B. Dirlam, and Robert F. Lanzillotti, *Pricing in Big Business* (Washington, D.C.: The Brookings Institution, 1958). See especially pp. 127–219.
[2]*Ibid.*, pp. 150–151.

ances in established goals. Frequently the attempts to level out the peaks and valleys of prices are a counterpart to other policies, e.g., target return.[13]

In those industries faced with aggressive competition one is likely to find a policy revolving around attempts to maintain or improve market position. Table 16-1 cites A & P, Sears Roebuck, Standard Oil (Indiana), and Swift, as adherents to this policy. It should be observed that the industries within which these companies operate are all keenly competitive. The retail institutions (A & P and Sears) adopted a low price policy in conjunction with their merchandising policies and of course have been successful in building market share profitably.

Pricing to meet or follow competition is a well-known and widely practiced policy. The firm that adopts this policy believes that a price above competition would only curtail sales. There also is a belief that an industry's prices are determined by the market and that little control over price can be exercised by the firm. Lower prices than competition would only serve to reduce total revenue and not increase sales significantly. In other words, meeting or following competition is in correspondence with the concepts of oligopolistic pricing.

In earlier sections and also in Chapter 8 much has been said about pricing and product differentiation. A price policy related to product differentiation is seldom practiced without its being contributory to other price policies. The firm that has such a policy as an important factor in its pricing places much emphasis on its position in the industry and on the value of its brand name and other merchandising features.

Product differentiation is a significant aspect of price policy when a company features products that can offer the purchaser special satisfactions for which he will pay a price that yields a better than average return on the capital invested. To exploit this policy successfully, a company must have a product line that lends itself to innovations with marketable advantages over comparable standard products. Beyond that, the emphasis on making a product "different" in the consumer's estimate may be an indication of the research-mindedness of the company's management or its strong inclination to develop opportunities for upgrading product rather than cutting price.[14]

Note that the principal policies or goals of the firms listed in Table 16-1 have collateral pricing goals as well. The available empirical evidence on pricing policies supports the view that many companies have difficulty in isolating a single policy as more important than another. Observation by the authors strengthens the position that most price policies are multipurpose and that a combination of the major policies cited is more typical in real price situations.

[13] *Ibid.*, p. 165–166.
[14] *Ibid.*, p. 217.

Table 16-1. Pricing Goals of Twenty Large Industrial Corporations

Company	Principal Pricing Goal	Collateral Pricing Goals	Rate of Return on Investment (After Taxes) 1947–1955[a]		Average Market Share[b]
			Avg.	Range	
Alcoa	20% on investment (before taxes); higher on new products [about 10% effective rate after taxes]	(a) "Promotive" policy on new products (b) Price stabilization	13.8	7.8–18.7	Pig & ingot, 37%; sheet, 46%; other fabrications, 62%[c]
American Can	Maintenance of market share	(a) "Meeting" competition (using cost of substitute product to determine price) (b) Price stabilization	11.6	9.6–14.7	Approx. 35% of all types of cans[d]
A & P	Increasing market share	"General promotive" (low-margin policy)	13.0	9.7–18.8	n.a.
du Pont	Target return on investment —no specific figure given	(a) Charging what traffic will bear over long run (b) Maximum return for new products—"life cycle" pricing	25.9	19.6–34.1	n.a.
Esso (Standard Oil of N.J.)	"Fair-return" target—no specific figure given	(a) Maintaining market share (b) Price stabilization	16.0	12.0–18.9	n.a.

Table 16-1—(Continued)

Company	Principal Pricing Goal	Collateral Pricing Goals	Rate of Return on Investment (After Taxes) 1947–1955[a] Avg.	Range	Average Market Share[b]
General Electric	20% on investment (after taxes); 7% on sales (after taxes)	(a) Promotive policy on new products (b) Price stabilization on nationally advertised products	21.4	18.4–26.6	—[e]
General Foods	33 1/3% gross margin: ("1/3 to make, 1/3 to sell, and 1/3 for profit"); expectation of realizing target only on new products	(a) Full line of food products and novelties (b) Maintaining market share	12.2	8.9–15.7	n.a.
General Motors	20% on investment (after taxes)	Maintaining market share	26.0	19.9–37.0	50% of passenger automobiles[f]
Goodyear	"Meeting competitors"	(a) Maintain "position" (b) Price stabilization	13.3	9.2–16.1	n.a.
Gulf	Follow price of most important marketer in each area	(a) Maintain market share (b) Price stabilization	12.6	10.7–16.7	n.a.

Company					
International Harvester	10% on investment (after taxes)	Market share: ceiling of "less than a dominant share of any market"	8.9	4.9–11.9	Farm tractors, 28–30%; combines, cornpickers, tractor plows, cultivators, mowers, 20–30%; cotton pickers, 65%; light & light-heavy trucks, 5–18%; medium-heavy to heavy-heavy, 12–30%
Johns-Manville	Return on investment greater than last 15-year average (about 15% after taxes); higher target for new products	(a) Market share not greater than 20% (b) Stabilization of prices	14.9	10.7–19.6	n.a.
Kennecott	Stabilization of prices		16.0	9.3–20.9	n.a.
Kroger	Maintaining market share	Target return of 20% on investment before taxes[g]	12.1	9.7–16.1	n.a.
National Steel	Matching the market—price follower	Increase market share	12.1	7.0–17.4	5%
Sears Roebuck	Increasing market share (8–10% regarded as satisfactory share)	(a) Realization of traditional return on investment of 10–15% (after taxes) (b) General promotive (low margin) policy	5.4	1.6–10.7	5–10% average (twice as large a share in hard goods v. soft goods)

Table 16-1—(Continued)

Company	Principal Pricing Goal	Collateral Pricing Goals	Rate of Return on Investment (After Taxes) 1947–1955[a]		Average Market Share[b]
			Avg.	Range	
Standard Oil (Indiana)	Maintain market share	(a) Stabilize prices (b) Target-return on investment (none specified)	10.4	7.9–14.4	n.a.
Swift	Maintenance of market share in livestock buying and meat packing		6.9	3.9–11.1	Approximately, 10% nationally[h]
Union Carbide	Target return on investment[i]	Promotive policy on new products; "life cycle" pricing on chemicals generally	19.2	13.5–24.3	—[j]
U.S. Steel	8% on investment (after taxes)	(a) Target market share of 30% (b) Stable price (c) Stable margin	10.3	7.6–14.8	Ingots and steel, 30%; blast furnaces, 34%; finished hot-rolled products, 35%; other steel mill products, 37%[k]

[h] This represents the average share of total industry shipments of the four largest firms in 1954. Cf. Concentration in American Industry, Report of Subcommittee on the Judiciary, U.S. Senate, 85th Cong, 1st Sess, Washington 1957, p. 315.

[i] In discussions with management officials various profit-return figures were mentioned, with considerable variation among divisions of the company. No official profit target percentage was given, but the author estimates the average profit objective for the corporation to be approximately 35% before taxes, or an effective rate after taxes of about 18%.

[j] Chemicals account for 30% of Carbide's sales, most of which are petro-chemicals, a field that the company opened thirty years ago and still dominates; plastics account for 18%—the company sells 40% of the two most important plastics (vinyl and polyethylene); alloys and metals account for 26% of sales—top U.S. supplier of ferroalloys (e.g., chrome, silicon, manganese), and the biggest U.S. titanium producer; gases account for 14% of sales—estimated to sell 50% of oxygen in the U.S.; carbon, electrodes, and batteries account for 12% of sales—leading U.S. producer of electrodes, refractory carbon, and flashlights and batteries; and miscellaneous—leading operator of atomic energy plants, a leading producer of uranium, the largest U.S. producer of tungsten, and a major supplier of vanadium. Cf. "Union Carbide Enriches the Formula," Fortune, Feb. 1957, pp. 123 ff.; Standard and Poor's Industry Surveys, "Chemicals-Basic Analysis," Dec. 20, 1956, p. C44; and "Annual Report for 1955 of the Union Carbide and Carbon Corporation."

[k] The range of the corporation's capacity as a percentage of total industry capacity varies from 15% to 54%, as of January 1957. For more detail see Administered Prices, Hearings Before the Subcommittee on Antitrust and Monopoly of the Senate Committee on the Judiciary, 85th Cong, 1st Sess, Pt. 2, Steel, Washington 1958, pp. 335-36.

SOURCE: Robert F. Lanzillotti, "Pricing Objectives in Large Corporations," American Economic Review, Vol. 48, No. 5, December 1958, pp. 921-940.

[a] Federal Trade Commission, Rates of Return (After Taxes) for Identical Companies in Selected Manufacturing Industries, 1940, 1947-1955, Washington [1957], pp. 28-30, except for the following companies whose rates were computed by the author using the methods outlined in the Commission Report: A & P, General Foods, Gulf, International Harvester, Kroger, National Steel, Sears Roebuck, and Swift.

[b] As of 1955, unless otherwise indicated. Source of data is company mentioned unless noted otherwise.

[c] U.S. v. Alcoa et al., "Stipulation Concerning Extension of Tables III-X," dated May 31, 1956, U.S. District Court for the Southern District of New York.

[d] As of 1939, U.S. Department of Justice, Western Steel Plants and the Tin Plate Industry, 79th Congress, First Session, Doc. No. 95, p. L 1.

[e] The company states that on the average it aims at not more than 22 to 25 percent of any given market. Percentages for individual markets or products were not made available, but it is estimated that in some markets, e.g., electrical turbines, General Electric has 60 percent of the total market. Cf. Standard and Poor's, Industry Surveys, "Electrical-Electronic-Basic Analysis," August 9, 1956, p. E 21.

[f] Federal Trade Commission, Industrial Concentration and Product Diversification in the 1000 Largest Manufacturing Companies: 1950, Washington, D.C., January 1957, p. 113.

[g] Target return on investment evidently characterizes company policy as much as target market share. In making investment decisions the company is quoted as follows: "The Kroger Co. normally expected a return on investment of at least 20% before taxes." See McNair, Burnham, and Hersum, Cases in Retail Management, New York 1957, pp. 205 ff.

PRICING PRACTICES

Over the years a number of price practices have evolved on the American business scene. The origin of some of them is not discernible, but the reasoning behind their use has wide agreement. Some of the practices grew out of industry custom, some because of assumed shapes of demand curves, and others to satisfy customer goodwill, consistency of business dealings, and more simplified operational procedures.

One Price to All Buyers

This practice by retailers and industrial firms results in the same price to all buyers when the purchase is made under the same conditions. As consumers we see this practice prevailing for most of the goods we purchase, in contrast to the bargaining carried on in the markets of foreign countries. Industrial firms use one price, which is often adjusted because of the quantities purchased, services performed by the buyer, or other cost-saving factors. The basis for a single price to all buyers of the same quantities and under the same conditions is its ease of administration. It simplifies the selling process and removes price making from the sales task. It also nullifies the need for bargaining, which, of course, not all buyers can accomplish equally.

Price Lining

Price lining means that prices will be set at specified levels for given classes or lines of merchandise. Men's suits in a clothing store, for example, may have the price lines of $59.95, $69.95, and $79.95. This procedure is duplicated in many retail firms and for much of their merchandise. Usually the number of price lines for a given kind of merchandise are few so as to classify the customer more easily and speed the sale rather than add confusion by a vast array of prices. This practice not only facilitates the selling process, but also simplifies the planning, accounting, and buying for the retail firm. As shown in Box 15-5 of the previous chapter, automobile pricing serves as a somewhat more complex system of price lining.

Odd-Even Pricing

Many businessmen apparently believe that consumers will react more favorably if prices end in certain numbers. Hence, numerous prices are quoted in odd figures such as 59¢, 89¢, $1.09, and so on rather than the next higher or lower even amount. When the businessman believes that odd prices expand sales, he is reasoning as if the demand curve looked like that in Figure 16-2a. This and the other demand curves in the figure were origi-

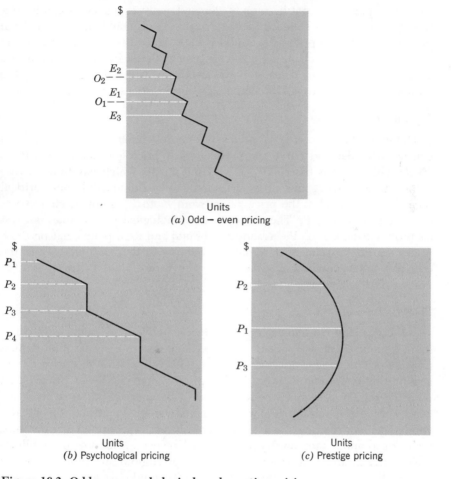

Figure 16-2. Odd-even, psychological, and prestige pricing.

SOURCE: Adapted from Edward R. Hawkins, "Price Policies and Theory," *Journal of Marketing,* Vol. 18, No. 3, January 1954, pp. 233–240.

nally developed by Edward R. Hawkins in one of the few attempts to integrate price theory with price practices. The odd-even demand curve tells us that each price ending in an odd figure will produce more sales volume than the next lower (and next higher) even price. E_1, E_2, and E_3 are the even-price points whereas O_1 and O_2 are the odd-price points. Is there any evidence to support the belief that odd prices generate more sales volume than even prices? No, there is not, but despite the lack of empirical evidence it is widely held to be an effective pricing practice. Odd pricing came into popularity not because of demand analysis, but as an administrative device. Retailers believed that their sales clerks could easily pocket the proceeds of an even-price sale. An odd price forced the sales person to ring up the sale and give change. Until such time as better evidence is produced to support the kind of demand curve associated with odd-even prices, the question of the validity and effectiveness of odd prices will remain unclear.

Psychological Pricing

Quite similar to odd-even prices but more authentic is psychological pricing. The demand curve for psychological pricing is shown in Figure 16-2b. This curve is based on pricing experiments which have shown that certain price ranges have little effect on sales volume until some critical point is reached. Thus the price range from P_1 to P_2 is not as effective as the range from P_3 to P_4. The concept of psychological pricing does not rest (as is often assumed) on the assumption of odd and even points, but on those prices that are psychologically more attractive to the consumer. Thus, the critical point is reached as price moves downward from P_2 to P_3 and the next critical point is P_4, and so on.

Prestige Pricing

Because many consumers have the faculty of judging quality by price, some products carry a prestige price. The demand curve that depicts prestige pricing is shown in Figure 16-2c. This tells us that the price P_1 will generate more volume than the higher price P_2 and the lower price P_3. At point P_2 some buyers would be forced out of the market, but at point P_3 the quality-price relationship is not prestigious enough to attract the greater volume gained by pricing at P_1. This curve is most appropriate for fine furs, high-priced autos, rare jewelry, and so on. However, some low-priced items such as health and beauty aids, though not prestigious, are more successful at a medium price; if the price were lower it would only lead to suspicions of poor quality (for instance, aspirin at 59¢ per 100 versus the same product at 19¢ per 100).

GEOGRAPHICAL PRICING PRACTICES

Every manufacturing and distributive institution is aware of the importance of transportation costs. In some instances the transportation bill for manufacturers involves an expenditure of many millions of dollars. In this country, where the distances are great, the markets dispersed, and the transportation systems elaborate, the costs incident thereto become significant. Consumers seldom come into direct contact with this aspect of pricing except when purchasing an automobile. Automobile prices are quoted f.o.b. (free on

BOX 16-2

Terms Frequently Used in Delivered Pricing Systems

Basing-point mill: Any mill which quotes a "base price" from which a "delivered price" is arrived at by adding the actual freight to the customer's location.

Base price: What a basing-point mill combines with actual freight cost to determine what delivered price to quote provided its combination of base price and actual freight cost is lower than that of any other basing-point mill.

Freight equalization: The practice of charging a customer, not the seller's actual transportation costs, but the lower transportation cost at which the customer could get delivery from a competing seller.

Market interpenetration: The extension of seller's operations beyond the range of their respective transportation-cost advantages.

Mill net return: The difference between a producer's delivered price and his actual cost of making delivery.

Nonbasing-point mills: Producers who do not quote "base prices" and are left out of account in determining *the* basing-point mill and *the* delivered price to be quoted on any given piece of business.

Nonlocal seller: One who is making the sale in a territory in which his transportation costs impose a competitive disadvantage.

Phantom freight: The amount by which a nonbasing-point "mill net return" exceeds the base price of *the* basing-point mill for a given delivered-price quotation. (The same as the difference between its actual freight cost and that of *the* basing-point mill.)

Postage-stamp pricing: Quoting the same delivered price to all customers (usually to all customers in the United States), regardless of location.

Variable f.o.b. pricing: Quoting an f.o.b. price but not necessarily the same one to every customer. The "variable" means customer-to-customer differences, not time-to-time changes.

Zone pricing: Dividing the market into zones and quoting a single delivered price for each zone.

SOURCE: "Delivered Pricing and the Law" (Washington, D.C.: Chamber of Commerce of the United States, 1948), p. 9.

board) Detroit, some other assembly point, or port of entry. On purchase the consumer learns the delivered price is somewhat higher because of transportation charges.

In general, geographic pricing practices may be divided into two categories: f.o.b. pricing and delivered pricing. With f.o.b. pricing the seller quotes the same uniform price to all customers. The f.o.b. price includes the cost of preparing the goods for shipment and placing them on board the mode of transportation selected by the buyer. The buyer takes delivery and pays the transportation. The net return to the seller is the same regardless of the location of the buyer, but the cost to the buyer varies according to transportation cost.

An alternative to f.o.b. pricing is delivered pricing. A delivered-pricing system includes both the price of the goods and the transportation costs of getting the goods to the customer. Under this system the seller often receives varying net prices because transportation costs vary with distances. Delivered pricing systems include zone prices, postage-stamp pricing, basing-point pricing, and freight equalization. These and other usual terms used in delivered pricing are identified in Box 16-2. The particular method used is an important decision, since it may affect the firm's competitive position, location of plant and suppliers, and the profitability of sales.[15]

Questions:

1. How would you proceed to price a new industrial product?
2. Develop a pricing structure for an agricultural product as it proceeds from the farmer through wholesale markets through processors through wholesalers through retailers to consumers.
3. To what extent do we in the United States have price competition?
4. Price competition is really cost competition. Explain. Are loss leaders a form of price competition?
5. Is there any psychology involved in pricing? Explain.

Statements to Consider

The price leader is usually the largest firm in the industry; if there are two or more dominant concerns, one may serve as leader as a matter of custom, or more than one may lead in separate territories, or in turn.

Different price levels prevail because the commodities are in different places, rather than because a period of time has elapsed during which prices for the commodity have changed in all markets.

[15] Jules Backman, *Price Practices and Price Policies*, pp. 174–175.

The price structures of individual retail firms selling to consumers are usually much simpler than those at the manufacturing or wholesale levels for the same goods.

Inelasticity of demand, or even the belief that demand is inelastic, acts as a strong deterrent to price flexibility.

All aspects of pricing by dealers are related to the buying habits and attitudes of buyers.

SELECTED REFERENCES

Jules Backman, *Price Practices and Price Policies* (New York: The Ronald Press Company, 1953).

Donald V. Harper, *Price Policy and Procedure* (New York: Harcourt, Brace and World, 1966).

Alfred R. Oxenfeldt, *Pricing for Marketing Executives* (San Francisco: Wadsworth Publishing Company, 1961).

° Joel Dean, "Pricing a New Product," *The Controller*, Vol. 23, No. 4, April 1955, pp. 163–165.

Clare E. Griffin, "When Is Price Reduction Profitable?" *Harvard Business Review*, Vol. 38, No. 5, September–October 1960, pp. 125–132.

° Edward R. Hawkins, "Price Policies and Theory," *Journal of Marketing*, Vol. 18, No. 3, January 1954, pp. 233–240.

° H. W. Huegy, "Price Decisions and Marketing Policies," in Hugh G. Wales (ed.), *Changing Perspectives in Marketing* (Urbana: University of Illinois Press, 1951), pp. 228–242.

Generalizations Were Taken From:

Rayburn D. Tousley, Eugene Clark, and Fred E. Clark, *Principles of Marketing* (New York: The Macmillan Company, 1962).

Roland S. Vaile, E. T. Grether, and Revis Cox, *Marketing in the American Economy* (New York: The Ronald Press Company, 1952).

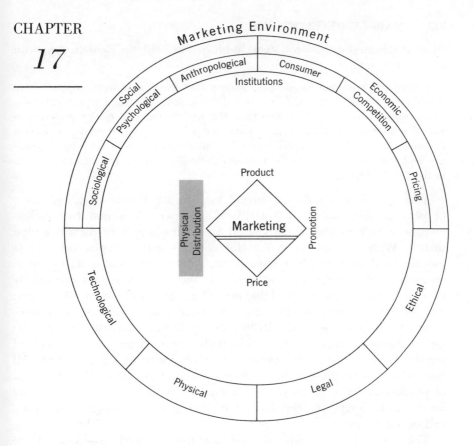

Marketing Logistics

THE ENVIRONMENT OF MARKETING LOGISTICS • LOGISTICS DECISION AREAS •
IMPLICATIONS FOR MARKETING • AN EXAMPLE OF COMPANY LOGISTICS

In an article on distribution systems published in 1965, the *German-American Trade News* said:

Indeed if it were not for a supply system that works anywhere anytime, there would be no foreign cars in the United States. Nothing serves as a greater deterrent to the sale of an imported product than the loss of time and money caused by a lack of replacement parts. It is one of the principal reasons why several good foreign car makes have failed to succeed in the U.S. market, while others, led by Volkswagen and Mercedes, continue to strengthen their highly respected market positions in the United States.[1]

This quotation implies the current importance of marketing logistics— or physical distribution, as it is likewise known. To almost two million owners of Volkswagens in the United States, the supply of parts is a vital matter. Without a proper system for speedily getting replacement parts into the hands of those who require them, Volkswagen might as well close its doors to United States buyers. Actually, the logistics system created by importers includes many things that are not readily visible to the VW owner. The importer travels abroad to tap new sources and to learn latest developments; he designs a regional distribution system throughout this country; he utilizes various transportation services both here and from overseas points of supply; he relies upon a computerized system for control of inventory. All these elements of physical distribution contribute to making the right kind of product available in the proper amount at the place where the demand for it exists. Together they form the "key link between manufacturing and demand creation."[2]

The task of moving materials and products is indeed an old one. Even before the exchange process developed, man engaged in the moving of goods. Today, when it is estimated that eighteen tons of materials are hauled annually for each person in our country, physical distribution has become an area of great concern.[3]

In many ways it is difficult to visualize the magnitude of the logistics task. The Flow of Goods Chart (Figure 2-1) depicts the movement of goods from producer to consumer in pipeline fashion through a variety of marketing intermediaries. Further examination of the chart will indicate the enormity of the job of physically handling the staggering volume and value of materials. The logistics task can also be illustrated by a map of steel warehouses located strategically across the nation or by a modern food wholesaling facility with

---

[1]"How 4 U.S. Importers Perfected Distribution Systems To Put Foreign Car Parts on Tap Anywhere, Anytime," *German-American Trade News*, Vol. 19, No. 3, March 1965, p. 14.
[2]Wendell M. Stewart, "Physical Distribution: Key to Improved Volume and Profits," *Journal of Marketing*, Vol. 29, No.1, January 1965, p. 65.
[3]James W. Millard, *Physical Distribution* (Pontiac, Mich.: General Motors Corporation, February 1961), page 5.

its readily apparent inbound and outbound flows of goods as well as its impressive inventory of merchandise.

Traffic and transportation, warehousing, inventory control, order processing, materials handling, and production constitute the principal components of marketing logistics. In addition, there are procurement as well as selling, inbound as well as outbound flows of goods, and internal as well as external considerations. In the case of oil and gasoline, the flow of crude petroleum through offshore rigs, refineries, pipes, railroad cars, trucks, storage trucks, and pumps to the automobile illustrates the logistics task from beginning to end (see Figure 17-1).

Years ago Shaw noted that the essential element in business was the application of motion to material.[4] Brass ingots are shipped to a manufacturer of faucets. The ingots are placed in an electric furnace, the molten brass is poured into molds, the product is conveyed through dipping tanks, cleaners, polishers, assemblers, and packagers before it is finally shipped to plumbing wholesalers who ship it to plumbers who in turn finally place the faucet on the sink in some home. Shaw was right: placing material in motion is indeed an essential element.

This motion occurs at a number of points. In a simple situation there is motion inbound to a processor, motion within the plant, and motion outbound toward the customer.[5] Typically, marketing has been concerned with outbound motion but recently the logistics concept has brought an appreciation of the total movement of goods. This accumulation of movements adds significantly to the importance of logistics to marketing.

We now see how time, place, and possession utilities relate to physical distribution. P. D. Converse sums up the matter as follows:

One part of marketing deals with buying and selling, with creating desires and demands for goods, of transferring title to the goods. This part of marketing creates possession utility. The other part deals with the physical handling of goods, transporting them from farm and mine to mill and factory and from factory to processing plant to the consumers and storing when and where necessary. This part of marketing creates time and place utilities.[6]

Alderson has suggested a different approach: "Marketing starts out with the available supply of diversified products and creates ultimate utility through what is essentially a process of sorting."[7] This sorting concept further clar-

[4] Arch W. Shaw, *Some Problems in Market Distribution* (Cambridge: Harvard University Press, 1915), p. 5.
[5] Donald V. Harper, "Transportation: A Forgotten Function of Marketing," *Business Review,* Spring 1964, p. 47.
[6] Paul D. Converse, "The Other Half of Marketing," *Boston Conference on Distribution,* 1954, p. 23.
[7] Wroe Alderson, *Marketing Behavior and Executive Action* (Homewood, Ill.: Richard D. Irwin, 1957), pp. 195–199.

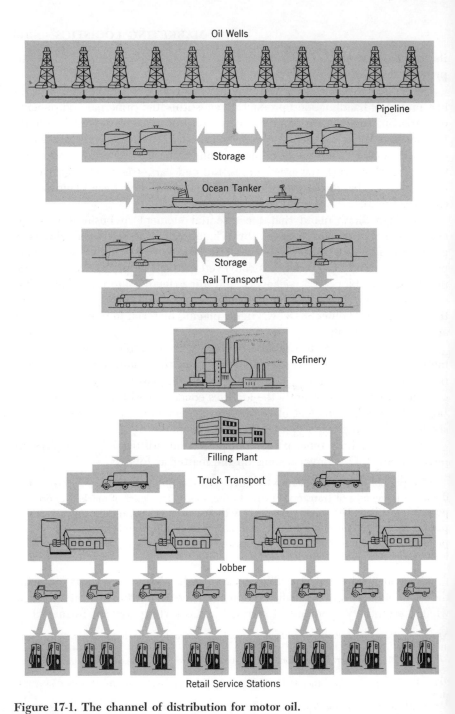

Figure 17-1. The channel of distribution for motor oil.

SOURCE: Martin L. Bell, *Marketing, Concepts and Strategies*, (Boston: Houghton Mifflin Company, 1966), p. 129.

ifies the importance and role of logistics. Sorting consists of four stages: (1) sorting out (grading of apples, lumber, or beef); (2) accumulation of homogeneous supplies with larger supplies; (3) allocation (both internally and externally), where supply is broken down according to situational requirements; and (4) assorting, where supplies are put together to meet demand requirements. These four stages are each accomplished by movement of goods. In a typical situation, beef is sorted out according to government grading systems; meat is accumulated at various stages at the farmer's feeding lot, the stockyards, and beyond; packers make various allocations of the product depending on market conditions; and the retailer builds up an assortment of meat as he anticipates consumer needs. Throughout this entire marketing process (the matching of needs to products), there is movement of goods which ultimately results in the satisfaction of needs.

THE ENVIRONMENT OF MARKETING LOGISTICS

Marketing logistics take place in the ever-changing, kaleidoscopic, total environment of marketing. This environment influences logistics and, reciprocally, logistics operations influence the environment.

Consumers are served by logistics. Their behavior demands the movement of goods, which ultimately aids in the satisfaction of their wants. Industrial consumers demand speed in delivery, housewives want fresh vegetables in winter, department stores carry both deep and wide lines in order to attract customers, jewelers accumulate attractive lines of watches and costume jewelry, mail-order houses ship fashion items by air express—these examples all reflect the fitting together of marketing efforts and consumer desires through physical distribution.

Logistics interact with many aspects of the environment. *Technology* has brought about changes in shipping (refrigerated cars), inventory (computers), handling (palletizing), warehousing (construction of efficient layouts), and many other marketing activities. Genesco, Inc., is one of many firms which has completely automated its distribution system. From an inventory of 1.5 million pairs of shoes, the company coordinates the output of 17 manufacturing facilities with the demands of thousands of retailers, and aided by a computer, it can ship 40,000 pairs to 1,500 dealers in one eight-hour day.[8]

The constant struggle to remain competitive definitely includes logistics. Owing to competition, delivery time is an important selling point, for example, and efficient handling of goods means a competitive advantage in speed and costs. Indeed, for many purchases—whether by industry, government, or ultimate consumer—availability is a key determinant in consummating the sale.

[8] "A Computer Ships the Shoes," *Business Week*, July 11, 1964, p. 96.

The *geography* of an area in part determines logistical policies. Handling the logistics problems in the Philippines is a much different situation from that of Japan or the United States. Geographic realities necessitate a wide variety of distribution facilities. Then, too, the structure of *intermediaries* also relates to logistics. Both the accumulation and the allocation functions are obviously influenced by the marketing structure, and vice versa. The marketing structure is a factor to consider when moving goods and materials. Drop shippers (wholesalers who are merchants that do not take possession) and decentralized warehousing develop in areas where product handling costs are high.

Many other environmental factors must be reckoned with in the development of an optimal logistics plan. Population density and distribution, plant location, availability of transportation, legal restrictions (rates, weight limitations, and so on), product characteristics, and demand patterns all affect physical handling. In addition, forecasts of economic conditions govern buyers in their inventory accumulation.

All these factors and more complicate the environment in which logistics must operate. Since a change in technology could conceivably alter today's logistics, the marketer should be alert to any development which bears on physical distribution. The manager who ignores his environment and its changes definitely courts trouble, whereas the manager who understands the environmental influence should be able to devise a sensible logistics plan.

LOGISTICS DECISION AREAS

As bystanders, we watch the trucks roll down the highway, observe the automobiles loaded on double-deck freight cars, and hear the cargo jets pass overhead. We appreciate the inventories of commodities carried by retailers and are aware of the assembly task involved in manufacturing a telephone. However, we are not always mindful of the decisions that each buyer, seller, and producer must make concerning the movement of goods. Optimizing logistical operations is a necessity for managers and even for the ultimate consumer.

The *locating* of facilities constitutes one prime decision area. Manufacturing facilities and warehousing locations must be planned and selected carefully since costs and time can be of major importance. The economics of location can be a complicated subject which the firm cannot ignore. For example, proximity to markets and transportation are factors as important to logistics as proximity to a labor force is to production (see Box 17-1).

There is no single facility for all *transportation* needs and hence a variety of means are available (Box 17-2). Probably many buyers pay for faster service than is necessary, but others fail to recognize the gains that speedy transporta-

BOX 17-1

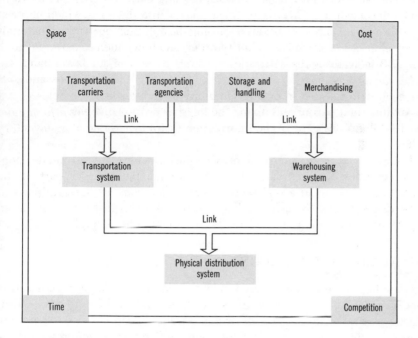

Physical Distribution System

SOURCE: William Lazer, "Distribution and the Marketing Mix," *Transportation and Distribution Management*, December 1962, p. 16.

BOX 17-2

General Relationships of Service Characteristics of the Five Modes of Transportation

Speed	Air	Highway	Rail	Water	Pipeline
Frequency	Pipeline	Highway	Air	Rail	Water
Dependability	Pipeline	Highway	Rail	Water	Air
Capability	Water	Rail	Highway	Air	Pipeline
Availability	Highway	Rail	Air	Water	Pipeline

SOURCE: J. L. Heskett, Robert J. Ivie, and Nicholas A. Glaskowsky, Jr., *Business Logistics*, (New York: The Ronald Press Company, 1964), p. 71.

tion bring about. For example, a manufacturer of furniture may provide fast delivery at greater expense in order to avoid warehousing costs.

Excessive purchases and storage generate high carrying costs, whereas insufficient quantities may result in stockouts and cause a costly shutdown of production facilities. This places the manager in a dilemma which he must solve through *inventory* decisions regarding the optimum quantity of materials to buy at a time (economical quantity order) and how much to carry on hand. Box 17-3 indicates a characteristic inventory pattern of stocks on hand.

Packaging decisions compromise among protection, attractiveness, and cost. For each item shipped in or out, handling procedures must be devised.

An important part of optimizing the logistics process involves *information*. Box 17-4 illustrates some of the information useful in arriving at an inventory policy.

Just as marketing research data provide the bases for many market development activities, logistics data serve to optimize the logistics part of the marketing function. In a real sense, logistics decisions are integral parts of marketing strategy. As such, marketers can look upon these decisions as an important and essential element of the total marketing complex.

IMPLICATIONS FOR MARKETING

Good logistics planning is based in large measure on adequate information concerning costs, speed, needs, and so forth. As part of the marketing effort, logistics is vital to the movement of goods from conception to consumption.

For one thing, logistics adds value to goods. Iron ore required by a Pittsburgh mill has less value in Minnesota than at the mill. Unsorted goods at a warehouse are less valuable than sorted goods. Logistics provides time and place utility, or as Alderson explained, it adds value all through the sorting process.

There is a great deal of engineering in logistics and indeed, improvements in many of its aspects are actually the accomplishments of an engineering staff. Pallet boards, handling equipment, conveyor systems, and various transportation facilities suggest the importance of engineering in the movement of goods. In a field so dependent on engineering techniques, frequent changes are bound to occur. As technology develops—piggyback, computer systems, scientific inventory control, radio-operated warehouses, and so on—logistics improves, since entrepreneurs strive to attain a competitive advantage.

Logistics is best understood by considering the nature of the entire system involved. This includes movements within the plant as well as external movements. Related activities comprise production, finance, traffic; and purchasing; and any integrated program for the logistics system necessarily encompasses them all.

What is the Characteristic Inventory Pattern of Stocks on Hand in the Typical Company?

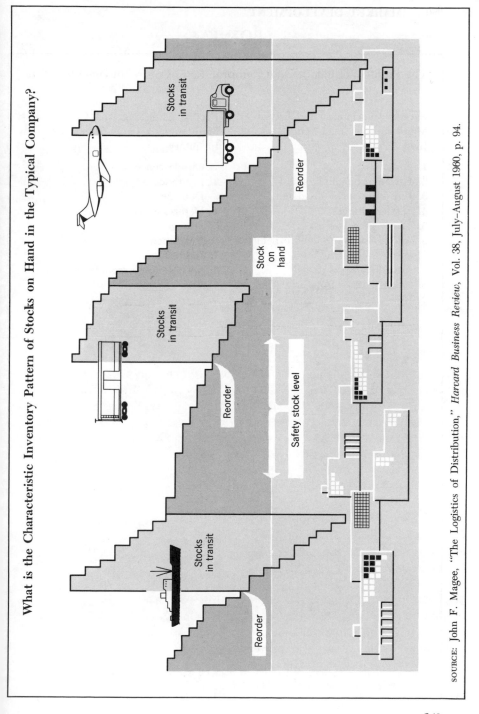

SOURCE: John F. Magee, "The Logistics of Distribution," *Harvard Business Review*, Vol. 38, July–August 1960, p. 94.

BOX 17-4

The Problem of Balance and Compromise in Control of Inventory Size

A	*B*
Factors Associated with Costs of Maintaining a Small Materials Inventory	Factors Associated with Costs of Maintaining a Large Materials Inventory

A
Factors Associated with Costs of
Maintaining a Small Materials
Inventory

1. Order costs
2. Excess of handling costs
3. Loss of quantity discounts
4. Service charges
5. Costly shortages
6. Added follow-up and expediting costs
7. Added transportation
8. Possible losses from price rises
9. Etc.

B
Factors Associated with Costs of
Maintaining a Large Materials
Inventory

1. Obsolescence
2. Insurance
3. Damage
4. Deterioration
5. Storage costs
6. Investment
7. Interest
8. Possible losses from price declines
9. Etc.

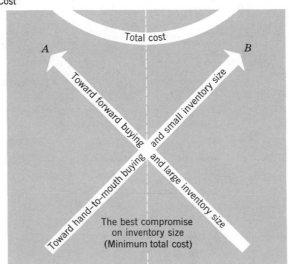

SOURCE: Stanley E. Bryan, "The Fundamental Elements of Effective Materials Control," *Purchasing*, Vol. 30, No. 5, May 1951, p. 97.

This desire for integrating several functions has caused some difficulty, as there has not been one best way of organizing for logistics. The material management concept has not been universally adopted, and managers in many organizations have not integrated all the elements of logistics. Whereas it seems to make sense to do so and include the entire system, further understanding and appreciation are probably necessary for many executives (see Box 17-5).

Logistics is an expensive function. Each movement of goods and each handling of them or storage costs money, and these costs accumulate. Con-

BOX 17-5

Recent Attention to Physical Distribution

If physical distribution is so important to the success of a firm's operation, why are possible returns from its effective management only now gaining attention? Several recent developments can be held primarily responsible for this:

1. Attention to the importance of all things described by the term "marketing concept."

2. Increasing demand on the part of consumers, who can now afford it, for more convenience in purchasing.

3. The tendency for marketing institutions to cut inventories in order to improve stock turnover, thereby shifting the responsibility for inventory maintenance backward in the channels of distribution to manufacturers.

4. The growth of multiple-product lines, which can increase the prospective gains from combined physical distribution methods.

5. Awareness of the fact that physical distribution (particularly transportation) costs are not, or need not be, static in nature.

6. Improved technology in transportation or movement systems that has recently offered a growing number of possibilities for physical distribution.

7. Recognition that only comparatively small gains in manufacturing efficiency are any longer possible in many firms, and that more fruitful areas for operational improvement exist elsewhere.

8. The wartime development of mathematical techniques which have brought problems of physical distribution, just as other marketing problems, within reach of realistic solution.

9. Design and manufacture of computers capable of performing the "busy work" of physical distribution analysis.

SOURCE: J. L. Heskett, "Ferment in Marketing's Oldest Area," *Journal of Marketing*, Vol. 26, No. 4, October 1962, p. 41.

siderable potential savings exist because of the relatively large costs incurred in the logistics area. Savings can accrue from many directions, such as an improved choice of transportation, better inventory control, more efficient conveyor system, more secure warehousing. Small savings rapidly grow into substantial amounts, and one should recognize that lowering of costs increases profits.

One study has suggested that *physical distribution costs* vary from approximately 10 percent of sales in the machinery industry to 30 percent in the food industry.[9] A study by A. T. Kearney & Company provides a functional breakdown of physical distribution costs.[10]

Functional Activity	*Percent of Sales*
Administration	2.4
Transportation	
Inbound	2.1
Outbound	4.3
Receiving and shipping	1.7
Packaging	2.6
Warehousing	
In-plant	2.1
Field	1.6
Inventory carrying costs	
Interest	2.2
Taxes, insurance, obsolescence	1.6
Order processing	1.2
TOTAL	21.8

Though approximate, these costs suggest that management may save considerable sums by improving the logistics part of its operations. Competition will force it to do so eventually. The information now available to the manager enables him to make intelligent decisions regarding *trade-offs*. A trade-off typically involves a reduction of costs in one area and their increase in other areas. A shift of air freight from rail may certainly raise transportation costs but may very well lower warehousing and inventory costs (see Box 17-6). Thus each logistics decision can be a trade-off in costs, with the decision being made because the net result is a gain for the company.

The matter of handling costs and trade-offs can be readily seen if one simplifies and groups costs into three classifications. These are (1) operating costs required for the actual movement of the goods, including transportation, loading, packing, and order costs; (2) possession costs, or inventory costs of

[9] Richard E. Snyder, "Physical Distribution Costs," *Distribution Age*, Vol. 62, December 1963, pp. 35–42.
[10] Adapted from Stewart, *Op. cit.*, p. 67.

BOX 17-6

Distribution Cost to Country—D

Based on 1964 Statistics, Expressed in Dollars per Pound

Cost Element	1964 Surface	1964 Air	1966 Proposed Air
Inland freight (to N.Y.)	$0.0189	$0.1488	$0.0734
Service and consolidation	0.0103 ⎫		
Delivery and cartage	0.0126 ⎪		
Document prep and postage	0.0145 ⎬	0.0110	0.0110
Penalty, strikes, and delays	0.0028 ⎪		
Wharfage and warehousing	0.0003 ⎭		
Insurance cost	0.0042	0.0061	0.0030
Ocean freight/air freight	0.0780	0.3268	0.2000
Customs documents and claims handling	0.0097	0.0042	0.0042
Unloading and wharfage	0.0131	0.0170	0.0034
Inland freight (within Europe)	0.0700	0.0300	0.0300
TOTAL TRANSPORTATION COST/POUND	$0.2344	$0.5439	$0.3250

Mode of Transportation	Percent	Weight in Pounds	Cost/ Pound	Cost per year
1964 surface	65	202,670	$0.2344	$ 47,505.00
1964 air	35	107,025	0.5439	58,210.00
Total Transportation Cost, 1964				$105,715.00
1966 "All air"		309,695	0.3250	100,650.00
Transportation savings in 1966				$ 5,065.00
"Pipeline" reduction based on 1964 export dollars (surface $716,037) (8%) (30 days)/(360 days)				4,725.00
Safety stock reduction estimated by subsidiaries ($50,000) (8%)				4,000.00
Estimated warehousing cost advantage:				
($ safety stock = 50,000) (warehousing = $93,200)				
(Grand total $ inventory = 1,134,000)				4,109.00
TOTAL ANNUAL SAVINGS				17,899.00

SOURCE: P. M. Le Mieux, L. A. Wickstrom, L. L. Pressler, "All Air Freight Distribution" (Minneapolis: Honeywell, International Division, 1966), p. A-11.

various kinds; and (3) service costs which accrue from poor logistics in one way or another, usually in the form of sales losses. The trade-off often includes only one's own firm but at other times encompasses costs which the supplier, buyer, or both generate and those controlled by the intermediate firm. The following business situations illustrate the kinds of decisions and trade-offs that are properly considered problems of logistics.[11]

Switch to air transportation from rail	Reduce warehousing costs Increase transportation costs (see Box 17-6)
Hire more clerical help	Take advantage of slower, cheaper transportation Increase labor costs Speed up order processing
Combine shipments	Lower truckload and carload rates Risk decreasing customer service
Place fewer orders	Decrease order processing costs Increase inventory problems perhaps
Increase the number of warehouses	Reduce service time to customers Increase warehousing costs
Palletize handling of products	Reduce handling costs Requires customer cooperation
Computerize the inventory operation	Increase efficiency, lower costs Involves labor training and new techniques

AN EXAMPLE OF COMPANY LOGISTICS

One company that has studied its distribution in some depth is Eastman Kodak, which organized a distribution center as early as 1948. Its distribution center integrates the logistics of photographic equipment, supplies, and related products.[12] The prime objective of the center is customer service—"To get the right product to the right place, at the right time, and to properly account for it." The center is concerned with coordinating worldwide planning in all company photographic plants, and its personnel are trained to be "sympathetic" to the problems of both production and marketing. Its ten major responsibilities include the following:

1. Estimate sales.
2. Schedule production.
3. Control inventory.

[11] This material is based primarily on two sources: (1) "New Strategies to Move Goods," *Business Week*, September 24, 1966, p. 112; and (2) Heskett *et al.*, *Op. cit.*, pp. 448–451.
[12] Russ Cornell, "Kodak Distribution Has 10 Responsibilities," *Distribution Age*, Vol. 63, No. 9, September 1964, pp. 33–40.

4. Handle and warehouse the products.
5. Account for production, inventories, shipments.
6. Handle and account for returned goods.
7. Be responsible for the business systems.
8. Distribute advertising materials.
9. Handle transportation.
10. Coordinate worldwide distribution.

It is obvious that physical distribution at Eastman has become a focal point for management and likewise that the company's perspective of logistics is a broad one, encompassing some production as well as marketing tasks.

The acquiring, possessing, handling, and shipping of goods costs money. It is a cost which can in many instances be reduced when management focuses its attention on the many aspects of logistics. A good program of logistics makes the firm more competitive, provides a better service for customers and improves the efficiency of the marketing task. As John Magee has stated:

One thing seems sure: the choice of distribution system each company makes will have a significant impact on product design, plant investment, and organization. Industrial logistics and trends in logistics technology will receive increasing attention from business, along with markets, capital resources, and product development, in the formulation of corporate plans for the decade ahead.[13]

Questions

1. Does the problem of marketing logistics apply only to tangible physical products? How about services? Insurance?
2. What are some of the important limitations on the automation of a distributor system?
3. Do you think the improvements in physical handling have outstripped the gains made in other marketing operations?
4. If you were to develop a cost-reduction program for a company, what would you include from physical distribution?

Statements to Consider

The trading-area structure for any store includes a core, shape, size, arteries of movement, competition, internal components, and external boundaries.

In a buyers' market the competition among manufacturers on the one hand and the opportunity for mass purchases at attractive prices on the other lead to integration of marketing functions.

---

[13] Magee, *op. cit.*, p. 101.

Economies of scale in distribution are greatest when horizontal and vertical integration are combined.

The economic justification then for independent wholesalers is the fact that the use of their services lowers the cost of marketing.

Most firms can market their products efficiently prior to the beginning of the dispersion process without combining them with the products of other firms.

The channel of distribution tends to be relatively longer for goods of low unit value, small size, general consumption, and staple nature, which are bought frequently and habitually by large numbers of people.

The distance which goods tend to travel to market is a direct function of the difference of price differentials in two markets and the cost of transportation between them.

As cities increase in size, two fairly definite tendencies begin to appear in the location of wholesale markets. Wholesalers of some goods tend to congregate in a common center. Wholesalers of other goods tend to follow their customers.

SELECTED REFERENCES

J. L. Heskett, Robert M. Ivie, and Nicholas A. Glaskowsky, Jr., *Business Logistics: Management of Physical Supply and Distribution* (New York: The Ronald Press Company, 1964).

Frank H. Mossman and Newton Morton, *Logistics of Distribution Systems* (Boston: Allyn and Bacon, 1964).

° Paul D. Converse, "The Other Half of Marketing," *Boston Conference on Distribution*, 1954, pp. 22–25.

° John F. Magee, "The Logistics of Distribution," *Harvard Business Review*, Vol. 38, No. 4, July–August 1960, pp. 89–101.

Generalizations Were Taken From:

William Applebaum and Saul B. Cohen, "Store Trading Areas in a Changing Market," *Journal of Retailing*, Vol. 37, Fall 1961, pp. 14–25.

Theodore N. Beckman, Nathaniel H. Engle, and Robert D. Buzzell, *Wholesaling* (New York: The Ronald Press Company, 1959).

Roland S. Vaile, E. T. Grether, and Reavis Cox, *Marketing in the American Economy* (New York: The Ronald Press Company, 1952).

Rayburn D. Tousley, Eugene Clark, and Fred E. Clark, *Principles of Marketing* (New York: The Macmillan Company, 1962).

Robert Bartels, "Can Marketing Be a Science?" *Journal of Marketing*, Vol. 15, January 1951, pp. 319–328.

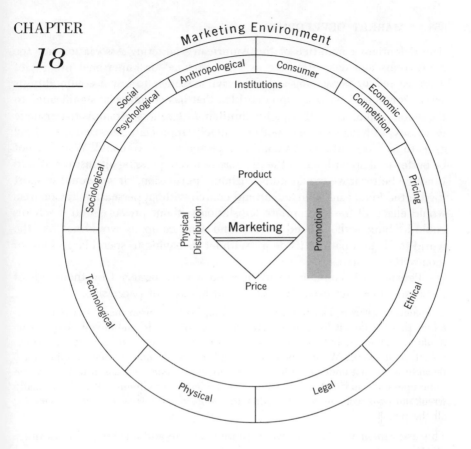

Persuasion in the Market Place—I

THE ROLE OF PERSUASION   *Persuasion and the Exchange Process   Persuasion and the Environment* • INSTRUMENTS OF PERSUASION   *The Institutions   The Instruments   The Promotion Mix*

357

The definitions committee of the American Marketing Association not too many years ago defined selling as "the personal or impersonal process of assisting and/or persuading a prospective customer to buy a commodity or service or to act favorably upon an idea that has commercial significance to the seller." All of us are thoroughly familiar with sellers' attempts to persuade us to buy, although we may not completely appreciate these efforts. Many of us think we would like to eliminate persuasion if we could. Would it not be better to shop without all the persuasive forces pressing against us? Would it not be better if we would study without "persuasion," if we would support the United Fund campaign and attend church without persuasion, if Congress would enact all the appropriate legislation without pressure, and if schools could be built without bond drives? And what company would not like the world to "beat a path to its door" without its having to spend large sums of money for persuasion?

Persuasion is common to us because we are besieged by thousands of persuasive messages each day. As Tosdal has said of persuasion:

Sometimes it is in bad taste, sometimes misleading, often inept; but it is so familiar that we take it for granted. At times we tolerate it, embrace it, and in particular condemn it; but by and large we are influenced by it to a degree which is little understood. We do not comprehend its social and economic implications. Because we do not understand it, we pass judgment upon the basis of its abuses. We sometimes endorse views which would tend to destroy or eliminate it and eventually wreck our own economy and its ability to maintain and raise standards of living for all the people.[1]

This assessment would seem to be more accurate and meaningful than those of Dexter Masters:

In the jungle of the market place, indeed, the intelligent buyer must be alert to every commercial sound, to every snapping twig, to every rustle that may signal the uprising arm holding the knife pointed toward the jugular vein.[2]

The aim of selling is to make something out of nothing, or, at least, more out of less.[3]

A recent government report concluded: "Although mass advertising may once have provided an impetus to industrialization, the conclusion is inescapable that the preponderance of contemporary advertising as it has developed contributes mainly to a massive waste of human and natural resources."[4]

[1]Harry R. Tosdal, Selling In Our Economy (Homewood, Ill.: Richard D. Irwin, 1957), p. 4.
[2]Dexter Masters, The Intelligent Buyer's Guide to Sellers (Mount Vernon, N. Y.: Consumers Union, 1965), p. 21.
[3]Ibid., p. 56.
[4]Consumers Union of the United States, Inc., Standards and the Consumer: A Special Report to the National Bureau of Standards by Consumers Union of U.S., Inc. (Springfield, Va.: The Clearinghouse for Federal Scientific and Technical Information, 1965), p. 81.

Lord Leverhume has been quoted as saying, "I know about half my advertising is wasted, but I do not know which half."[5] As a society, we feel that production is good, but that consumption is bad. We applaud the Hershey Chocolate Corporation because we say it is successful in business without having to resort to persuasive efforts (see Box 18-1).

Hershey has annual sales exceeding $200 million and profits exceeding $20 million. Its ratios of profit to sales and to invested capital are excellent, its asset to liability ratio is 12:1, and its stock is steady on the exchange. As a top company officer stated: "All we do is make a good product, sell it at the lowest possible price, and do some promotional work with retailers and distributors."[6]

Hershey's policies are not opposed to advertising and indeed the company sponsors cooperative advertising with retailers and advertises in trade publications. It uses considerable point-of-sale advertising, and the millions of wrappers seen at more than one million retail outlets (including vending machines) are excellent reminders to buy Hershey products. Hershey was in the business early and established its name with many promotions and with the aid of 10,000 distributors and 600,000 retailers. It produced a quality product which it sold vigorously. Advertising people like to ask: "What could the company have done with a strong advertising program?"

Let there be no question about persuasion in the marketing process. It is used to influence, to convince, to coax, to move people to buy a company's product or service (see Box 18-2). Advertising and personal selling together represent the twin forces of persuasion, integral parts of industry's operations. Just as they are important, so are they controversial.

Persuasion is an important part of our lives. Forgetting the persuasion used in religious work, welfare programs, international affairs, political activities, and other nonbusiness facets of life, persuasion remains important as a part of our buying and selling activities. Almost every business buys and sells, and almost every manufacturer, wholesaler, and retailer persuades. They are in business to earn a profit, and persuasion is one method used to develop sales and profits.

Employment in selling is impressive, since millions of people earn their livelihoods by selling (see Table 18-1), but employment is not the *raison d' être*. Selling and advertising are utilized to persuade people to buy a given product or service. The continuance of persuasion stands on its own contribution to industries' selling programs, not on the amount of employment it provides.

---

[5] John Hobson, "The Influence and Techniques of Modern Advertising," Three Cantor Lectures from the *Journal of the Royal Society of Arts*, London, July 1964, p. 4.
[6] Lawrence M. Hughes, "How Is Hershey Doing—Without Advertising?" *Sales Management*, Vol. 84, No. 10, May 20, 1960, pp. 33–114.

BOX 18-1

Marketing Pictograph
The Power of Advertising

HERSHEY GETS BY WITHOUT ADVERTISING . .

but

AMERICAN CHICLE, WITH ADVERTISING, GROWS FASTER

The owners of Hershey Chocolate Corporation from the very beginning in 1893 have resisted the arguments of media sellers and advertising agencies. Their goodies promote themselves . . . at least that's their answer. How long will Hershey hold out?

In recent years their sales curve has been far from healthy. Dollar volume has only inched along, with a meager sales gain of 7% since 1951; or less than half the rate of gain of the nation's population (17%).

Earnings per share, thanks largely to lower cocoa bean prices, have held up better than sales, with a gain of 46%, 1958 over 1951.

The striking similarities between American Chicle and Hershey are that both (1) sell low-priced confections (2) which in the main are marketed at pre-inflation prices, (3) have a type of business where labor costs are small, (4) and gross profit margins are high except when raw materials shoot skyward.

The striking difference is that American Chicle aggressively promotes its growing product line by advertising in every type of medium. Last year's expenditures were in excess of $5 million, or around 8% of sales.

Since 1951 American Chicle's sales have gone up 68% (Hershey's 7%), and earnings per share by 102% (Hershey by 46%).

What do the comparative tables prove? Nothing, probably, that hasn't long been apparent to objective observers . . . that Hershey, *with* advertising, could make markedly faster progress than it makes *without* advertising.

SOURCE: *Sales Management,* Vol. 83, No. 4, August 7, 1959, p. 69.

BOX 18-2

The Son Shows the Way

A man lived by the side of the road and sold hot dogs.
He was hard of hearing so he had no radio.
He had trouble with his eyes so he read no newspapers.
But he sold good hot dogs.
He put up a sign on the highway telling how good they were.
He stood by the side of the road and cried: "Buy a hot dog, Mister."
And people bought.
He increased his meat and roll orders.
He bought a bigger stove to take care of his trade.
He got his son home from college to help him.
But then something happened . . .
His son said, "Father, haven't you been listening to the radio?
If money stays 'tight,' we are bound to have bad business.
There may be a big depression coming on.
You had better prepare for poor trade."
Whereupon the father thought, "Well, my son has gone to college.
He reads the papers and he listens to the radio, and he ought to know."
So the father cut down on his meat and roll orders.
Took down his advertising signs.
And no longer bothered to stand on the highway to sell hot dogs.
And his hot dog sales fell almost overnight.
"You're right son," the father said to the boy.
"We are certainly headed for a depression."

SOURCE: *Sales Management,* Vol. 86, No. 6, March 17, 1961. p. 37.

If we had a totalitarian system in which we could abolish personal selling, advertising, and other forms of persuasion, would this be a desirable alternative? An interesting diversion is to speculate about a business system which lacks persuasion but at the same time fits our ideals as they pertain to free enterprise and our political philosophy. Let us select an industry that has been criticized for its lack of social responsibility—the drug industry. Bauer and Field have contrasted the Soviet and the United States drug industries. In the Soviet Union where there were low promotion costs, no brand names, and no private responsibility, Bauer and Field did not find adequate information, well-informed physicians, adequate quality, sufficiently low prices, or ample supplies of pharmaceuticals. Of course, this is not to say that our system of drug promotion is good and the Soviet system bad. Bauer and Field have concluded, however, that vigorous promotion is not necessarily

Table 18-1. Employment in Selling, United States, 1960

	Number Employed	Percent Increase 1950–1960
Advertising agents and salesmen	34,762	2.8
Auctioneers	4,139	−24.2
Demonstrators	25,722	83.3
Hucksters and peddlers	56,760	139.7
Insurance agents, brokers, and underwriters	369,230	33.7
Newsboys	197,333	98.3
Real estate agents and brokers	195,742	36.9
Stock and bond salesmen	29,018	157.0
Salesmen and sales clerks (n.e.c.)	3,888,635	13.8
Manufacturing	474,436	42.0
Wholesale trade	504,295	22.1
Retail trade	2,724,313	7.4
Other industries (incl. not reported)	185,591	36.8

SOURCE: United States Department of Commerce, Census of Population: 1960, Detailed Characteristics, (Washington, D.C.: U.S. Government Printing Office, 1963), p. 52.

socially undesirable (see Box 18-3), that brand naming is also not undesirable, that customer preference serves to stimulate full lines of drugs, and that our system has shorter research-to-market time periods than the Soviet system.[7]

Persuasion is not a twentieth-century anomaly. Neither is it a development of the affluent society. Buyers and sellers have existed for centuries, and with

[7] Raymond A. Bauer and Mark G. Field, "Ironic Contrast: US and USSR Drug Industries," Harvard Business Review, Vol. 40, No. 5, September–October 1962, pp. 90, 97.

BOX 18-3

More Advertising Is Urged in Soviet

by Theodore Shabad

Moscow, April 25, 1964—Does the Soviet Union's planned economy need more advertising? An emphatic yes has appeared in Izvestia, the Government newspaper.

Reporting on a survey of advertising needs and facilities, the newspaper called for a system of billboards, posters and other promotional methods to help the consumer make up his mind.

SOURCE: New York Times, April 26, 1964, p. 1.

them have arisen the situations in which each exerts some attempt to achieve maximum satisfaction or gain. Hollander has described some of early commerce—trading companies in Mesopotamia in 2500 B.C., price systems in the King of Ur Mannu's codes in 2100 B.C., Phoenician salesmen who sailed the Red Sea and the Persian Gulf in 1200–1500 B.C.[8] Miriam Beard has written that the businessman had been developing his skill at bargaining "enormously long" ago and that the traders were then "wise with the cunning of untold ages."[9] Brink has located evidence of early singing commercials, product sampling, and other sales-promotion techniques which were used hundreds of years ago.[10]

But age does not justify the presence of persuasion any more than does the number of jobs in selling, or the recent expansion of persuasion in the Soviet Union. Persuasion remains an effective way of urging people to buy— that is why it exists today. It is far from perfect, but remains an integral part of our system.

THE ROLE OF PERSUASION

Persuasion facilitates the exchange of goods, aiding in the marketing process and expediting the profitable sales of the product. As one authority has pointed out, it is the "ultimate expression of the competitive effort."[11]

In normal times it is the seller who employs the various forms of persuasion, but during wartime shortages it is usually the buyer. In the Soviet Union, buyer-expediters have been more influential than any sales-oriented personnel. In our society, almost every business firm employs some kind of promotional strategy. Some attempt is made to persuade the buyer, to shift the demand curve to the right of where it would otherwise be. Critics call this effort "manipulation of demand," but one need not read anything sinister into it. It should be abundantly clear that the role of the many selling forces is to persuade people to buy a given product.

Persuasion and the Exchange Process

The essence of marketing is the exchange of goods for money. Much effort is expended to facilitate this exchange, a transfer of title from seller to buyer.

[8] Stanley C. Hollander, *Sales Devices Throughout the Ages* (New York: Joshua Meier Company, 1953), p. 6.
[9] Miriam Beard, *A History of the Business Man*, (New York: The MacMillan Company, 1938), p. 11.
[10] Edward L. Brink and William T. Kelley, *The Management of Promotion* (Englewood Cliffs, N.J.: Prentice-Hall, 1963), p. 28.
[11] John M. Rathmell, "The Salesman and Competition," in Taylor W. Meloan and Charles M. Whitlo (eds.), *Competition in Marketing* (Los Angeles: University of Southern California, Graduate School of Business Administration, 1964), p. 94.

This action is the goal of both buyer and seller, and persuasion facilitates the process.

Accomplishment of the exchange involves a cost. The goods must be financed, transported, stored, checked, marked with prices, displayed, and so forth. Marketing research activities have to be paid for, as do the costs of persuasion. Both are employed in order to make the selling task easier and, it is hoped, more efficient. Ideally, successful selling strategies contribute toward efficient marketing operations.

Persuasion and the Environment

The marketing environment is a framework in which all buying and selling are consummated. Persuasion must operate within this framework.

Technology, for example, both aids and limits the persuader. Selling techniques have changed dramatically as faster transportation for salesmen and improved printing processes for advertising have developed. The mail-order catalog is now a colorful book of products, attractively presented. Persuasion is closely related to technology in another way, that of aiding the adopting of new technologies and new products, such as computers, office copying equipment, and improved dentrifices. The case for persuasion is a strong one in connection with the development of markets for new products.

Persuasion must take place according to the legal and ethical rules of society. Violators should be prevented from continuing unacceptable practices. Successful promotion conforms to social norms, but abuses do occur and should certainly be discouraged. Consumer refusal to purchase represents a most effective deterrent to promotional abuses.

To be successful, the selling effort must reflect an understanding of the consumer in his environment. What does he need, what does he want, how much can he pay, where does he live, and how much does he know about the product? These are some of the questions which must be considered, for they give answers about buyers which improve the effectiveness of the persuasion process.

Much has been written of a "marketing concept." To many businessmen this has meant a new understanding of the importance of knowing the consumer and the environment. Many firms now develop products for a segment of the market, whereas before they produced a new product and then gave it to the salesmen for "distribution." The marketing concept is not subtle; it is an important and an obvious one for any businessman to grasp. The success any company has in persuading people to buy its products depends on a thorough understanding of the environment in which it operates. Competition, institutions of business, consumers, laws, and technology are all forces which apply to the person who develops a program for persuading people to buy. This is the intelligent way to approach the problem and it carries benefits for the buyer as well as for the seller.

INSTRUMENTS OF PERSUASION

The late Carl Hovland did much to explain the process of communication. He and his colleagues performed many experiments in an effort to understand more thoroughly the refinements of the communication or persuasive process. He pointed out that in a persuasive communication the sender (seller) submitted a key element in the form of a "recommended *opinion.*" This opinion, explained Hovland, causes the receiver (buyer) to react with at least two responses. He will think of his own answer, in this case the brand he is currently using, and also of the brand recommended by the seller. If the new opinion (the recommended brand) has been persuasive enough, the buyer will be influenced by it and may well choose the new brand.[12]

Hovland further pointed out that a communication contained three main classes or stimuli. The first of these relates to the observable character of the communication's personal source. A second class involves the setting in which the person is exposed to the communication. The third class of stimuli comprises the arguments and appeals.[13]

Our understanding of the communication process is enhanced if we use Hovland's organization of material. He saw the persuasive communication as involving a communicator, a communication content, audience predispositions, and responses.[14] Facilitating these four elements of persuasive communications are all kinds of attempts at persuasion.

The persuasion attempt is not as simple as first appears. As Hovland and others have discovered, there are many fine points to the process. Should a salesman or an advertisement present the competitive view as well as one's own? Under what conditions should a salesman omit a relevant argument? What effect does a warning have on the receiving of information? That is, if a person is warned that he may receive information with which he has not agreed in the past, will this warning cause him to be more or less receptive to this negative information? Should the seller's views be presented first or last relative to those of a competitor? What is the role of persuasion *after* the purchase? (This introduces the notion of cognitive dissonance.)

---

[12] Carl I. Hovland, Irvin L. Janis, and Harold H. Kelley, *Communication and Persuasion*, (New Haven: Yale University Press, 1953), p. 11.
[13] *Ibid.*, p. 12.
[14] *Ibid.*, pp. 13, 14.

The Institutions

The institutions of persuasion are the institutions of marketing. That is, almost every seller at every level of distribution utilizes some form of persuasion. The manufacturer may have his own sales force, supplemented by agents, and aided by advertising and other types of selling effort. The wholesaler may have extensive coverage of the retailers in his area through his sales force. The retailer utilizes the familiar clerk and attractive self-service displays. Reference to Figure 18-1 gives a reasonably good idea of the institutions and points of exchange where persuasion is used. It should be clear

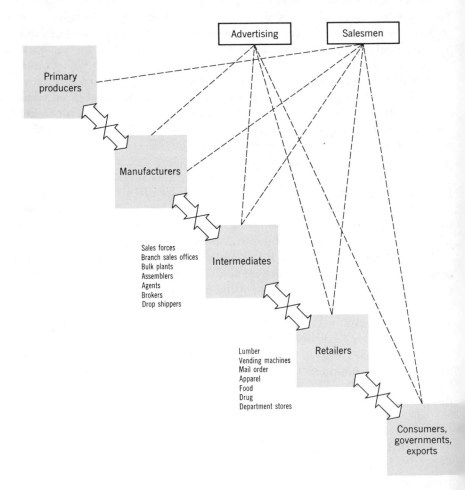

Figure 18-1. *Points of persuasion*

that selling is a marketing function which is performed by almost every business firm. Each of these businesses, large and small, has its own concept of effective selling, and its selling efforts are obvious features of our competitive system.

The Instruments

The term "instruments" is used here as the tools or the means utilized by the marketing institutions to persuade buyers. The salesman represents one of the oldest and most important ways for sellers to effect a marketing transaction. Millions of people are engaged in selling, as we have seen. Most of us seek out these salesmen more than they seek us. Perhaps the reader has had contact with a salesman who tried to sell him a product in which he had no interest. As a result, salesmen may be thought to be persistent and wasters of one's time. As needs increase, however, and we come into the market for insurance, securities, household items, and many other goods and services, the image of the salesman may well change in our minds. As we learn the role of the salesman in developing a market for a product for which we are responsible, our appreciation of the good salesmen will increase. The consumer who is served by dependable insurance agents, intelligent securities salesmen, and honest clerks derives much more satisfaction from his purchase than the less fortunate, and the purchasing agent who learns from salesmen of new ways to use an old product, or of new products, encourages them to call on him.

Some companies operate with their own sales force; others utilize agents of various kinds to handle the selling function; some use both. Mail-order houses rely on the catalog in lieu of the personal salesman. All have some system for taking orders and for developing what they consider to be their market. The salesman is the coordinator of the company's marketing program, and in most cases he is the seller's principal contact with the buyer.

Superior selling is needed. The development of an adequate sales function is one of the firm's vital cogs. Good people need to be recruited. (What makes a good salesman?) Salesmen have to be trained. (What is important in selling?) What ought to take place in those few minutes when the seller is interacting with the buyer? (Dressing neatly and knowing the product is not a sufficient answer.) Salesmen must be motivated. (What system of compensation is best for salesmen? What should be the relationship between commission and salary?) A salesman needs a territory. (How large should it be? How frequently does he need to call on a customer?)

Another powerful instrument of persuasion is advertising. Each of us is probably exposed to a thousand advertisements every day. Advertising is a large industry as shown in Table 18-2.

Advertising is a message to a potential buyer. The message can be sent

Table 18-2. Advertising Services in the United States, 1963

Advertising Services	Number of Establishments	Receipts ($1,000)	Payroll Entire Year ($1,000)
Advertising agencies	7,432	5,822,357	583,661
Outdoor advertising services	1,631	244,972	80,178
Radio, television, and publishers' representatives	1,486	206,700	75,459
Miscellaneous advertising	2,347	110,118	26,845
Direct-mail advertising services	2,471	309,664	121,549

SOURCE: United States Department of Commerce, Bureau of the Census, Selected Services, United States (Washington, D.C.: United States Government Printing Office, 1965), pp. 1–7.

rapidly. It can be low-cost on a per-unit basis, it can be narrowed through careful media selection, or it can be broadcast widely through television, radio, newspapers, and magazines. Almost all marketers use advertising, either as a supplement to personal selling or even in lieu of it. In 1964 the advertising volume was estimated at $15 billion (see Table 18-3).

Obviously, advertising differs in many ways from product to product and from company to company. The different allocations of advertising dollars are illustrated by the figures on automobile advertising (Box 18-4).

The task is the difficult one of effectively allocating advertising dollars. Figure 18-2 pictures the problem facing marketing managers. How much should be spent? How should the money be distributed among the media? As the seller approaches the saturation level, persuading one to buy becomes more difficult. Something needs to be known about this saturation level. We need to understand the promotional elasticity involved. To complicate the problem further, the promotional elasticity varies from product to product, from time to time, and from market to market. A model may be used to determine advertising appropriations, but no panacea has yet emerged.

The challenge is to make advertising an effective persuasive communication. It should fit our economic situation (see Box 18-5). We like it to be clever, informative, and in good taste. The seller wants to propagandize, to persuade, to sell. He learns to mold his advertising program so that the cost per unit sold is reasonable. He conducts research before the program is developed, he pretests his ads, he checks exposure, and he measures the effects in a variety of ways. In the final analysis, it will be the sales figures that tell him about his advertising program. Were the customers persuaded to buy?

Though dominated by advertising and personal selling, persuasion takes many forms in the marketplace. The variations in products, customers, mar-

Table 18-3. Estimated Annual United States Advertising Expenditures: 1947-1966

Allocations (Millions of Dollars)

Year	Total	News-papers	Maga-zines	Business Publi-cations	Farm Publi-cations	Television	Radio	Direct Mail	Outdoor	Point-of-Purchase Displays	Agency Income	Other Expenditures
1947	4,241	1,192	434	150	41	2	365	566	113	187	265	926
1948	4,907	1,410	482	163	42	9	408	671	115	194	309	1,104
1949	5,331	1,503	463	162	43	34	415	724	115	199	338	1,335
1950	5,864	1,641	481	164	42	106	444	749	132	202	373	1,530
1951	6,497	1,747	545	182	44	236	450	833	137	235	414	1,674
1952	7,161	1,879	592	210	46	324	470	907	145	262	459	1,867
1953	7,784	2,002	650	220	48	432	476	1,003	158	290	501	2,004
1954	8,080	2,059	646	228	48	593	449	1,040	172	288	520	2,037
1955	8,997	2,320	668	250	50	745	453	1,229	176	311	597	2,198
1956	9,674	2,476	680	275	53	897	480	1,308	189	345	675	2,296
1957	10,313	2,510	695	319	56	943	517	1,324	201	318	737	2,693
1958	10,414	2,459	652	302	55	1,030	523	1,419	219	344	757	2,654
1959	11,358	2,705	718	354	58	1,164	560	1,597	221	362	815	2,804
1960	11,900	2,821	769	383	55	1,269	598	1,658	239	387	859	2,862
1961	12,048	2,818	774	384	53	1,318	591	1,687	209	405	870	2,939
1962	12,919	2,930	797	378	50	1,486	636	1,758	203	416	955	3,310
1963	13,639	3,087	832	413	47	1,597	681	1,760	202	490	1,005	3,525
1964	14,571	3,318	869	453	47	1,793	732	1,873	207	549	1,075	3,655
1965[a]	15,570	3,505	939	489	53	1,965	793	1,995	215	590	1,172	3,854
1966[b]	16,810	3,817	1,015	528	54	2,187	885	2,105	217	620	1,266	4,116

SOURCE: Charles Y. Yang, Seymour Banks and Richard W. Strain, "Economy Soars, U.S. Advertising Volume Rises 8% to $16.8 Billion in 1966, AA's Yang Estimates Show," *Advertising Age*, Vol. 37, No. 51, December 19, 1966, p. 54. [a] Revised. [b] Preliminary.

BOX 18-4

How New Car Ad Investments Were Allocated in '64 and '65

(In thousands of dollars)

	Total 1965	Newspapers (including supplements) 1964	Newspapers (including supplements) 1965	Magazines (general and farm) 1964	Magazines (general and farm) 1965	Network TV 1964	Network TV 1965	Spot TV 1964	Spot TV 1965	Network radio 1964	Network radio 1965	Spot radio 1964	Spot radio 1965
American Motors	20,071	7,634	5,458	4,474	3,737	3,652	4,688	3,427	3,090	1,171	1,029	2,516	2,069
Corporate	78	3	—	715	78	—	—	—	—	—	—	—	—
Rambler	17,160	7,631	4,096	3,759	2,874	3,652	4,005	3,427	3,087	1,171	1,029	2,516	2,069
Marlin	2,833	—	1,362	—	785	—	683	—	3	—	—	—	—
Chrysler Corp.	71,255	17,594	16,413	10,766	10,293	22,048	20,770	7,977	8,315	1,082	929	12,192	14,535
Corporate	7,009	3,347	1,786	3,230	1,732	5,024	1,332	17	59	—	929	12,192	1,171
Barracuda	1,543	427	392	291	257	513	894	—	—	—	—	—	—
Chrysler	9,853	2,561	2,070	2,179	2,166	1,769	2,279	1,102	1,340	—	—	—	1,998
Chrysler-Plymouth div.	3,762	—	2,570	875	1,192	—	—	—	—	—	—	—	—
Dart	3,759	1,622	1,261	628	415	2,526	2,083	4	—	—	—	—	—
Dodge	21,791	4,081	4,436	1,554	1,731	4,689	6,260	4,013	3,568	—	—	—	5,796
Dodge div.	286	193	2	197	284	97	—	—	—	—	—	—	—
Imperial	2,485	256	235	901	722	625	748	41	100	—	—	—	680
Plymouth	17,281	3,097	2,613	614	1,502	4,752	5,163	2,635	3,129	—	—	—	4,874
Valiant	2,661	1,422	893	63	230	1,603	1,445	165	93	—	—	—	—
Simca	825	588	155	234	62	450	566	—	26	—	—	—	16
General Motors	120,175	37,887	39,303	31,918	33,115	23,788	21,658	8,259	8,724	6,067	5,429	10,734	11,946
Corporate	11,128	3,144	2,323	3,553	4,534	600	—	46	121	—	951	10,734	3,199
Buick	12,441	3,363	3,458	2,882	5,215	714	30	762	758	—	934	—	2,046
Buick special	966	418	751	11	215	31	—	—	—	—	—	—	—
Buick div.	341	4	16	2,118	325	—	—			—	—	—	909

Note: This page is a large table rotated 90°. The top of the table (column headers and the first data row) is cut off at the page edge; only partial figures are visible there. Figures are reconstructed by column position and may contain alignment uncertainty.

Make	(1)	(2)	(3)	(4)	(5)	(6)	(7)	(8)	(9)	(10)	(11)	(12)	(13)
[upper row / headers cut off]				5,110	4,663	5,31_	5,625	4,500	3,102		2,912		1,663
Chevrolet div.	4,121	2,845	2,035	906	744	1,424	1,342	—	—	—	—	—	1,663
Chevelle	5,124	—	—	2,320	1,934	2,302	3,190	—	—	—	—	—	—
Chevy II	2,463	—	—	1,018	786	2,286	1,677	—	—	—	—	—	—
Corvair	8,222	3,649	4,428	1,505	1,047	2,597	2,747	—	—	—	—	—	—
Corvette	324	38	123	138	173	—	28	—	—	—	—	—	—
Oldsmobile	15,989	3,744	4,155	3,392	4,695	4,231	3,394	846	1,249	—	572	—	1,924
Oldsmobile—F-85	805	840	479	736	104	586	222	—	—	—	—	—	—
Toronado	609	—	609	—	—	—	—	—	—	—	—	—	—
Pontiac	13,146	3,738	3,273	5,001	4,345	1,716	2,105	1,338	1,270	—	—	—	2,153
Pontiac div.	1,277	11	3	158	1,274	—	—	—	—	—	—	—	—
Tempest	1,162	1,452	1,056	1,056	12	704	94	4	—	—	—	—	—
Opel	889	699	550	639	307	—	—	2	—	—	—	—	32
Vauxhall	3	—	3	—	—	—	—	—	—	—	—	—	—
Ford Motor Co.	81,962	18,884	22,197	17,737	20,316	16,626	16,782	10,284	10,008	1,319	946	10,994	11,713
Corporate	8,730	561	1,137	5,601	5,773	170	185	—	62	1,319	—	10,994	1,573
Comet	5,435	3,368	2,242	1,759	1,642	1,242	1,384	67	167	—	532	—	—
Ford	37,723	5,838	8,884	1,973	3,528	8,210	9,025	8,888	8,785	—	—	—	6,969
Ford div.	3,819	2,988	2,372	1,286	1,075	284	372	—	—	—	—	—	—
Falcon	2,576	1,073	657	487	773	1,398	1,146	—	—	—	—	—	—
Lincoln	2,403	701	486	1,613	1,523	45	—	563	394	—	—	—	—
Mercury	7,969	2,560	2,662	2,512	2,646	1,155	1,697	746	550	—	414	—	—
Lincoln-Mercury div.	3,534	161	291	25	72	—	—	—	—	—	—	—	3,171
Mustang	7,208	1,348	3,148	1,726	1,728	3,499	2,321	9	11	—	—	—	—
Thunderbird	1,662	110	102	660	1,035	623	525	—	—	—	—	—	—
Bronco	468	—	8	—	333	—	127	11	—	—	—	—	—
English Fords	435	176	208	95	188	—	—	—	39	—	—	—	—

NOTES: When a campaign covered two or more makes (for instance, Chrysler and Plymouth), the cost was divided equally between the makes. Dealer service advertising is included; parts advertising is excluded. Spot TV includes dealer campaigns as reported by TvB. Radio investments for 1964 have been assigned to "corporate" as no breakout by make is available. All investment figures are gross time or space billings, except network-TV investments, which are estimated net time and program costs.

SOURCE: _Printer's Ink_, Vol. 293, No. 1, July 8, 1966, page 13.

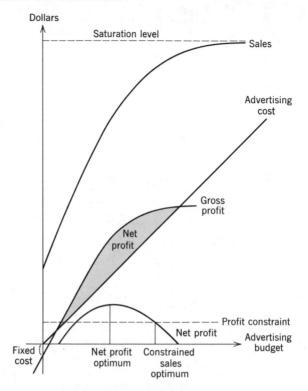

Figure 18-2. The relation of profits to advertising expenditure.

SOURCE: Wroe Alderson, "The Productivity of Advertising Dollars," *Cost and Profit Outlook*, Vol. 11, No. 2, February 1958, p. 1.

kets, resources, and channels and in competitive practices stimulate the development of different ways to promote products. The alternatives are many. Hundreds of millions of dollars are spent each year on point-of-sale promotion. The package itself has become an important promotional piece. Contests, services, gifts, favors, trading stamps, catalogs, premiums, bonuses, and many other devices such as samples represent a few of the ways in which sellers attempt to persuade people to buy their products. Sellers also have word-of-mouth advertising working for them. As a seller, one sits back and contemplates, "How can we get those people to buy?" The question is basic and it is old, but it is not an easy one. Competitors have the same freedom to persuade, and thus we must pit our persuasive talents against those of the entire industry.

BOX 18-5

Quotes from Practical Advertising Men

David Stewart, Kenyon & Eckhardt Advertising Agency:

. . . there are four facts about modern advertising, which, taken together, are highly disturbing . . .

1. Advertising has become far more necessary to U.S. business than ever before . . .
2. Advertising has become far more costly . . .
3. Each dollar of expenditure returns less in sales results than it did a few years ago.
4. Advertising . . . has become bogged down in red tape, in systems, procedures, viewpoints and operating methods which prevent it from doing a meaningful job.

He indicated that businessmen have a responsibility to the entire economy to eliminate advertising waste and inefficiency.

Clarence Eldridge, retired Vice President of Marketing, General Foods:

It may seem paradoxical to imply that the influence of advertising is declining at a time when expenditures for advertising have reached an all time high.

1. With respect to a great many categories of products, there is no substantial difference between competitive products.
2. The believability of advertising is being seriously jeopardized by the attempt to create "psychological differences," psychological superiorities, in products where no such differences or superiorities exist.
3. The sheer volume of advertising . . . there is too much of it.

SOURCE: Comments from speeches given before the National Retail Merchants Association as reported in "Progressive Grocer," *Progress*, July 1964, New York, pp. 1–2.

The Promotion Mix

The elaborate array of persuasion techniques is impressive but confusing to the one who must develop a marketing program from among the alternatives. The seller must make decisions about the mix or blend of promotional techniques which he wishes to utilize in his marketing development program (see Box 18-6). The concept of a mix, conceived by a pioneer of advertising, Neil Borden, conveys the notion of combining persuasive forces into one promotion strategy. The marketer attempts to find a promotion mix which will be effective and at the same time within the budget. A part of the decision

BOX 18-6

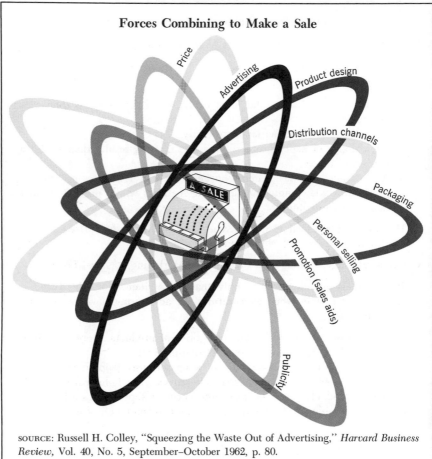

Forces Combining to Make a Sale

source: Russell H. Colley, "Squeezing the Waste Out of Advertising," *Harvard Business Review*, Vol. 40, No. 5, September–October 1962, p. 80.

involves the ratio of advertising to personal selling. Advertising does certain jobs not assigned to personal selling, and vice versa (see Box 18-7).

It is difficult to generalize on these matters. One study made by E. H. Lewis showed different ratios of advertising to personal selling in one metropolitan area, as Figure 18-3 indicates. Lewis concluded:

The development of a satisfactory sales-promotion mix by an individual company requires continuous study of the market and the competitive situation in it. The optimum mix probably is seldom attained, but companies must continue to experiment with the several methods of sales promotion and to use them in various combinations in order to make their sales efforts more effective.[15]

[15]Edwin H. Lewis, "Sales Promotion Decisions," *Business News Notes*, University of Minnesota, No. 18, November 1954, p. 5.

BOX 18-7

Effectiveness of Personal Selling and the Tasks of Advertising

One marketing scholar cites the following factors which he believes account for the effectiveness of personal selling:

1. Less opportunity for self-selection of messages by person being influenced.
2. Flexibility of timing and message to fit individual conditions.
3. Immediate and personal award for compliance—through the approval and friendship of the influencer (salesman).
4. Trust by the prospect in an intimate and respected source to select factors relevant to the prospect's specific case.
5. Decision on the basis of positive personal factors when there is no other element leading to a specific choice.

SOURCE: Rathmell, *Op.cit.*, p. 99.

Another scholar sees advertising as having many tasks to perform, which do not arise when selling is done face-to-face at the point of sale:

1. It must create or point out a need by identifying the circumstances under which it arises.
2. It must link the need to the possibility of fulfilling it with a general product, so that when the need arises the respondent will think of the product that will fulfill it.
3. It must differentiate the particular brand and its sponsor from other products which might satisfy the need approximately as well.
4. It must connect the particular branded product with the place and the conditions under which it can be obtained.
5. It must show that the need is urgent and that the task of buying is easy.
6. It must give a rational basis for action, for people do not like to buy goods which they cannot justify to their own consciences.
7. It must stimulate the respondent to make a firm decision on which he will act at a later time.

SOURCE: Edmund D. McGarry, "The Propaganda Function in Marketing," *The Journal of Marketing*, Vol. 23, No. 2, October 1958, pp. 131–139.

The promotion mix is only one of many major marketing decisions, and as such it has to dovetail with the rest of the marketing program. The "freedom of the marketing manager to manipulate the four elements of the marketing mix (product, place, price, perception) is not unlimited."[16] The

[16] Edgar Crane, *Marketing Communications* (New York: John Wiley and Sons, 1965), p. 35.

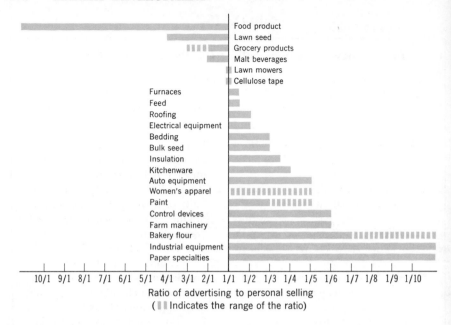

Figure 18-3. Sales promotion mix by type of product.

SOURCE: Edwin H. Lewis, "Sales Promotion Decisions," *Business News Notes*, University of Minnesota, No. 18, November, 1954, p. 5.

elements are not independent; there are limits to the marketer's manipulation of price, product, and place. Thus, as Crane indicates, the promotion mix which is a blend in itself must also blend into the overall marketing mix.

Questions

1. What do you see as the purposes of advertising? Does advertising achieve these goals?
2. Why are so few advertisements directed toward increasing primary demand?
3. What would be the result if all firms in any given industry discontinued their advertising efforts?
4. What types of advertising do you think are a waste of economic resources? Why are they used?
5. Aside from wasting resources, what types of advertisements are socially detrimental?

Statements to Consider

People tend to see and hear communications that are favorable or congenial to their predispositions.

The more trustworthy, credible, or prestigious the communicator is perceived to be, the less manipulative his intent is considered and the greater the immediate tendency to accept his conclusions.

People use their own changes of opinion, however recent or immediate, as blocks against further modification of opinion under the pressure of communications.

The communication of facts is typically ineffective in changing opinions in desired directions against the force of audience predispositions.

The higher a person's level of intelligence, the more likely it is that he will acquire information from communications.

Word-of-mouth or personal communication from an immediate and trusted source is typically more influential than media communication from a remote and trusted source, despite the prestige of the latter.

SELECTED REFERENCES

David K. Berlo, *The Process of Communication: An Introduction to Theory and Practice* (New York: Holt, Rinehart and Winston, 1960).

Neil H. Borden and Martin V. Marshall, *Advertising Management*, Rev. Ed. (Homewood, Ill.: Richard D. Irwin, 1959).

Edgar Crane, *Marketing Communications: A Behavioral Approach to Men, Messages, and Media* (New York: John Wiley and Sons, 1965).

Albert W. Frey, *Advertising*, 3rd. Ed. (New York: The Ronald Press Company, 1961).

Neil H. Borden, "Findings of the Harvard Study on the Economic Effects of Advertising," *Journal of Marketing*, Vol. 16, No. 4, April 1942, pp. 89–99.

° Edmund D. McGarry, "The Propaganda Function in Marketing," *Journal of Marketing*, Vol. 23, No. 2, October 1958, pp. 131–139.

° C. H. Sandage, "The Role of Advertising in Modern Society," in Hugh G. Wales (ed.), *Changing Perspectives in Marketing* (Urbana: University of Illinois Press, 1951), pp. 185–196.

Daniel Starch, "Do Ad Readers Buy the Product?" *Harvard Business Review*, Vol. 36, No. 3, May–June, 1958, pp. 49–58.

Generalizations Were Taken From:

Bernard Berelson and Gary A. Steiner, *Human Behavior* (New York: Harcourt, Brace and World, 1964).

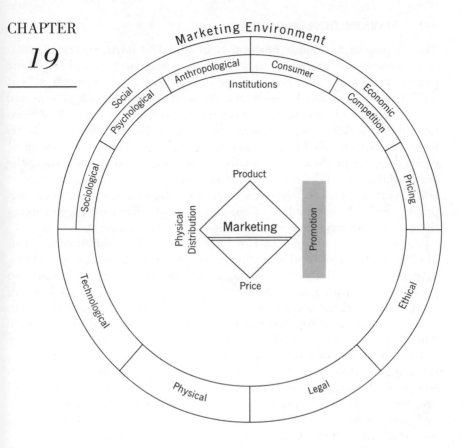

Persuasion in the Market Place—II

ETHICS AND PERSUASION • DEVELOPMENT OF A PERSUASION PROGRAM   *Goals*
Research •
ADDENDA: 1. *The Economic Effects of Advertising* • 2. *Generalizations Relating to the Com-munication and Persuasive Process*

379

The purpose of the selling function is to stimulate buying action. Persuasive attempts are geared in some way to precipitate a purchase. Some persuasion is subtle and may achieve a favorable image through a "soft sell." Other persuasion is direct and insistent. Either way, it is expected that persuasion will inform people about the product and widen or deepen the chosen market. Some would say that the "principal thing that advertising can accomplish for the seller is to accelerate the growth curve of demand for the product. . . ."[1] Another view sees advertising shortening the time to inform.[2] A third states that "there seems to be little to indicate that any important trend of fashion has ever been changed by any form of sales promotion."[3] These samplings of comments about advertising suggest something about the way persuasion may operate or fail to operate.

To be effective, communications have to reach the right audience. This implies a real need to choose the proper advertising and selling media. Magazines are carefully selected and so are salesmen. Communications also provide buyers with a rationale for their buying action. The product tastes good, looks good, the neighbors have one, or only the sophisticated own it, whereas communications directed to the industrial buyer, attempt to convince him of the durability, the safety features, or the economy of operation.

Conditioning of buyers is done through persuasion. Golby illustrates how this might be done (Box 19-1). The Golby example demonstrates an important principle in persuasion: no particular part of the communication should ever be regarded as acceptable or believable in isolation from the rest of it.

There are many magic formulas for successful promotion. Hobson cites one which Sir William Crawford espoused: "concentration—domination—repetition." This simply means that the market is pinpointed or segmented, that all forms of persuasion are then gathered to create a dominant impact on the minds of the segment already selected and, finally, that repetition is important to sellers because, as is commonly known, readers of advertisements forget rapidly. Therefore marketers advertise frequently, hoping that repetition will aid in the development of their market segment.[4]

A persuasive communication works when it influences the buyer. Ideally the buyer is motivated to commit himself to buying action. Persuasion attempts are launched in a "noisy" atmosphere where competitors are trying their best to recruit the same customers. Final acceptance by the buyer, however, depends on many factors.

---

[1] Ralph S. Alexander, Frank M. Surface, and Wroe Alderson, *Marketing* (Boston: Ginn and Company, 1949), p. 341.
[2] Roland S. Vaile, E. T. Grether, and Reavis Cox, *Marketing in the American Economy* (New York: The Ronald Press Company, 1952), p. 276.
[3] Paul H. Nystrom, *Fashion Merchandising* (New York: The Ronald Press Company, 1932), p. 35.
[4] Hobson, *Op. cit.*, p. 23.

BOX 19-1

An Example of A Conditioning Communication

1. A nice complexion makes a woman more attractive.	"That's true."	Most women would likely agree.
2. Toilet soap can help to keep the complexion nice.	"Yes, it can."	Follows first statement.
3. Particularly a mild and gentle toilet soap.	"I suppose so."	Follows second statement.
4. Lanolin helps to make a toilet soap mild and gentle.	"Yes."	Follows third statement.
5. Brand Y contains lanolin.	"I see."	Notice the increase in particular-ness and decrease in generality. This prepares the way for the factual statement in statement 5. No. 5 completes the argument and prepares way for conclusion.
6. Therefore Brand Y will keep her complexion nice and make her more attractive.	"I suppose that's true."	Conclusion now acceptable because of prior conditioning.

SOURCE: Colin Golby, "Toward a Theory," *Scientific Business,* February 1965, p. 331.

ETHICS AND PERSUASION

We are told by critics that selling raises the costs of products, which should not happen; that selling influences people to buy the wrong things, to buy the right things for the wrong reasons, and to buy harmful goods; that selling effort is untruthful and insincere, resulting in fraud, sharp practice, and deceit; and that selling causes people to be too materialistic. Each reader can undoubtedly recall many selling practices which he would classify as unethical. We resent any attempt by anyone to wield power over us or any force which interferes with competition. We abhor any device which makes prices higher than they "should be." We dislike being cheated in any way. Our goal as consumers is to make wise decisions in order to be able to derive maximum satisfaction from our expenditures of limited funds. If persuasion obstructs attainment of this end, we consider it unethical.

Probably the best answer is that selling is an old and accepted practice not likely to be eliminated. We should press for an attitude which makes the persuaders responsible people. Those people who use the marketplace, who take advantage of our free expression, should not abuse the privilege.

Most businessmen point out that relatively few are guilty of such abuse. They also point out that many safeguards exist in addition to laws. They are not in business to sell only once; to succeed, they need repeat sales. This in itself imposes restraints on persuasion. Moreover, does not the buyer know that someone is selling him, that someone is trying to persuade him? "To be forewarned is to be forearmed." Does not a buyer trim out the unacceptable persuasion? Does anyone believe there is a "tiger in the tank?"

Materialism as expressed and promoted through advertising may disturb many of us. But is materialism actually the result of persuasion? One of the authors traveled in the Soviet Union several years ago and found the Soviet people, who had seen little advertising and who met few salesmen, to be as materialistic if not more so than United States citizens.

It is also possible to cite benefits of advertising. Tosdal, for example, believes that advertising

> Energizes the whole economic system.
> Justifies and permits production, usually in advance of sale.
> Enables improvements in production to be adopted.
> Enables research to be carried on to find new end products.[5]

To this list could be added many further benefits. However, the answer to unethical selling does not lie in a counterargument of benefits. Rather it lies in improved selling techniques which are ethical to any reasonable man. When the intent is to sell through deceitful methods, consumers should discourage the seller in the best way they know. At times this may call for legislative help.

The following advertisement (Box 19–2) illustrates that sellers do provide information and that advertising can be useful to a buyer who wants to learn something about a product. This advertisement would probably be rated exceptional by many readers. Does it persuade?

DEVELOPMENT OF A PERSUASION PROGRAM

Much fun has been poked at Henry Ford for his remark, "Any customer can have a car painted any color that he wants so long as it is black."[6] Critics

---

[5] *Ibid.*, p. 323.
[6] Alfred D. Chandler, Jr., *Giant Enterprise* (New York: Harcourt, Brace and World, 1964), p. 37.

BOX 19-2

The New RCA Whirlpool 2-Motor Vacuum Picks Up Everything But Men And Money

(JUST ONE OF 38 GOOD REASONS WHY IMPECCABLE HOUSEWIVES ARE SMITTEN WITH IT)

1. Your carpets will look like they've been shampooed. The nap stands up, the color looks bright again and you won't believe the difference in your carpet's outlook until you watch this two-motor job dig out years of hidden dirt.

2. With two motors instead of one, the RCA WHIRLPOOL canister/upright cleaner has twice the suction power of an ordinary upright cleaner. This eliminates the need for beater bars that can whip the daylights out of your good carpets.

3. The Super Celoc (that's the name of this model here) is not plastic or toy-like. It's built to last long after the buffers and puffers quit.

4. The canister is so slender it will stand on the stairs while you race up and down.

5. It's a cinch to store. You can stand it on end in a closet, or on a shelf, or tuck it under a bed.

6. The canister motor is approximately one and one-half horsepower. That's a lot of horsepower for a vacuum (ask big daddy why).

7. The canister has a furniture guard (the upright does, too) for all around protection against bumping and banging.

8. There are no locks, no latches. A hinged, covered compartment is built into the cleaner to carry the tools for your whole home-cleaning system.

9. The tools fit inside easily and you have all attachments at hand when and where you need them.

10. Still with us? Grand!

11. The unit is cast aluminum everywhere it counts. There isn't another like it in the stores.

12. Look inside at the size of our canister motor and compare it with any other in the store. You're buying dependable power here.

13. No need to open and poke—there's a special Power Eye indicator on the canister that lets you know when to change the bag. It also alerts you when the machine is not working at its maximum and you can see just how much suction is being produced at all times.

14. Our dust bags are large (over two feet long), high density, double wing bags. It takes a lot more dust to fill one of these than the average size vacuum bag can hold. So you go a whole lot longer without the bother of changing.

15. The cord is super-flexible, light, vinyl-jacketed. It's 22 feet long (longest cord in a home cleaner). Means less stop and start in your cleaning.

16. The motor drives two fans and creates a hard-working air stream that dust and dirt bow down to.

17. The Super Celoc upright part of the combination has its own separate electric motor. This added power literally slurps out grit and dirt that can really ruin rugs. The canister does a great job on bare floors and furniture, etc. Great housewives know they need both an upright and a canister to run an immaculate house.

18. The hose has a steel core so tough you can tie a knot in it.

19. The electric motor-driven revolving brush in the upright picks up thread, lint, dog hair, and Siamese cat hair (the slipperiest hair of all) in one fell sweep.

20. Many cleaners rub dirt in—the Super Celoc takes it out. McCall's use-tested.

21. Cleaner can't tip over. The wheels won't mar a polished floor.

22. The canister motor has two speeds—Normal and "Let's get out of here."

23. One big convenient front toe pedal operates both the canister and the upright motors.

24. The exclusive wide-sweep design (only two inches high) on the upright makes it possible for it to sneak in under beds, radiators, couches, and low-slung chairs.

25. The upright is downright flexible. The handle goes all the way down to the floor (there's no bag), so that getting under things is a cinch.

26. The headlight on the upright lights up the dreariest corners.

27. Our upright revolving brush is driven from the side thus avoiding the center dirt track you get with other uprights.

28. MORE? Grand!

29. Our wands click lock, will never fall apart or jam together. Our cleaning tools are oversized—they work faster. Our brushes are removable so they can be washed and replaced.

30. The RCA WHIRLPOOL vacuum has an air-filter system with four dirt traps. These dirt traps hold back the fine dust that ordinarily gets blown back into the room.

31. The bags are a snap to replace—no latches—flip-top, self-locking lid opens wide for changing. And our bags never, never touch the top of the motor, so dirt can't seal off good suction. More dirt goes in—more dirt stays in.

32. The hose locks right into the suction opening of the canister and holds securely until you press a button.

33. The suction control for delicate fabrics is at your fingertips. Just select the amount you want. The switch is right at the head of the hose handle.

34. This cleaner comes with two 20-inch chrome-plated steel wands, a crevice tool and de-mother, a vinyl dusting brush, a vinyl floor-wall brush and a vinyl fabric tool with oscillation brush.

35. Our Super Celoc comes in colors all meant to cheer you up—Desert Fawn, Metallic, and Harvard Brown.

36. This vacuum was tested under the toughest home usage life tests. It will probably be inherited by your granddaughter.

37. We will put you and your new RCA WHIRLPOOL vacuum in the fine care of your neighborhood RCA Service Company (the same folks that service your color television). They have an instant supply of parts and they are experts.

38. Convinced? Then head for these stores. Abraham & Straus, B. Altman & Co., Bloomingdale's, Bamberger's, Gimbels, Macy's, Sterns, and other fine stores in New York and around the country. Or, if you're lazy and want to watch one of our men work, call Oreck Corporation, LT 1-0743, and we'll have him show you the RCA WHIRLPOOL vacuum right in your own living room. No cost or obligation, of course, but it would be nice if you'd buy the guy a cup of coffee.

ORECK CORPORATION, EXCLUSIVE NATIONAL DISTRIBUTORS, ONE ROCKEFELLER PLAZA, NEW YORK CITY
RCA WHIRLPOOL APPLIANCES ARE PRODUCTS OF WHIRLPOOL CORPORATION, BENTON HARBOR, MICHIGAN. TRADEMARKS RCA AND ® USED BY AUTHORITY OF TRADE.

Reprinted with permission of Oreck Corporation (RCA).

view this remark in today's environment, forgetting that Ford said it in 1909. His marketing strategy was simple: build a mass-produced car; sell it at a low price; create strong dealerships. Ford wanted his salesmen to know every prospective buyer in their territory: "If your territory is too large to permit this, you have too much territory." [7] The promotional efforts of Ford mirrored the rest of his company's strategy. His marketing mix (product, channels, promotion, and price) was indeed a successful one for many years.

As the environment changed, General Motors adapted faster than Ford. It hired Richard Grant, one of the day's dynamic salesmen, who had learned to sell from John Henry Patterson of National Cash Register Company. Grant's marketing orientation played a major role in General Motors' development, enabling it to sell automobiles by the millions. Like those of Ford, his principles were simple: (1) Have the right product. (2) Know the potential of each market area. (3) Constantly educate your salesmen on the product. (4) Constantly stimulate your sales force. (5) Cherish simplicity in all presentations. (6) Use all kinds of advertising. (7) Constantly check up on your salesmen, but be reasonable with them.[8] This merchandising strategy worked for years. The persuasive function was well recognized, and the price and product mix of Ford lost ground fast to the promotion-mix emphasis that Grant was giving General Motors. The struggle among the automobile manufacturers continues even to this day.

Goals

It is axiomatic that a program of persuasion should be keyed to goals. But goals are not automatically determined; neither are they permanent or single in number. Typically the persuasion goals are multiple, although each promotion plan is developed to perform a particular job.

The marketing plan may call for the development of a primary market. The persuasion plan must then be developed accordingly. A few years ago there were new concepts of office copying equipment. Office managers had to be persuaded that the concept was a good one—this was developing of a primary market. In the beginning competitors may in effect work toward a "common" goal because they know that at this stage the job is not one of selling Thermofax or Xerox but of selling dry-copying equipment. Steel companies may join together in association advertising, promoting the use of stainless steel; only later will United States Steel be concerned about developing a selective demand. The aluminum companies may work together in persuading people to use more aluminum, for siding for homes as an example; then Alcoa, Reynolds, and others change their promotion

[7] *Ibid.*, p. 35.
[8] *Ibid.*, p. 160.

goals to selective selling. Weyerhauser may work with other lumber companies in promoting plywood; later there will be selective selling for Weyerhauser's Foursquare product.

As products and product concepts become accepted, the emphasis typically shifts to the development of selective demand. Actually this is where most of society's criticism is directed. The primary-demand type of campaign may be more informative and less competitive in nature. Once the market has been developed, it becomes necessary to create and maintain brand shares. There was a time when Eastman Kodak had to persuade people to take pictures with color film. Camera companies and film companies devoted much energy to this primary-demand task. By 1965 the market environment was different. The 3M Company was selectively selling its Dynacolor film just as Eastman was selling its Kodacolor (see Box 19–3). Eastman and others at the same time were concerned with developing primary markets for their Super 8 film, cooperating with Polaroid and others in this effort.

There are many different demand situations. Derived demand conditions necessitate one kind of promotion program. The manufacturer who is selling batteries depends to some extent on new car sales. The replacement market for his batteries is very different and must be developed separately. This is likewise true for tires and many other products. The demand for steel is derived because steel sales depend on automobile, refrigerator, industrial construction, and other sales.

It becomes clear that promotion serves many needs. AT & T may wish to maintain an image of a service company which is owned by many ordinary people. IBM may need informed salesmen to introduce a new type of computer. Missionary salesmen who know the product thoroughly may accompany regular salesmen for months in an effort to develop a new market for a given product. An automobile wholesaler may take along a missionary paint-spray salesman to demonstrate a new piece of equipment. A bottling-company salesman may handle both sales and delivery. Advertising may be used to introduce a product or it may bolster the personal selling effort. All forms of promotion can perform many different tasks; the job of the marketer is to match the goals with the specific kind of promotion required by the marketing task.

The marketer who develops the marketing mix for his company must take a number of factors into consideration. He must evaluate the relative merits of his products, their uses, the relative price, the company's image, the customers—where, how many, what kinds, and so on—the institutions used in distribution, and many other factors in selecting the basis for the marketing effort. This effort is an important allocation of the firm's resources and represents important commitments on its part for some time in the future.

BOX 19-3

Radio Program Prepared and Produced by . . .
Batten, Barton, Durstine & Osborn, Inc.

3M COMPANY   Typed: March 3, 1966
RA 96-007   As Recorded
DYNACHROME
60-SEC. ANNOUNCEMENT #M-66-37-60 "GROUCHO"

SOUND: *STORE NOISES UNDER*

GROUCHO: Am I a Dynachrome Convert? You bet your life!
ANNCR: (SOTTO VOCE) Folks, here's one of thousands of camera
          fans who's changed to new Dynachrome Color Film. (TO
          GROUCHO) May I help you, sir?
GROUCHO: You can if you have Dynachrome color film.
ANNCR: Ooh! Aren't you Groucho Marx?
GROUCHO: Watch your language; there may be children listening.
ANNCR: Oh. Are you incognito?
GROUCHO: No, I'm in a hurry. How about that Dynachrome?
ANNCR: Mmm, let's see . . . Dynachrome . . .
GROUCHO: That's it—the one from 3M Company.
ANNCR: Oh, yeeees. Sure you wouldn't rather have . . .
GROUCHO: No, I wouldn't rather have. Got to be sure of the color . . . may
          be shooting some colorful friends—Rose La Rue, Peaches Melba,
          Scarlet Schwartz.
ANNCR: Ummm, yes. Say, look at this price: Dynachrome really saves
          you money!
GROUCHO: Certainly. If they'd shot "GONE WITH THE WIND" in Dyna-
          chrome, they'd've saved millions.
ANNCR: Groucho, I'd say you're a real . . .
GROUCHO: A real Dynachrome Convert? You bet your life.

SOUND: *(CASH REGISTER RING)*

ANNCR: Why don't you join the Dynachrome Converts? Get Dyna-
          chrome for color slides and movies—film so good, you'll forget
          it cost less.

Research

It is almost obvious that the marketer will need many facts in his possession
to develop an effective persuasion program. Some information is available to
him from his own company's records, some is available from secondary data
such as government sources and association publications, and still other

information is gathered through marketing research. Some research is performed prior to the program, some during the marketing effort, and some after (see Box 14-2). Research to improve estimates of the effects of advertising is the key to scientific budgeting."[9]

Research is the basis for marketing-development decisions. It needs to be blended with executive judgment, for it cannot possibly provide all the answers. An early example of the role of research in developing a promotion program was that of H. G. Weaver, who forty years ago found that 25 percent of General Motors' sales could be directly credited to dealer efforts. This research finding formed the basis of the distribution program.[10]

Research is commonplace in promotion: Markets and people are surveyed before, during, and after marketing development efforts; copy themes and spot commercials are pretested; test markets are utilized; coincidental telephone surveys are made during television and radio programs; readership studies are performed; and consumer panels test many aspects of the marketing program as well as the product itself. Indeed, it has become almost standard procedure for even the sales effort to be critically examined (see Box 19-4).

Research sharpens the persuasion tool. Identification of the market prior to the development program enables the company to direct its efforts more precisely than otherwise. When it is known that a gelatin dessert is purchased because it is quick and easy to prepare, the advertising copy can be directed to this point. Offering complicated recipes under these conditions has been found to be wasteful and even to dampen buying action.

The marketer would like to know the precise effect on the market of an advertisement or a sales call. He would like to know how much the demand curve will shift to the right if he spends a given number of dollars, but this is difficult to ascertain. Well aware that the effects of his promotion program are buried among price changes, new products, competitors' actions, economic conditions, fashion changes, inventory levels, and other factors, the marketer must nevertheless go as far as he can in an attempt to make his marketing effort efficient and successful (see Box 19-5).

Three basic questions have been posed by Britt, who believes that the effectiveness of advertising could be greatly improved if advertisers would ask and answer them.

1. What facts do we have about the product or service to be advertised; and how can we integrate this information with other phases of our marketing mix?
2. What facts do we have about the people who might buy our product or service; and how can we use this information in developing our advertising messages?

[9] Joel Dean, *Managerial Economics* (New York: Prentice-Hall, 1951), p. 385.
[10] Chandler, *Op. cit.*, p. 163.

BOX 19-4

Relationship between Number of Salesmen and Percentage of Operating Profit to Sales Volume and Investment

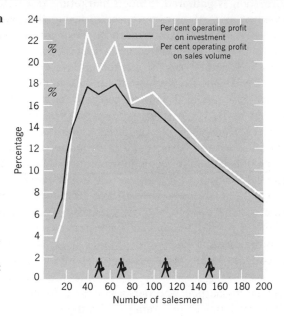

NOTE: Irregularities in percentage curves are due to increased plant investment and corresponding fixed costs as volume reaches certain points.

Relationship between Number of Salesmen and Total Sales Volume and Total Operating Profit in Dollars

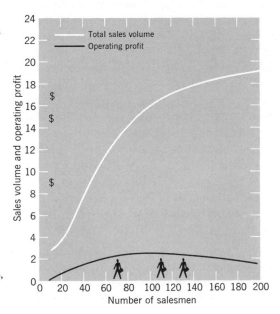

SOURCE: Walter J. Semlow, "How Many Salesmen Do You Need?" Harvard Business Review, Vol. 37, No. 3, May–June 1959, pp. 126–132.

BOX 19-5

Model for General Advertisers with Small Market Shares and a Relatively Undifferentiated Product

We shall assume that the firm for whom we are constructing the model is small enough so that its advertising expenditures will not elicit "defensive" expenditures by other firms; that is, the firm's appropriation may be set as if other firms' advertising will not be changed in response. Furthermore, the small firm's advertising for a product that is not physically differentiated competes for sales against other firms, rather than against the same firm's advertising in other periods. (Later this assumption will be loosened to deal with larger firms.) Our firm may sell either an expensive durable product, *e.g.* a washing machine, or a repeat purchase item, *e.g.* bread.

The dependent variable will be "net revenue," R, equal to total revenue minus cost of goods sold, delivery costs, and other nonselling variable costs. We shall assume that these deducted "production" costs are a linear function of output. This assumption is not likely to vitiate our conclusions over the ranges of operation we shall consider.

Let

T = advertising period ($T = 1$, 2, $\cdots$ m),

t = revenue period ($t = 1$, 2, $\cdots$ n),

$T = t$

$R_{T,t}$ = net revenue caused by advertising in period T, realized in period t, undiscounted (gross revenue less all production costs).

$V_{T,t}$ = present value net revenue

A_T = advertising expenditure in period T.

P_T = profit from advertising in period T

b = retention rate, equal to 1 minus the decay rate of customer purchases from period to period (in absence of further advertising).

ρ = discount rate of the cost of money to the firm.

$\sum_{T=1}^{t} R_{T,t}$ = sum of sales in period t, caused by all prior advertising in periods 1, 2, $\cdots$ t.

By definition, the total sales in period t, $\sum_{T=1}^{t} R_{T,t}$, are the sum of those sales attributable to advertising° in period T, plus the sales that would occur in period t even if no advertising occurs in t. The latter may also be thought of as sales in period t caused by advertising in all periods prior to T. Therefore:

$$(1) \quad \sum_{T=1}^{t} R_{T,t} = \sum_{T=1}^{t-1} R_{T,t} + R_{T=t,t}.$$

By definition of the retention rate,

$$(2) \quad \sum_{T=1}^{t-1} R_{T,t} = b \sum_{T=1}^{t-1} R_{T,t-1}, \; i.e.,$$

sales in the present period caused by

° Assume that we are dealing with a firm in which the sales caused by advertising can be logically partitioned from sales caused by other factors. In some cases, such as cigarettes, advertising may actually be the prime mover of sales.

BOX 19-5—(*Continued*)

prior advertising equal sales in the last period diminished by the decay rate. So

$$(3) \quad \sum_{T=1}^{t} R_{T,t}$$

$$= b\sum_{T=1}^{t-1} R_{T,t-1} + R_{T=t,t}.$$

The sales caused in period t by A_t are

$$(4) \quad \sum_{T=1}^{t} R_{T,t} - b\sum_{T=1}^{t-1} R_{T,t-1}.$$

It is this core idea upon which the model is built.

It is known that the sales caused in period $t + 1$ by $A_{T=t}$ will equal $R_{T=t,t}$ diminished by the decay rate, $(1 - b)$. Similarly, sales in $t + 2$ will equal those in $t + 1$ diminished by $(1 - b)$, and so on, *ad infinitum*.

The basic result of this model is then:

$$\sum_{t}^{\infty} R_{T=t,t} = \left(\sum_{T=1}^{T=t} R_{T,t} - b\sum_{T=1}^{t-1} R_{T,t-1}\right)$$

$$(5) \qquad + b\left(\sum_{T=1}^{T=t} R_{T,t} - b\sum_{T=1}^{t-1} R_{T,t-1}\right)$$

$$+ b^2\left(\sum_{T=1}^{T=t} R_{T,t} - b\sum_{T=1}^{t-1} R_{T,t-1}\right)$$

$$\cdots + b^{\infty}\left(\sum_{T=1}^{T=t} R_{T,t} - b\sum_{T=1}^{t-1} R_{T,t-1}\right).$$

In other words, the total sales caused by advertising A_t in all periods equal the total of the sales caused by A_t in each future period; this is true by definition. The sales caused by A_t in each future period equal the total sales in that period, less sales that would have occurred anyway.

Since the terms within each bracket are identical, the entire expression can be simplified to:

$$(6) \quad \sum_{t}^{\infty} R_{T=t,t}$$

$$= \frac{1}{1 - b}\left(\sum_{T=1}^{t} R_{T,t} - b\sum_{T=1}^{t-1} R_{T,t-1}\right).$$

So all that is needed to estimate the total sales caused by A_t are sales in $t - 1$, sales in t, and the retention rate.

To allow for the diminished value of a dollar in revenue in the future, as compared to current revenue, we modify with the discount rate. The *present value* of the advertising in the present period, $A_{T=t}$, is then obtained.

$$(7) \quad \sum_{t}^{\infty} V_{T=t,t}$$

$$= \frac{1}{1 - b\rho}\left(\sum_{T=1}^{t} R_{T,t} - b\sum_{T=t}^{t-1} R_{T,t-1}\right).$$

The profit from advertising in the present period is:

$$(8) \qquad P_T = \sum_{t}^{\infty} V_{T=t,t} - A_{T=t}.$$

This enables us to compare the profitability of given advertising levels, assuming we know the sales in each period, the sales that would occur during this period with each given level of advertising, and the retention rate. The most profitable level of advertising can then be selected by inspection. This simple idea is the main finding; apparently, it is the first time it has been so stated.

The profit-maximizing rule can be expressed thus: advertise until

$$(9) \qquad \Delta A_{T=t} = \Delta \sum_{t}^{\infty} V_{T=t,t}.$$

BOX 19-5—(*Continued*)

To illustrate, assume a firm with:

Retention rate b from year to year = .65

Last year's sales

$$\sum_{T=1}^{t-1} R_{T,t-1} = \$1,387,000.00$$

This year's sales

$$\sum_{T=1}^{t} R_{T,t} \text{ for } A_T \text{ of } \$564,000$$
$$= \$1,289,000.00$$

Discount rate $\rho = .90$

The value in sales of this year's advertising = ($\$1,289,000 - \$1,387,000 \times .65) + .65$ ($\$1,289,000 - \$1,387,000 \times .65$) .90 + .65 × .65

($\$1,289,000 - \$1,387,000 \times .65$) .90 × 90, *etc.*

As a shortcut, calculate

(10) $\left[\dfrac{1}{1 - .90 \times .65} \right]$

$\cdot (\$1,289,000 - .65 \times \$1,387,000)$
$$= \$929,000.$$

This example is based on 1960 data from Palda's [15] study of Lydia Pinkham. Similar computations for years before 1960 are shown in Table 19.1. The retention rate of .65 is an approximation based on Palda's estimates. The discount rate of .90 seems appropriate for a small business, such as Lydia Pinkham.

Table 19-1. Application of Advertising Model to Lydia Pinkham Data

(1) Year	(2) Sales in t caused by prior advertising, in thousands of dollars	(3) Advertising in t, in thousands of dollars	(4) Profit from advertising, in thousands of dollars
	$\left[\sum_{T=1}^{t} R_{T,t} - d\sum_{T=1}^{t-1} R_{T,t-1} \right] \left(\dfrac{1}{1-b\rho} \right)$ $-$ A_T $=$ $\sum_{t}^{\infty} V_{T=t,t}$		
1960	387 × 2.4	564	365
1959	484 × 2.4	644	518
1958	312 × 2.4	639	110
1957	492 × 2.4	770	411
1956	596 × 2.4	802	628
1955	538 × 2.4	789	502
1954	452 × 2.4	811	274
1953	683 × 2.4	964	675
1952	768 × 2.4	920	923
1951	527 × 2.4	766	499
1950	497 × 2.4	974	219
1949	643 × 2.4	981	562
1948	662 × 2.4	941	648
1947	519 × 2.4	836	410

SOURCE: Julian L. Simon, "A Simple Model for Determining Advertising Appropriations," *Journal of Marketing Research*, Vol. 2, No. 3, August 1965, pp. 286–287.

3. What facts do we have about channels of communication; and how can we use this information in selecting our advertising media?[11]

Inspired by research, bolstered by theories of persuasion, and aided by accumulated experience, the marketer develops his promotion plan. This plan, synchronized with the rest of the marketing plan, becomes the firm's marketing effort. Oversimplified, the General Motors experience illustrates this point, as seen in the following charge to the company's marketing team:

Establish a complete line of motor cars from the lowest to the highest price that would justify production. Develop the best value in each price class which large volume, effective manufacturing methods, aggressive engineering and efficient means of distribution, all supported by large resources, make possible.[12]

Simple as such instructions may seem, marketing programs are not easy to develop. The big question in all of them is how to estimate the impact of any part of the marketing effort. Persuading people to buy a product appears to be an easy task until one is required to do it for one's own product.

Almost any marketing situation presents an interesting problem. Assume that you are in charge of the merchandising program at Macy's in New York. Your staff suggests that hair wigs for women have proven most successful and that the market for male hairpieces is also feasible. What would you do? The advertisement which announced Macy's program presents its answer to the way it would persuade men to purchase hairpieces (Box 19-6). What is your opinion of this approach?

Finally, note these statements made by various students of persuasion:

Advertising is but one of many factors which lead to purchase or repurchase of a product or service. The purpose is to create or reinforce favorable attitudes toward the product or service.

No single exposure of a single-print advertisement or commercial is likely to change consumer attitudes immediately toward buying a product or service. Instead, consumer attitudes usually change gradually.[13]

Three factors have come together to produce advertising as we know it: the growth of mass production techniques; the increase and redistribution of wealth giving mass purchasing power; and the availability since the turn of the century of regular channels of mass communication. I see no reason to suppose that any of these causal factors is going to diminish or indeed fail to grow.

Industry is going to require salesmanship for as long as production exceeds spontaneous and necessary demand.[14]

---

[11] Steuart Henderson Britt, "Advertising Research in Action," in Meloan, *Op. cit.*, p. 73.
[12] Chandler, *Op. cit.*, p. 150.
[13] Britt, *Op. cit.*, p. 73.
[14] Hobson, *Op. cit.*, p. 34.

Nearly everyone is engaged in marketing in the sense of offering goods or his own services in the market and in buying the goods and services of others. Everyone makes promises of performance and payment, and individuals live up to their promises in varying degrees. The promises made as an aspect of mass marketing are different. Here we are promising each other through our industrial leaders a better way of life, the fruits of technology and enterprise, the physical means and instruments for supporting desired patterns of activity. . . . At a minimum, the marketer must believe in what he is doing if he is to convince anyone else. He, at least, should be prepared to live in the kind of world his efforts seem calculated to produce.[15]

Selling effort is the energizer of our economic machine. Its power may be misapplied, but its necessity in influencing our people to want higher and rising standards of living cannot be denied. Selling effort is necessary to make people both desire and achieve a higher level of living. Selling is necessary that firms which introduce unfamiliar products may live and old firms may continue to exist and perform their services for the public. The development and functioning of the production structure necessary for a high standard of living has depended and will continue to depend upon the energizing influence of selling effort, whether that effort be in the form of advertising or personal selling, or in the manifold minor aspects of marketing persuasion.[16]

If the ballyhoo and confetti of the competitive advertising man's carnival dies away, there will come a time of comparative quiet. It is at such times that the higher instincts and emotions are likely to emerge, and business may direct itself into channels dictated by a better social philosophy than now holds way.[17]

Questions

1. What factors must be considered in the development of the complete selling function?
2. Compare and contrast the selling operations of firms engaged in manufacturing, wholesaling, and retailing.
3. Can you evaluate advertising and selling?
4. What suggestions would you make to improve the selling functions of marketing?
5. Under what conditions would you emphasize personal selling over advertising, and vice versa?

Statements to Consider

Stimulation of selective demand cannot be easily accomplished for a product the identity of which is not obtrusive to the purchaser.

[15] American Marketing Association, *Theory in Marketing*, edited by Reavis Cox, Wroe Alderson, and Stanley J. Shapiro (Homewood, Ill.: Richard D. Irwin, 1964), pp. 104–105.
[16] Tosdal, *Op. cit.*, p. 328.
[17] Roland S. Vaile, *Economics of Advertising* (New York: The Ronald Press Company, 1927), p. 176.

BOX 19-6

Studio 34 is a private area adjacent to Macy's Men's Store on the 2nd floor at Herald Square. It provides a complete service where you can buy custom-made hairpieces or have them cleaned or repaired (even if you bought them somewhere else). What happens when you come to Studio 34? First you have a private consultation. Our expert shows you the different kinds of hairpieces, explains how they're custom-made of the finest human hair from Europe, shows you pictures of how they look on other men. You then discuss the kind of hairpiece that would be right for you. He measures you carefully, takes a snip of your hair as a sample for color. Then, in two or three weeks, your hairpiece is ready. You come in, it's fitted to you, combed in with your own hair so the difference is visually non-existent. Then you learn how to put it on, how to comb it, how to take it off. That's all there is to it...but we doubt if you'll be able to pass a mirror for weeks without looking at yourself and enjoying the sight.

So if you're one of the tens of thousands of men who have thought about a hairpiece but have never done anything about it, do it now.

Come to Studio 34 any time during Macy store hours. Or call LA 4-6000, ext. 2770 for an appointment. There is no charge for a consultation; you're under no obligation. Come this week and you can discuss your hairpiece with Joe Carlow, one of the country's top experts, so expert that he's written a book called "Carlow on Hairpieces". Why not call for your appointment now?

BOX 19-6—(*Continued*)

The questions most men ask about hairpieces:

Q. Is a hairpiece for me..or only for actors?

A. Modern hairpieces are for any man who is losing or has lost his hair. Thousands and thousands of men in every walk of life are wearing and enjoying them. It's as contemporary as trying to stay trim and fit ... instead of slumping into middle-aged thickness as past generations did.

Q. Will people know I'm wearing it?

A. Your friends and relatives will, of course ... at first. Then they'll forget it. Other people will never realize it, because new techniques have made hairpieces virtually impossible to detect. Just think of the close-ups on TV and the movie screen of men who wear hairpieces. You never even suspect.

Q. Will a hairpiece make me look younger?

A. Naturally, but don't expect it to work miracles. You'll look younger ... but not like a boy. Experts suggest that you don't get a hairpiece that takes you all the way back to your youth. A little thinning of the temples, a little pepper and salt coloring is a lot more believable.

Q. What will it feel like?

A. It will feel like hair, because it is hair. Macy's hairpieces are custom-made of only the best European human hair, with a fine texture. Your hairpiece will be light and comfortable. In fact, after a short time, you'll hardly know you're wearing it. You'll comb it and brush it just like your own hair.

Q. What if I get caught in the rain?

A. Exactly what happens to your own hair ... it'll get wet. All you have to do is comb it out.

Q. Does it have to be cleaned?

A. A hairpiece needs cleaning much less often than your own hair, because there's no oil. But it will need cleaning, which Macy's will do for you. Eventually most men find that they want two hairpieces, so they can wear one while the other is being cleaned.

Q. Do I have to take my hairpiece off at night?

A. No. You can sleep in it, wear it for a week or so without ever removing it.

Q. Are there different kinds of hairpieces?

A. Dozens and dozens, from a little forehead piece to a full hairpiece to cover the whole head. They fall into 4 basic types: executive, continental, Ivy League, and casual. Naturally, you choose the one that's right for you.

Q. Is it expensive?

A. Yes ... and no. Considering the custom-work involved and what a hairpiece will do for you, the cost is modest (and, at Macy's, thrifty as well). Partial pieces run around $70 ... about what you'd pay for a good suit. Full hairpieces start from $150 to $250. And, of course, you can charge it to your Macy Account.

Come to Studio 34, Macy's 2nd floor, Broadway Building, 35th Street side, adjacent to the Men's Store.

Reprinted with permission of Macy's, New York.

An individual's psychological characteristics play a role in his response to advertising.

Advertising will not reverse unfavorable trends based on changed socioeconomic conditions.

Stimuli that are pleasant, highly valued, and consistent with expectations are perceived more quickly and correctly.

The "propensity to communicate" is shown to be a scalable, predisposing attitude directly and positively correlated with the number and types of media to which the message recipient is exposed, the impact these media have, and the probability of inducing behavior with respect to new food products.

A significant difference exists between the ratio of ad outlays to sales of consumer goods and industrial goods industries.

SELECTED REFERENCES

William J. Stanton and Richard H. Buskirk, *Management of the Sales Force*, Rev. Ed. (Homewood, Ill.: Richard D. Irwin, 1964).

Richard R. Still and Edward W. Cundiff, *Sales Management: Decisions, Policies, and Cases* (Englewood Cliffs, N.J.: Prentice-Hall, 1958).

Harry R. Tosdal, *Selling in our Economy: An Economic and Social Analysis of Selling and Advertising* (Homewood, Ill.: Richard D. Irwin, 1957).

Herbert E. Krugman, "Salesmen in Conflict: A Challenge to Marketing," *Journal of Marketing*, Vol. 23, No. 1, July 1958, pp. 59–61.

° Harry R. Tosdal, "Objectives of Selling," in Harry R. Tosdal, *Selling in Our Economy* (Homewood, Ill.: Richard D. Irwin, 1957), pp. 79–90.

Generalizations Were Taken From:

Michael Halbert, *The Meaning and Sources of Marketing Theory* (New York: McGraw-Hill Book Company, 1965).

ADDENDUM 1.

The Economic Effects of Advertising

Excerpts from Neil H. Borden, "Findings of the Harvard Study on The Economic Effects of Advertising," *The Journal of Marketing*, Vol. 6, No. 4, April 1942, pp. 89–99.

I. The Effects of Advertising on Demand
    A. For many products advertising tends to speed up favorable trends of demand; that is, if underlying conditions are favorable to an increase in demand for the product.
    B. In the case of a declining trend in demand, for example, cigars, advertising is powerless to halt or reverse the trend. It can do no more than temporarily delay it.
    C. Where possibilities of expanding a market do not exist, or where there is a declining trend of demand, cooperative industry advertising campaigns have not been able to succeed.
    D. By aiding in the expansion of markets through accelerating a rising trend of demand, advertising also helps to increase the elasticity of demand.
    E. The expansion of the market also makes it possible for new competitors to enter.
    F. The building of the market by means of advertising and other promotional devices not only makes price reductions attractive or possible for large firms; it also creates an opportunity to develop private brands, which generally are offered at lower prices.
    G. As a general rule, businessmen, particularly manufacturers, have not fully recognized the opportunities for increasing sales volume and profits through the exploitation of demand elasticity. In general they have been too ready to assume that demand is inelastic, and have not been sufficiently willing to experiment with price strategy.
    H. Possibilities for the use of advertising by individual companies vary widely. If the right combination of conditions is present, the effect of advertising is to increase the demand for the particular company's product. There are situations, however, in which it does not pay a company to advertise, because of insufficient product differentiation, lack of strong consumer buying motives, insufficient size and frequency of sale, and so on, for instance, matches, wheat, and nails.

I. Where advertising does operate to increase the demand for the individual concern, it tends to make the consumer demand for that product inelastic.

J. In the longer run, however, competitive forces tend to weaken the condition of a company which relies on advertising to bring about an inelasticity of its individual demand and thus enable it to ignore price competition, especially during periods of depression.

II. The Effects of Advertising on Costs—The Effects of Advertising on Total Marketing Costs

Advertising is not in itself the cause of high distribution costs. Advertising is a part of present-day high distribution costs, but it is not a basic cause of the high proportion of these costs.

III. The Effects of Advertising On Price

The long-run effect of advertising and aggressive selling costs on price is closely related to the concept of innovation and growth costs. Since the burden of developing demand is a substantial and costly one, pioneers in any business fairly often must make large outlays before they begin to get any return on their investment. After they have developed a demand, the path is easier for the imitators who follow them, since the latter do not have to incur the same developmental expenses but at the same time are able to take some of the market.

IV. The Effects of Advertising on Quality and Range of Merchandise

Advertising tends to improve the quality and range of merchandise offered to consumers.

V. The Effect of Advertising on Consumer Choice

A. Advertising and aggressive selling have had their most direct and important influence on consumer choice in widening the range of merchandise available to consumers, particularly through product differentiation.

B. Significant product differentiations for the consumer are those things which give him satisfaction.

C. The main task of advertising for business concerns is to make sales mutually satisfactory to buyers and sellers at low cost.

D. Advertising has been the principal source of information available to consumers.

VI. Final Conclusions on the Economic Problem

On balance, the general conclusion to be drawn from the evidence is that the functional objectives of advertising in a dynamic economy are socially desirable and that advertising as it is now conducted, though certainly not free from criticism, is an economic asset and not a liability.

ADDENDUM 2.

Generalizations Relating to the Communication and Persuasive Process

From Bernard Berelson and Gary A. Steiner, *Human Behavior* (New York: Harcourt, Brace and World, 1964).

1. People tend to see and hear communications that are favorable or congenial to their predispositions. . . . (p. 529)

2. Interest remains the single most significant determinant of exposure, and the major countering factor to self-selection of communications is sheer accessibility. . . . (p. 531)

3. People interested in a topic tend to follow it in the medium that gives it the fullest and most faithful treatment. (p. 532)

4. The use, and perhaps the effectiveness, of different media varies with the educational level of the audience—the higher the education, the greater the reliance on print; the lower the education, the greater the reliance on aural and picture media. (p. 532)

5. People tend to misperceive and misinterpret persuasive communications in accordance with their own predispositions, by evading the message or by distorting it in a favorable direction. (p. 536)

6. The more trustworthy, credible, or prestigious the communicator is perceived to be, the less manipulative his intent is considered to be and the greater the immediate tendency to accept his conclusions. (p. 537)

7. In cases where the audience approves of the communicator but disapproves of his conclusions, it tends to dissociate the source from the content. (p. 538)

8. The nature of the source is especially effective in the case of ambiguous or unstructured topics. (p. 539)

9. People use their own changes of opinion, however recent or immediate, as blocks against further modification of opinion under the pressure of communications. (p. 541)

10. The effect of communication programs that try to convert opinions on controversial issues is usually slight. (p. 542)

11. The communication of facts is typically ineffective in changing opinions in desired directions against the force of audience predispositions . . . (p. 543)

12. The higher a person's level of intelligence, the more likely it is that he will acquire information from communications. (p. 544)

13. The more communications are directed to the group's opinion leaders rather than to rank-and-file members, the more effective they are likely to be. (p. 550)

14. Word-of-mouth or personal communication from an immediate and trusted source is typically more influential than media communication from a remote and trusted source, despite the prestige of the latter. (p. 550)

15. The explicit drawing of conclusions by the communicator is more effective in bringing about audience acceptance than relying upon the audience to draw its own conclusions from the material presented. (p. 553)

Marketing
in Perspective

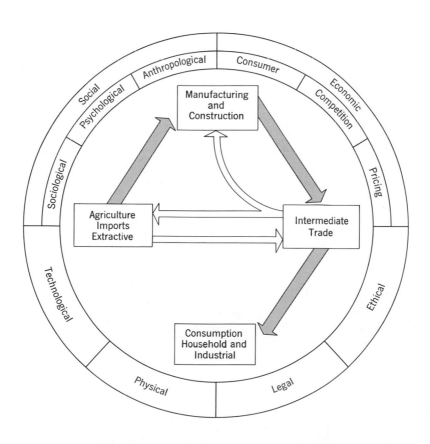

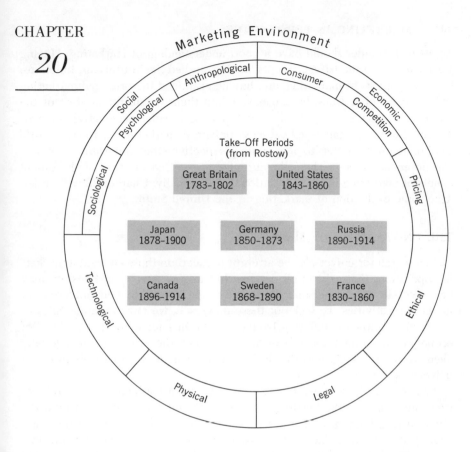

Take–Off Periods
(from Rostow)

Great Britain 1783-1802	United States 1843-1860	
Japan 1878-1900	Germany 1850-1873	Russia 1890-1914
Canada 1896-1914	Sweden 1868-1890	France 1830-1860

Marketing Environment · Anthropological · Consumer · Economic · Competition · Pricing · Ethical · Legal · Physical · Technological · Sociological · Psychological · Social

Universality of Marketing and Economic Development

THE UNIVERSALITY OF MARKETING • MARKETING AND ECONOMIC DEVELOPMENT
The Nature of Development   Problems in Development   Tasks of Marketing   Evidence of Accomplishment

By now the reader should have a good understanding of marketing. Having been exposed to the basic concepts, having studied the institutions, functions, and components of marketing, and having examined the principal marketing management operations, he can now relate them within the context of the total environment and logically develop some broader perspectives of marketing. First, we shall briefly discuss universal marketing in today's world and relate this matter to a second perspective, the important economic development process. The following chapter will cover some of the salient points of marketing in the international area. Finally, Chapter 22 will undertake some evaluation of marketing in the United States.

THE UNIVERSALITY OF MARKETING

In a search for universals, we attempt to ascertain those elemental marketing operations that exist in all nations. Just as joy, sorrow, and anxiety may be universals in our personal lives, we might expect to find universals in marketing activities. To seek out these universals, we must examine cultures which are completely different from our own. In some countries the level of economic development is unbelievably different, the value system is equally alien to our thinking, and this lack of homogeneity serves to obscure any universal patterns.

An isolated village which functions in autonomous fashion is clearly remote from our image of the bustling city. It is difficult for us to understand the different social emphasis or the lack of economic self-interest. Yet there are many people in such places who have no aspiration to improve their income: rigid cultural ties inhibit the person interested in achievement from entering market pursuits. There is no place for the legitimate aspiration of individuals; there is no mobility, nor any possibility for assuming responsibility for one's self-betterment. The producer consumes what he himself produces, aiding his neighbors only if they lack the basics of life. He may be condemned if he accumulates wealth. Spiritually oriented communities can be considered in the same way. They have few contacts with the outside world and there is a sameness in life. In some instances there is a strong mistrust of the other individual, especially the foreigner. Imagine conducting business where one had no faith in a contract! Certainly there are no universal patterns here.

We could dismiss these situations as premarket or as primitive economies and in this way ignore them. They do, however, exist today and have their own systems of distribution. We cannot condemn them but we can wonder about their very different orientations.

Primarily we are interested in the universals of marketing which relate to the society that has a market for land, labor, and goods. In such societies there is bargaining, and active supply and demand factors affect the exchange of goods. There are both risk and a possibility of profit.

Concerning the matter of universals, Reavis Cox has observed:

In the absence of such true universals, or perhaps as complements to them if they can be made, we seek what we may call "limited generalizations." These will take us as near as we can come to universals and give us a basis for classifying societies according to their systems of marketing. By the use of such limited generalizations we may be able to differentiate primitive or underdeveloped economies from fully developed ones or to find significant differences between ancient and modern cultures. Perhaps we can find here a basis for a differentiation of western from eastern or Iron Curtain countries.[1]

The form or system of buying and selling exists in most societies. The market may be quite primitive or most complex. Regardless, there is some means whereby sellers can dispose of their goods and buyers can fulfill their many needs (see Box 20-1).

[1] Reavis Cox, "The Search for Universals in Comparative Studies of Domestic Marketing Systems," from *Marketing and Economic Development,* ed. Peter D. Bennett, American Marketing Association Proceedings, (Chicago: American Marketing Association, 1965), p. 146.

BOX 20-1

Market Places and Market Principle

(African Communities)

Market Places

		Present	Absent
Market Principle	Peripheral	Guro Fulani	Lele Sonjo Arusha
	Dominant	Copperbelt	

Market Place—Specific site where buyers meet

Market Mechanism or Market Principle—Determination of prices of labor, resources and output by forces of supply and demand.

SOURCE: Paul Bohannan and George Dalton (eds.), *Markets in Africa* (Garden City, N.Y.: Doubleday and Company, 1965), p. 3.

The dynamics of the marketing system might be considered one identifiable marketing universal. The needs and desires of consumers change, the technology of production changes, and the marketing institutions and operations adjust accordingly. There is usually a type of money system which facilitates the exchange process. There also develops some specialization and as this increases, the complexity of the marketing task similarly increases. Box 20-2 notes some implications of this complexity.

All kinds of goods must find their way to the consumer. Governments market their goods and private citizens market theirs. This activity necessitates basic economic decisions, and in our society marketing aids in their determination. Perhaps this assistance is an important universal function of the marketing process.

Information may be considered another universal of marketing. Every transaction is built upon some information which is available to the buyer and seller in a variety of ways. Obviously the quantity and quality of the information vary from condition to condition but its utilization is rather universal.

BOX 20-2

The Complex System

If every decision embodies no less than an infinite number of variables, then a complex society embodies an infinite number raised to an infinite power. And if the beginning of wisdom for decision makers is to realize that they can deal with only a tiny fraction of what is possibly relevant, the beginning of wisdom for students of society is to realize that social decisions, market, political, or other, can deal with an even tinier fraction of what is relevant. Viewed in this light, the model of a market system is an extremely sensitive decision process about human wants for private goods. "It incorporates a delicately calibrated system of penalties and rewards which records the preferences of individuals and creates pressures to honor those preferences."* It is theoretically capable of observing and responding to every want of every person for exchangeable private goods if the Effective Preference is strong enough to overlap that of others. Thus far no one has even imagined a more sensitive technique of social decision making, and it is difficult to conceive that one is possible.

SOURCE: Alfred Kuhn, *The Study of Society* (Homewood, Ill.: Richard D. Irwin, and the Dorsey Press, 1963), p. 610.

*Alfred R. Oxenfeldt, *Economic Systems in Action* (New York: Rinehart and Company, 1957), p. 8.

The study of marketing has impressed many of us with its intangibility, complexity, costs, immensity, and the surprising number of ways it creeps into business decisions. The search for universals reinforces the notion that marketing has to seek its own adaptation in each environment. Although retailing and wholesaling *per se* may not be universals, some form of marketing institution typically exists even in temporary or primitive markets. Persuasion may not be universally used, but usually there is some communication which influences the process of exchange. In all cases, the goods must physically be taken from producer to consumer and some marketing system develops accordingly (see Box 20-3).

Even though the foregoing falls far short in identifying a list of marketing universals, some perspective of them can do more than aid one's understanding of the process of distribution. Perhaps it can "give us a better understanding than we now have of what goes on in other countries. Indirectly and in the long run it will help people who trade across international boundaries. Most importantly, however, it will help us to understand better what goes on in the United States itself."[2]

[2] Cox, *Ibid.*, p. 162.

BOX 20-3

Characteristics of the Exchange System

The characteristics of exchange systems deal with the:

1. Interaction of buyers and sellers;
2. Systematization of exchange values (prices), so that we may see whether and how they affect one another;
3. Degree to which buying and selling of specific goods and services are specialized functions;
4. Range of goods and services for which buying and selling are conventionally valid;
5. Degree to which exchange transactions enter into the stages of production from raw resources to consumable product or service;
6. Degree and nature of competition in buying and selling;
7. Degree to which buying and selling may be differentiated through the interposition of a medium of exchange.

All these variables are essential aspects of the marketing principle.

SOURCE: Cyril S. Belshaw, *Traditional Exchange and Modern Markets* (Englewood Cliffs, N.J.: Prentice-Hall, 1965), pp. 8–9.

MARKETING AND ECONOMIC DEVELOPMENT

The literature of marketing suggests that marketers believe that economic development is enhanced by placing considerable emphasis on distributive activities. Writers in marketing have expressed this view many times. An Egyptian authority writes that marketing is "capable of being used as one of the most effective factors in underdeveloped countries," but it is rarely so used.[3] An American expert has stated: "There is ample evidence that marketing methods used by marketing-minded entrepreneurial leadership have helped to stimulate demand expansion in the United States."[4] He believes the same thing can happen in less developed countries. A Philippine marketer finds that his government's planning is production-oriented and that marketing is taken for granted. He recognizes that industrial growth depends on the effectiveness and efficiency of the marketplace: "Programs for economic development in any country can be successful only when marketing orientation is a basic part of it, when marketing planning and implementation are integrated into it."[5]

Marketers believe that economic developers have overlooked the potential of marketing in their planning. The latter think that marketing problems can be more obstructive than many other deterrents to the process of industrialization and contend that marketing is at fault in many economic failures.[6] It is not an argument whether marketing is the main force behind development, but whether marketing should be considered in the planning because it is an essential ingredient of development. As one economist put it: "Whether markets pull development or lag behind it, it is evident that much planning in the area of economic development today neglects distribution."[7]

Economic development is no panacea, and there have been many failures. It certainly seems reasonable to suggest that improved marketing should serve as a positive contribution to the economic development of a nation. Before examining the role of marketing in development, we should be clear as to what we mean by economic development. Therefore we should look at some

[3] A. Coskun Samli, "Exportability of American Marketing Knowledge," *Business Topics*, Vol. 13, No. 4, Autumn 1965, p. 34.
[4] Frank G. Coolsen, "Marketing and Economic Development," from *Emerging Concepts in Marketing*, ed. William S. Decker, American Marketing Association Proceedings (Chicago: American Marketing Association, 1962), p. 35.
[5] Emilio Maceda, "Marketing in a Developing Economy," *Marketing Horizons*, Vol. 2, No. 5, May 1963, p. 19.
[6] A. A. Sherbini, "Marketing in the Industrialization of Underdeveloped Countries," *The Journal of Marketing*, Vol. 29, No. 1, January 1965, p. 28.
[7] Charles P. Kindleberger, *Economic Development* (New York: McGraw-Hill Book Company, 1958), p. 107.

of the problems which have come to light in recent years as many efforts have been applied to a wide variety of situations.

The nature of development

There are many theories of economic development. Rostow's controversial theory includes five stages (see Box 20-4):

1st—traditional society, essentially poor and stagnant.

2nd—transitional society, pre-conditions for take-off are being established.

3rd—take-off, resistances to steady growth are finally overcome and the economy takes off as growth becomes the normal condition.

4th—drive to maturity, modern technology extended over the economic front.

5th—age of high mass consumption, or the affluent society.[8]

It is not essential for us to adopt any particular theory of economic development. What is relevant is for us to recognize the multifaceted nature of the process and to feel the tremendous changes that take place through the development. A country does not simply develop. It needs economic self-reliance and freedom in what is likely to be a competitive trading system. It will come to know mass production, mass communication, mass distribution, and mass consumption. It will develop a set of institutions, habits, in-

[8]"Take-off, Catch-up, Satiety," *Business Week*, No. 1597, April 9, 1960, p. 97.

BOX 20-4

The Rostow Timetable—Tentative, Approximate Take-off Periods and Maturity Dates

Nation	Take-off Period	Maturity
Great Britain	1783–1802	1850
France	1830–1860	1910
United States	1843–1860	1900
Germany	1850–1873	1910
Sweden	1868–1890	1930
Japan	1878–1900	1940
Russia	1890–1914	1950
Canada	1896–1914	1950
Argentina	1935–	not yet
Turkey	1937–	not yet
India	1952–	not yet
China	1952–	not yet

SOURCE: "Take-off, Catch-up, Satiety," *Business Week*, No. 1597, April 9, 1960, p. 100.

centives, and motivations so that the inputs necessary to a continuous increase in output are self-generating.[9]

The undeveloped country typically has low income, overpopulation in agriculture, and low productivity in most economic effort. It has not organized its economic efforts and energies: it has not brought together its resources, wants, and capacities (see Box 20-5).

The drive begins, spreads, and saturates. This does not mean that the nation suddenly jumps into development in disjointed fashion, for the drive may simply accelerate the process. It must relate the political, social, economic, and other institutions in the process. The growth process probably unfolds continuously once it starts, but seldom is this easily and smoothly accomplished. The process of development is difficult for the people and far-reaching in its effects. The evolution of the process is shown in Box 20-6.

[9] Edward S. Mason, "The Planning of Development," *Scientific American*, Vol. 209, No. 3, September, 1963, p. 235.

BOX 20-5

Aspects of Modernization of the Modern Economy

Achievement orientation—unsatisfied wants.

Maximization of satisfaction principle at work.

Organization of resources.

Important entrepreneurial functions omnipresent.

Basis of exchange.

Entrepreneur is key figure in coordination.

Bureaucracy not overlooked.

Modern accounting penetrates subsistent sector, links it with commercial sector.

Value orientations system governs goals and modes of behavior—allocative system associated with it distributes resources. The direct allocation of resources is blended by political authority and the acquisition of resources freely through the use of a medium of exchange.

Mobility of production factors.

Adaptability of production factors in market economy.

Flow of information.

Physical communications.

Dynamic orientation.

Complexity.

SOURCE: Cyril S. Belshaw, *Traditional Exchange and Modern Markets* (Englewood Cliffs, N.J.: Prentice-Hall, 1965), adapted from Chapter 5.

Evolution of the Marketing Process

Stage	Sub-stage	Examples	Marketing Functions	Marketing Institutions	Channel Control	Primary Orientation	Resources Employed	Comments
Agricultural and raw materials (Mk.(f) = Prod.)	Self-sufficient	Nomadic or hunting tribes	None	None	Traditional authority	Subsistence	Labor Land	Labor intensive No organized markets
	Surplus commodity producer	Agricultural economy —i.e., coffee, bananas	Exchange	Small-scale merchants, traders, fairs	Traditional authority	Entrepreneurial Commercial	Labor Land	Labor and Land Intensive Product specialization Local markets
Manufacturing (Mk.(f) = Prod.)	Small-scale	Cottage industry	Exchange Physical distribution	Merchants, wholesalers, export-import	Middlemen	Entrepreneurial Financial	Labor Land Technology Transportation	Labor intensive Product standardization and grading Regional and export markets
	Mass production	US economy from 1885–1914	Demand creation. Physical distribution	Merchants, wholesalers, traders, and specialized institutions	Producer	Production and finance	Labor Land Technology Transportation Capital	Capital intensive Product differentiation National, regional and export markets
Marketing (Prod.(f) = Mk.)	Commercial— Transition	US economy from 1915 to 1929	Demand creation Physical distribution Market information	Large-scale and chain retailers increase in specialized middlemen	Producer	Entrepreneurial Commercial	Labor Land Technology Transportation Capital Communication	Capital intensive Changes in structure of distribution National, regional and export markets
	Mass distribution	US economy from 1950 to present	Demand creation. Physical distribution Market information Market and product planning, development	Integrated channels of distribution Increase in specialized middlemen	Producer Retailer	Marketing	Labor Land Technology Transportation Capital Communication	Capital and land intensive. Rapid product innovation National, regional and export markets

SOURCE: John M. Hess and Philip R. Cateora, *International Marketing* (Homewood, Ill.: Richard D. Irwin, 1966), page 172.

411

Problems in Development

Experience with the development process has taught one lesson well: the job is not easy. "We now know that the job is both difficult and long. Indeed, the task is only beginning to be clearly defined. To a very large extent Western technology cannot be simply adopted in less-developed countries—it has to be adapted." [10] Students, observers, and practitioners in development are now thinking more about the problems associated with development, and it is clear that some of the difficulty lies in the marketing area. Though this text is primarily concerned with marketing, the reader should recognize that marketing is only one aspect of the total developmental process.

Let us examine some of the problems which have been reported, especially those of a marketing nature. One of the first is the lack of manpower trained for the job. Almost all phases of marketing have shown weaknesses in this area. It takes time to develop capable personnel and foreign firms operating in undeveloped areas have not traditionally expended sufficient effort to upgrade domestic manpower. Many students from various nations are studying in western societies and some of these will return to take their place in business, including marketing, but this is a slow process. Moreover, there are jobs in marketing which require in-service training and this need must also be satisfied.

Another problem has been the importation of merchandise. The wrong products are imported many times and there is a lack of priority in the importation. Further, there are simple mistakes which create disorder. For example, some items may be imported in assembled form when they should enter in knocked-down or unassembled form. Little thought has been given to the blend of imported and domestic goods. The accent on imports often causes problems such as people associating quality with imported merchandise. Indeed, consumers have extremely strong preferences and some imported brands are in effect generic terms for certain products. In the Philippines, for example, one can "Colgate" one's teeth. Sherbini refers to this import preference as "domophobia," a mistrust and disbelief in quality of domestic products.[11] Typically imported items carry high margins and high prices. Starved demand conditions are frequently accentuated. Sometimes importers and domestic sellers injuriously compete with one another, with the result that the marketing system becomes an entanglement.

Further, there has been little marketing planning. The items may be ready for distribution before marketing is ever considered and consequently they have low probabilities of success. Product attributes are not carefully

[10] Michael L. Hoffman, "Development Needs the Business Man," *Lloyd's Bank Review*, New Series, No. 68, April 1963, pages 31–41.

[11] Sherbini, *Op. cit.*, p. 31.

planned because consumer orientation has not become a way of life, and therefore many products do not correspond to market demand.

Inventory problems arise because there is a lack of information between the various levels of distribution. The manufacturers do not know what the rate of sale will likely be, and as a result the inventory levels in the pipelines of distribution are not at all geared to sales. Nor does the credit system function smoothly. In many cases the retailer or wholesaler has no credit and thus buys on a hand-to-mouth basis. The same is true with the consumer who may purchase one egg at a time.

The lack of physical facilities hampers marketing efforts all along the way from producer or importer to ultimate consumer. Lack of refrigeration prevents the proper storage of many items in homes, in stores, and at the wholesale firms. Costs of marketing can soar under these conditions. Lack of transportation facilities likewise pushes marketing costs upward and make the marketing of items unnecessarily inefficient. Geographic and physical facilities tend to perpetuate the existence of separate markets. Sometimes each market requires its own language or dialect. They may have different cultures although located fairly close to one another. The urban market may have an element of the discriminating, upper-class, affluent consumer who may be highly style- and dress-conscious. Almost next door may be the poor peasant who barely subsists. The conspicuous consumer who lives next to the poverty-stricken is a common sight in large cities. The lack of development of market structures, long distances between markets, poor transportation and communication facilities, and the low level of capital—all breed small markets. And small markets without question impede specialization.[12] Thriving marketplaces have great difficulty in being launched in these environments.

There is inertia at all levels of distribution. Efforts to expand the economy where inertia is working against the development process mean, of course, that speed of development is difficult if not impossible. The old traditions and institutions can cause people to resist any and all attempts to change their ways. "Whatever the technology that activates industrial revolutions, the disturbance of old traditions and institutions and the imposition of unfamiliar rhythms of work and leisure are bound to bring social upheavals."[13] The farmer resists suggestions that would help him get a higher yield; retailers resist changing their inefficient and costly operated stores (see Box 20-7). The consumer does not submit easily. In contrast, the development process requires rather profound changes in human motivations

---

[12] Reed Moyer, "The Structure of Markets in Developing Economies," *Business Topics*, Vol. 12, No. 4, Autumn 1964, p. 44.

[13] Asa Briggs, "Technology and Economic Development," *Scientific American*, Vol. 209, No. 3, September 1963, p. 58.

BOX 20-7

Common Defects in Firms in Underdeveloped Countries

1. Absence of a sufficiently vigorous "growth mentality" reflected in:

   a. Failure to plow back profits adequately, tendency toward "milking" firms;
   b. Failure to keep up with technological progress abroad;
   c. Preference for a stagnating enterprise that stays "within the family" over expansion that is bought at the cost of partial surrender of control.

2. Difficulties in administration, management, and "human relations," shown in such symptoms as:

   a. Excessive centralization of decision making and inability or unwillingness to delegate authority;
   b. Ineffective staff work and coordination;
   c. Failure to pay adequate salaries to key personnel in spite of high turnover and recognized scarcity;
   d. Failure to impart to subordinates a feeling of participation and spirit of initiative;
   e. Neglect of personal relations and morale;
   f. Neglect of public relations.

3. Difficulties in carrying out functions not directly connected with the central production process, evidenced in:

   a. Defective advance planning (engineering studies, market research, provision for finance);
   b. Defective cost accounting and control in general;
   c. Defective maintenance.

SOURCE: A. O. Hirschman, *The Strategy of Economic Development*, (New Haven: Yale University Press, 1958), Chapter 8.

and values and calls for the highest priority in all nations of the world. People have to want it.

Another problem which was not appreciated some years ago is the role of government in development. Government today plays a much larger and more important role than formerly and marketing people must learn to work with it. Most undeveloped countries lack the strong competitive private sector as we know it. The planning of marketing operations must accommodate the thinking of both government and private entrepreneurs. Planning for marketing will not always be optimal, in view of political and other considerations. The distinctive aims of government need to be recognized even if they are not always appreciated.

Lack of information was alluded to briefly in connection with inventory levels. In the less developed countries the marketer is forced to make marketing decisions without having basic socioeconomic information available. As a result he may make serious mistakes. Or, more likely, he will be overly cautious because of the uncertainties; in this way he does not develop the market to its proper dimensions. The role of marketing research as described in Chapters 12 and 13 is hardly a realistic picture in undeveloped countries.

In our advanced societies, we are accustomed to a large, complex marketing structure which operates in a surprisingly efficient manner. It is decentralized, profit-oriented, privately owned, and individually operated. Yet the consumers find the goods to satisfy their many needs and desires. We overlook the importance of the informal organization which is a part of this marketing labyrinth. Within the operations of the more formal marketing structure is a vast informal system; verbal orders, implied meanings, and off-hand communications strengthen the formal operation. By contrast, the underdeveloped nations lack both the adequate formal structure and the informal. Lack of confidence in one another prevents informal communications from developing. Economic development efforts should not ignore this important facet of marketing if the ultimate system is to be a viable one.

Experience in development programs has enlightened many persons. It has brought marketing problems to the surface whereas they were not recognized a few years ago. Probably more problems than solutions have been presented, but it is necessary first to identify the problems before proper solutions can be decided upon and later implemented.

Tasks of marketing

The foregoing material on the problem areas has suggested many tasks of marketing in relation to a developmental program. Our earlier work in the environmental area suggested the importance of understanding the total environment in which marketing operates, the importance of understanding the people, the geography, the culture, the history, the sociology, the economics, and the psychology of the people. Only in this way, it has been shown, can marketing operate efficiently in our own society. Only in this way can marketing develop and operate efficiently in the less developed nations of the world.

The tasks of marketing are many. Each of these ideally play a role, a positive role, in aiding a nation to improve its standard of living.

We can think of the role of marketing in a developing economy as that of an integral facilitating function for the overall program. Marketing is expected to deliver the rewards of increased productivity. It is the conveyor of development. The channels will carry the new products; retailers will stock the items; consumers will purchase the merchandise. But, of course, the process is more complicated and difficult than this implies. The marketer should gather and use new information so that his planning is improved. He can improve his decisions on products, pricing, promotion, channels, on the wholesale and retail outlets, and on delivery, storage, and inventory functions. Each improved decision can mean better profits, lower prices, or both.

The marketing operation must mirror the nation. One does not graft a modern distributive system to primitive production units, and vice versa.[14] An efficient and orderly marketing process will reflect its environment, and it is the responsibility of the marketer to see that this happens.

Rostow has indicated that each industry has an optimum position and that development efforts should be made accordingly.[15] This can also be a task of the marketer as he attempts to exploit the strengths and overcome the weaknesses of his existing marketing system (see Box 20-8). Rivers in one country might be highly utilized for the transportation of goods whereas in another country, such as the island economies of the Philippines, an inter-island physical distribution system must develop.

Samli stresses the task of providing additional time, place, and possession utilities.[16] This seems to be a sensible and basic approach. The marketer might well approach his task while clearly keeping in mind that he wants to expand the marketing utilities. The notion certainly adds perspective to the process.

An important task is to make certain that the development process includes the small businessman. "I suggest that the forgotten man in the in-

[14] George L. Mehren, "Market Organization and Economic Development," *Journal of Farm Economics*, Vol. 41, No. 5, December 1959, p. 1311.
[15] Rostow, *Op. cit.*, p. 102.
[16] Samli, *Op. cit.*, p. 36.

BOX 20-8

Export Marketing Aid

If we are to export practical marketing aid to developing nations, we must know the strengths and weaknesses of our marketing methods under different environmental conditions. Marketing, we know, is a powerful energizer for economic growth. The task now is to develop a body of hypotheses through historical and comparative analysis that will lead to useful theories or ideas concerning what to expect and what to do at various stages of market and marketing development.

SOURCE: Frank G. Coolsen, "Marketing and Economic Development," from *Emerging Concepts in Marketing*, ed. William S. Decker, American Marketing Association Proceedings (Chicago: American Marketing Association, 1962), p. 37.

ternational technical assistance effort is the struggling businessman in a really backward country or region, trying to make something useful to sell to his fellow countrymen."[17] This is both appealing and important. Marketing ultimately reaches the individual in both the production and the consumption ends. Grass-roots marketing therefore, should, not be overlooked.

Perhaps as well as anyone else, Peter Drucker has set forth the tasks and role of marketing in development:

> Marketing occupies a critical role in respect to the development of such "growth" areas. Indeed marketing is the most important "multiplier" of such development. . . . Marketing is central in this new situation [the race between economic development and international world-wide class war]. For marketing is one of our most potent levers to convert the danger into the opportunity. . . . Marketing is also the most easily accessible "multiplier" of managers and entrepreneurs in an "under-developed" growth area. . . . Marketing is critical in economic development because marketing has become so largely systematized, so largely both learnable and teachable. It is the discipline among all our business disciplines that has advanced the furthest.[18]

Drucker recognizes that marketing can crystallize and direct demand for maximum productive effectiveness and efficiency, that it can guide production purposefully toward maximum consumer satisfaction and consumer value, and that it can create discrimination and give rewards to those who contribute excellence.

These are "big" thoughts; they certainly focus one's attention to the tasks at hand. They show that marketing does have a vital role to play in development. Much remains to be done, obviously, and much of this is the marketer's responsibility.

Evidence of accomplishment

The development picture is not complete if we think only in terms of problems and tasks. There have been accomplishments which give credibility to the ideas set forth earlier (see Table 20-1). There have been individual company success stories such as Sears in some Latin and South American countries. Sears undertook a big job. By successfully identifying and solving problems, the company has helped improve credit and the institutional structure, expanded demand, and created employment opportunities through the stimulation of industry. This was the result of adding some marketing capabilities to a developing economy.[19]

There have been many improvements in the marketing of agricultural

---

[17] Hoffman, *Op. cit.*, p. 38.
[18] Peter F. Drucker, "Marketing and Economic Development," *Journal of Marketing*, Vol. 22, No. 3, January 1958, pp. 252–259.
[19] Coolsen, *Op. cit.*, p. 35.

Table 20-1. Israel: Purchases of Durable Goods, 1963-1964

	Locally Produced			Imported		
	1963	1964	Percent Change	1963	1964	Percent Change
Washing machines	18,703	19,573	4.7	7,299	8,942	22.5
Tape recorders	528	324	−38.6	10,896	13,724	26.0
Television sets	218	47	−78.4	1,876	14,162	654.9
Sewing machines	8,123	8,880	9.3	4,605	4,175	−9.3
Car radios	4,126	9,059	119.6	2,717	2,342	−13.8
Motor scooters	1,215	842	−30.7	4,530	2,568	−43.3

SOURCE: Bank of Israel, Annual Report 1964, Jerusalem, May 1965, p. 73.

products. Producers in many countries receive higher profits for their efforts; there is less waste, more market information available, and better planning; and the acceptance of improved production methods has stimulated improved distribution, and vice versa.

A nation can discover that its economic system can be built on choice rather than on direction. The Soviet Union is experiencing such a change now. There may be a large element of government in the overall process, but the improved standard of living can demonstrate effectively that consumer votes are most useful in the allocation and distribution of resources (see Table 20-2.)

Graduates of business schools today are called on to aid business in less developed nations. Both government employees and company representatives are seeking ways to speed up the development of the area in which they are working. It is clear that no one will have all the answers. Difficult problems will be inherited, but at least some basic work is already being undertaken.

Marketing can serve as a catalyst for the transmutation of latent resources into actual resources, of desires into accomplishments, and the development of responsible economic leaders and informed economic citizens.[20]

If I am correct that men must, in the generation ahead, diffuse the process of modernization out over long neglected rural regions, creating new efficient networks of distribution, we shall see not merely new and challenging tasks for those who command the skills of distribution but a new theoretical respect and appreciation for the art of that widening of the market which, for so long, was taken for granted.[21]

[20]Drucker, Op. cit., p. 259.

Table 20-2. USSR—Sales of Domestic
Appliances (thousands)

	1913	1940	1965
Clocks and watches	700	2,500	30,600
Sewing machines	272	175	—
Television sets	—	0.3	3,700
Refrigerators	—	—	1,675
Washing machines	—	—	3,400

SOURCE: Central Statistical Board of the USSR Council of Ministers, *Forty Years of Soviet Power* (Moscow: Foreign Languages Publishing House, 1958), p. 299 and *Current Digest of Soviet Press*, Vol. XVIII, No. 5, February 23, 1965, p. 4.

Questions

1. How does the influence of aspiration affect marketing in countries of varying degrees of economic development?
2. Is marketing a necessity in all types of economic systems?
3. Why has marketing not played a vital role in economic planning?
4. Develop a marketing plan for an underdeveloped nation.
5. Which should come first in an underdeveloped country, technological development or development of the marketing system?

Statements to Consider

Products in a classless society are viewed from a utilitarian perspective.

People in affluent countries want greater individuality in products.

One can relate marketing and styles of marketing activity to the states of economic development.

Marketing is related not to the type of political organization—capitalism versus communism—but to the affluence of society.

Income and expenditure patterns in the United States and Great Britain exhibit the following similarities: (1) a tendency to cling to higher good-and-service standards of living, (2) a faster rise in discretionary spending power than in disposable income, and (3) a slower rise in expenditures on consumer durables than in total discretionary spending.

[21] Walt W. Rostow, "The Concept of a National Market and Its Economic Growth Implications," from *Marketing and Economic Development*, ed. Peter D. Bennett, American Marketing Association Proceedings (Chicago: American Marketing Association, 1965), p. 20.

SELECTED REFERENCES

Robert T. Holt and John E. Turner, *The Political Basis of Economic Development* (New York: D. Van Nostrand Company, 1966).

Reed Moyer, *Marketing in Economic Development*, International Business Occasional Paper No. 1 (East Lansing: Institute for International Business Management Studies, Graduate School of Business Administration, Michigan State University, 1965).

Secretary-General of the United Nations Conference on Trade and Development, *Towards a New Trade Policy for Development* (New York: United Nations, 1964).

° Peter F. Drucker, "Marketing and Economic Development," *Journal of Marketing,* Vol. 22, No. 3, January 1958, pp. 252–259.

° Richard D. Robinson. "The Challenge of the Underdeveloped National Market," *Journal of Marketing,* Vol. 25, No. 6, October 1961, pp. 19–25.

Generalizations Were Taken From:

Ernest Dichter, "The World Customer," *Harvard Business Review,* Vol. 40, July–August 1963, pp. 113–122.

Marshall I. Goldman, "Marketing—A Lesson for Marx," *Harvard Business Review,* Vol. 38, January–February 1960, pp. 79–86.

Leslie C. Wright, "Spending Patterns in the U.K. and U.S.," *Scottish Journal of Political Economy,* February 1959, pp. 71–77.

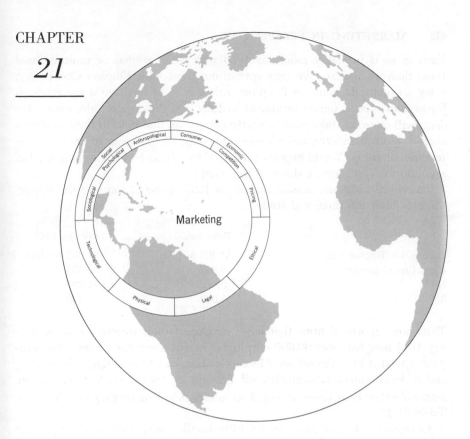

International Marketing

Reasons for International Marketing • COMPETITION • THE ENVIRONMENT • COM-
MUNICATIONS • CHANNELS • PRODUCT • PROMOTION • OTHER MARKETING
FUNCTIONS • OVERALL PROGRAMS • ADDENDA. 1. SELECTED ASPECTS OF AN
EXPORT SHIPMENT 2. MARKETING FORECASTS FOR EXPORTS TO FOREIGN MAR-
KETS

Each of us is probably more involved with international or multinational trade than we realize. We may spread our toast with Filipino Cocohoney, carry an umbrella made in Belgium, ride a scooter or drive a car made in Japan, and view a movie produced in Italy. On the export side, many students will some day take positions with companies that market their products abroad. More than ever, today's marketer must be prepared to enter the international arena. World exports exceed $185 billion and each company has an opportunity to gain a share of this market.

Individual company annual reports in 1965 reflected some of the importance of their multinational trade.

	Total Sales	Foreign Sales
Caterpillar Tractor Co.	$1,405 million	$ 607 million
Carnation Company	539	153
IBM	3,672	1,085
3M	1,000	300

These are reports of firms that have developed their international marketing. IBM now has over 60,000 employees in 102 countries, where the company operates 321 sales offices, 218 service bureaus, 15 manufacturing plants, and 6 development laboratories, all through its World Trade Corporation. Selected other companies engaged in international marketing are shown in Table 21-1.

Companies do not have to be billion-dollar corporations to enjoy the fruits of trading abroad. A study made during the 1950s in Minnesota found that 250 firms engaged in some amount of exporting even though many of them were small in size. The multination market may be reached directly or it may be exported to in an indirect manner. For example, batteries produced in St. Paul, Minnesota, may be placed on tractors manufactured in Iowa, and these may be exported to a variety of countries. The same kind of procedure also operates in reverse; radios assembled in this country may use component parts produced in Japan.

The dynamics of the marketplace are characteristic of the international as well as the domestic market. Attitudes toward world trade have changed dramatically over the years. Many firms in the past did little to develop their international marketing, but as the world has shrunk in size and as the purchasing power of the growing population has improved, the passive company is now enthusiastically examining its potential in the world marketplace.

Reasons for International Marketing

Basically, the reason for marketing internationally is the same as for marketing domestically. Someone has a need or want and someone else has a

Table 21-1. *Big Business Around the World*

Foreign Rank of Company	U.S. Rank of Company	Sales Volume ($000)	Name of Company	Location
1		6,824,644	Royal Dutch-Shell	Netherlands–Britain
	4	4,941,352	General Electric	New York
10		1,452,794	Fiat	Italy
	32	1,448,831	Firestone Tire & Rubber	Akron, Ohio
20		1,020,000	Rheinische Stahlwerke	Germany
	54	1,009,471	American Motors	Detroit
30		898,250	Gutehoffnungshütte	Germany
	60	896,239	Singer	New York
40		778,589	Matsushita	Japan
	76	767,113	Electrical Industrial	
50		672,984	Martin Marietta Aluminum	New York Canada
	89	667,193	Honeywell	Minneapolis
60		636,392	English Electric	Britain
	96	636,317	Atlantic Refining	Philadelphia
70		572,070	International Nickel	Canada
	109	571,050	American Home Products	New York
80		532,785	Hoesch	Germany
	118	530,976	Hercules Powder	Wilmington, Delaware
90		476,280	General Electric	Britain
	132	464,046	Sunray DX Oil	Tulsa, Oklahoma
100		426,860	Bowater Paper	Britain
	141	422,153	McGraw-Edison	Elgin, Illinois
110		388,021	Idemitsu Kosan	Japan
	157	385,958	Champion Papers	Hamilton, Ohio
120		362,858	Isuzu Motors	Japan
	166	362,314	Zenith Radio	Chicago
130		336,638	L'Air Liquide	France
	177	335,291	Warner-Lambert Pharmaceutical	Morris Plains, New Jersey
140		319,564	L. M. Ericsson Telephone	Sweden
	190	318,408	Worthington	Harrison, New Jersey
150		293,446	Seita	France
	209	293,164	Liggett & Myers Tobacco	New York
160		265,090	Electric & Musical Industries	Britain

Table 21-1. Big Business Around the World (Cont.)

Foreign Rank of Company	U.S. Rank of Company	Sales Volume ($000)	Name of Company	Location
	229	265,014	Bristol-Myers	New York
170		248,030	Nippon Electric	Japan
	251	247,401	Brown Shoe	St. Louis
180		236,424	British Oxygen	Britain
	262	236,287	Consumers Cooperative Association	Kansas City, Missouri
190		213,882	SAAB, Swedish Aircraft	Sweden
	280	212,586	Abbott Laboratories	N. Chicago, Illinois
200		208,170	Algoma Steel	Canada
	288	207,129	Hershey Chocolate	Hershey, Pennsylvania

SOURCE: Reprinted with permission from "The Fortune Directory," *Fortune*, July–August, 1965.

product or service to satisfy it. The buyer and seller both have opportunities to gain through the exchange. The manufacturer of hydraulic presses sees an opportunity to expand his sales and profit by selling abroad. There are users of Caterpillar tractors in Liberia who can use the hydraulic press to remove pins in broken treads. Hence the buyer of the press and the seller engage in international marketing for mutual benefits. The theory of comparative or absolute advantage explains in part the allocation of resources and the subsequent trading which is carried on between nations.

It is important to recognize that international trade statistics are aggregate figures. Actually the totals represent thousands of individual transactions consummated within the complex international environment. One tractor may have been shipped from Illinois to Liberia; 1000 bags of cement may have been shipped from New York to Argentina; and one case of antibiotics may have gone from Michigan to Egypt. Recognizing the individual transaction gives one a better picture of international marketing than simply looking at balance-of-payment figures.

Table 21-2 shows the total exports and imports for the United States in 1965. Of this total, $415 million worth of tractors were exported. This figure represents many companies which sell their products abroad, many buyers in various countries, and the costs of each of the marketing functions performed each time a sale was made. A single tractor may have been shipped from Iowa to Manila and from there to a government agency on the south-

Table 21-2. Foreign Trade of the United States

Value

Exports (mdse.), incl. reexports, total .... mil. $	...	27,346.2
Excl. Dept. of Defense shipments.................. do	...	26,567.1
Seasonally adjusted .... do	...	
By geographic regions:		
Africa...................................... do	...	1,224.1
Asia....................................... do	...	5,495.8
Australia and Oceania .... do	...	850.7
Europe..................................... do	...	8,851.6
Northern North America .... do	...	5,587.1
Southern North America .... do	...	2,094.6
South America............................... do	...	2,141.7
By leading countries:		
Africa:		
United Arab Republic (Egypt) .... do	...	157.6
Republic of South Africa...................... do	...	437.8
Asia; Australia and Oceania:		
Australia, including New Guinea................ do	...	700.7
India...................................... do	...	928.0
Pakistan.................................... do	...	335.9
Malaysia .... do	...	89.5
Indonesia................................... do	...	41.5
Philippines.................................. do	...	336.3
Japan .... do	...	2,057.5
Europe:		
France..................................... do	...	901.8
East Germany............................... do	...	12.6
West Germany .... do	...	1,501.8
Italy .... do	...	864.4
Union of Soviet Socialist Republics .... do	...	44.4
United Kingdom .... do	...	1,564.8
North and South America:		
Canada .... mil.$	...	5,586.7
Latin American Republics, total .... do	...	3,750.6
Argentina .... do	...	266.0
Brazil.................................... do	...	328.6
Chile..................................... do	...	235.3
Colombia .... do	...	196.4
Cuba .... do	...	(¹)
Mexico................................... do	...	1,105.2
Venezuela .... do	...	623.7

Table 21-2. Foreign Trade of the United States (Cont.)

Exports of U.S. merchandise, total . . . . do . . . 27,003.3
    Excl. military grant-aid . . . . do . . . 26,224.5
  By economic classes:
    Crude materials . . . . do . . . .
    Crude foodstuffs . . . . do . . . .
    Manufactured foodstuffs and beverages . . . . do . . . .
    Semimanufactures . . . . do . . . .
    Finished manufactures . . . . do . . . .
      Excl. military grant-aid . . . . do . . . .
  By principal commodities:
    Agricultural products, total . . . . do . . . 6,228.9
      Animal and vegetable oils and fats . . . . do . . . .
      Cotton, unmanufactured . . . . do . . . .
      Fruits, vegetables, and preparations . . . . do . . . .
      Grains and preparations . . . . do . . . .
      Meat and meat preparations . . . . do . . . .
      Tobacco and manufactures . . . . do . . . .
    Nonagricultural products, total . . . . do . . . 20,777.0
      Automobiles, parts, and accessories . . . . do . . . .
      Chemicals and related products . . . . do . . . .
      Coal and related fuels . . . . do . . . .
      Iron and steel prod. (excl. adv. mfs.) . . . . do . . . .
      Machinery, total . . . . do . . . .
        Agricultural . . . . do . . . .
        Tractors, parts, and accessories . . . . do . . . .
        Electrical . . . . do . . . .
        Metalworking . . . . do . . . .
        Other industrial . . . . do . . . .
      Petroleum and products . . . . do . . . .
      Textiles and manufactures . . . . do . . . .

General imports, total . . . . do . . . 21,366.4
    Seasonally adjusted . . . . do . . . .
  By geographic regions:
    Africa . . . . do . . . 875.1
    Asia . . . . do . . . 4,528.4
    Australia and Oceania . . . . do . . . 453.5
    Europe . . . . do . . . 6,293.0
    Northern North America . . . . do . . . 4,837.1
    Southern North America . . . . do . . . 1,741.1
    South America . . . . do . . . 2,626.2

Table 21-2. Foreign Trade of the United States (Cont.)

By leading countries:
  Africa:
    United Arab Republic (Egypt) . . . . do . . .   16.1
    Republic of South Africa . . . . do . . .   225.1
  Asia; Australia and Oceania:
    Australia, including New Guinea . . . . do . . .   314.1
    India . . . . do . . .   348.0
    Pakistan . . . . do . . .   44.8
    Malaysia . . . . do . . .   211.9
    Indonesia . . . . do . . .   165.3
    Philippines . . . . do . . .   369.1
    Japan . . . . do . . .   2,414.1
  Europe:
    France . . . . do . . .   615.3
    East Germany . . . . do . . .   6.5
    West Germany . . . . do . . .   1,341.6
    Italy . . . . do . . .   619.7
    Union of Soviet Socialist Republics . . . . do . . .   42.6
    United Kingdom . . . . do . . .   1,405.3
  North and South America:
    Canada . . . . do . . .   4,831.9
    Latin American Republics, total . . . . do . . .   3,676.6
      Argentina . . . . do . . .   122.1
      Brazil . . . . do . . .   511.9
      Chile . . . . do . . .   209.4
      Colombia . . . . do . . .   276.7
      Cuba . . . . do . . .   (^{1})
      Mexico . . . . do . . .   637.9
      Venezuela . . . . do . . .   1,020.6
Imports for consumption, total . . . . mil. $ . . 21,281.8
  By economic classes:
    Crude materials . . . . do . . . .
    Crude foodstuffs . . . . do . . . .
    Manufactured foodstuffs and beverages . . . . do . . . .
    Semimanufactures . . . . do . . . .
    Finished manufactures . . . . do . . . .
  By principal commodities:
    Agricultural products, total . . . . do . . .   4,092.2
      Cocoa (cacao) beans, incl. shells . . . . do . . .   120.5
      Coffee . . . . do . . .   1,060.2
      Rubber, crude (incl. latex and guayule) . . . . do . . .   182.3

Table 21-2. Foreign Trade of the United States (Cont.)

Sugar (cane or beet) . . . . do . . .   444.7
Wool and mohair, unmanufactured . . . . do . . .   235.1
Nonagricultural products, total . . . . do . . . 17,195.3
  Furs and manufactures . . . . do . . .   128.8
  Iron and steel prod. (excl. adv. mfs.) . . . . do . . . .
  Nonferrous ores, metals, etc.:
    Bauxite, crude . . . . do . . .   143.0
    Aluminum semimfs (incl. calcined bauxite) . . . . mil. $ . .   270.5
    Copper, crude and semimfs . . . . do . . .   302.2
    Tin, including ore . . . . do . . .   168.6
  Paper base stocks . . . . do . . .   451.7
  Newsprint . . . . do . . .   789.6
  Petroleum and products . . . . do . . . 2,063.3

Indexes

Exports (U.S. mdse., excl. military grant-aid):
  Quantity . . . . 1957–59 = 100   144
  Value . . . . do   152
  Unit value . . . . do . . . .   [r]106
Imports for consumption.
  Quantity . . . . do . . . .   [1]153
  Value . . . . do . . . .   [1]152
  Unit value . . . . do . . . .   [1]99

Shipping Weight and Value

Waterborne trade:
  Exports (incl. reexports):
    Shipping weight . . . . thous. sh. tons . . .   171,810
    Value . . . . mil.$ . . .   16,927.1
  General imports:
    Shipping weight . . . . thous. sh. tons . . .   255,454
    Value . . . . mil.$ . . .   14,934.6
Airborne trade:
  Exports (incl. reexports):
    Shipping weight . . . . thous. sh. tons . . .   228.7
    Value . . . . mil.$ . . .   [r]2,289.4
  General imports:
    Shipping weight . . . . thous. sh. tons . . .   96.1
    Value . . . . mil.$ . . .   [r]1,315.9

SOURCE: "Current Business Statistics," *Survey of Current Business,* Vol. 46, No. 6, June 1966, pp. 21–23.

ern island of Mindanao. Selling, buying, financing, packaging, advertising, insuring, shipping, and all the other marketing functions were performed in order to sell and deliver that single tractor.

COMPETITION

Marketing abroad, of course, has its competitive nature. In addition to all the competitive aspects of business found in domestic marketing, there are political overtones, military motivation, dumping, restrictions, and deep-seated attitudes. Frequently it is heard that the United States cannot continue to compete against other nations because of the price differential. Obviously our marketers must be competitive or they will lose their markets to rivals. Box 21-1 indicates that for some consumer goods the United States position in the United Kingdom has deteriorated.

Price is only one competitive factor. A firm can still compete in the world market with a high price if its product is superior, if its marketing program is a good one, if it provides excellent delivery and servicing, and perhaps if its credit policy is favorable. In other words, a seller in the international field has to decide upon his strategy and his marketing mix, and compete vigorously.

The task of marketing internationally may keep many firms out of a market. For a Canadian firm to enter the United States shoe market requires more than a favorable decision to lower our shoe tariffs. United States customers would have to be convinced that Canadian shoes represented good values. There would be extensive advertising, adequate distribution, and other marketing investment before the Canadian company could make any profits in our market. In other words, to sell in foreign markets, a company must develop a strong marketing program or utilize the program of an indigenous marketer.

THE ENVIRONMENT

The experienced foreign trader always warns the novice about understanding the foreign environment. Moreover, this text has stressed the environmental approach to all of marketing. Still, the necessity of learning as much as possible about the foreign consumer and his environs must be noted. The legal, ethical, technical, cultural, institutional, and economic segments of the overall culture are real, important, and frequently fascinating. The success of an international marketing program will depend in large measure on one's understanding of the environment in which one wishes to do business.

Nations will differ from one another in many ways, most of which are obvious. The following classification of market groups suggests many differences among nations:

BOX 21-1

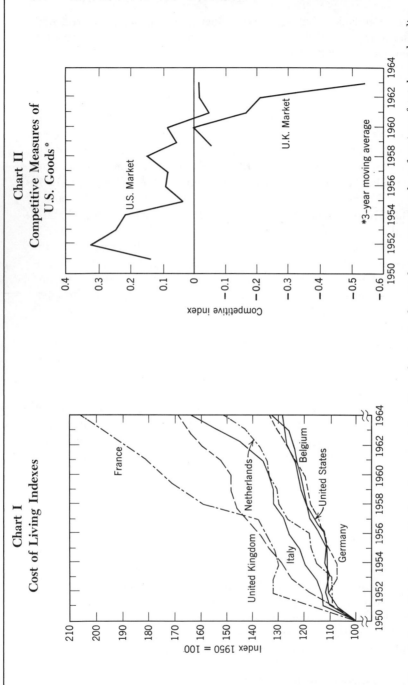

Chart I
Cost of Living Indexes

Chart II
Competitive Measures of
U.S. Goods *

Chart I shows the price levels of various countries. Since foreign-trade articles represent only a fraction of total merchandise manufactured, sold or bought in a country, the general price index may not provide an accurate competitive picture.

Chart II depicts the ability of the U.S. to sell consumer goods in the U.K, as compared to all other foreign countries which sell in the U.K. except the U.K. The trends show a deterioration in the U.S. competitive position than that shown for the U.S. market.

1. Almost classless society, contented countries (for example, Scandinavian countries).
2. Affluent countries (for example, United States, West Germany, Switzerland)
3. Countries in transition (Italy, Japan, England)
4. Revolutionary countries (Venezuela, Brazil, Spain, China)
5. Primitive countries (some African nations)
6. New class society (USSR)[1]

COMMUNICATIONS

Language remains important in international marketing. Negotiations and persuasion, for example, require adequate lines of communication, and knowledge of the buyer's language is extremely important. In addition to normal language problems, there are those of the "silent language" about which Edward Hall has written:

Language of Time—time required to make a decision.
Language of Space—the distance maintained between two persons carrying on a conversation.
Language of Things—money versus friendship versus tastefull arrangements versus dependability.
Language of Friendship—time to develop friends and loyalty of friends.
Language of Agreements—rules and customs.[2]

CHANNELS

International marketing is consummated through channels of marketing institutions just as is domestic marketing. The channels may be short, as between a large company in the United States and its branches abroad. They may be long and involved, as when a seller in this country ships through an intermediary and the goods are received through another intermediary or two in the importing nation (see Box 21-2).

Japan's channels are a case in point. Products imported from the United States or any other country must eventually be sold through Japan's domestic channels. There one may find three wholesale links, since the channels tend to be longer than those to which we are accustomed. The reasons are the long narrow country, the buying habits which encourage intensive retail distribution for many products, the atomistic size of a large proportion of producers, the manufacturers' often performing little or no part of the mar-

[1] Ernest Dichter, "The World Customer," *Harvard Business Review*, Vol. 40, No. 4, July–August 1962, pp. 113–122.
[2] Edward T. Hall, "The Silent Language in Overseas Business," *Harvard Business Review*, Vol. 38, No. 5, September–October 1960, p. 107.

BOX 21-2

Organization for Foreign Sales

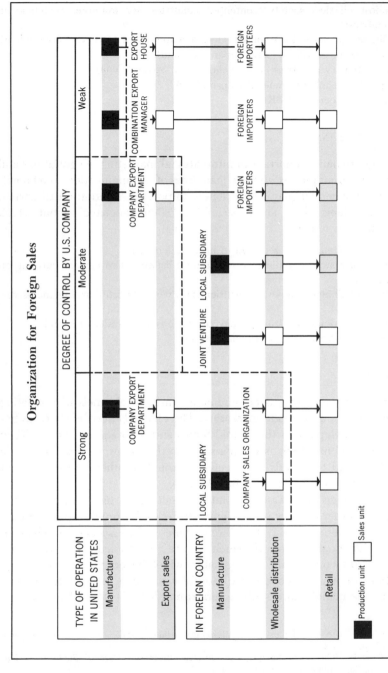

* Shading indicates levels at which the U.S. company has strong control over the sales program.

SOURCE: John Fayerweather, *International Marketing* (Englewood Cliffs, N.J.: Prentice-Hall, 1965), p. 108.

432

keting task, and the general discouragement of large-scale operations.[3] There has been a growth of retailing and hence new channels have developed; for years there has been a small, cottage industry combined with giant combines. The overall result is a different type of channel situation facing the seller from abroad. Though he may not come into direct contact with the Japanese market, the foreign seller will undoubtedly become aware of this different channel situation.

Channels are closely tied to a company's organization. This can be seen from the diagram in Box 21-2. A company wishing to handle its own exporting can sell directly to the buyer abroad or he may turn over his exporting to a middleman who specializes in foreign marketing. The same is true with the importer who may buy through import houses or who may buy directly. Many department stores send their buyers to foreign countries, where they place direct orders with foreign manufacturers. The alternatives are many and the decision will rest on the type of products, the size of the foreign business, and other factors not unlike domestic distribution decisions. As in domestic marketing, there have developed marketing institutions to handle each kind of situation.

PRODUCT

If companies in the United States have learned that products must fit the consumer, international marketing will come easier. Robinson has summarized the need for this sensitivity as he considered the environmental factors influencing the value of an exportable product (see Box 21-3). *Product design* obviously calls for adaptation to the foreign markets. Automobile speedometers may register in kilometers, the steering wheel may be on the right side, and the headlights may have different kinds of bulbs. Dials on equipment may conform to the metric system. Power-driven units may be replaced by hand operations. The illustrations are many: the product must fit all facets of the culture and economy.

Second, management must recognize that the products may not induce the same kind of *economic and social* benefits which accrue to buyers in this country. A product may be successful here because of its labor-saving attributes, but abroad this may be entirely irrelevant. A product such as a cola drink may be excluded in some countries because of the shortage of foreign exchange for a luxury item. Third, the buyer or seller must reckon with the *political implications* in his marketing. In international marketing this is a particularly important segment of the environment.

[3] George A. Elgass, "Marketing in Japan: An Expanding Economy," in William D. Stevens (ed.), *The Social Responsibilities of Marketing* (Chicago: American Marketing Association, 1962) p. 429.

BOX 21-3

Environmental Factors Considered in the Design of an Exportable Product

Level of technical skills——————→	Product simplification
Level of labor cost————————→	Automation or manualization of product
Level of literacy—————————→	Remarking and simplification of product
Level of income————————→	Quality and price change
Level of interest rates——————→	Quality and price change (Investment in high quality might not be financially deisrable.)
Level of maintenance——————→	Change in tolerances
Climatic differences——————→	Product adaptation
Isolation (heavy repair—————→ difficult and expensive)	Product simplification and reliability improvement
Differences in standards—————→	Recalibration of product and resizing
Availability of other products———→	Greater or lesser product integration
Availability of materials—————→	Change in product structure and fuel
Power availability————————→	Resizing of product
Special conditions————————→	Product redesign or invention

SOURCE: Richard D. Robinson, "The Challenge of the Underdeveloped National Market," *Journal of Marketing*, Vol. 25, October 1961, p. 22.

PROMOTION

The entire persuasion process of the international marketer must adapt to the culture in which the merchandise is to be sold. In some instances the foreign nature of the materials makes them desirable but in other cases it does not. Regardless, the market must be understood. Many words are "taboo," and these must be known by the advertiser. Lists of such words can be obtained in order to avoid offending the local population. United States businessmen continually travel through foreign countries in order to promote their products, and foreign marketing men tour our country doing the same thing.

Advertising is used in all advanced countries and even used to some extent in state-controlled nations such as the USSR (see Box 21-4 and Table 21-3). Successful advertising campaigns in Yugoslavia have changed consumer habits. In one case, consumers were successfully encouraged to purchase canned soup instead of preparing it in the home as had been done for many years. In another instance, industrial firms were persuaded to substitute paperboard packing for wooden packing cases.[4]

The United States firm may use its own advertising agency abroad or it may use one located in the foreign country. The foreign buyer must be persuaded to buy: consequently the persuasion will have to be in his language

[4]Mihoril Skobe, "Marketing and Advertising in Yugoslavia," in Peter D. Bennett (ed.), *Marketing and Economic Development* (Chicago: American Marketing Association, 1965), p. 99.

BOX 21-4

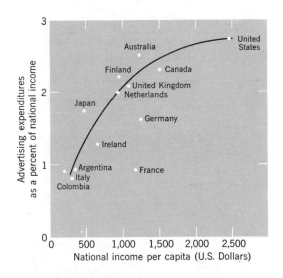

Intensity of advertising effort.

SOURCE: John Fayerweather, *International Marketing*, 1965, reprinted by permission of Prentice-Hall, Inc., Englewood Cliffs, N.J., p. 83. Derived from data on advertising expenditures compiled by the author for The International Advertising Association and published in *The International Advertiser*, August 1963. Certain adjustments have been made in the incomplete published data to give the approximate total expenditures for this graph. The data are mostly for 1962, though for some countries 1960 or 1961 data are used.

Table 21-3. *Distribution of Total National Advertising Expenditures by Medium (in percent)*

	Belgium	Brazil	France	Israel	Japan	Lebanon	Peru	Turkey	United Kingdom	United States
Newspapers	27.1	32.5	22.4	49	38.7	28	31.5	30.0	31.2	29.8
Magazines	14.5	11.6	28.1	6	6.0	22	3	7.4	17.4	12.9
Outdoor and transportation	10.6	8.1	8.1	8	8.6	10	5	21.1	6.8	1.4
Cinema	3.1	Neg.	7.1	5	1.8	9	4	2.7	1.1	Neg.
Radio	2.2	14.0	⎱ 9.1	4.7	7.3	None	18	4.8	Neg.	5.7
Television	0.3	9.3	⎰	None	28.9	18	27.5	None	18.2	15.0
Direct	17.4	21.0	⎱ 12.5	10	4.7	4	2	23.1	9.1	15.6
Exhibitions, etc.	7.7	NA	⎰	10	⎱ 2.1	3	NA	NA	3.8	"Misc."
Display and point of sale	7.7	NA	11.5	NA	⎰	2	2	4.1	7.1	"Misc."
Promotional schemes	"Misc."	2.9	NA	3	NA	NA	5	NA	3.5	"Misc."
Reference publications	NA	NA	NA	NA	NA	"Misc."	NA	NA	"Misc."	"Misc."
Miscellaneous	9.4	0.6	1.2	4.3	1.9	4	2	6.8	1.8	19.6
Total	100	100	100	100	100	100	100	100	100	100

NA—not available   Neg.—negligible   "Misc."—included in "Miscellaneous"

SOURCE: Fayerweather, *Op. cit.*, pp. 83 and 90.

and style in order to be effective. Individual company advertising expenditures are shown for selected firms in Table 21-4.

Images of foreign products also are important. A study by a young Japanese student showed the differences among images held by Minnesota businessmen of foreign made products (see Box 21-5). Whereas the young student saw his country as the producer of Sony radios, Honda cycles, and Toyota automobiles, the Minnesota businessmen held images of Japanese products which were produced thirty years ago.[5]

OTHER MARKETING FUNCTIONS

The international marketer will find some foreigners highly sophisticated in marketing knowledge and others entirely lacking it. Regardless, all marketing functions must be carried out. In international marketing, some functions take on greater importance and require more effort than corresponding functions in domestic marketing. Insuring the shipment is an example. Marine insurance must cover a more complex shipment and with greater chance for pilferage (see Box 21-6). The transportation function likewise constitutes a larger proportion of the total cost and is very important for a variety of reasons such as time.

Marketing research will be necessary to provide the seller with the needed market information (Box 21-7).

Financial arrangements require greater care and Letters of Credit must be obtained. Government controls are many and permission to import or export must be carefully checked. Many of the functions taken for granted in domestic shipments loom large in foreign shipments. Tariff regulations, for example, are different for each country. Embargoes, quotas, prohibitions, and regulations for sanitation, political, military, or other reasons are common.

Despite the many difficulties of marketing abroad, the opportunities are considerable and many firms successfully and profitably carry on extensive foreign trade operations. To be successful, it behooves the international marketer to adapt his operations to fit the foreign situation.

OVERALL PROGRAMS

The foreign market must be planned and developed as carefully as any other (see Box 21-8). The marketing factors will influence organization (branch plants or licensed operators, for example), investment, product line, and other features of resource allocation. The marketing mix should be

[5] Akira Nagashima, "Minnesota Businessmen's Image of Foreign Made Products by Semantic Differential Method, "Unpublished Master's Thesis, University of Minnesota, 1965.

Table 21-4. 50 Leading Advertisers in International Media: 1963

1.	Ford Motor Co.	$688,083
2.	Martini & Rossi	633,431
3.	British-American Tobacco	629,064
4.	P. Lorillard Co.	560,935
5.	Carreras-Rothmans	549,018
6.	Pan American World Airways	508,381
7.	Matsushita Elec.	445,421
8.	Shell International Co.	442,649
9.	Champion Spark Plug Co.	430,903
10.	Esso International	413,905
11.	Coca-Cola Export Co.	398,705
12.	British Overseas Airways	388,164
13.	Chrysler International	370,656
14.	Eastman Kodak Co.	366,613
15.	Trans World Airline	361,305
16.	Alitalia	344,515
17.	Daimler Benz	336,750
18.	Sony Corp.	296,355
19.	Omega Watch Co.	287,372
20.	Philips Industries	286,567
21.	Mobil Overseas Oil Co.	268,956
22.	KLM Royal Dutch Airlines	259,244
23.	Rolex Watch Co.	256,881
24.	First National City Bank of N.Y.	250,050
25.	Philip Morris Overseas	242,703
26.	Outboard Marine Int'l	242,435
27.	Imperial Chemical	238,313
28.	Deutsche Lufthansa	236,649
29.	Dubonnet	234,583
30.	Fiat	226,010
31.	Scandinavian Airlines	218,039
32.	Liggett & Myers Tobacco	213,279
33.	Firestone International	205,561
34.	Boeing Aircraft Co.	197,685
35.	Allis-Chalmers International	194,677
36.	International Harvester Export Co.	193,592
37.	George Ballantine & Son	187,181
38.	IBM World Trade Corp.	184,647
39.	Wm. Grant & Sons	180,823
40.	Ford Works	180,505
41.	Burroughs Corp.	175,480
42.	John Deere	171,534
43.	Air India International	168,465
44.	Japan Air Lines	166,104

Table 21-4. 50 Leading Advertisers in International Media: 1963 (Cont.)

45. R. J. Reynolds Tobacco	162,724
46. Cinzano Cio	162,568
47. Texaco	156,211
48. Bank of America	156,010
49. Tokyo Shibaura Electric	150,934
50. Eterna	148,776

Note: Listing does not include locally-placed advertising by international companies, among whom may be found some of the largest international advertisers in the world.

SOURCE: Reprinted with permission of John M. Hess and Philip R. Cateora, *International Marketing*, Richard D. Irwin, Inc., Homewood, Illinois, 1966, page 544. Originally published in *Rome Report* of Expenditures in International Media, 1964.

BOX 21-5

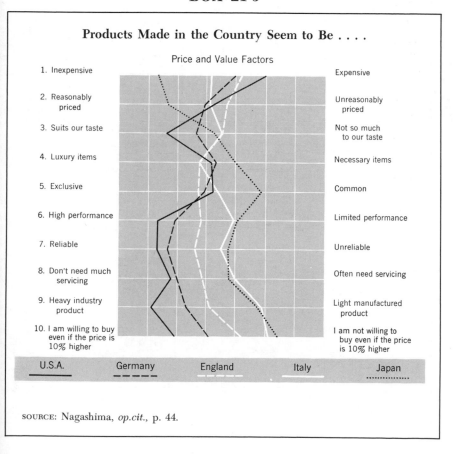

SOURCE: Nagashima, *op.cit.*, p. 44.

BOX 21-6

Stowage Plan for Moore—McCormack Lines, Inc. (cargo from South Africa to United States ports)

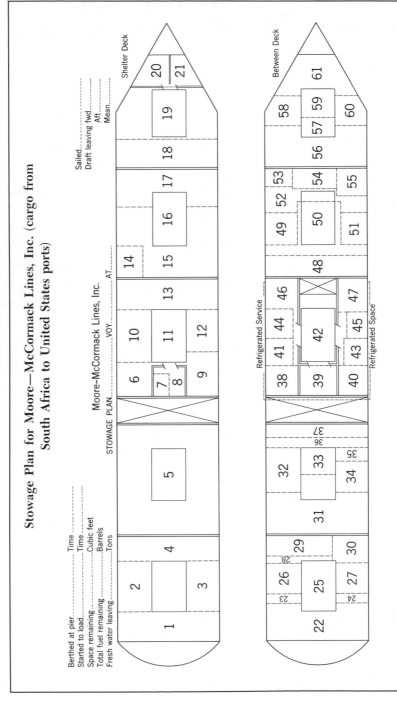

Berthed at pier........................Time..............
Started to load........................Time..............
Space remaining........................Cubic feet..............
Total fuel remaining........................Barrels..............
Fresh water leaving........................Tons..............

Moore—McCormack Lines, Inc.

STOWAGE PLAN........................VOY..............AT..............

Sailed..............
Draft leaving fwd..............
Aft..............
Mean..............

Shelter Deck

Between Deck

Refrigerated Service

Refrigerated Space

SOURCE: Carl E. McDowell and Helen M. Gibbs, *Ocean Transportation* New York: McGraw-Hill Book Company, 1954), p. 178.

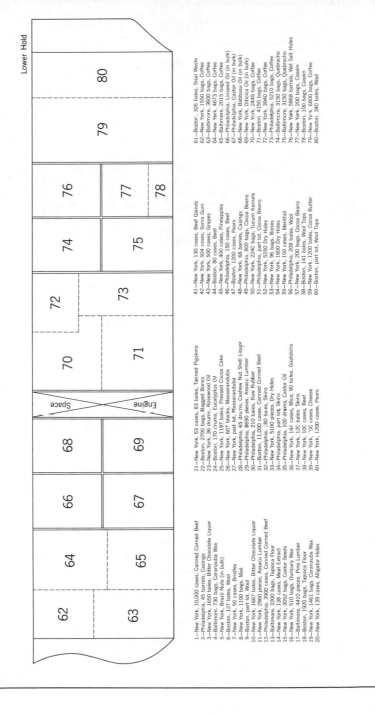

Lower Hold

1—New York, 10,000 cases, Canned Corned Beef
2—Philadelphia, 45 barrels, Casings
3—New York, 1650 bales, Bitter Chocolate Liquor
4—Baltimore, 730 bags, Caranauba Wax
5—New York, Brazil Nuts (in bulk)
6—Boston, 127 bales, Wool
7—New York, 50 cases, Bristles
8—New York, 1100 bags, Mali
9—Boston, part lot, Wool
10—New York, 1667 bales, Bitter Chocolate Liquor
11—New York, 2960 pieces, Assacu Lumber
12—Philadelphia, 3900 cases, Canned Corned Beef
13—Baltimore, 2200 bags, Tapioca Flour
14—New York, 138 cases, Meat Extract
15—New York, 3052 bags, Castor Seeds
16—New York, 510 bags, Ouricury Wax
17—Baltimore, 4410 pieces, Pine Lumber
18—Boston, 1920 bags, Tapioca Flour
19—New York, 1461 bags, Caranauba Wax
20—New York, 139 cases, Alligator Hides

21—New York, 53 cases, 83 bales, Tanned Pigskins
22—Boston, 2700 bags, Bagged Bones
23—New York, 36 drums, Rosewood Oil
24—Baltimore, 170 drums, Eucalyptus Oil
25—New York, 1197 bales, Pressed Cocoa Cake
26—New York, 607 blocks, Massaranduba
27—New York, part lot, Massaranduba
28—Philadelphia, 65 drums, Cashew Nut Shell Liquor
29—Philadelphia, 8690 pieces, Assacu Lumber
30—Philadelphia, 210 bales, Raw Rubber
31—Boston, 11,000 cases, Canned Corned Beef
32—Philadelphia, 80 bales, Skins
33—New York, 5100 pieces, Dry Hides
34—Philadelphia, part lot, Skins
35—Philadelphia, 100 drums, Castor Oil
36—New York, 144 cases, Mica; 90 bales, Goatskins
37—New York, 120 bales, Skins
38—New York, 100 cases, Beef
39—New York, 100 cases, Cheese
40—New York, 1200 cases, Pears

41—New York, 130 cases, Beef Glands
42—New York, 504 cases, Sorva Gum
43—New York, 500 cases, Grapes
44—Boston, 80 cases, Beef
45—New York, 400 cases, Pineapples
46—Philadelphia, 150 cases, Beef
47—Boston, 1200 cases, Pears
48—New York, 68 barrels, Casings
49—Philadelphia, 800 bags, Cocoa Beans
50—New York, 2240 bags, Tucum Kernels
51—Philadelphia, part lot, Cocoa Beans
52—New York, 5250 Dry Hides
53—New York, 96 bags, Bones
54—New York, 1800 Dry Hides
55—New York, 150 cases, Menthol
56—Philadelphia, 208 bales, Wool
57—New York, 200 bags, Cocoa Beans
58—Boston, 141 bales, Wool Tops
59—New York, 1200 bales, Wool Tops
60—Boston, part lot, Wool Tops

61—Boston, 326 bales, Sisal Waste
62—New York, 1550 bags, Coffee
63—Baltimore, 3600 bags, Coffee
64—New York, 4673 bags, Coffee
65—Baltimore, 2015 bags, Coffee
66—Philadelphia, Linseed Oil (in bulk)
67—Philadelphia, Castor Oil (in bulk)
68—New York, Babbasu Oil (in bulk)
69—New York, Oiticica Oil (in bulk)
70—New York, 2445 bags, Coffee
71—Boston 4150 bags, Coffee
72—New York, 3940 bags, Coffee
73—Philadelphia, 5210 bags, Coffee
74—Baltimore, 3150 bags, Quebracho
75—Baltimore, 3150 bags, Quebracho
76—New York, 5868 barrels, Wet Salt Hides
77—New York, 200 bags, Casein
78—Boston, 100 bags, Casein
79—New York, 6800 bags, Coffee
80—Boston, 340 bales, Wool

441

BOX 21-7

Picture-Type Audience Preference, Latin America*

Country	1st	2nd	3rd	4th	5th	6th
Brazil	Musical	Drama	Action	Comedies	Slapstick	Mystery
Chile	Musical	Action	Drama	Slapstick	Mystery	Comedies
Colombia	Musical	Drama	Action	Mystery	Comedies	Slapstick
Cuba	Musical	Drama	Action	Mystery	Comedies	Slapstick
Mexico	Action	Drama	Musical	Mystery	Comedies	Slapstick
Panama	Musical	Action	Drama	Comedies	Mystery	Slapstick
Peru	Musical	Drama	Action	Mystery	Comedies	Slapstick
Puerto Rico	Musical	Drama	Action	Mystery	Comedies	Slapstick
Venezuela	Musical	Action	Drama	Mystery	Comedies	Slapstick

* Argentina omitted because comparable up-to-date figures are lacking.

Picture-Type Audience Preference, Near East

Country	1st	2nd	3rd	4th	5th	6th
Egypt	Action	Musical	Mystery	Slapstick	Comedies	Drama
Iraq	Action	Musical	Drama	Mystery	Slapstick	Comedies
Lebanon	Action	Musical	Drama	Mystery	Slapstick	Comedies

Picture-Type Audience Preference, Far East

Country	1st	2nd	3rd	4th	5th	6th
Hong Kong	Musical	Action	Slapstick	Drama	Mystery	Comedies
India	Musical	Action	Slapstick	Drama	Mystery	Comedies
Indo China	Action	Musical	Drama	Mystery	Slapstick	Comedies
Indonesia	Action	Musical	Slapstick	Drama	Mystery	Comedies
Japan	Action	Musical	Drama	Slapstick	Mystery	Comedies
Malaya	Musical	Action	Slapstick	Drama	Comedies	Mystery
Philippines	Action	Musical	Drama	Mystery	Slapstick	Comedies
Siam	Musical	Action	Slapstick	Drama	Comedies	Mystery

SOURCE: Ronald Carroll, "Selecting Motion Pictures for the Foreign Market," *Journal of Marketing*, Vol. 17, No. 2, October 1952, p. 167.

planned in order to achieve an effective marketing program abroad. Each facet of the mix must be geared to the overall international operation.

Sears, Roebuck de Mexico, S.A., opened the doors of its first store in Mexico on February 27, 1947. Within six years it was one of the largest companies in the country, with sales of $15 million. Many lessons had to be

BOX 21-8

Fifteen Rules and Warnings

1. Adapt the product to the market.
2. Gauge the impact of custom and tradition.
3. Exploit markets in proper sequence.
4. Remain politically tolerant.
5. Build a strong local management.
6. Beware of language barriers.
7. Study differences in advertising.
8. Identify the company with the local scene.
9. Know the trade channels.
10. Understand the consumer's views of price and quality.
11. Appraise the degree of acceptance of free enterprise.
12. Explore government regulations.
13. Insulate against restrictive legislation.
14. Invest for the long pull.
15. Interchange information between the home office and the foreign office.

SOURCE: Arthur C. Nielsen, Jr., "Do's and Don't's in Selling Abroad," *The Journal of Marketing*, Vol. 23, No. 4, April 1959, pp. 405–411.

learned about doing business abroad, but by adapting to each situation the operation has been most successful (Box 21-9).

Today every marketer should consider the possibilities of buying from or selling to foreign countries. The opportunities may be great; each experience is unique.

In Spain, for example, the marketer finds ultraconservatism in virtually every respect: economic, political, religious, and social. An efficient marketing structure is a necessary concomitant of any real economic advancement. Two primary markets exist, Madrid and Barcelona. The standard of living is low with the average annual per capita income only $360. Goods are sold through *agentes comerciales,* and governmental controls determine the market structure of some products such as drugs. Retailing is small-scale, but advertising is expanding. Despite an absence of market data, the outlook for development is rather good.[6]

In India one finds both a public sector and a private sector of the economy. A seller's market prevails in most consumer goods and industrial products. The transport system is fairly well developed. Advertising is quite well

[6]Edwin H. Lewis, "Marketing in Spain," *Journal of Marketing,* Vol. 28, No. 4, October 1964, p. 17.

BOX 21-9

Six Years of Sears in Mexico City

Store	Cloth and Clothing	Furniture and Home Fixtures	Electrical Appliances	Auto Supplies
Palacio de Hierro	40%	10%	2%	—
Salinas y Rocha	18	14	4	—
Sears in Mexico City	24	15	7	5%
Puerto de Liverpool	29	4	2	—
Centro Mercantil	4	2	3	—
Puerto de Veracruz	14	1	—	—
Any specialty shop	25	26	34	15
Stalls in open markets . . .	16	5	1	—
Private artisans (dress-makers, cabinet makers, etc.)	6	6	—	—
Other department stores. .	18	3	2	—
Others	4	4	5	1

SOURCE: Richardson Wood and Virginia Keyser, *Sears, Roebuck de Mexico, S.A.* (Washington, D.C.: National Planning Association, 1953), p. 15.

established, with over 125 advertising agencies, some of which are international. Market research is inadequate, as are the channels of distribution. One small television station operates for approximately 500 receivers.[7]

Similar capsule summaries could be made for each nation of the world. For each individual market the exporter plans his marketing strategy so that he can profitably market his merchandise there.

Questions

1. How does trading between nations begin? What are the motivations? Who gains from it?
2. International marketing is not new and yet we continue to hear that it is a fraction of what it could and perhaps should be. Why?
3. What nonlegal reasons prevent a firm from entering a foreign market? Concentrate on marketing reasons.
4. In what ways does the marketing environment in foreign nations differ from that of the United States?

[7] Shrivaram Nair, "The Progress of Modern Marketing Methods in India," *International Marketing Federation Newsletter*, No. 6, May 1965, p. 1.

Statements to Consider

Organizing international marketing programs requires the ability to grasp the complexities of the economic, political, and commercial relationships of the nations of the world and to formulate effective marketing programs to fit them.

The foundation for understanding the workings of trade among nations is the "theory of comparative advantage."

The origins of consumer demands are universal.

Industrial buyers around the world are much more similar than individual consumers.

In many countries, especially in the developing nations, channels of distribution are largely ineffective in transmitting information.

The large differences in buying abilities abroad have considerable bearing on the promotion appeals.

SELECTED REFERENCES

John Fayerweather, *International Marketing* (Englewood Cliffs, N.J.: Prentice-Hall, 1965).

John M. Hess and Philip R. Cateora, *International Marketing* (Homewood, Ill.: Richard D. Irwin, 1966).

J. Frederick Dewhurst, "European Customers in a Changing Environment," in Donald W. Scotton (ed.), *Marketing Adjustments to the Environment* (Urbana: University of Illinois, 1961), pp. 96–106.

°Ernest Dichter, "The World Customer," *Harvard Business Review*, Vol. 40, No. 4, July–August, 1962, pp. 113–122.

Generalizations Were Taken From:

John Fayerweather, *International Marketing* (Englewood Cliffs, N.J.: Prentice-Hall, 1965).

ADDENDUM 1. Selected Aspects of an Export Shipment

Buyer's Inquiry

CIF Calculation

A SPECIMEN EXPORT TRANSACTION

DATE _September 16, 19—_

QUOTATION ☐   OFFER ☒   SALE ☐

BASIS (check) FAS VESSEL

C&F _____

CIF _X Santos_

MATERIAL _Portland Cement_
CONSIGNEE _Brazil Imports of São Paulo_
PORT _____ _Santos_

QUANTITY _10,000 bags_

BASE PRICE _$.76_	per _bag_	$7,600.00
SHIPPING BASE	PACKED IN _6-ply paper_	
(check)		
Ex Factory	MEAS. _____	
FOB Cars	GROSS _95#_	
FAS Vessel _New York_	TARE _1#_	
	NET _94#_	
	Profit Markup	
	(5¢ per bag)	500.00
INLAND FREIGHT _____ lbs.	@ _____	_____
CARTAGE _____ lbs.	@ _____	_____
HANDLING _____	@ _____	
OCEAN FREIGHT _950,000#_	@ _$18.00/2,240 #_	7,633.93
SURCHARGE _____	@ _25%_	1,908.48
_____	@ _+10¢/2,240#tax_	
PORT & HANDLING CHARGE _____	_+$6.00 per B/L_	48.41
HEAVY LIFT CHARGE _____	@ _____	
MARINE INSURANCE _$19,790_	@ _$1.30%_	257.27
(Coverage _A/R—2% shortage_)		
CONSUL FEES _____		42.00
MISCELLANEOUS _____		
	TOTAL	$17,990.09

TOTAL UNIT PRICE _$1.80_ PER _bag_

SOURCE: Philip MacDonald, _Practical Exporting_ (New York: The Ronald Press Company, 1949), p. 287.

Exporter's Firm Offer

Buyer's Acceptance
  Documents
      Purchase order
      Sales contract
      Letters of credit
      Letters of confirmation
      Shipper's export declaration
      Steamship delivery permit
      Steamship dock receipt
      Railroad documents
      Ocean bill of lading
      Brazilian Consular invoices
      On-board certification
      Sight drafts
      Insurance policy

ADDENDUM 2. Marketing Forecasts for Exports to Foreign Markets

Follow the arrows to read this table

	Trend of the Market	U.S. Share of the Market
Increasing	↗	↗
Steady	→	→
Declining	↘	↘

		AFRICA		AMERICAN REPUBLICS		
SITC NUMBER	COMMODITY	NIGERIA	SOUTH AFRICA	ARGENTINA	COLOMBIA	VENEZUELA
51250	Acids and their derivatives					
54170	Medicaments					
58120	Selected plastics; polymers and copolymers					
64120	Printing and writing paper					
65160	Yarn and thread of synthetic fiber					
65360	Synthetic fiber fabrics					
67430	Iron and steel plates and sheets less than 3 mm. thick					
69420	Nuts, bolts, screws, rivets, and washers					
71110	Steam generating boilers					
71220	Agricultural harvesting, threshing, and sorting machinery					
71420	Calculating, accounting machines, electric computers, etc.					
71510	Metal working machine tools					
71710	Textile machinery					
71810	Paper making machinery					
71830	Food processing machines, except household					
71840	Construction and mining machinery					
71910	Heating and cooling equipment					
71930	Mechanical handling equipment					
72210	Electric power machinery					
72500	Household electric equipment					
73230	Buses					

International Commerce

U.N. market share reports

SOURCE: *International Commerce*, Bureau of International Commerce, Vol. 72, No. 24, June 13, 1966, cover.

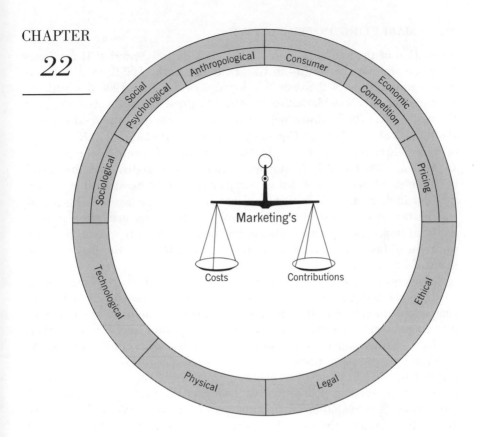

An Evaluation of Marketing

THE PROBLEM • FUNCTIONS • EVALUATION OF MARKETING IN OUR SYSTEM •
GLOSSARY OF MARKETING DEFINITIONS

Evaluation of the marketing process has gone on for centuries. It continues today throughout the world—in Great Britain, in the USSR, in the United States, and in some of the underdeveloped areas. In June 1966 the National Commission on Food Marketing reported in great detail on its findings in the vast market for food products. Much to the dismay of the food industry the reports of the National Commission on Food Marketing imply criticism of the industry and tend to emphasize the wastes of nonprice competition. In August 1966 the British Monopoly Commission stated that the Board of Trade should encourage British companies to institute at least a 40 percent cut in marketing expenses to accompany a price reduction. This report was particularly critical of the detergent industry. The marketing process has been under constant surveillance, and today's efforts represent the accumulation of discussions, recommendations, and actions on the part of thousands of businessmen.

Throughout these pages we have learned that marketing operates in an environment influenced by technology, laws, ethics, economic conditions, competitive factors, and the subjective judgments of millions of consumers. As we have seen, marketing responds to these environmental forces. Further, we have discussed marketing tasks and indicated marketing's role in the allocation of company resources; and we have shown how marketing research has aided in the decision-making processes of physically distributing the goods, persuading people to buy, financing the exchange of goods and services, and the overall merchandising aspects of marketing. To be sure, we are all interested in the crucial question—Is marketing doing a good job?

As consumers and as citizens we have the privilege of asking this question and we expect an adequate explanation of the marketing operation. If marketing is not doing a good job we should expect changes. As company employees, stockholders, and managers, we want an accurate answer to the question. If our marketing operations are faulty we should obviously initiate action to improve them. The manager, perhaps more than the citizen and perhaps more than members of Congress, is asking the same question and asking it daily. If marketing is not doing a good job, the firm will not remain competitive.

T. J. Kreps, a professor and former presidential economic adviser, has examined the social performance of business in a study for the Temporary National Economic Committee. The lead paragraph of his monograph provides valuable perspective.

Business is not merely nor even in the first instance a struggle of individuals for wealth. It is a way of life, a system of providing goods and services. It is not a segment of the community, cooperating or warring with other segments such as labor, consumers, or farmers. It is not superior or inferior to the community. It is the community engaged in getting its daily bread. Its goals, its ethics, its welfare are inseparable from the goals and aspirations and welfare of the community. No matter how much or how often the business phases of social or community activity may be abstracted, analyzed, and separately discussed, the fundamental and organic unity between business and the community is indissoluble.[1]

The question of evaluating marketing can be examined from many points of view. For example, as public-minded citizens we might ask the following questions: Are not the costs of transporting an automobile from Detroit to Los Angeles excessive? Does not advertising raise the cost of a package of cigarettes? Do we need 107 varieties of men's cosmetics? Are not 42 price lines of fishing rods too many? Could we not get along without three service stations at an intersection? Is not $80 a lot to pay the salesman for selling a new automobile? Is it a healthy sign to see manufacturers setting up their own wholesaling and retailing establishments? Are not the big retailers making it impossible for the small businessman to operate? Does the farmer deserve a higher percentage of the dollar spent for food items? Why should housewives feel compelled to boycott their food stores?

Managers are hired to make profit for their companies. To accomplish this they must remain competitive and measure their competitiveness in a variety of ways, such as the amount of profit, sales volume, share of the market, and percentage change of sales. They, too, are asking questions similar to those in the pervious paragraph. An automobile company found that a completed automobile could be shipped for $274 by truck and $140 by three-tier rack railroad car from Detroit to Los Angeles. Every company evaluates its dollars spent for advertising: are the expenditures necessary to keep the desired share of the market or to develop an adequate volume of sales? A cosmetic manufacturer asks if the new brand of men's after-shave lotion will uncover a new segment of a profitable market. A fishing rod manufacturer asks how much each segment of the market will spend for fishing rods, and he finds that there are vast differences among fishermen in this respect. A petroleum company finds in its research that the intersection of Highways 62 and 494 is the best location for a new service station. An automobile dealer finds that it has to pay a certain commission on an automobile in order to attract high-quality salesmen; to do differently would attract only low-quality salesmen and the marketing process would be less efficient. A manufacturer may find that it can integrate vertically and reduce its costs. A retailer may find that it can integrate backward or forward and reduce its costs. Another manufacturer may find that promotion brings about a higher volume of sales and this in turn results in some economies of size. A creamery checks over the route which milk takes in going from the cow to the table. At what point, the creamery asks, can it reduce its costs? (See Box 22-1.)

---

[1]Theodore J. Kreps, "Measurement of the Social Performance of Business," Temporary National Economic Committee, Investigation of Concentration of Economic Power, Monograph No. 7 (Washington, D.C., 1940).

BOX 22-1

Questions on Milk Distribution

A rise of a penny or two in the price of bread and milk—as has occurred in recent weeks—can produce remarkable effects, not only in the economy, but also in the emotions. A politician, whose name is forgotten but whose words endure, once said:

"Milk is one of the world's great enigmas. It is obtained from contented cows, calmly grazing in warm country pastures. It nurtures babies, nourishes growing children, strengthens the aged and is considered one of nature's sublimest creations. It also rouses normally quiet men to towering rages, brings the flower of womanhood shrieking into the political arena and threatens to topple the mighty from their thrones of power."

The cry has been heard in Washington. The Senate Agriculture Committee has called for an inquiry, and Agriculture Secretary Orville L. Freeman came to New York last week and announced that he had asked the Federal Trade Commission to look into the situation on a national level. The FTC immediately complied.

Milk travels a circuitous route from the cow to the table. With every step, a little more money is tacked on until the milkman delivers it to the door.

From the farm, the milk goes to a country station where production from many farmers is accumulated each day. The milk is inspected, tested, cooled and shipped in tank trucks to the city. There it is again sampled, pasteurized, homogenized and packaged. Finally, it is delivered to homes or sold in stores.

According to industry sources, country handling and transportation cost $1\frac{1}{2}$ cents, and processing costs $2\frac{1}{2}$ cents, bringing the cost at the city plant to 16.8 cents. The milk container costs 1.9 cents and local delivery is 4.5 cents. Thus the average cost of milk delivered into a store is now approximately 23.2 cents. This does not cover the cost of milk delivered to the home which may average as much as 5 cents a quart more than store-sold milk.

The marketing manager must examine each facet of the marketing operation. His profits depend on the quality of the job he can do. Can we tell if marketing is doing a good job by looking at a breakdown of costs? Consider the figures in Box 22-2 or Box 22-3. As managers or as John Q. Citizen, where would we reduce the marketing costs shown in the examples?

THE PROBLEM

The process of evaluating almost any operation is a difficult one. It is not easy to determine the standards by which we will judge. Also, it is difficult

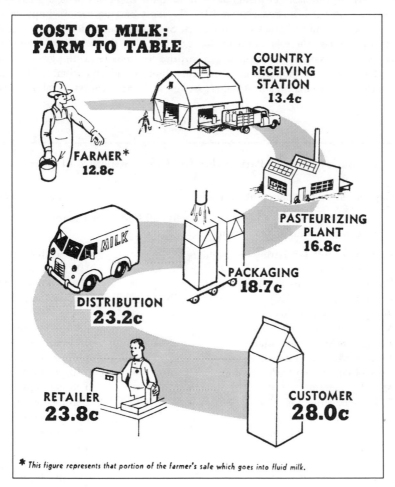

COST OF MILK: FARM TO TABLE

COUNTRY RECEIVING STATION 13.4c

FARMER* 12.8c

PASTEURIZING PLANT 16.8c

PACKAGING 18.7c

DISTRIBUTION 23.2c

RETAILER 23.8c

CUSTOMER 28.0c

* *This figure represents that portion of the farmer's sale which goes into fluid milk.*

SOURCE: Robert E. Dallos, "Milk: Case History Of a Rising Price," *New York Times,* August 7, 1966.

to isolate each small part of a complicated problem. As managers can we evaluate marketing by looking only at our profit figures, or our brand share, or our prices? Can we possibly evaluate marketing without also evaluating production, research, technology, finance, and other aspects of total performance? As citizens we would like to make an acid test of the marketing program; that is, we would like to make a social audit of marketing. But as Kreps has stated;

Concerning the basic elements of such an audit there has been a great deal of controversy. But it has been centered for the most part on certain imponderables that are not capable of exact measurement. Such imponderables are, of course, of great importance. There is no doubt, for example, that the American people want their economic system of free private enterprise to promote (1) the growth, health, and education of the population; (2) resourcefulness and invention; (3) the democratization of business organization; (4) reason and effectiveness in labor organiza-

BOX 22-2

Barley Costs as Part of the Total Cost Structure of Beer

Cost of barley production at farm level: $25.00 per acre

Average yield of barley in bushels per acre: 20 bushels per acre;
  some yields as high as 50 bushels

Price of a bushel of barley on the farm:	0.90 per bushel
Country elevator margin	0.05 per bushel
Freight to Minneapolis Market	0.25 per bushel
Commission firm's charge	0.02 per bushel
Terminal handling charge	0.04 per bushel
Minneapolis price for barley	$ 1.26 per bushel
Freight to Milwaukee Market	0.13 per bushel
Procurement and interest charges	0.06 per bushel
Cost of converting barley to malt	0.40 per bushel
Maltster margin	0.05 per bushel
Milwaukee price for malt	$ 1.90 per bushel
Cost of converting malt to beer	1.00 per bushel
Advertising costs for beer	2.50 per bushel
Transportation costs for beer	0.70 per bushel
Packaging costs for beer	1.30 per bushel
Federal tax on beer	9.00 per bushel
State tax on beer	2.00 per bushel
Brewers margin	1.00 per bushel
Beer Cost to wholesaler	$19.40 per bushel
Wholesaler margin	3.40 per bushel
Cost to retailer	$22.80 per bushel° (or 95¢ per 6-pack)
Sales price to consumer	$27.60 per bushel (or $1.15 per 6-pack)

° 1 bushel = 24 6-packs

SOURCE: Harvard Business School, Pabst Brewing Company, Case, 1961.

tion; (5) international peace; (6) the enlargement of individual liberty; (7) increased opportunity for each individual to develop to the full all his intellectual, aesthetic, spiritual, and economic capacities.[2]

In addition to the technical difficulties of evaluating, there is a problem which may be unique to marketing. This problem was explained in the Twentieth Century Fund's classic study, *Does Distribution Cost Too Much?*

The idea that it costs too much to distribute goods and that modern methods of distribution are wasteful and inefficient has taken root in the public mind. Every day the consumer is exposed to sights and sounds which seem to confirm this impression—the spectacle of four gasoline stations, one on each corner of a crossroads, the constant bombardment of costly radio programs selling everything from cigarettes to pianos, and the frequent complaint of the farmer who gets only four or five cents of the fifteen cents we pay for a quart of milk.

Quite naturally the automobile driver and the cigarette smoker and the housewife begin to wonder if all the costs of placing goods at their disposal are necessary and warranted. And since they themselves have to pay all these costs, they question so great a toll on their purchasing power. Added to this is the general belief that while invention and scientific management have increased the efficiency and lowered the costs of making goods, the cost of distributing them has remained high.[3]

As citizens, we have not really learned that the cost of a product includes more than the raw materials. We seem to fear that our expenditures will include too large an amount for parasitic operations, for waste in the distributive network, or for useless persuasion. We simply have not recognized the essentiality of the marketing process.

Other issues come to light after we point out the separate roles of individuals as producers and as consumers. As society develops, the individual no longer produces for himself, and an organization of intermediaries develops to bridge the gap between producer and consumer. The relationships which develop explain some of our problems of understanding the process. As consumers, we are well aware of the "objective" dollars we spend for goods and services, but we should also recognize that many of our values from these goods and services are "subjective." We may buy a food item because of its flavor, a necktie because of its appearance, and a hi-fi system because of its tone. The manager, on the other hand, sees his expenditure for raw materials and for other goods and services as rather objective amounts. He also records his sales in objective dollar figures. In the course of a year he makes many decisions which are designed to reduce his objective costs and increase his objective values or income—in other words, he seeks to increase

[2] Kreps, *Op. cit.*, p. 2.
[3] Paul W. Stewart and J. Frederic Dewhurst, *Does Distribution Cost Too Much?* (New York: Twentieth Century Fund, 1939), p. 3.

BOX 22-3

Distribution of consumer's dollar according to marketing function, leading farm food products, 1964

Item	Butter (pound)	Cheese, American process (half pound)	Evaporated milk (14½-ounce can)	Ice cream (half gallon)	Fresh milk (half gallon) In stores	Fresh milk (half gallon) Home delivery	Beef, choice (pound)	Pork (pound)	Lamb, choice (pound)
(1) Retail price	Cents 74.4	Cents 36.7	Cents 14.9	Cents 80.4	Cents 47.7	Cents 52.8	Cents 70.8	Cents 52.3	Cents 70.0
(2) Retailing	7.6	7.6	1.5	18.6	7.3	20.8	17.0	12.3	17.5
(3) Wholesaling, transportation, other distribution.	8.2	5.9	1.2	19.4	7.5		2.3	1.6	2.4
(4) Processing	5.6	8.1	5.8	20.6	9.8	8.9	5.3	10.1	7.4
(5) Assembly				2.6	1.4	1.4	3.8	1.7	3.2
(6) Farm value	53.0	15.1	6.4	19.2	21.7	21.7	42.4	26.6	39.5
(7) Percent of retail price: (8) Farm share	71	41	43	24	45	41	60	51	56

458

Distribution of consumer's dollar according to cost items, leading farm food products, 1964

Item	Butter (pound)	Cheese, American process (half pound)	Evaporated milk (14½-ounce can)	Ice cream (half gallon)	Fresh milk (half gallon)		Beef choice (pound)	Pork (pound)	Lamb, choice (pound)
					In stores	Home delivery			
	Cents	Cents	Cents	Cents	Cents	Cents	Cents	Cents	Cents
(1) Retail price	74.4	36.7	14.9	80.4	47.7	52.8	70.8	52.3	70.0
(2) Marketing margin	21.4	21.6	8.5	61.2	26.0	31.1	28.4	25.7	30.5
(3) Labor	6.7	6.3	1.3	22.5	10.2	16.2	12.1	14.5	14.3
(4) Buildings and equipment	4.1	3.4	.7	11.2	3.1	1.8	3.7	2.8	4.6
(5) Containers and supplies	2.3	2.1	3.0	7.9	3.0	2.6	1.4	1.2	1.7
(6) Advertising, promotion	2.2	1.3	.9	3.9	1.6	1.3	2.0	1.8	2.1
(7) Transportation, including local	1.4	1.3	.8	5.1	2.4	5.0	3.5	1.7	2.6
(8) Administrative and other	2.4	3.5	1.0	7.5	3.2	2.6	3.7	2.1	3.2
(9) Profits before income tax	2.3	3.7	.8	3.1	2.5	1.6	2.0	1.6	2.0
(10) Farm production	53.0	15.1	6.4	19.2	21.7	21.7	42.4	26.6	39.5
(11) Percentage of marketing margin:									
(12) Labor	31	29	15	37	39	52	43	56	47
(13) Buildings and equipment	19	16	8	18	12	6	13	11	15
(14) Containers and supplies	11	10	36	13	12	8	5	5	6
(15) Advertising, promotion	10	6	11	6	6	4	7	7	7
(16) Transportation	7	6	9	8	9	16	12	7	8
(17) Administrative and other	11	16	12	13	12	9	13	8	10
(18) Profits before income tax	11	17	9	5	10	5	7	6	7
(19) Total	100	100	100	100	100	100	100	100	100

SOURCE: National Commission on Food Marketing, *Food From Farmer to Consumer*, Washington, D.C., 1966, pp. 14–17.

459

his profits. But his objective income from sales may be subjective expenditures for the consumer.[4]

To add to the confusion, many of us see transportation costs, credit costs, and retailing operations as not adding value to the goods. We see an added cost but not an added value. When viewed in this light, marketing does add to the ultimate cost, but it also adds to the total value in relation to the value added to the goods by the various marketing processes. Just as there is "Value Added by Manufacturing" there is "Value Added by Marketing."

FUNCTIONS

Can a company or would any consumer eliminate the functions of marketing? Does not a buyer want to be able to contact a seller, and vice versa? Do not the manufacturer, the wholesaler, and the retailer have to impose a price on the goods? Should not the business firm ascertain the desires of a consumer so that it can help him to fulfill them? Does not someone have to transport the goods from producer through the channels to the consumers? Do we not expect the seller to maintain some liability in connection with the products he has sold? Do not companies need to be permitted to persuade people to buy?[5]

Let us face the situation properly: the consumer expects and demands much in the way of marketing services. He expects choice. He expects availability. He expects financial help in making purchases. He expects delivery. He expects adequate packaging. He expects adequate inventory. When traveling on a vacation, he expects that the petroleum producers will have distributed their products in such a way that he can procure gasoline when needed. He expects that there will be restaurants located along all the roads. It should be clear that in adjusting to the environment, marketing obviously has had to answer to the desires and needs of the consumer.

Still, most of us would agree that there are excesses and abuses in the marketing process. We would probably agree that these should be eliminated, but further examination would also convince us that some of the excesses represent the price we pay for our system. Each system has its own excesses, wastes, and prices. We find superfluous advertising, an excessive number of brands, a multiplicity of middlemen, and various restraints of trade. Some of these excesses and abuses will disappear; perhaps others will take their place. The manager is constantly doing the best he can to improve the problem areas. If he does not improve the efficiency of his marketing, he will have

[4] Alfred Kuhn, *The Study of Society: A Unified Approach* (Homewood, Ill.: Richard D. Irwin, and The Dorsey Press, 1963), p. 567.
[5] E. D. McGarry, "Some Functions of Marketing Reconsidered," in Reavis Cox and Wroe Alderson (eds.), *Theory in Marketing* (Chicago: Richard D. Irwin, 1950), pp. 263–279.

considerable difficulty remaining competitive in the marketplace. The functions of marketing are an integral part of business—a necessary part of society in our country, in the Far East, or in the Soviet Union.

EVALUATION OF MARKETING IN OUR SYSTEM

Most of us believe in an economic system in which there is considerable freedom. We want freedom to buy and sell, to produce and to consume. We want a system that operates without violence, according to law. We believe in the gains from competition, and we stress competitive effort in many ways. All this is a part of our total environment, and any evaluation of the marketing process should recognize the kind of a system in which marketing exists.

As consumers, we like to have brand choice and manufacturer choice. We want to think that the price system accurately reflects supply and demand. We hope that manufacturers and distributors make intelligent decisions based on information. We want a marketing system which helps deliver a good standard of living. But we also want efficiency in our marketing. Specialization and standardization provide the consumer some measure of efficiency. Labor-saving devices, new marketing institutions, adjustments to the dynamics of society, competition, research, and the training of people also reflect the efficiency of the distributive process.[6]

As a citizen, a stockholder, an employee, a consumer, a student, or merely an observer of the passing scene, each reader will in the years ahead ask himself many times about the quality of the marketing job. Perhaps he will find ways in which the marketing process can be improved; certainly he owes it to himself to make this one of his goals. There are a number of questions one might ask. Does the system work? Will reducing the number of distributors increase the efficiency of the system? How many retailers are too many? Is efficiency enough? Is distribution unfair? Is distribution abusive? After exhaustive study, Reavis Cox concluded:

> Obviously, in a very important sense, the system works. The society dependent upon it not only has survived; it has grown and prospered enormously. Year after year stupendous quantities of goods and services are produced, processed, sorted, moved about, transferred from owner to owner, and eventually delivered to millions of terminal buyers. Billions of transactions supported by billions of units of transportation, storage, finance, and all the rest are arranged and carried into effect. The end result: A much vaunted level of living.[7]

[6] See Theodore N. Beckman, "Criteria of Marketing Efficiency," *The Annals of the American Academy of Political and Social Science*, Vol. 209, May 1940, p. 133.
[7] Reavis Cox, *Distribution in a High-Level Economy* (Englewood Cliffs, N.J.: Prentice-Hall, 1965), p. 167.

Cox also concluded, "Specifically, it [marketing] must be judged in our society by what it does to serve rather than abuse the consumer interest, however that interest may be conceived."[8]

Another authority suggests:

The legitimacy of the system is high, since all transactions within it are voluntary and the government exercises no formal authority. . . .

In this connection it may be well to survey the difficulty of the problem. Any industrial society must make decisions about goods—what to produce, with what factors, and so forth—for the whole society. This decision requires some sort of technique for aggregating many preference systems into a single preference system—at least in a society which pays attention to individual preferences. Viewed in this light, it is difficult to imagine any technique of social decision making which could give more continuous and detailed attention to individual preference.[9]

A third expert has stated: "It [the marketing system] incorporates a delicately calibrated system of penalties and rewards which records the preferences of individuals and creates pressures to honor those preferences."[10]

The faculty of the Marketing Department at the Ohio State University has prepared a statement concerning the nature of marketing. The statement suggests that "the ends served by the marketing process are, hopefully, the more complete satisfaction of human, business, and public wants, and at the same time provision for the highest attainable degrees of utilization of our technological and human resources." The statement further points out the divergent viewpoints concerning the nature of marketing. As we attempt to evaluate this part of our whole productive process, we should be aware of these viewpoints. For example, the statement indicates that marketing has been described as *a business activity; a trade phenomenon; a frame of mind; a coordinative, integrative function in policy making; a sense of business purpose; an economic process; a structure of institutions; the process of exchanging or transferring ownership of products; a process of concentration, equalization, and dispersion; the creation of time, place, and possession utilities; a process of demand and supply adjustment; and other things as well.*[11]

If marketing is not doing a good job, where is it failing? If marketing costs too much, who gets the surplus? If there are excesses in marketing, how should they be eliminated? Each question has to be answered with the consumer in mind.

Perhaps marketing, as one component of the total business and economic

[8] *Ibid.*, p. 173.
[9] Kuhn, *Op. cit.*, p. 585.
[10] Alfred R. Oxenfeldt, *Economic Systems in Action* (New York: Reinhardt and Company, 1957), p. 8.
[11] The Marketing Faculty, *Statement of the Philosophy of Marketing* (Columbus: Ohio State University 1964).

operation, is analogous to the cell in the human body. The cells specialize and cooperate with one another. Their importance lies not in any one of them by itself, but in what it contributes to the whole. This, then, is our evaluation of the marketing process. In the authors' opinions, it definitely contributes to our society in a positive way. There are faults which remain to be corrected, efficiencies yet to be gained. The contributions, however, have been enormous.

Questions

1. On balance, do you consider marketing a plus factor in society or a negative factor?
2. To serve society best, what is the role for marketing?
3. If you think marketing costs too much, who is it that gets too much?
4. How can marketing be made more efficient? Who should decide?
5. Can you measure the efficiency of the marketing operation? Can you measure the utility of the marketing: the Value Added by Marketing?

Statements to Consider

A reason for the existence of high marketing costs is the fact that marketing requires a great amount of human labor to perform its work.

The services rendered to consumers by the marketing system constitute a reason for high marketing costs.

In distribution, the economies of scale are sometimes much less than in manufacturing; they may even be nonexistent.

As production becomes larger in scale and more specialized, as products are manufactured to stock and not to order, and as consumers demand a greater and greater variety of goods, marketing becomes more and more important and more and more costly.

SELECTED REFERENCES

Harold Barger, *Distribution's Place in the American Economy Since 1869* (Princeton, N.J.: Princeton University Press, 1955).

Reavis Cox, Wroe Alderson, and Stanley J. Shapiro, *Theory in Marketing*, Second Series (Homewood, Ill.: Richard D. Irwin, 1964).

Reavis Cox, in association with Charles S. Goodman and Thomas C. Fichandler, *Distribution in a High-Level Economy* (Englewood Cliffs, N.J.: Prentice-Hall, 1965).

John A. Howard, *Marketing Theory* (Boston: Allyn and Bacon, 1965).

° Stanley C. Hollander, "Measuring the Cost and Value of Marketing," *Business Topics*, Vol. 9, No. 3, Summer 1961, pp. 17–27.

° Paul Mazur, "Soliloquy in Marketing," in *Marketing: A Maturing Discipline*, Proceedings of the Winter Conference of the American Marketing Association, December 1960, pp. 10–17.

° Roland S. Vaile, "Efficiency Within the Marketing Structure," *Journal of Marketing*, Vol. 5, No. 4, April 1941, p. 350.

Generalizations Were Taken From:

Rayburn D. Tousley, Eugene Clark, and Fred E. Clark, *Principles of Marketing* (New York: The Macmillan Company, 1962).

Roland S. Vaile, E. T. Grether, and Reavis Cox, *Marketing in the American Economy* (New York: The Ronald Press Company, 1952).

Glossary Of
Marketing Definitions[1]

[1]Compiled by Ralph S. Alexander and the Committee on Definitions of the American Marketing Association, *Marketing Definitions: A Glossary of Marketing Terms* (Chicago: American Marketing Association, 1960), pp. 9–23.

A

ADVERTISING—Any paid form of non-personal presentation and promotion of ideas, goods, or services by an identified sponsor. It involves the use of such media as the following:

Magazine and newspaper space
Motion pictures
Outdoor (posters, signs, skywriting, etc.)
Direct mail
Novelties (calendars, blotters, etc.)
Radio and television
Cards (car, bus, etc.)
Catalogues
Directories and references
Programs and menus
Circulars

This list is intended to be illustrative, not inclusive.

Comment. Advertising is generally but not necessarily carried on through mass media. While the postal system is not technically considered a "paid" medium, material distributed by mail is definitely a form of presentation that is paid for by the sponsor. For kindred activities see "Publicity" and "Sales Promotion."

Advertising Research—See Marketing Research.

AGENT—A business unit which negotiates purchases or sales or both but does not take title to the goods in which it deals.

Comment. The agent usually performs fewer marketing functions than does the merchant. He commonly receives his remuneration in the form of a commission or fee. He usually does not represent both buyer and seller in the same transaction. Examples are: broker, commission merchant, manufacturers agent, selling agent, and resident buyer. The Committee recommends that the term Functional Middleman no longer be applied to this type of agent. It is hardly logical or consistent in view of the fact that he performs fewer marketing functions than other middlemen.

ASSEMBLING—The activities involved in concentrating supplies or assortments of goods or services to facilitate sale or purchase.

Comment. The concentration involved here may affect a quantity of like goods or a variety of goods. It includes the gathering of adequate and representative stocks by wholesalers and retailers.

AUTOMATIC SELLING—The retail sale of goods or services through currency operated machines activated by the ultimate-consumer buyer.

Comment. Most, if not all, machines now used in automatic selling are coin operated. There are reports, however, of promising experiments with such devices that may be activated by paper currency; machines that provide change for a dollar bill are already on the market.

AUXILIARY   EQUIPMENT—See EQUIPMENT.

B

BRANCH HOUSE (Manufacturer's)— An establishment maintained by a manufacturer, detached from the head-quarters establishment and used primarily for the purpose of stocking, selling, delivering, and servicing his prodcut.

BRANCH OFFICE (Manufacturer's)— An establishment maintained by a manufacturer, detached from the head-quarters establishment and used for the purpose of selling his products or providing service.

Comment. The characteristic of the branch house that distinguishes it from the branch office is the fact that it is used in the physical storage, handling, and delivery of merchandise. Otherwise the two are identical.

BRANCH STORE—A subsidiary retailing business owned and operated at a separate location by an established store.

BRAND—A name, term, sign, symbol, or design, or a combination of them which is intended to identify the goods or services of one seller or group of sellers and to differentiate them from those of competitors.

Comment. A brand may include a brand name, a trade mark, or both. The term brand is sufficiently comprehensive to include pratically all means of identification except perhaps the package and the shape of the product. All brand names and all trade marks are brands or parts of brands but not all brands are either brand names or trade marks. Brand is the inclusive general term. The others are more particularized.

See also NATIONAL BRAND and PRIVATE BRAND.

BRAND MANAGER—See product Management.

BRAND NAME—A brand or part of a brand consisting of a word, letter, group of words or letters comprising a name which is intended to identify the goods or services of a seller or a group of sellers and to differentiate them from those of competitors.

Comment. The brand name is that part of a brand which can be vocalized—the utterable.

BROKER—An agent who does not have direct physical control of the goods in which he deals but represents either buyer or seller in negotiating purchases or sales for his principal.

Comment. The broker's powers as to prices and terms of sale are usually limited by his principal.

The term is often loosely used in a generic sense to include such specific business units as free-lance brokers, manufacturer's agents, selling agents, and purchasing agents.

BUYING POWER—See Purchasing Power.

C

CANVASSER—See House-to-House Salesman.

CASH AND CARRY WHOLESALER —See Wholesaler

CHAIN STORE—CHAIN STORE SYSTEM—A group of retail stores or essentially the same type, centrally owned and with some degree of centralized control of operation. The term Chain Store may also refer to a single store as a unit of such a group.

Comment. According to the dictionary, two may apparently be construed to constitute a "group."

CHANNEL OF DISTRIBUTION—The structure of intra-company organization units and extra-company agents and dealers, wholesale and retail, through which a commodity, product, or service is marketed.

Comment. This definition was designed to be broad enough to include (a.) both a firm's internal marketing organization units and the outside business units it uses in its marketing work and (b.) both the channel structure of the individual firm and the entire complex available to all firms.

COMMERCIAL AUCTION—An agent business unit which effects the sale of goods through an auctioneer,who, under specified rules, solicits bids or offers from buyers and has power to accept the highest bids of responsible bidders and, thereby, consummates the sale.

Comment. The auctioneer usually but not always is a paid employee of an auction company which is in the business of conducting auctions.

COMMISSION HOUSE (sometimes called Commission Merchant)—An agent who usually exercises physical control over and negotiates the sale of the goods he handles. The commission house usually enjoys broader powers as to prices, methods, and terms of sale than does the broker although it must obey instructions issued by the principal. It generally arranges delivery, extends necessary credit, collects, deducts its fees, and remits the balance to the principal.

Comment. Most of those who have defined the commission house state that it has possession of the goods it handles. In its strict meaning the word "possession" connotes to some extent the idea of ownership; in its legal meaning it involves a degree of control somewhat beyond that usually enjoyed by the commission merchant. Therefore, the phrase, "physical control," was used instead.

The fact that many commission houses are not typical in their operations does not subtract from their status as commission houses.

COMMISSARY STORE—See Industrial Store

COMMODITY EXCHANGE—An organization usually owned by the member-traders, which provides facilities for bringing together buyers and sellers of specified commodities, or their agents, for promoting trades, either spot or futures or both, in these commodities.

Comment. Agricultural products or their intermediately processed derivatives are the commodities most often traded on such exchanges.

Some sort of organization for clearing future contracts usually operates as an adjunct to or an arm of a commodity exchange.

COMPANY STORE—See Industrial Store.

CONSUMER RESEARCH—See Marketing Research.

CONSUMERS' COOPERATIVE—A retail business owned and operated by ultimate consumers to purchase and distribute goods and services primarily to the membership—sometimes called purchasing cooperatives.

Comment. The Consumers' Cooperative is a type of cooperative marketing institution.

Through federation, retail units frequently acquire wholesaling and manufacturing institutions. The definition confines the use of the term to the cooperative purchasing activities of ultimate consumers and does not embrace collective buying by business establishments or institutions.

CONSUMERS' GOODS—Goods destined for use by ultimate consumers or households and in such form that they can be used without commercial processing.

Comment. Certain articles, for example, typewriters, may be either consumers' goods or industrial goods depending upon whether they are destined for use by the ultimate consumer or household or by an industrial, business, or institutional user.

CONVENIENCE GOODS—Those consumers' goods which the customer usually purchases frequently, immediately, and with the minimum of effort in comparison and buying.

Examples of merchandise customarily bought as convenience goods are; tobacco products, soap, newspapers, magazines, chewing gum, small packaged confections, and many food products.

Comment. These articles are usually of small unit value and are bought in small quantites at any one time, although when a number of them are bought together as in a supermarket, the combined purchase may assume sizeable proportions in both bulk and value.

The convenience involved may be in terms of nearness to the buyer's home, easy accessibility to some means of transport, or close proximity to places where people go during the day or evening, for example, downtown to work.

COOPERATIVE MARKETING—The process by which independent producers, wholesalers, retailers, consumers, or combinations of them act collectively in buying or selling or both.

D

DEALER—A firm that buys and re-sells merchandise at either retail or wholesale.

Comment. The term is naturally ambiguous. For clarity, it should be used with a qualifying adjective, such as "retail" or "wholesale."

DEPARTMENT STORE—A large retailing business unit which handles a wide variety of shopping and specialty goods, including women's ready-to-wear and accessories, men's and boy's wear, piece goods, small wares, and home furnishings, and which is organized into separate departments for purposes of promotion, service and control.
Examples of very large department stores are Macy's, New York, J. L. Hudson Co. of Detroit, Marshall Field & Co. of Chicago, and Famous, Barr of St. Louis. Two well-known smaller ones are Bresee's of Oneonta, New York, and A. B. Wycoff of Stroudsburg, Penn.

Comment. Many department stores have become units of chains, commonly called "ownership groups," since each store retains its local identity, even though centrally owned. The definition above stresses three elements: large size, wide variety of clothing and home furnishings, and departmentization. Size is not spelled out in terms of either sales volume or number of employees, since the concept keeps changing upwards. Most department stores in 1960 had sales in excess of one million dollars.

DIRECT SELLING—The process whereby the firm responsible for production sells to the user, ultimate consumer, or retailer without intervening middlemen.
The Committee recommends that when this term is used, it be so qualified as to indicate clearly the precise meaning intended (direct to retailer, direct to user, direct to ultimate consumer, etc.).

Comment. The phrase "firm responsible for production" is substituted for "producer" in the old definition so as to include the firm that contracts out some or all of the processes of making the goods it sells direct, for example the drug house that has its vitamin pills tableted by a contractor specializing in such work.

DISCOUNT HOUSE—A retailing business unit, featuring consumer durable items, competing on a basis of price appeal, and operating on a relatively low markup and with a minimum of customer service.

DISCRETIONARY FUND—Discretionary income enlarged by the amount of new credit extensions, which also may be deemed spendable as a result of consumer decision relatively free of prior commitment or pressure of need.

Comment. These are the definitions of the National Industrial Conference Board, which publishes a quarterly Discretionary Income Index Series. Discretionary Income is calculated by deducting from disposable personal income (a.) a computed historical level of outlays for food and clothing; (b.) all outlays for medical services, utilities, and public transportation; (c.) payment of fixed commitments, such as rent, home owner taxes, net insurance payments, and installment debt; (d.) homeowner taxes; and (e.) imputed income and income in kind.

DISCRETIONARY INCOME—That portion of personal income, in excess of the amount necessary to maintain a defined or historical standard of living, which may be saved with no immediate impairment of living standards or may be as a result of consumer decision relatively free of prior commitment or pressure of need.

DISPOSABLE INCOME—Personal income remaining after the deduction of taxes on personal income and compulsory payment, such as social security levies.

Comment. This is substantially the Department of Commerce concept.

DISTRIBUTION—The Committee recommends that the term Distribution be used as synonymous with Marketing.

Comment. The term Distribution is also sometimes used to refer to the extent of market coverage.

In using this term marketing men should clearly distinguish it from the sense in which it is employed in economic theory, that is, the process of dividing the fund of value produced by industry among the several factors engaged in economic production.

For these reasons marketing men may be wise to use the term sparingly.

DISTRIBUTION COST ANALYSIS—See Marketing Cost Analysis.

DISTRIBUTOR—In its general usage, this term is synonymous with "Wholesaler."

Comment. In some trades and by many firms it is used to designate an outlet having some sort of preferential relationship with the manufacturer. This meaning is not so widely used or so standardized as to justify inclusion in the definition.

The term is sometimes used to designate a manufacturer's agent or a sales representative in the employ of a manufacturer.

DROP SHIPMENT WHOLESALER—See Wholesaler.

E

EQUIPMENT—Those industrial goods that do not become part of the physical product and which are exhausted only after repeated use, such as Machinery, Installed Equipment and Accessories, or Auxiliary Equipment.

Installed Equipment includes such items as boilers, linotype machines, power lathes, bank vaults.

Accessories include such items as gauges, meters, and control devices.

Auxiliary Equipment includes such items as trucks, typewriters, filing cases, and industrial hoists.

EXCLUSIVE OUTLET SELLING—That form of selective selling whereby sales of an article or service or brand of an article to any one type of buyer are confined to one retailer or wholesaler in each area, usually on a contractual basis.

Comment. This definition does not include the practice of designating two or more wholesalers or retailers in an area as selected outlets. While this practice is a form of Selective Selling, it is not Exclusive Outlet Selling.

The term does not apply to the reverse contractual relationship in which a dealer must buy exclusively from a supplier.

F

FABRICATING MATERIALS—Those industrial goods which become a part of the finished product and which have undergone processing beyond that required for raw materials but not as much as finished parts.

Comment. Examples are plastic moulding compounds.

FACILITATING AGENCIES IN MARKETING—Those agencies which perform or assist in the performance of one or a number of the marketing functions but which neither take title to goods nor negotiate purchases or sales.

Common types are banks, railroads, storage warehouses, commodity exchanges, stock yards, insurance companies, graders and inspectors, advertising agencies, firms engaged in marketing research, cattle loan companies, furniture marts, and packers and shippers.

FACTOR—(1.) A specialized financial institution engaged in factoring accounts receivable and lending on the security of inventory.

(2.) A type of commission house which often advances funds to the consigner, identified chiefly with the raw cotton and naval stores trades.

Comment. The type of factor described in (1) above operates extensively in the textile field but is expanding into other fields.

FACTORING—A specialized financial function whereby producers, wholesalers, and retailers sell their accounts receivable to financial institutions, including factors and banks, often on a non-recourse basis.

Comment. Commercial banks as well as factors and finance companies engage in this activity.

FAIR TRADE—Retail resale price maintenance imposed by suppliers of branded goods under authorization of state and federal laws.

Comment. This is a special usage of the term promulgated by the advocates of resale price maintenance and bears no relation to the fair practices concept of the Federal Trade Commission; nor is it the antithesis of unfair trading outlawed by the antitrust laws.

G

GENERAL STORE—A small retailing business unit, not departmentized, usually located in a rural community and primarily engaged in selling a general assortment of merchandise of which the most important line is food, and the more important subsidiary lines are notions, apparel, farm supplies, and gasoline. These stores are often known as "country general stores."

Comment. This is roughly the Bureau of the Census usage.

GRADING—Assigning predetermined standards of quality classifications to individual units or lots of a commodity.

Comment. This process of assignment may be carried on by sorting.

This term is often defined so as to include the work of setting up classes or grades. This work is really a part of standardization.

H

HOUSE-TO-HOUSE SALESMAN—A salesman who is primarily engaged in making sales direct to ultimate consumers in their homes.

Comment. The term Canvasser is often employed as synonymous with House-to-House Salesman. Due to its extensive use in fields other than marketing this usage is not recommended.

I

INDEPENDENT STORE—A retailing business unit which is controlled by its own individual ownership or management rather than from without, except insofar as its management is limited by voluntary group arrangements.

Comment. This definition includes a member of a voluntary group organization. It is recognized that the voluntary group possesses many of the characteristics of and presents many of the same problems as the chain store system. In the final analysis, however, the members of the voluntary groups are independent stores, cooperating, perhaps temporarily, in the accomplishment of certain marketing purposes. Their collective action is entirely voluntary and the retailers engaging in it consider themselves to be independent.

INDUSTRIAL GOODS—Goods which are destined to be sold primarily for use in producing other goods or rendering services as contrasted with goods destined to be sold primarily to the ultimate consumer.

They include equipment (installed and

accessory), component parts, maintenance, repair and operating supplies, raw materials, fabricating materials.

Comment. The distinguishing characteristics of these goods is the purpose for which they are primarily destined to be used, in carrying on business or industrial activities rather than for consumption by individual ultimate consumers or resale to them. The category also includes merchandise destined for use in carrying on various types of institutional enterprises.

Relatively few goods are exclusively industrial goods. The same article may, under one set of circumstances, be an industrial good, and under other conditions a consumers' good.

INDUSTRIAL STORE—A retail store owned and operated by a company or governmental unit to sell primarily to its employees.

Non-governmental establishments of this type are often referred to as "Company Stores" or "Commissary Stores." In certain trades the term "Company Store" is applied to a store through which a firm sells its own products, often together with those of other manufacturers, to the consumer market.

Comment. Many of these establishments are not operated for profit. The matter of the location of the control over and responsibility for these stores rather than the motive for their operation constitutes their distinguishing characteristic.

INSTALLED   EQUIPMENT—See **Equipment.**

J

JOBBER—This term is widely used as a synonym of "wholesaler" or "distributor."

Comment. The term is sometimes used in certain trades and localities to designate special types of wholesalers. This usage is especially common in the distribution of agricultural products. The characteristics of the wholesalers so designated vary from trade to trade and from locality to locality. Most of the schedules submitted to the Bureau of the Census by the members of the wholesale trades show no clear line of demarcation between those who call themselves jobbers and those who prefer to be known as wholesalers. Therefore, it does not seem wise to attempt to set up any general basis of distinction between the terms in those few trades or markets in which one exists. There are scattered examples of special distinctive usage of the term "Jobber." The precise nature of such usage must be sought in each trade or area in which it is employed.

L

LIMITED   FUNCTION   WHOLESALER—See **Wholesaler.**

LOSS LEADER—A product of known or accepted quality priced at a loss or no profit for the purpose of attracting patronage to a store.

Comment. This term is peculiar to the retail trade—elsewhere the same item is called a "leader" or a "special."

M

MAIL-ORDER HOUSE (retail)—A retailing business that receives its orders primarily by mail or telephone and generally offers its goods and services for its sale from a catalogue or other printed material.

Comment. Other types of retail stores often conduct a mail order business, usually through departments set up for that purpose, although this fact does not make them mail order houses. On the other hand, some firms that originally confined themselves to the mail order business now also operate chain store systems. For example, Sears Roebuck and Company and Montgomery Ward and Company are both mail order houses and chain store systems.

MAIL-ORDER   WHOLESALER—See **Wholesaler.**

MANUFACTURER'S AGENT—An agent who generally operates on an extended contractual basis; often sells within an exclusive territory; handles non-competing but related lines of goods; and possesses limited authority with regard to prices and terms of sale. He may be authorized to sell a definite portion of his principal's output.

Comment. The manufacturer's agent has often been defined as a species of broker. In the majority of cases this seems to be substantially accurate. It is probably more accurate in seeking to define the entire group not to classify them as a specialized type of broker but to regard them as a special variety of agent since many of them carry stocks. The term "Manufacturer's Representative" is sometimes applied to this agent. Since this term is also used to designate a salesman in the employ of a manufacturer, its use as a synonym for "Manufacturer's Agent" is discouraged.

MANUFACTURER'S STORE—A retail store owned and operated by a manufacturer, sometimes as outlets for his goods, sometimes primarily for experimental or publicity purposes.

MARKET—(1.) The aggregate of forces or conditions within which buyers and sellers make decisions that result in the transfer of goods and services.
(2.) The aggregate demand of the potential buyers of a commodity or service.

Comment. The business man often uses the term to mean an opportunity to sell his goods. He also often attaches to it a connotation of a geographical area, such as the "New England market," or of a customer group, such as the "college market" or the "agricultural market." Retailers often use the term to mean the aggregate group of suppliers from whom a buyer purchases.

MARKET ANALYSIS—A sub-division of marketing research which involves the measurement of the extent of a market

and the determination of its characteristics.

Comment. See also Marketing Research. The activity described above consists essentially in the process of exploring and evaluating the marketing possibilities of the aggregates described in (2.) of the definition of Market.

MARKET POTENTIAL (also Market or Total Market)—A calculation of maximum possible sales opportunities for all sellers of a good or service during a stated period.

MARKET SHARE (or Sales Potential)—The ratio of a company's sales to the total industry sales on either an actual or potential basis.

Comment. This term is often used to designate the part of total industry sales a company hopes or expects to get. Since this concept usually has in it a considerable element of "blue sky," this usage is not encouraged.

MARKETING—The performance of business activities that direct the flow of goods and services from producer to consumer or user.

Comment. The task of defining Marketing may be approached from at least three points of view.
(1.) The "legalistic" of which the following is a good example: "Marketing includes all activities having to do with effecting changes in the ownership and possession of goods and services." It seems obviously of doubtful desirability to adopt a definition which throws so much emphasis upon the legal phases of what is essentially a commercial subject.
(2.) The "economic" examples of which are: "That part of economics which deals with the creation of time, place, and possession utilities."
"That phase of business activity through which human wants are satisfied by the exchange of goods and services for some valuable consideration."
Such definitions are apt to assume somewhat more understanding of economic concepts

than are ordinarily found in the market place. (3.) The "factual or descriptive" of which the definition suggested by the Committee is an example. This type of definition merely seeks to describe its subject in terms likely to be understood by both professional economists and business men without reference to legal or economic implications.

This definition seeks to include such facilitating activities as marketing research, transportation, certain aspects of product and package planning, and the use of credit as a means of influencing patronage.

MARKETING BUDGET—A statement of the planned dollar sales and planned marketing costs for a specified future period.

Comment. The use of this term is sometimes confined to an estimate of future sales. This does not conform to the general use of the term "budget" which includes schedules of both receipts and expenditures. If the marketing budget is to be used as a device to facilitate marketing control and management, it should include the probable cost of getting the estimated volume of sales. The failure to allow proper weight to this item in their calculations is one of the most consistently persistent and fatal mistakes made by American business concerns. It has led to much of the striving after unprofitable volume that has been so costly.

A firm may prepare a marketing budget for each brand or product or for a group of brands or products it sells or for each group of customers to whom it markets. See also Sales Budget.

MARKETING COOPERATIVE—See Producers' Cooperative Marketing.

MARKETING COST ACCOUNTING— The branch of cost accounting which involves the allocation of marketing costs according to customers, marketing units, products, territories, or marketing activities.

MARKETING COSTS ANALYSIS— The study and evaluation of the relative profitability or costs of different marketing units, commodities, territories, or marketing activities.

Comment. Marketing Cost Accounting is one of the tools used in Marketing Cost Analysis.

MARKETING FUNCTION—A major specialized activity or group of related activities performed in marketing.

Comment. There is no generally accepted list of marketing functions, nor is there any generally accepted basis on which the lists compiled by various writers are chosen.

The reason for these limitations is fairly apparent. Under this term students of marketing have sought to squeeze a heterogeneous and non-consistent group of activities. Some of them are broad business functions with special marketing implications; others are peculiar to the marketing process. The function of assembling is performed through buying, selling, and transportation. Assembling, storage, and transporting are general economic functions; selling and buying are more nearly individual in character. Most of the lists fail sadly to embrace all the activities a marketing manager worries about in the course of doing his job.

MARKETING MANAGEMENT—The planning, direction and control of the entire marketing activity of a firm or division of a firm, including the formulation of marketing objectives, policies, programs and strategy, and commonly embracing product development, organizing and staffing to carry out plans, supervising marketing operations, and controlling marketing performance.

Comment. In most firms the man who performs these functions is a member of top management in that he plays a part in determining company policy, in making product decisions, and in coordinating marketing operations with other functional activities to achieve the objectives of the company as a whole.

No definition of his position is included in this report because there is no uniformity in the titles applied to it. He is variously designated Marketing Manager, Director of Marketing, Vice President for Marketing, Director or Vice President of Marketing and Sales, General Sales Manager.

MARKETING PLANNING—The work of setting up objectives for marketing activity and of determining and scheduling the steps necessary to achieve such objectives.

Comment. This term includes not only the work of deciding upon the goals or results to be attained through marketing activity but also the determination in detail of exactly how they are to be accomplished.

MARKETING POLICY—A course of action established to obtain consistency of marketing decisions and operations under recurring and essentially similar circumstances.

MARKETING RESEARCH—The systematic gathering, recording, and analyzing of data about problems relating to the marketing of goods and services. Such research may be undertaken by impartial agencies or by business firms or their agents for the solution of their marketing problems.

Comment. Marketing Research is the inclusive term which embraces all research activities carried on in connection with the management of marketing work. It includes various subsidiary types of research, such as (1) Market Analysis, which is a study of the size, location, nature, and characteristics of markets, (2) Sales Analysis (or Research), which is largely an analysis of sales data, (3) Consumer Research, of which Motivation Research is a type, which is concerned chiefly with the discovery and analysis of consumer attitudes, reactions, and preferences, and (4) Advertising Research which is carried on chiefly as an aid to the management of advertising work. The techniques of Operations Research are often useful in Marketing Research.

The term Market Research is often loosely used as synonymous with Marketing Research.

MERCHANDISING—The planning and supervision involved in marketing the particular merchandise or service at the places, times, and prices and in the quantities which will best serve to realize the marketing objectives of the business.

Comment. This term has been used in a great variety of meanings, most of them confusing. The usage recommended by the Committee adheres closely to the essential meaning of the word. The term is most widely used in this sense in the wholesaling and retailing trades.

Many manufacturers designate this activity as Product Planning or Management and include in it such tasks as selecting the article to be produced or stocked and deciding such matters as the size, appearance, form, packaging, quantities to be bought or made, time of procurement, and price lines to be offered.

MERCHANT—A business unit that buys, takes title to, and resells merchandise.

Comment. The distinctive feature of this middleman lies in the fact that he takes title to the goods he handles. The extent to which he performs the marketing functions is incidental to the definition. Wholesalers and retailers are the chief types of merchants.

MIDDLEMAN—A business concern that specializes in performing operations or rendering services directly involved in the purchase and/or sale of goods in the process of their flow from producer to consumer.

Middlemen are of two types, MERCHANTS and AGENTS.

Comment. The essence of the middleman's operation lies in the fact that he plays an active and prominent part in the negotiations leading up to transactions of purchase and sale. This is what distinguishes him from a Marketing Facilitating Agent who, while he performs certain marketing functions, participates only incidentally in negotiations of purchase and sale.

This term is very general in its meaning. It also possesses an unfortunate emotional content. Therefore, the Committee recommends that whenever possible more specific terms be used, such as agent, merchant, retailer, wholesaler.

MISSIONARY SALESMAN—A salesman employed by a manufacturer to call on customers of his distributors, usually to develop good will and stimulate demand, to help or induce them to promote the sale of his employer's goods, to help them train their salesmen to do so, and, often, to take orders for delivery by such distributors.

MOTIVATION RESEARCH—A group of techniques developed by the behavioral scientists which are used by marketing researchers to discover factors influencing marketing behavior.

Comment. These techniques are widely used outside the marketing sphere, for example, to discover factors influencing the behavior of employees and voters. The Committee has confined its definition to the marketing uses of the tool.

Motivation Research is only one of several ways to study marketing behavior.

N

NATIONAL BRAND—A manufacturer's or producer's brand, usually enjoying wide territorial distribution.

Comment. The usage of the terms National Brand and Private Brand in this report, while generally current and commonly accepted, is highly illogical and non-descriptive. But since it is widespread and persistent, the Committee embodies it in this report.

P

PERSONAL SELLING—Oral presentation in a conversation with one or more prospective purchasers for the purpose of making sales.

Comment. This definition contemplates that the presentation may be either formal, (as a "canned" sales talk), or informal, al-

though it is rather likely to be informal, either in the actual presence of the customer or by telephone although usually the former, either to an individual or to a small group, although usually the former.

PHYSICAL DISTRIBUTION—The management of the movement and handling of goods from the point of production to the point of consumption or use.

PRICE CUTTING—Offering merchandise or a service for sale at a price below that recognized as usual or appropriate by its buyers and sellers.

Comment. One obvious criticism of this definition is that it is indefinite. But that very indefiniteness also causes it to be more accurately descriptive of a concept which is characterized by a high degree of indefiniteness in the mind of the average person affected by price cutting.

Traders' ideas of what constitutes price cutting are so vague and indefinite that any precise or highly specific definition of the phenomenon is bound to fail to include all its manifestations. If you ask a group of traders in a specific commodity to define price cutting, you will get as many conflicting formulas as there are traders. But if you ask those same traders at any particular time whether selling at a certain price constitutes price cutting, you will probably get a considerable degree of uniformity of opinion. It is percisely this condition which the definition is designed to reflect.

PRICE LEADER—A firm whose pricing behavior is followed by other companies in the same industry.

Comment. The price leadership of a firm may be limited to a certain geographical area, as in the oil business, or to certain products or groups of products, as in the steel business.

PRIVATE BRANDS—Brands sponsored by merchants or agents as distinguished from those sponsored by manufacturers or producers.

Comment. This usage is thoroughly illogical, since no seller wants his brand to be private in the sense of being secret and all brands are private in the sense that they are special and not common or general in use. But the usage is common in marketing literature and among traders. Therefore the Committee presents it in this report.

PRODUCERS' COOPERATIVE MARKETING—That type of cooperative marketing which primarily involves the sale of goods or services of the associated producing membership. May perform only an assembly or brokerage function but in some cases, notably milk marketing, extends into processing and distribution of the members' production.

Comment. Many producers' cooperative marketing associations also buy for their members. This fact does not subtract from their status as producers' cooperatives; This is especially true of the farm cooperatives.

The term does not include those activities of trade associations that affect only indirectly the sales of the membership. Such activities are the maintenance of credit rating bureaus, design registration bureaus, and brand protection machinery.

PRODUCT LINE—A group of products that are closely related either because they satisfy a class of need, are used together, are sold to the same customer groups, are marketed through the same type of outlets or fall within given price ranges. Example, carpenters' tools.

Comment. Sub-lines of products may be distinguished, such as hammers or saws, within a Product Line.

PRODUCT MANAGEMENT—The planning, direction, and control of all phases of the life cycle of products, including the creation or discovery of ideas for new products, the screening of such ideas, the coordination of the work of research and physical development of products, their packaging and branding, their introduction on the market, their market development, their modification,

the discovery of new uses for them, their repair and servicing, and their deletion.

Comment. It is not safe to think of Product Management as the work of the executive known as the Product Manager, because the dimensions of his job vary widely from company to company, sometimes embracing all the activities listed in the definition and sometimes being limited to the sales promotion of the products in his care.

PRODUCT MIX—The composite of products offered for sale by a firm or a business unit.

Comment. Tooth paste is a product. The 50 cent tube of Whosis ammoniated tooth paste is an item. Tooth pastes and powders, mouth washes, and other allied items compose an oral hygiene product line. Soaps, cosmetics, dentifrices, drug items, cake mixes, shortenings and other items may comprise a product mix if marketed by the same company.

PUBLICITY—Non-personal stimulation of demand for a product, service or business unit by planting commercially significant news about it in a published medium or obtaining favorable presentation of it upon radio, television, or stage that is not paid for by the sponsor.

Comment. Retailers use the term to denote the sum of the functions of advertising, display, and publicity as defined above.

PURCHASING POWER (Buying Power)—The capacity to purchase possessed by an individual buyer, a group of buyers, or the aggregate of the buyers in an area or a market.

R

RACK JOBBER—A wholesaling business unit that markets specialized lines of merchandise to certain types of retail stores and provides the special services of selective brand and item merchandising and arrangement, maintenance, and stocking of display racks.

Comment. The Rack Jobber usually, but not always, puts his merchandise in the store of the retailer on consignment. Rack Jobbers are most prevalent in the food business.

RESALE PRICE MAINTENANCE— Control by a supplier of the selling prices of his branded goods at subsequent stages of distribution by means of contractual agreement under fair trade laws or other devices.

RESIDENT BUYER—An agent who specializes in buying, on a fee or commission basis, chiefly for retailers.

Comment. The term as defined above, is limited to agents residing in the market cities who charge their retail principals fees for buying assistance rendered, but there are resident buying offices that are owned by out-of-town stores and some that are owned cooperatively by a group of stores. The former are called *private* offices and the latter *associated* offices. Neither of them should be confused with the central buying office of the typical chain, where the buying function is performed by the office directly, not acting as a specialized assistant to store buyers. Resident Buyers should also be distinguished from apparel *merchandise brokers* who represent competing manufacturers in the garment trades and have as customers out-of-town smaller stores in search of fashion merchandise. These brokers are paid by the manufacturers to whom they bring additional business, on a percentage of sales basis.

RETAILER—A merchant, or occasionally an agent, whose main business is selling directly to the ultimate consumer.

Comment. The retailer is to be distinguished by the nature of his sales rather than by the way he procures the goods in which he deals. The size of the units in which he sells is an incidental rather than a primary element in his character. His essential distinguishing mark is the fact that his typical sale is made to the ultimate consumer.

RETAILER COOPERATIVE—A group of independent retailers organized to buy cooperatively either through a jointly owned warehouse or through a buying club.

Comment. Their cooperative activities may include operating under a group name, joint advertising and cooperative managerial supervision.

RETAILING—The activities involved in selling directly to the ultimate consumer.

Comment. This definition includes all forms of selling to the ultimate consumer. It embraces the direct-to-consumer sales activities of the producer whether through his own stores, by house-to-house canvass, or by mail order. It does not cover the sale by producers of industrial goods, by industrial supply houses, or by retailers to industrial, commercial, or institutional buyers for use in the conduct of their enterprises.

S

SALES AGENT—See Selling Agent.

SALES ANALYSIS—A subdivision of Marketing Research which involves the systematic study and comparison of sales data.

Comment. The purpose of such analysis is usually to aid in marketing management by providing sales information along the lines of market areas, organizational units, products or product groups, customers or customer groups, or such other units as may be useful.

SALES BUDGET—The part of the marketing budget which is concerned with planned dollar sales and planned costs of personal selling during a specified future period.

SALES FORECAST—An estimate of sales, in dollars or physical units for a specified future period under a proposed marketing plan or program and under an assumed set of economic and other forces outside the unit for which the forecast is made. The forecast may be for a specified item of merchandise or for an entire line.

Comment. Two sets of factors are involved in making a Sales Forecast; (1) those forces outside the control of the firm for which the forecast is made that are likely to influence its sales, and (2) changes in the marketing methods or practices of the firm that are likely to affect its sales.

In the course of planning future activities, the management of a given firm may make several sales forecasts each consisting of an estimate of probable sales if a given marketing plan is adopted or a given set of outside forces prevails. The estimated effects that several marketing plans may have on Sales and Profits may be compared in the process of arriving at that marketing program which will, in the opinion of the officials of the company, be best designed to promote its welfare.

SALES MANAGEMENT—The planning, direction, and control of the personal selling activities of a business unit, including recruiting, selecting, training, equipping, assigning, routing, supervising, paying, and motivating as these tasks apply to the personal sales force.

Comment. These activities are sometimes but not generally designated Sales Administration or Sales Force Management.

SALES MANAGER—The executive who plans, directs, and controls the activities of salesmen.

Comment. This definition distinguishes sharply between the manager who conducts the personal selling activities of a business unit and his superior, the executive, variously called Marketing Manager, Director of Marketing, Vice President for Marketing, who has charge of all marketing activities. The usage of this form of organization has been growing rapidly during recent years.

SALES PLANNING—That part of the Marketing Planning work which is concerned with making sales forecasts, devising programs for reaching the sales target, and deriving a sales budget.

SALES POTENTIAL—See Market Share.

SALES PROMOTION—(1.) In a specific sense, those marketing activities, other than personal selling, advertising, and publicity, that stimulate consumer purchasing and dealer effectiveness, such as display, shows and exhibitions, demonstrations, and various non-recurrent selling efforts not in the ordinary routine. (2.) In retailing, all methods of stimulating customer purchasing, including personal selling, advertising, and publicity.

Comment. This definition includes the two most logical and commonly accepted usages of this much abused term. It is the suggestion of the Committee that insofar as possible, the use of the term be confined to the first of the two definitions given above.

SALES QUOTA—A projected volume of sales assigned to a marketing unit for use in the management of sales efforts. It applies to a specified period and may be expressed in dollars or in physical units.

Comment. The quota may be used in checking the efficiency or stimulating the efforts of or in remunerating individual salesmen or other personnel engaged in sales work.

A quota may be for a salesman, a territory, a department, a branch house, a wholesaler or retailer, or for the company as a whole. It may be different from the sales figure set up in the sales budget. Since it is a managerial device, it is not an immutable figure inexorably arrived at by the application of absolutely exact statistical formulas.

SALES RESEARCH—See Marketing Research and Sales Analysis.

SELECTIVE SELLING—The policy of selling to a limited number of customers in a market.

SELF SELECTION—The method used in retailing by which the customer may choose the desired merchandise without direct assistance of store personnel.

SELF SERVICE—The method used in retailing whereby the customer selects his own merchandise, removes it from the shelves or bulk containers, carriers it to a check-out stand to complete the transaction and transports it to the point of use.

SELLING—The personal or impersonal process of assisting and/or persuading a prospective customer to buy a commodity or a service or to act favorably upon an idea that has commercial significance to the seller.

Comment. This definition includes advertising, other forms of publicity, and sales promotion as well as personal selling.

SELLING AGENT—An agent who operates on an extended contractual basis; sells all of a specified line of merchandise or the entire output of his principal, and usually has full authority with regard to prices, terms, and other conditions of sale. He occasionally renders financial aid to his principal.

Comment. This functionary is often called a Sales Agent.

SERVICE WHOLESALER—See Wholesaler.

SERVICES—Activities, benefits, or satisfactions which are offered for sale, or are provided in connection with the sale of goods.

Examples are amusements, hotel service, electric service, transportation, the services of barber shops and beauty shops, repair and maintenance service, the work of credit rating bureaus. This list is merely illustrative and no attempt has been made to make it complete. The term also applies to the various activities such as credit extension, advice and help of sales people, delivery, by which the seller serves the convenience of his customers.

SHOPPING CENTER—A geographical cluster of retail stores, collectively handling an assortment of goods varied enough to satisfy most of the merchandise wants of consumers within convenient travelling time, and, thereby, attracting a general shopping trade.

Comment. During recent years, the term has acquired a special usage in its application to the planned or integrated centers developed in suburban or semi-suburban areas usually along main highways and featuring ample parking spaces.

SHOPPING GOODS—Those consumers' goods which the customer in the process of selection and purchase characteristically compares on such bases as suitability, quality, price and style.

Examples of goods that most consumers probably buy as Shopping Goods are: millinery, furniture, dress goods, women's ready-to-wear and shoes, used automobiles, and major appliances.

Comment. It should be emphasized that a given article may be bought by one customer as a Shopping Good and by another as a Specialty or Convenience Good. The general classification depends upon the way in which the average or typical buyer purchases.

See Comment under Speciality Goods.

SPECIALITY GOODS—Those consumers' goods with unique characteristics and/or brand identification for which a significant group of buyers are habitually willing to make a special purchasing effort.

Examples of articles that are usually bought as Specialty Goods are: specific brands and types of fancy foods, hi-fi components, certain types of sporting equipment, photographic equipment, and men's suits.

Comment. Price is not usually the primary factor in consumer choice of specialty goods although their prices are often higher than those of other articles serving the same basic want but without their special characteristics.

SPECIALTY STORE—A retail store that makes its appeal on the basis of a restricted class of shopping goods.

STANDARDIZATION—The determination of basic limits or grade ranges in the form of uniform specifications to which particular manufactured goods may conform and uniform classes into which the products of agriculture and the extractive industries may or must be sorted or assigned.

Comment. This term does not include Grading which is the process of sorting or assigning units of a commodity to the grades or classes that have been established through the process of Standardization. Some systems of standardization and grading for agricultural products are compulsory by law.

STOCK or INVENTORY CONTROL—The use of a system or mechanism to maintain stocks of goods at desired levels.

Comment. Such control is usually exercised to maintain stocks that are (a) representative in that they include all the items the customer group served expects to be able to buy from the firm involved, (b) adequate in that a sufficient quantity of each item is included to satisfy all reasonably foreseeable demands for it, and (c) economical in that no funds of the firm are held in inventory beyond those needed to serve purposes (a) and (b) and in that it facilitates savings in costs of production.

STORAGE—The marketing function that involves holding goods between the time of their production and their final sale.

Comment. Some processing is often done while goods are in storage. It is probable that this should be regarded as a part of production rather than of marketing.

SUPERETTE—See Supermarket.

SUPERMARKET—A large retailing business unit selling mainly food and grocery items on the basis of the low margin appeal, wide variety and assortments, self-service, and heavy emphasis on merchandise appeal.

Comment. In its bid for patronage the Supermarket makes heavy use of the visual appeal of the merchandise itself.

The Committee realizes that it would be foolhardy in this day of rapid change to try to indicate how large a store must be to be a Supermarket. At the time of this report the latest figures indicate that the average store recognized by the Supermarket Institute as belonging to the class has annual sales of somewhat under $2,010,000, and that about 45 percent of them sell more than that amount each year. Both of these figures have been changing rapidly and may continue to do so. A Superette is a store, somewhat smaller than a Supermarket, and possessing most of the same characteristics.

T

TRADE-MARK—A brand or part of a brand that is given legal protection because it is capable of exclusive appropriation; because it is used in a manner sufficiently fanciful, distinctive, and arbitrary, because it is affixed to the product when sold, or because it otherwise satisfies the requirements set up by law.

Comment. Trade-mark is essentially a legal term and includes only those brands or parts of brands which the law designates as trademarks. In the final analysis in any specific case a Trade-mark is what the court in that case decides to regard as a Trade-mark.

TRADING AREA—A district whose size is usually determined by the boundaries within which it is economical in terms of volume and cost for a marketing unit or group to sell and/or deliver a good or service.

Comment. A single business may have several trading areas; for example, the Trading Area of Marshall Field for its store business is different from that for its catalogue business.

TRAFFIC MANAGEMENT—The planning, selection, and direction of all means and methods of transportation involved in the movement of goods in the marketing process.

Comment. This definition is confined to those activities in connection with transportation that have to do particularly with marketing and form an inseparable part of any well-organized system of distribution. It includes control of the movement of goods in trucks owned by the marketing concern as well as by public carrier. It does not include the movement of goods within the warehouse of a producer or within the store of a retail concern.

TRUCK WHOLESALER—See Wholesaler.

U

ULTIMATE CONSUMER—One who buys and/or uses goods or services to satisfy personal or household wants rather than for resale or for use in business, institutional, or industrial operations.

Comment. The definition distinguishes sharply between Industrial Users and Ultimate Consumers. A firm buying and using an office machine, a drum of lubricating oil, or a carload of steel billets is an Industrial User of those products, not an Ultimate Consumer of them. A vital difference exists between the purposes motivating the two types of purchases which in turn results in highly significant differences in buying methods, marketing organization, and selling practices.

V

VALUE ADDED BY MARKETING—The part of the value of a product or a service to the consumer or user which results from marketing activities.

Comment. There is urgent need of a method or formula for computing Value Added

by Marketing. Increased attention is being devoted to developing such a formula. At present none of those suggested have gained enough acceptance to justify inclusion in this definition or comment.

VARIETY STORE—A retailing business unit that handles a wide assortment of goods, usually in the low or popular segment of the price range.

Comment. While some foods are generally handled, the major emphasis is devoted to non-food products.

VOLUNTARY GROUP—A group of retailers each of whom owns and operates his own store and is associated with a wholesale organization or manufacturer to carry on joint merchandising activities and who are characterized by some degree of group identity and uniformity of operation.

Such joint activities have been largely of two kinds; cooperative advertising and group control of store operation.

Comment. A Voluntary Group is usually sponsored by a wholesaler. Similar groups sponsored by retailers do not belong in this category. Groups of independent stores sponsored by a chain store system are usually called "Agency Stores."

W

WHOLESALER—A business unit which buys and resells merchandise to retailers and other merchants and/or to industrial, institutional, and commercial users but which does not sell in significant amounts to ultimate consumers.

In the basic materials, semi-finished goods, and tool and machinery trades merchants of this type are commonly known as "distributors" or "supply houses."

Comment. Generally these merchants render a wide variety of services to their customers. Those who render all the services normally expected in the wholesale trade are known as Service Wholesalers; those who render only a few of the wholesale services are known as Limited Function Wholesalers. The latter group is composed mainly of Cash and Carry Wholesalers who do not render the credit or delivery service, Drop Shipment Wholesalers who sell for delivery by the producer direct to the buyer, Truck Wholesalers who combine selling, delivery, and collection in one operation, and Mail Order Wholesalers who perform the selling service entirely by mail.

This definition ignores or minimizes two bases upon which the term is often defined; first, the size of the lots in which wholesalers deal, and second, the fact that they habitually sell for resale. The figures show that many wholesalers operate on a very small scale and in small lots. Most of them make a significant portion of their sales to industrial users.

CROSS-REFERENCES

The chart that follows indicates references to two other works and the chapters in MARKETING IN A CHANGING ENVIRONMENT in which they occur. The cross-referenced works are:

J. Howard Westing and Gerald Albaum, *Modern Marketing Thought* (New York: The Macmillan Company, 1964).

Holloway and Hancock, *The Environment of Marketing Behavior*, Selections from the Literature (New York: John Wiley and Sons, 1964).

		Westing and Albaum	Holloway and Hancock
Part I. *The Basis and Conceptual Framework of Marketing*			
Ch. 1	Marketing and Society	1, 69, 70	1, 2
Ch. 2	The System of Marketing	3, 7–19, 65, 66	3, 28, 29, 30
Ch. 3	Marketing in Capitalistic and Planned Economies		4
Part II. *Marketing Environment and Market Forces*			31, 32
Ch. 4	The Environment of Consumer Behavior—I	4	5, 6, 7, 8, 9
Ch. 5	The Environment of Consumer Behavior—II	5	10, 11, 12
Ch. 6	The Environment of Consumer Behavior—III		13, 14
Ch. 7	The Visible and Dynamic Force of Technology	2	25, 26, 27
Ch. 8	The Economic Environment- Competition	29, 30	23, 24
Ch. 9	Demand Analysis	31	15
Ch. 10	Marketing and the Law	20–28	16, 17, 18, 19, 20
Ch. 11	The Ethical Dimension in Marketing		21, 22
Part III. *Market Development*			33
Ch. 12	Marketing Intelligence—I	61–64	34, 35
Ch. 13	Marketing Intelligence—II		36, 37

		Westing and Albaum	Holloway and Hancock
Ch. 14	Planning for Marketing Development	32, 33, 44–46	48, 49, 50
Ch. 15	Market Development; The Product	34–37	43, 44
Ch. 16	Market Development: The Price	47–52	45, 46, 47
Ch. 17	Marketing Logistics	53–57	41, 42
Ch. 18	Persuasion in the Market Place—I	6, 38–43, 58	38, 39
Ch. 19	Persuasion in the Market Place—II		40

Part IV. *Marketing in Perspective*

Ch. 20	Universality of Marketing and Economic Development		52, 53
Ch. 21	International Marketing	71–73	51
Ch. 22	An Evaluation of Marketing	74	54, 55, 56

Name Index

Adams, Cedric, 57n.
Adelman, M. A., 199
Albaum, Gerald, 211n., 485
Alderson, Wroe, 14, 29, 141, 159, 308, 343, 348, 372n., 380n., 393n., 463
Alexander, Ralph S., 23n., 28, 380n., 465
Alexis, Marcus, 75, 108
Anshen, Melvin, 262
Applebaum, William, 356

Bach, George Leland, 42n., 151n., 174
Backman, Jules, 156n., 315, 323–324, 338n., 339
Baker, Henry C., 284
Banks, Seymour, 369n.
Barger, Harold, 463
Barnett, H. G., 141
Bartels, Robert, 356
Bauer, Raymond A., 361–362
Baumhart, Raymond C., 205n., 206n.
Beard, Miriam, 363
Beckman, Theodore N., 29, 175, 356, 461n.
Bell, Martin L., 13
Belshaw, Cyril S., 13, 407n., 410n.
Benson, Purnell H., 308
Berelson, Bernard, 377, 399
Berenback, William, 217
Berg, Thomas L., 308
Berlo, David K., 377
Bilkey, Warren J., 106n.
Bliss, Perry, 86
Blomstrom, Bruce, 28
Boddy, Francis M., 50
Bohannan, Paul, 405n.
Borden, Neil H., 373, 377, 397
Boulding, Kenneth E., 6–7

Bourne, Francis S., 60n., 62n., 71
Bowen, Howard R., 204, 207, 217
Bowman, B. F., 137n.
Boyd, Harper W. Jr., 237, 284
Briggs, Asa, 413n.
Bright, James R., 141
Brink, Edward L., 363
Britt, Steuart Henderson, 71, 284, 308, 387–392
Brown, William F., 199
Bryan, Stanley E., 350n.
Buell, Victor P., 224n., 284
Buskirk, Richard H., 396
Buzzell, Robert D., 29, 175, 356

Canoyer, Helen G., 90n.
Cardozo, Richard N., 258n.
Carroll, Ronald, 442n.
Carson, Rachel, 194
Cassady, Ralph Jr., 228, 237
Cateora, Philip R., 411n., 439n., 445
Chamberlain, John, 44n.
Chamberlin, Edward Hastings, 149–150
Chandler, Alfred D., 382n., 387n., 392n.
Chase, Stuart, 193
Clark, Eugene, 28, 159, 262, 339, 356, 464
Clark, Fred E., 28, 159, 262, 339, 356, 464
Clark, J. M., 202
Clark, Lincoln H., 93n.
Clasen, Earl A., 218
Clewett, Richard M., 28
Cohen, Saul B., 356
Coleman, James, 71
Coleman, Richard P., 67n., 78n.
Colley, Russell H., 374n.
Conrad, Jones, 139n.

487

Converse, Paul D., 24n., 343, 356
Cook, Fred J., 212n.
Coolsen, Frank G., 408n., 416n.
Corey, Raymond E., 130n.
Cornell, Russ, 354n.
Cox, Donald F., 98
Cox, Reavis, 14, 29, 159, 262, 308, 339, 356, 380n., 393n., 405, 461–462, 463, 464
Crane, Edgar, 375n., 376, 377
Crawford, William, 380
Cross, James S., 28
Cundiff, Edward W., 174, 396
Cunningham, Ross M., 28, 79n.

Dallos, Robert E., 455n.
Dalton, George, 405
David, D. Ronald, 227n.
Davis, Allison, 61n.
Dean, Joel, 156–158, 324–325, 339, 387n.
Dewhurst, J. Frederick, 445, 457n.
Dichter, Ernest, 262, 420, 431n., 445
Dirlam, Joel B., 327
Douglas, Paul, 198
Drucker, Peter F., 135, 273, 276, 289, 417, 420
Duncan, C. S., 235
Dunn, S. Watson, 204n.

Eastman, R. O., 243
Elgass, George A., 433n.
Engle, Nathaniel H., 29, 175, 356
Entenberg, Robert D., 28

Fayerweather, John, 432n., 435n., 436n., 445
Ferber, Robert, 84n., 108, 225, 237, 246n., 262
Fichhandler, Thomas C., 463
Field, Mark G., 361–362
Foote, Nelson N., 87
Ford, Henry, 382–384
Fox, Willard M., 240n.
Frederick, J. George, 243
Frey, Albert W., 377
Friedman, Milton, 83

Galbraith, John Kenneth, 206–207
Gale, Harlow, 243
Gardner, Burleigh B., 61n.
Gardner, Mary R., 61n.
Garrett, Thomas M., 218
Gibbs, Helen M., 440n.
Glaskowsky, Nicholas A. Jr., 347n., 356

Golby, Colin, 380, 381n.
Goldman, Marshall I., 50, 420
Goldstein, R. C., 291n.
Goldstrucker, Jack, 28
Goodman, Charles S., 463
Grant, Richard, 384
Green, Paul E., 262
Grether, E. T., 14, 29, 159, 262, 308, 339, 356, 380n., 464
Griffin, Clare Elmer, 290, 339

Halbert, Michael, 396n.
Hall, Edward T., 431
Hancock, Robert S., 485
Handel, Gerald, 67
Hanson, Hans B., 50
Hare, Paul A., 99n., 102n.
Harper, Donald V., 324n., 339, 343n.
Hart, Philip, 208
Hauser, Philip M., 71
Haverman, Robert H., 174
Hawkins, Edward R., 335, 339
Herzog, Herta, 308
Heskett, J. L., 347n., 351n., 356
Hess, John M., 411n., 439n., 445
Hill, Richard M., 28
Hirschman, A. O., 414n.
Hobart, David M., 243
Hobson, John, 359n., 380, 392n.
Hoffman, Michael L., 412n.
Hollander, Stanley C., 28, 363, 464
Holloway, Robert J., 71, 224n., 249n., 485
Holt, Robert T., 420
Houthakker, H. S., 174
Hovland, Carl, 365
Howard, John A., 174, 200, 464
Howard, Marshall C., 199, 200
Huegy, Harvey W., 24n., 339
Hughes, Lawrence M., 359n.
Humphrey, Hubert H., 197

Ivie, Robert J., 347n., 356

Janis, Irvin L., 365n.
Johnson, Samuel C., 139n., 297n.
Jones, Conrad, 297n.

Kaplan, A. D. H., 327
Katona, George, 84, 93n., 107n., 108, 169, 174, 175, 262

Katz, Elihu, 71
Keith, Robert J., 285
Kelley, Eugene J., 217, 242n., 284
Kelley, Harold H., 365n.
Kelley, William T., 363n.
Keynes, J. M., 82
Keyser, Virginia, 444n.
Kindleberger, Charles P., 408n.
Kintner, Earl W., 199
Knopf, Kenyon A., 174
Kornhauser, Arthur, 104
Kreps, Theodore J., 452–453, 455–457
Krugman, Herbert E., 396
Kuehn, Alfred A., 250n.
Kuhn, Alfred, 14, 406n., 460n., 462n.

Laird, Donald A., 87
Lamm, Earl, 254n.
Lansing, John B., 66
Lanzillotti, Robert F., 327, 333n.
Laver, James, 65
Lazarfeld, Paul F., 80, 104
Lazer, William, 242n., 271n., 284, 347n.
Lazo, Hector, 81n.
Leftwich, Richard H., 148n., 153n., 158, 174
Leman, Graham, 308
LeMieux, P. M., 353n.
Lester, Bernard, 28
Leverhume, Lord, 359
Levitt, Theodore, 138n., 141
Lewis, Edwin H., 374, 376n., 443
Likert, Renis, 102
Lippitt, Vernon G., 104n., 174
Lockley, Lawrence C., 243n.
Loeb, Benjamin S., 82

MacDonald, Philip, 446n.
Maceda, Emilio, 408n.
Magee, John F., 349n., 355, 356
Maines, N. R., 223n.
Mansfield, Edwin, 141
Marquand, J. P., 207
Marshall, Martin V., 377
Martineau, Pierre, 28, 71
Mason, Edward S., 198, 410n.
Masters, Dexter, 217, 358
May, Catherine, 210
Mazur, Paul, 464
McConnell, Campbell R., 163n.
McDowell, Carl E., 440n.

McGarry, Edmund D., 377, 460n.
McGuire, Joseph W., 217, 218
McInnes, William C., 14
McKay, Edward S., 282n.
McNeal, James U., 108
Mehren, George L., 416n.
Menzel, Herbert, 71
Meriam, R. S., 159
Millard, James W., 342
Mitchell, Robert V., 24n.
Morgan, James N., 66
Morton, Newton, 356
Mossman, Frank H., 356
Moyer, Reed, 413n., 420
Mueller, Era, 93n.

Nagashima, Akira, 437n., 439n.
Nair, Shrivaram, 444n.
Newman, Joseph W., 108, 235
Nicosia, Francesco M., 107
Nielsen, Arthur C., 253n.
Nielsen, Arthur C. Jr., 443n.
Nystrom, Paul H., 174, 243, 380n.

Ogden, William F., 272n.
Otteson, Schuyler F., 28
Oxenfeldt, Alfred R., 237, 339, 406n., 462n.

Packard, Vance, 207, 208n., 210–211
Panschar, William G., 28
Paradise, Louis J., 83n.
Parlin, Charles, 243
Patterson, James M., 28
Patterson, John Henry, 384
Pegrum, Dudley F., 186n., 199
Phelps, D. Maynard, 159, 228n., 237
Phillips, Charles F. Jr., 199
Pilgrim, F., 308
Pitcher, Alvin, 123n.
Polanyi, Karl, 14
Poltiz, Alfred, 79n.
Pressler, L. L., 353n.
Proxmire, William, 197

Rainwater, Lee, 67n.
Rathmell, John M., 363n., 375n.
Reynolds, A. E., 141
Reynolds, W. B., 141
Robbins, David W., 200
Robbins, George W., 14

Roberts, Harry V., 237
Robinson, Richard D., 420, 434n.
Rogers, Everett M., 141n.
Rostow, Walt W., 409, 416, 419n.

Samli, A. Coskun, 408n., 416
Sandage, C. H., 377
Sargent, Hugh, W., 97n.
Schlink, F. J., 193
Schmookler, Jacob, 141
Schumpeter, Joseph A., 141
Scott, Walter Dill, 243
Semlow, Walter J., 388n.
Shapiro, Stanley J., 141, 393n., 463
Shaw, Arch W., 14, 224, 243, 343
Sherbini, A. A., 408n., 412
Shuchman, Abraham, 308
Simon, Julian L., 391n.
Sinclair, Upton, 193
Sissors, Jack Z., 25n.
Skobe, Mihoril, 435n.
Slichter, Sumner H., 135
Smith, Adam, 54
Smith, Richard Austin, 181n.
Smith, Wendell R., 285
Snyder, Richard E., 352n.
Stanton, William J., 396
Starch, Daniel, 377
Steiner, Gary A., 377, 399
Stelzer, Charles F., 199
Stewart, Paul W., 457n.
Stewart, Wendell M., 342n., 352n.
Still, Richard R., 174, 396
Stouffer, Samuel A., 123n.
Strain, Richard W., 369n.
Surface, Frank M., 380n.

Tallman, Gerald B., 28
Tanner, Henry, 48n.
Taylor, Lester D., 174
Terpstra, Vern, 141

Thorelli, Hans B., 48n., 50
Tosdal, Harry R., 140n., 358, 382, 393n., 396
Tousley, Rayburn D., 28, 159, 262, 339, 356, 464
Towney, R. H., 207
Toynbee, Arnold, 217
Trevithick, Richard, 290
Tull, Donald S., 262
Turner, John E., 420

Urwick, Lyndall F., 278, 281n.

Vaile, Roland S., 14, 29, 85–86, 159, 262, 308, 339, 356, 380n., 393n., 464
Van Vlack, Philip W., 215n.
Veblen, Thorstein, 59
Verdoorn, P. J., 225, 237, 246n., 262

Walton, Clarence C., 210n.
Warne, Colston E., 208n.
Wasson, Chester R., 308, 309n.
Weaver, H. G., 387
Westfall, Ralph, 237
Wells, William D., 105n.
West, John, 92n.
Westing, J. Howard, 211n., 485
White, Percival, 231–232
Whitney, Simon N., 198
Whyte, William H. Jr., 64n.
Wickstrom, L. A., 353n.
Wilcox, Clair, 179, 193n., 199
Wolgast, Elizabeth H., 103n.
Wood, Richardson, 444n.
Woods, Walter A., 87
Working, Elmer J., 174
Wright, Leslie C., 420

Yang, Charles Y., 369n.
Young, Agnes, 78

Zober, Martin, 284

Subject Index

Absolute-income hypothesis, 82
Advertisers, in international media, 438–439
Advertising, allocated for new cars in '64 and
    '65, 370–371
  benefits of, 382
  criticisms of, 207
  economic effects of, 397–398
  effectiveness, 387–392
  effect on consumer choice, 398
  effects on costs, 398
    on demand, 397–398
    on price, 398
    on quality, 398
  instrument of persuasion, 367–373
  in international marketing, 435–436
  media analysis, 255
  model for determining appropriations, 389–
    391
  personal selling, 375
  in Soviet Union, 362
  wastefulness of, 358
Advertising expenditures, estimated annual
    U.S., 369
  and profits, 372
Advertising services in the U.S., 1963, 368
Advertising standards in television, 215–216
African markets, 405
Age, consumption and, 65–66
Alcoa, 130
Alternatives and consumption, 85
Aluminum Company of America, 130
American Tobacco Co. vs. United States, 181
Antitrust laws, 180–190
Aspirations, 59
Attitudes, 59
Automobile Information Disclosure Act, 194

Automobiles, dropout brands since 1920, 310–
    312

Behavior propositions, 116–117
Biological needs, 58
Borden Company, FTCV, 188–189
Brand Loyalty, 79
Brand shifting, model of, 250
Break-even analysis, 151–152, 172
  chart, 172
  point, 152
Brokerage allowances, 187–188
Bureau of Deceptive Practices, 194–195
Business ethics, 202–217
  intelligence, 222
Business Ethics Advisory Service, 213
Buyer-beware attitude, 57
Buying, attitudes toward, 56–58
  consuming and, 54
  impulse, 92
Buying power, and consumption, 68

Capitalistic System, 42–49
Celler-KeFauver Act, 188–190
Change, impact of, 122–123
Changing Times, 95
Channels of distribution, 21
  international, 431–433
  for motor oil, 344
Chevrolet automobile wiring diagram, 132–133
Clayton Act, 184–186
Climate, influence on consumption, 67
Codes of ethics, 213–217
  marketing research, 267
Cognitive dissonance, 365

Communication, classes of, 365
  conditioning, 381
  and the persuasive process, 399–400
  process of, 365
Competition, 144–157
  criteria, 157
  hallmarks of, 157
  in international marketing, 429
  nonprice, 156–158
  and product differentiation, 292–294
  pure, 144–146
Competitive decisions, 232–233
Complementary goods, 169–170
Concept of differentiation, 149–150
Conditioning communication, 381
Conformity, 62
Consumer, acceptance of products, 294
  behavior, 54–117
  behavior propositions, 116–117
  decisions, 90–107
  distribution of dollar on farm food products,
    458–459
  education, 90
  expectations with respect to future income
    and prices, 168–169
  expenditures and income changes, 83
  interaction, 98–103
  protection, 192–195
  tastes and preferences, 150, 167–168
Consumer action, biographic analysis of, 104
Consumer-Advisory Council, 198
Consumer Bulletin, 95, 97
Consumer decision making, diagram of, 114–
  115
Consumer-Product Rating, publications and
  buying behavior, 97
Consumer Reports, 95, 97
Consuming, buying and, 54
Consumption, aspirations, 59
  attitudes toward, 56–59
  biological needs, 58
  conspicuous, 59
  and discriminating forces, 74–81
  environmental forces of, 55–68
  experience and, 80
  and fashion, 63
  forces that influence, 58–68
  personal expenditures, 30
  by type of product, 109–113

Consumption, personality and, 58
  prestige and, 59
Convenience goods, 321
Corporations, combinations of, 179–180
  objectives, 273–278
Cost analysis, 255
Costs, determined by prices, 323
  distribution, 457
  effects of advertising on, 398
  of the firm, 172–173
  and price policies, 323–324
Credit, and consumption, 82
Cultural environment, 58

Data, collection of, 245
  selection of, 246
Death of a Salesman, 62
Deceptive practices, and the law, 191–195
Decision maker, 93
Decision-making, and consumption, 90–107
  diagram of, 114–115
  family patterns, 103
  and marketing-development, 270–272
  process of, 103–107
Decisions, competitive, 232–233
  information for, 94–98
  marketing, 226–235
  routine, 233–235
Delivered pricing, 338
Delivered pricing systems, terms, 337
Demand analysis, 161–175
  and the ability to buy, 163–166
  and complementary goods, 169–170
  definition of, 162
  derived, 385
  determinants of, 162–163
  effects of advertising on, 397–398
  and expectations of consumers, 168–169
  and number of buyers in the market, 170
  and the price of related and substitute goods,
    169–170
  and tastes and preferences of consumers,
    167–168
  and the willingness to buy, 166–167
Demand curves, 171
  and differentiated products, 151
  kinked, 154–155
  and monopolistic competition, 152
Department of Agriculture, 194

Department of Interior, 194
Differentiation, concept of, 149–150
Discounts, and Robinson-Patman Act, 188
Discretionary income, 163–165
Discriminating forces, 74–81
Discriminations in buying behavior, 76
Disposable income, 163–164
Distribution, channel, 21
  channel for motor oil, 344
  costs, 352–354, 457
  system of, 27
Drug industry, U.S. vs. Soviet Union, 361–362
DuPont pricing policy, 327
Durable-goods expenditures, 164–165

Eastman Kodak Co., distribution responsibilities, 354–355
Economic development, marketing and, 408–419
  nature of, 409–411
  problems in, 412 415
Economic effects of advertising, 397–398
Economic environment, 143–159
Economic forces and consumption, 81–84
Economic man, 166–167, 211
Economic systems, 42
Economic theory, limitations of, 155–156
Economy, modernization of, 410
Elasticity of demand, 170–173
  and differentiated products, 151
  formula, 170
  and kinked demand curve, 154–155
  and monopolistic competition, 152
  and pricing policies, 324–326
Electrical conspiracy, 181–182
Emotional aspects of industrial buying, 81
Engel's laws, 82
Environment, cultural, 58
  effect on international marketing, 429–431
  forces of, 27
  information, 225
  of marketing logistics, 345–346
  persuasion and, 364–365
ESOMAR, 22
Ethical behavior, and legal restraint, 203
Ethical codes, 213–217
Ethical dimension in marketing, 201–218
Ethical and social accomplishments of American business, 204

Ethics, and persuasion, 381–382
  and the product, 295
European Society for Opinion Surveys and Market Research, 222
Exchange process, persuasion and, 363–364
Exchange system, characteristics of, 407
Expectations factor, 84
Experimental design, 255–258
Export shipment, selected aspects of, 445–447
Export Trade Act, 185

Fair-trade laws, 196–197
Family size and consumption, 65–66
Fashion, 63
Federal Alcohol Administration Act, 193
Federal Aviation Act, 194
Federal laws, and deceptive practices, 191–195
Federal Reserve Board, 168
Federal Trade Commission, 184–185, 194
Federal Trade Commission Act, 184–185, 193
Feedback, 107
Firms in underdeveloped countries, common defects in, 414
Flow of goods and services, 16–18
F.o.b. pricing, 338
Food consumption, differences by urbanization, 77
Food and Drug Administration, 193–194
Food, Drug and Cosmetic Act, 193
Foreign markets, marketing forecasts for exports to, 448–449
  selling rules and warnings, 443
Foreign Trade of the U.S., 425–428
Form utility, 6
Fur Products Labeling Act, 193

General Motors, 392
General Motors, U.S. vs., 182–184
Geographical pricing practices, 336–338
Geography, and logistics, 346
German-American Trade News, 342
Goals, consumption and, 59
  and innovation, 135
  of persuasion, 384–385
Goods, convenience, 321
  shopping, 321
  specialty, 321
Goods and services, flow of, 16–18

Green Giant Company, marketing research job description, 263
Gross national product, relation of various components, 164
Group leaders, influence of, 61

Hazardous Substances Labeling Act, 194
Hershey Chocolate Corporation, 359

Igorot, 124
Impulse buying, 92
Income, 163–167
  and consumption, 82
  discretionary, 163–165
  disposable personal, 163–165
  distribution of, 166
Industrial buying, emotional aspects of, 81
Industrial marketing, committee review board, 28
Industrial marketing, principal characteristics of, 56
Inelastic, *see* Elasticity of demand, 170–173
Information, 222–226
  methods of gathering, 235–236
  sources of, 225–226, 247
Innovation, 122–125
  goals, 135
  and selling, 138–140
  and technology, 138–140
Institutions, of persuasion, 366–367
Instruments, of persuasion, 367–373
Intelligence, 222
  value of, 223–225
Interaction, elements of, 102
  among consumers, 98–103
Interaction-influence systems, 102
International cost of living indexes, 430
International marketing, 421–449
  channels, 431–433
  communications, 431
  competition, 429
  environment, 429–431
  firms engaged in, 423–424
  product and, 433–434
  programs, 437–444
  promotion, 434–437
  reasons for, 422–429
International Marketing Federation, 222
Inventory, 348–350
  control of size, 350

Inventory, pattern of stocks on hand, 349
Israel, purchases of durable goods, 1963–1964, 418

Journal of Marketing, 226

Kinked demand curve, 154–155

Language, 431
Lanham Trade-Mark Act, 185
Law, and deceptive practice, 191
  intent of, 178
  and marketing, 177–200
  and the product, 301
Legislation, and public demand for control of business, 178
  in the States against monopolies and trusts, 195–197
Life cycles, consumption and, 66–67, 74–75
  of products, 289–292
Life Study of Consumer Expenditures, 76n.
Location, consumption and, 67
Logistics, 341–355
  company example, 354–355
  decision areas, 346–348
  and geography, 346
  implications for marketing, 348–354
  and technology, 345

McGuire Act, 197
Macy's, 392–395
Management information, 227
Management and technology, 128–129
Marginal analysis, 147, 151
Marginal cost, 146–147
Marginal revenue, 147
Marital status, consumption and, 65–66
Market, 23–24
  definition of, 23
  domination by leading firms, 153
  information, 222–226
  physical attributes, 25
  planning, 280
  price, 144–147
  qualitative dimensions, 25
  segmentation, 24
  structures, 145
Marketing, aid to developing nations, 416
  channel, 21
  complexity of the system, 406
  components of, 22

Marketing, costs of the firm, 172-173
  criticisms of, 205
  decisions, 226-235
  definition of, 4
  economic character of, 10
  and economic development, 408-419
  ethical dimension, 201-218
  evaluation of, 451-463
  evolution of process, 411
  goals, 276
  international, 421-449
  and the law, 177-200
  logistics, 341-355
  measurement, 242
  multidisciplinary aspect of, 8-11
  network, 18-20
  plan, 279-281
  plan of study, 11-12
  political and ethical character of, 11
  product and environment, 292-301
  response to social system, 12-13
  setting objectives, 273-278
  social, character of, 9
  social and economic welfare of, 6-7
  tasks of, 415-417
  technological character of, 11
  university of, 404-407
Marketing concept, 129, 364
Marketing development, 269-283
  and decision making, 270-283
  nature of, 272-273
  plan, 278-281
  and products, 287-307
Marketing Horizons, 222
Marketing intelligence, 221-267
Marketing research, 135-137
  benefits, 223
  characteristics, 240-241
  code of ethics, 213, 262
  cost analysis, 255
  definition of, 240
  experimental design, 255-258
  interdisciplinary contributions to, 242
  media analysis, 255
  and motivational research, 253-255
  and operations research, 251-253
  panels, 251
  position descriptions, 263-264
  propositions, 235
  statistical techniques, 248

Marketing research, surveys, 248-251
  techniques for securing information, 248-258, 261
  trends, 241-243
Marketing system, 13
  objectives of, 43
Markets in Africa, 405
Mature product, 325
Media analysis, 255
  selection, 274-275
Membership groups, 60
Micro film, 295
Milk distribution, 454-455
Miller-Tydings Act, 197
Minnesota Mining and Manufacturing Company, 295, 298-299
Missionary salesmen, 131
Mixed-enterprise system, 8
Mobility, and consumption, 67-68
  and tastemaker theory, 69
Monopolistic competition, 148-149
  and pricing, 150-152
Monopoly, 144-152
  partial, 149
  pure, 144-148
  and Sherman Act, 181
Motivational research, 253-256

National Industrial Conference Board, 108, 168
Nations, differences among, 431
Negro consumption patterns, 75
New products, 230
  classification by product objective, 139, 296-297
  impact of, 126
  selection, 303
  versus mature products, 324-326
Nielsen, A.C., Co., 245
Non price competition, 156-158

Objectives, 273-278
Obsolescence, 134, 210-211
Occupation, consumption and, 67
Offer, 23
Offering differentiation, 149
Oligopolistic market structures, 148-149
Oligopoly, 145, 148, 152-155
  planning policies, 153
  and pricing, 153-155

Operations research, 254
and marketing research, 242–251
Opinion Research Corporation, 67m, 69m, 71
Organization for Economic Cooperation and
Development, 222

Panels, 251
Partial monopoly, 149
Patents, 120–121
Penetration Price, 324–326
Penicillin, comparison of production with
wholesale price, 128
Perception, 78–79
Permanent-income theory, 83
Personal consumption expenditures, 30
by type of product, 109–113
Personality, 58
Personal selling and advertising, 375
Persuasion, development of a program, 382–
393
and environment, 364–365
ethics and, 381–382
and the exchange process, 363–364
goals, 384–385
institutions of, 366–367
instruments of, 365–376
and market development, 307
in the market place, 357–399
points of, 366
and promotion mix, 373–376
research and, 386–393
role of, 363–365
tools, 367–373
Persuasive communication, 365
elements of, 365
Persuasive process communication and, 399–
400
Physical distribution, 21
costs, 352–354
developing the market, 306
recent attention given, 351
system, 347
Physical needs, 58
Picture-type audience preference of foreign
countries, 442
Place utility, 6, 343
Planned economies, 42–49
Planned obsolescence, 134, 210–211
Planning, 278–283
illustration of, 282–283

Planning, overall view of, 281–282
statement, 302
Plans and strategies, 301–303
Position descriptions in marketing research,
263–264
Possession utility, 6, 343
Predicting, 229
Predisposition to buy, 105
Preferences, 150, 167–168
Prestige, consumption and, 59
pricing, 335–336
social classes and, 60
Price, 20
criticisms of, 211–212
effects of advertising on, 398
establishing, 151
factors affecting behavior, 319–320
lining, 334
major influences on policies, 318–327
market development and, 313–338
penetration, 324–326
policies, 314, 327–333
of related and substitute goods, 169–170
skimming, 324–326
trends, 216–317
Price-discrimination, 185–188
Price-leaders, 196
Prices, interrelationship of, 314–318
Pricing, developing the market, 304–306
geography and, 336–338
goals of large industrial corporations, 329–
333
and monopolistic competition, 150–152
odd or even, 259, 334–336
and oligopoly, 152–155
practices, 334–336
Primitive societies, 124–125
Printers Ink, 100–101n, 126n
Private ownership, 44
Procter and Gamble Company, FTC vs., 190–
191
Products, 20
categories, 289
characteristics and price policies, 318–322
classification by product objective, 139, 296–
297
competition, 292–294
and the consumer, 294
criticisms of, 210–211
developing the market for, 301–307

Products, differentiation, 292
  differentiation and price policies, 322, 328
  and environment, 292–301
  ethics and, 295
  focus, 288
  information form, 293
  and international marketing, 433–434
  law and, 301
  life cycles, 289–292
  marketing development, 287–307
  in the marketing environment, 292–301
  planning statements, 302
  and technology, 294
  what makes them new, 309
Profit, and break-even analysis, 172
  as a regulator, 46–47
  relation to advertising expenditure, 372
Promotion, 21–22
  under different economic systems, 44
  and international marketing, 434–437
Promotion mix, 373–376
Psychic Vectors, 106–107
Psychological pricing, 335–336
Psychology, and marketing research, 242
Public Health Service, 194
Purchase decisions, 93–94
Purchase patterns, 77–78
Purchasers, behavioral characteristics of, 25
Purchasing power, 163–165
Pure competition, 144–146
Pure Food and Drug Act, 193
Pure monopoly, 144–148

Quality Stabilization Bill, 197

Race, and consumption, 75
Radio and Television Sets, 127
Razors, 134
Readiness-to-buy condition, 105
Reference groups, 60
  conformity and, 62–63
  influence on products and brands, 62
Relative-income hypothesis, 82
Resale-price maintenence, 196–197
Research, 135–137
  developing the market, 303–304
  and persuasion, 386–393
  phase of, 244
Researchers, 244

Restraining forces to consumption, 81–84
Retail establishments, 32
  number of persons per, 32
  sales, 32
Retail Sales, 33–34
Retail trade, United States, 31
Return on investment, 327
Robinson-Patman Act, 186–188
Rostow timetable, 409
Rule of reason, 181

Sale, forces behind, 374
  forecasting, 271
  foreign organization for, 432
  promotion mix by type of product, 376
  representatives, 131
Salesmen, 131
  number required, 388
Sales-promotion mix, 374
Schwegmann Brothers vs. Calvert Corporation,
  197
Schwegmann Brothers vs. Seagram Distillers
  Corporation, 197
Scientific Marketing, 222
Selling, criticisms of, 207
  definition of, 358
  employment in U.S., 1960, 362
  and innovation, 138–140
Selling in foreign markets, rules and workings,
  443
Services, geographic division of, 36
Services, receipts, 35
Services, standard metropolitan statistical areas,
  37
Sherman Antitrust Act, 180–184
Shopping goods, 321
Skimming price, 324–326
Social classes, 60
  and consumption, 75–81
  purchase patterns, 77–78
  social perspectives of, 61
Societies, advanced, 125
Sociology, and marketing research, 242
Sorting concept, 343–345
Sources of information, 247
Soviet Union, 42–48
  drug industry, 361–362
  sales of domestic appliances, 419
Specialization and exchange, 4–6
Specialty goods, 321

Standard metropolitan statistical areas, selected services, 37
top twenty ranked by retail sales, 33
Standard Oil Company, 179–180
Standard Oil Company vs. U.S., 181
Statistics, and marketing research, 242
Strategies, plans and, 301–303
Style, 63
Substitute goods, 169–170
Subsystem, 20
Survey Research Center of the University of Michigan, 168–169
Surveys, 248–251
System of Distribution, 24–27
System, planned, 42–49
Systems, economic, 42

Tariff Act, 193
Tastemaker theory, 69
Tastes, 150, 167–168
Technical Research, 137
Technological progress, 124
Technology, 120–139
  and consumption, 68
  disruptive aspect, 123
  and innovation, 138–140
  logistics and, 345
  and the product, 294–295
Television advertising standards, 215–216

Television code, 215–216
Television growth, 291
Television and radio sets, 127
Time utility, 6, 343
Total cost, 151–172
Total plan, 273
Total revenue, 151
Trade-off, 352–354
Transportation, 346–347
  comparison of modes, 347
Truth-in lending Bill, 198
Truth-in-packaging Bill, 198, 208
Tying-contracts, 185–186

Unethical behavior, 212–213
Unethical practices executives want to eliminate, 206
Unitary demand curve, 170–171
U.S.S.R., 42–48
  sales of domestic appliances, 419
Utility, and physical distribution, 343

Value added by marketing, 460

Wheeler-Lea Act, 184, 193
Wholesale Trade, 38–39
Wiring diagram, Chevrolet automobile, 132–133
Wool Products Labeling Act, 184, 193